Anonymous

The Rebellion Register

A History of the Principal Persons and Places

Anonymous

The Rebellion Register
A History of the Principal Persons and Places

ISBN/EAN: 9783337202552

Printed in Europe, USA, Canada, Australia, Japan

Cover: Foto ©Andreas Hilbeck / pixelio.de

More available books at **www.hansebooks.com**

THE

REBELLION REGISTER:

A HISTORY OF THE

PRINCIPAL PERSONS AND PLACES, IMPORTANT DATES, DOCUMENTS AND STATISTICS, MILITARY AND POLITICAL, CONNECTED WITH THE CIVIL WAR IN AMERICA.

TO WHICH IS ADDED

A CITIZEN'S MANUAL:

CONTAINING

NATIONAL DOCUMENTS, PROCLAMATIONS, AND STATISTICS POLITICAL PLATFORMS, GRANT'S REPORT, PARLIAMENTARY RULES, &c.,

ALPHABETICALLY ARRANGED.

COMPILED FROM OFFICIAL AND OTHER AUTHENTIC SOURCES,

By ROBERT A. CAMPBELL.

INDIANAPOLIS, IND.:

A. D. STREIGHT, PUBLISHER,

1867.

STEREOTYPED AT THE
FRANKLIN TYPE FOUNDRY,
CINCINNATI, O.

PREFATORY.

A GLANCE at the Title Page will show the general scope of this work. It has been the aim of the Author to condense into the smallest possible space, consistent with precision, clearness, and interest, the multitudinous incidents and dates presented. He has avoided all partisan views, mere speculation, and unprofitable detail. The documents, statistics, and extracts are from official sources, and given without comment. The historical part of the work has been carefully gathered from the abundant materials at the command of the Author, and as carefully culled and presented. In his labors it has been his constant care to make a fair, full statement of *facts*, rather than any display of rhetoric.

It is intended as a reliable and convenient reference book upon the topics presented, for the use of the various classes and parties of American citizens; and the Author hopes that the execution of the design may not be altogether unworthy the approbation already bestowed upon the plan.

REBELLION REGISTER.

Abbeville, Miss., deserted by the rebels and occupied by the Union forces December 2, 1862.

Abell, D. K., editor of the St. Joseph (Mo.) Tribune, arrested October 30, 1863, for publishing treasonable articles in his paper.

Abingdon, Va., was occupied by General Burbridge, who destroyed a large amount of stores, including a quantity of salt, December 14, 1864.

A. B. Ligur, a rebel steamer, was captured near New Orleans, November 1, 1862.

Abolition of Slavery in the District of Columbia. Bill passed the United States Senate April 3, (29 *v.* 14); passed the House (93 *v.* 39) April 11, and was approved by President Lincoln April 16, 1862.

Absentees from the army were ordered to their places August 11, 1862.

Accomac and Northampton Counties, Va., were taken possession of by the Union troops, and the rebels in them disbanded, November 18, 1861.

Acquia Creek, Va.—There was an engagement, May 31, 1861, between the rebel batteries near this place and the gun-boats Anacosta and Freeborn. After a two-hours' battle the gun-boats retired; but, renewing the attack next day, the batteries were silenced and a part of the town burned. There were undecisive attacks at the same point July 29 and August 16 of the same year. The place was evacuated by the rebels March 18, 1862, thus raising the blockade of the Potomac.

Actual Commencement of War, by the rebels opening fire upon Fort Sumter, at 4:30 A. M. April 12, 1861.

Acworth, Ga., was Sherman's head-quarters June 6, 1864.

Adair County, Ky., was the scene of severe skirmishing December 29, 1861.

Adairsville, Ga., was occupied by General Howard's corps, after defeating the rebels, May 18, 1864.

Adams, Charles Francis, United States Minister to London, received a congratulatory visit from the Emancipation Society of England January 16, 1863.

Adams. (See South Carolina Commissioners.)

Adamstown, Md. (See Second Invasion of Maryland.)

Adele, an Anglo-Confederate steamer, was captured July 6, 1862.

Admiral, an Anglo-Confederate ship, was captured off the coast of Georgia December 13, 1861.

Aiken, Rev. C. W., was betrayed to the rebels in South Carolina December 27, 1860.

Alabama.—Senator C. C. Clay, Jr., resigned his seat in the United States Senate December 10, 1860, and he, with his colleague, Benjamin Fitzpatrick, formally withdrew from that body January 21 following. Delegates to a State Convention were elected (result, in the State, over 60,000 for secession) December 24, 1860. They assembled at Montgomery January 7, 1861; four days later passed a secession ordinance, (61 *v.* 39,) and adjourned. They reassembled at the same place March 4, and on the 13th ratified the so-called Confederate Constitution, (85 *v.* 5.) December 24, 1860, the Governor issued his call for an extra session of the State Legislature, convening them January 14, to provide laws to carry into effect the action of the State Convention. Arms for the Alabama authorities were seized in New York city January 22, 1861. Jeff Davis made a requisition, April 9, upon Governor Moore for 3,000 troops, and on the 16th of the same month President Lincoln declared the State in insurrection.

Alabama, the Anglo-Confederate cruiser, *alias* "290," was built in England, and sailed from Liverpool July 29, 1862, for the Azores, where she received her armament. Captain Ralph Semmes assumed command August 24. This pirate captured and destroyed about eighty vessels belonging to merchants of the United States, including the gun-boat Hatteras, off the coast of Texas, January 11, 1863. Captain Semmes, his officers, and crew, had a public reception and welcome from the Government and city officials at Kingston, Jamaica, January 25, 1863. Arriving at Cherbourg, June 14, 1864, from a cruise in the Indian Ocean, she was, in accordance with the French law of neutrality, warned to leave that port, which she did on the morning of the 19th, first sending a challenge to the United States war steamer Kearsage, Captain Winslow. The battle commenced as soon as the vessels had reached a point beyond the French jurisdiction, (three leagues from shore,) and after a short engagement the pirate was sunk. Captain Semmes, most of his officers, and part of his crew—forty in all—made their escape upon the British yacht Deerhound, which landed them in England, where they were received with much enthusiasm.

Alabama, a United States war steamer, sailed in search of the Anglo-Confederate pirate Florida, February 20, 1863.

Albemarle, a rebel ram, was destroyed by Lieutenant W. B. Cushing with a torpedo-boat, on Roanoke River, October 28, 1864.

Albert, a United States gun-boat, was accidentally burned at Norforlk, Va., May 31, 1863.

Aldie, Va., the rebels at, capture a squad of fifty Union cavalry March 1, 1863, and the next day the Union boys captured thirty of Moseby's guerrillas near the same place. Cavalry skirmishing again commenced June 17, 1863, and continued at intervals until the 21st, when the rebels were routed.

Alert was captured by the Alabama September 9, 1862.

Alexandria, Va., was declared open as a port of entry September 24, 1863. (See Ellsworth.)

Alexandria, La., was captured by Admiral Porter May 8, 1863, and a few days later the place was occupied by General Banks's army. The city was again occupied March 16, 1864, by General A. J. Smith, Admiral Porter holding the river.

Alice, a schooner, was captured by the Alabama November 2, 1862.

Allatoona, Ga., Sherman flanked Johnston at, May 24, 1864. Hood moved upon this place October 5, 1864, and continued the attack unsuccessfully next day.

Allatoona Mountains, Ga., were occupied by Johnston's rebel army, and the position fortified, May 22, 1864. Sherman "flanked him" next day, when Johnston again retreated.

Allatoona Pass, Ga., was occupied by Stoneman and Garrard's cavalry June 2, 1864.

Alleghany Arsenal.—Great excitement was caused in Pittsburg December 24, 1860, upon the reception of an order to send a quantity of arms South, and the citizens *en masse* declared the thing should not be done. The order was revoked January 3, 1861.

Alleghany Camp, near Staunton, Va.—A battle was fought at this place December 13, 1861, between General Milroy's Union force of 750 men, and General Johnston's rebels, numbering 2,000. The battle opened at daylight, the Union troops retiring about 3 P. M. Loss: Union, 30; rebel, 100.

Altoona, Penn.—The Governors of the loyal States met at Altoona September 24, 1862, and adopted an address to the President, indorsing all the acts of the Government.

Amendment to the Constitution. (See page —.)

Ames, Bishop Edward, and Hon. Hamilton Fish were, on January 27, 1862, appointed commissioners to visit Richmond and other places in the South, to relieve the suffering and promote the comfort of the Federal prisoners in rebel hands. They returned February 14, having been refused admission within the Confederate lines, but having effected an arrangement for the exchange of prisoners.

Amite River, La.—Rebels dispersed at this place March 9, 1863.

Amnesty Proclamations.—During the rebellion three of these proclamations have been issued, as follows: The first and second by President Lincoln, December 8, 1863, and March 26, 1864, respectively, and the third by President Johnson, May 29, 1865. For these important documents in full, see pages 270 and 271.

Anderson, Major Robert, assumed command of Fort Moultrie November 18, 1860. Acting upon his views of the situation and the pending struggle, he spiked the guns, destroyed the carriages, and abandoning that point,

December 26, with his small force, established himself in Fort Sumter. This movement caused a great excitement in Charleston and other Southern cities, and was sustained by Congress January 7, 1861. By order of General Beauregard, April 7, communication between the fort and city was prohibited, and on the 11th he sent in a summons to surrender. Major Anderson replied that his "sense of honor and his obligations to his Government" would prevent his doing so. The demand was repeated and again refused at midnight. The bombardment commenced at 4:30 o'clock next morning by a fire from Fort Moultrie, followed by all the batteries, which nearly surrounded Sumter. Sumter replied at 7 o'clock, and a vigorous fire was kept up by both parties until 6 P. M. The Confederates fired at intervals during the night, and opened again in force at daylight of the 13th. The fort held fire until 7 A. M. During the morning the barracks of the fort took fire several times from the effects of shells. When the flames burst forth the Confederates redoubled their energies, and with such effect that at five minutes of 1 the garrison capitulated. The Federal loss was one man killed; he by the explosion of the last gun of the salute. It was rumored that the Confederate loss was comparatively heavy. The garrison were allowed the honors of war. Saluting their flag, and taking it and private and company property with them, they sailed, on the 14th, for New York, where they arrived on the 18th, and four days later received the thanks of the Government for their patriotism and bravery. Major Anderson was subsequently commissioned as Major-General, and, September 21, assigned to the command of the troops in Kentucky, which position he assumed October 5, and relinquished, on account of ill health, on the 8th.

Anderson's Cross Roads, Ky., was the scene of a brisk engagement and a rebel defeat, October 2, 1863.

Andersonville, Ga. (See Prisoners.)

Annandale, Va., was the scene of a spirited skirmish December 13, 1861. A battle was fought near this place February 14, 1863, in which the Unionists were defeated, with a loss of 17 killed and missing, and 21 wounded. The rebels captured the sutler's stores at this point June 28, 1863. A squad of Union cavalry was captured at Annandale, August 24, 1863, and Mosby's force was repulsed, with considerable loss, at the same place, just one year later.

Antietam, the battle of, was commenced September 16, 1862. General Hooker crossed the Antietam, near Sharpsburg, Md., to feel the rebel left and gain a position ready to attack in the morning. Considerable skirmishing ensued, which lasted till dark. The army slept on their arms. The next morning, about 5 o'clock, the real battle commenced, by Hooker's corps advancing against the rebel left. The fight raged fiercely and with varying success, both armies alternately advancing and retiring. At the fourth advance the Federals held the piece of woods in their front, which was felt to be the key of the position. On the left, at 1 o'clock P. M., Burnside had carried the stone bridge at the point of the bayonet; and at 4 P. M., he and Franklin in the center received orders to advance. Franklin moved his batteries forward and held his ground. Burnside carried the hills in his front; but the enemy being reinforced from the left, he was flanked, overpowered, and compelled to retire to his former position. It was now dark, and the battle closed. The forces engaged numbered about 100,000 on each side, the rebels having been reinforced by General Jackson's corps, after his capture of Harper's Ferry. The line of battle was four miles long. The field was fiercely contested, and the carnage was terrible. Preparations were immediately made to renew the contest on the morrow, but during the night the Confederates retreated. The Union loss in this fight was stated at 2,010 killed; 9,416 wounded; and 1,043 missing. The Confederates acknowledged a loss of 14,000, but General McClellan stated it to be 25,542. General Mansfield was killed; Generals Richardson and Rodman mortally wounded.

Anthony, a rebel Major, together with Lieutenant Davis, were convicted of recruiting for the rebels within the Union lines, and, January 2, 1864, sentenced to imprisonment in Fort Warren, for fifteen years.

Apache Canon, New Mexico, was the scene of a brisk engagement, March 28, 1862, between 1,300 Unionists, with six pieces of artillery, under Colonel J. P. Slough, and 2,000 Texans, with one piece of artillery, who were in ambush. Colonel Slough attacked the Texans in front, while Major Chivington, with a part of the force, attacked them in the rear. The fight lasted until 4 o'clock, when flags of truce were interchanged to bury the dead and care for the wounded. The rebels lost their entire train, comprising 64 wagons and 230 mules; about 150 killed, 200 wounded, and 93 prisoners. The Union loss was 20 killed, 54 wounded, and 35 prisoners.

Apalachicola, Florida, surrendered without resistance to the Union forces April 3, 1862.

Ariel, a California steamer, was captured by the "Alabama," December 7, 1862, and released upon giving bonds for $228,000, payable thirty days after the recognition of the Southern Confederacy.

Arizona, through action of a convention held at Mesilla, seceded March 16, 1861. The Confederate Congress subsequently erected a Territorial Government over it. On February 24, 1863, all of New Mexico west of a line from the point where the south-west corner of Colorado joins New Mexico, due south to the northern line, Mexico was constituted a separate territory, under the name of Arizona, and a temporary government provided therefor.

Arizona, a United States gun-boat, was burned below New Orleans, February 27, 1865, five of the crew perishing.

Arkadelphia, Ark., was the scene of a battle and rebel defeat February 15, 1863. Rebel loss, 25 men; Union loss, 14 men. September 8, the rebels were again defeated at this point. The place was occupied by Colonel Caldwell, with 700 Federal troops, October 28, after driving out the rebel rear guard and capturing several hundred prisoners. The place was occupied by 7,000 rebels, under Marmaduke and Price, January 6, 1864.

Arkansas.—The State Legislature, on January 16, 1861, resolved to submit to the people the question of calling a State Convention, the vote to be polled February 18. The result was (27,410 *v.* 15,820) in favor of a convention—delegates to which were elected, and met at Little Rock March 4. After resolving to submit the question of secession to the people, the Convention adjourned March 21, and met at the same place early in May, and on the 6th of that month passed (69 *v.* 1) a secession ordinance, which was ratified by the people, and on the 17th the State was admitted as one of the "Confederate States of America." The military board, on July 3, called for 10,000 men to repel the Union troops. President Lincoln declared the State in insurrection August 16. A provisional government was inaugurated at Little Rock January 20, 1864. The State, by a popular vote, on March 16, 1864, declared for a Free State Constitution, and the State Legislature ratified the Constitutional Amendment prohibiting slavery, April 1, 1865.

Arkansas City, Texas, surrendered to the Union forces March 17, 1863; 100 prisoners and 3 guns were taken.

Arkansas, the rebel iron-clad ram, on July 15, 1862, ran the blockade of the Yazoo River, and passed through the Union fleet, and anchored under the guns of the shore batteries. The gun-boats' fire had no effect on her. Several were killed and wounded on the fleet by the shots from the Arkansas. On the 22d, the Union ram Queen of the West attacked the Arkansas, endeavoring to sink her, but came off defeated. The Arkansas then made for Baton Rouge, where she was attacked by the Union gunboat Essex, and after a short engagement, was sunk August 6.

Arkansas Post, Ark.—A combined land and naval force was sent against this place. The land force, under General McClernand, landed about one mile below the place, under cover of the gun-boats, January 10, 1863. The day following the Union forces stormed the works, aided by the gun-boats, under Admiral Porter. The whole garrison surrendered. The Union loss was 100 killed and 500 wounded; rebel loss, 500 killed and wounded; 5,000 prisoners were taken, including General Churchill, commanding, and all the ammunition and stores. Two Texas regiments, ignorant of the change of affairs, and anxious to reinforce the rebels, marched into the camp on the 12th, and were added to the list of Union captures. The fort (Hindman) at this place was destroyed, and the place abandoned by the Unionists on the 29th.

Arlington, Va., was occupied by Sheridan's forces March 7, 1865.

Arlington Heights, opposite Washington, were fortified May 16, 1861.

Arrow Rock, Mo., was the scene of a skirmish October 13, 1863.

Arsenals.—At the outbreak of the rebellion, the possession of the arsenals was an important item to each party, and hence the efforts made to capture or destroy them. The arsenals at the following places were surrendered to or taken possession of by the State authorities as follows: Augusta, Georgia, January 24, 1861; Baton Rouge, Louisiana, January 10, 1861; Fayetteville, N. C., April 22, 1861; Liberty, Mo., April 20, 1861; Little Rock, Ark., February 8, 1861; Mobile, Ala., January 4, 1861; Napoleon, Ark., April 22, 1861. On April 28, 1861, a detachment of Illinois troops, under Captain Stokes, of the regular army, succeeded in removing, from the arsenal at St. Louis about twenty thousand stand of arms, besides one hundred and ten thousand cartridges, cannon, equipments, etc., and conveyed them to Springfield, Illinois. (See Harper's Ferry.)

Ashby's Gap, Va., was occupied by the Union forces November 4, 1862, and soon abandoned. The rebel pickets at this place were driven in on the 28th of the same month. The Union forces were repulsed here July 18 and 20, 1864, with a loss of nearly 500 men; and on February 19, 1865, a Union force of 110 men were surprised and captured by 40 guerrillas.

Ashland, Va., was dashed into by some Union cavalry May 29, 1862. They captured a train of quartermaster's and commissary stores. The town was occupicd by Union cavalry May 3, 1863.

Ashland Station, Va., was occupied by Sheridan's forces May 11, 1864. He destroyed two trains of cars, locomotives, engine-houses, Confederate store-house, and six miles of railroad.

Atchafalaya Bayou was reached and pontooned by General Bank's forces, in their retreat toward New Orleans, May 19, 1864.

Athens, Ala., garrisoned with 100 Union troops, was attacked January 26, 1864, by General Forrest, with 600 men, who, after a two hours' fight, was defeated; 5 rebels killed and a number wounded and captured; Union loss, 10 wounded. Again on September 23, 1864, the same General, with a force of 8,000 strong, attacked the place and defeated 500 Unionists.

Athens, Ky., was the scene of a brisk skirmish February 23, 1863. The guerrilla Morgan (brother to John) was taken prisoner.

Athens, Mo., was the scene of a skirmish August 5, 1861.

Atlanta, Ga., was occupied and fortified, by the rebel forces under Johnson, July 10, 1864. On the 20th, Sherman's army was within two and a half miles of the place, and threatening the main roads leading to and from the city. Johnson had been relieved from command of the rebels by General Hood, and forthwith proceeded to put in operation a style of tactics, which were directly the opposite of the slow movements of his predecessor. He made three assaults on the right of the position, at Peach-tree Creek, defended by General Joe Hooker, with the 20th Corps, but was "bloodily repulsed." He maneuvered skillfully, about daylight, and attacked a weak spot, or gap, in the lines, which were of unusual and dangerous length, extending some twelve miles. Hood sent out deserters to give false news of his having abandoned Atlanta; he also withdrew his skirmishers, the better to support the deception. He then fell on Sherman's forces, before the latter's order of battle was fully prepared, and when he had but just crossed the river. At one time, General Hood was nigh successful in piercing the weakened center. He would thus have retrieved the calamities of the campaign, but for some fortuitous circumstances, and the indomitable pluck of the 20th Corps, aided by General Newton of the 4th Corps, and part of Palmer's 14th Corps. Hood gained some slight advantages in the early part of the day, but at night had to relinquish them all. Late at night he retired to his earth-works, leaving over 1,300 prisoners. He had 1,200 killed and 4,000 wounded. Union loss, 1,700.

He made another attack on the left of the Union lines on the 22d. Logan's corps (the 15th), as also the 17th and Dodge's (16th Corps), felt the shock of his charges most severely. In the early part of the day he gained some temporary successes, as on the 20th. He took some works, which he was at a later time, obliged to relinquish; he was finally driven back with heavy loss. The enemy made six furious assaults on the 17th Corps. During the heat of battle, the rebel General Wheeler, with his raiders, attacked the rear of the 15th Corps, and captured 10 wagons. Their presence gave rise to the belief that Hood had outflanked the army; this caused a serious panic in the 15th Corps, who were also attacked at the same time in front, and driven from their main line of intrenchments to their second line, a distance of 500 yards to the rear; but they quickly reformed and took their old position. The gifted and valorous General James B. McPherson met his death early in the day. The rebels lost 3,100 killed, 5,000 wounded, 3,200 prisoners, 25 stand of colors, and 5,000 muskets. Union loss, 3,720, killed, wounded, and missing.

On the 28th, General Sherman attempted to extend his line to the right, by subtracting his left corps and sending them to the other extremity of the line, so as to reach the west of Atlanta. The enemy observing the movement, massed his troops in the same direction, and was successful in his onset. In the afternoon the fortune of battle had changed.

Atlanta was now heavily bombarded for some days. On August 26, after getting all things in readiness, General Sherman made a feint of retreating, in order to cover his "flanking" the place. On September 1, Hood blew up his magazine, destroyed 7 locomotives, 81 cars loaded with ammunition, small arms, and stores, partially destroyed 14 guns, and retreated south.

General Slocum entered the town September 2, at 11 o'clock A. M. It is estimated that the total Union loss from Chattanooga to Atlanta, in killed, wounded, and missing, is 31,500 men, 15 cannon, and 5 flags. The rebel loss for the same time, 44,000 men, 32 cannon, 30 flags, and 20,000 small arms.

On the 4th, General Sherman issued his order that

Atlanta must be held for military purposes exclusively, and sending all the inhabitants north or south, as they may choose. General Hood, on the 9th, protested, "in the name of God and humanity," against this order, but accepted a proposed truce for the removal. General Sherman's orders for the march from Atlanta were issued November 9. They direct troops to "forage liberally on the country," forbid trespassing by soldiers, and hold the country responsible for attacks by guerrillas. The public buildings were burned or blown up, the place rendered a desert, and evacuated November 14, and Sherman's forces were "marching to the sea."

Atzerodt, one of Booth's accomplices, was captured at Monocacy, near Baltimore, April 20, 1865. (See Harold.)

Auburn, Tenn., was the scene of a brisk but undecisive skirmish, March 20, 1863.

Auger, General, about October 20, 1864, adopted the plan of placing in conspicuous places, upon each train on the Manassas Gap Railroad, prominent secessionists, residents of the vicinity, as a protection against attacks from guerrillas. The plan accomplished the desired object.

Augusta, Ga. (See Arsenal.)

Augusta, Ky., was, on September 27, 1862, captured by rebel guerrillas, the garrison, after a stubborn fight, being compelled to surrender to superior forces. The rebels lost 90 killed and wounded. Union loss about 50.

Austin, Miss., was burned by Union forces, May 24, 1863.

Averysboro, N. C.—On March 16, 1865, the 14th Corps, of Sherman's army, had a fight with Hardee at this place, in which the latter was defeated, leaving all his dead in General Davis's hands, and retreating to Bentonsville. Union loss about 1,000 killed and wounded. Rebel loss less than half that number, on account of their works protecting them.

Avoyelles Prairie, La., was the scene of a short but spirited battle on May 16, 1864, between General Banks's retreating forces and the rebels, who were endeavoring to cut him off. The rebels were driven with great loss, considering the time and numbers engaged.

Aylett's, Va., was surprised and captured by Union

forces, under Colonel Fitspatrick, May 5, 1863. A party of 50 rebel cavalry were surprised and taken prisoners at the same time.

Bachelor's Creek, N. C., was, on May 20, 1864, the scene of an accidental explosion of four recently captured rebel torpedoes, killing and wounding several Union soldiers. (See Newbern.)

Bagley, a Union gun-boat, was blown up by torpedoes, on the Roanoke River, December 10, 1864.

Bahia. (See privateer Florida.)

Bailey's Dam was built partially across the Red River at the falls near Alexandria, raising the river at that point, and thus releasing Admiral Porter's fleet from its apparently hopeless situation above the falls. The force employed consisted of 3,000 men and 300 teams, under direction of Lieutenant-Colonel Bailey, who commenced operations May 2, 1864, and on the 13th the last of the fleet passed in safety, thus saving vessels valued at $2,000,000.

Bainbridge, Tenn.—Sturgis's cavalry attacked and drove the videttes out of this place January 14, 1864, but subsequently fell back before superior numbers. Three days later the rebels renewed the attack, and General Sturgis fell back to Strawberry Plains. The skirmishing lasted from daylight until 4 P. M., when Colonel McCook charged upon and completely routed them. Union loss, 150. Johnson's brigade of Rhoddy's army crossed the Tennessee River at this point, January 26, 1864.

Baker, Edward D., United States Senator from Oregon, was appointed Major-General of volunteers, September 21, 1861, and one month later was killed in battle, while gallantly leading his men near Ball's Bluff. (See Ball's Bluff.)

Baker's Creek, or Champion Hill, battle of, (25 miles west of Jackson, Miss.,) May 16, 1863. The forces engaged were about 25,000 on each side—the Unionists under General Grant, the rebels under Pemberton. The rebels were routed, and retired behind the Big Black River, with a loss of 16 pieces of artillery, 3,000 prisoners, 1,000 killed and wounded. Union loss, 1,700 killed or wounded.

Baldwin, Fla.—A force 5,000 strong, under General Seymour, advanced to and fortified this place February 18, 1864. Ten days later they evacuated the place, burning the stores, etc. The town was held by the rebels from that time till July 25, at which date General Birney, entering Florida by the St. Mary's River, drove out the rebels, and the place was occupied by Union forces.

Ball's Bluff, Va., battle of, October 21, 1861.—Colonel E. D. Baker, with 2,000 men, crossed the Potomac at Harrison's Island and Ball's Bluff, under orders from General Stone. About 4 P. M. they were suddenly attacked by a body of 5,000 Confederates, under General Evans. Being overpowered, they were driven back to the river, and many, for want of means to cross, were drowned or slaughtered on the banks. Baker fell at the first fire. General Stone was arrested and confined in Fort Lafayette, on suspicion of foul play. The Union loss was about 1,000 men, of whom nearly 300 were killed, and 500, including part of the wounded, taken prisoners.

Baltimore, Md.—An immense secession meeting was held at Baltimore, in Monument Square, on the evening of April 18, 1861. Violent disunion speeches were made, and the meeting adjourned with enthusiastic cheers for "the South" and for "President Davis." Next day the city was in the hands of the mob, with whom the 6th Massachusetts and 7th Pennsylvania regiments had a fight. Three soldiers were killed and eight wounded. Of the mob, eleven were killed and several wounded. The same day the Mayor of the city notified the President that no more troops could pass through the city without fighting their way. The mob on the following day, April 20, destroyed the telegraph lines and various bridges and culverts on the railroads, thus checking communication between Washington and the North. The city militia was speedily organized in the Southern interest, but was disbanded on May 6. General Butler took possession of Federal Hill, thus commanding the city, and re-establishing communications and travel through it on the 13th. June 15th the B. and O. R. R. was re-opened to Harper's Ferry. On the 17th, Marshal Geo.

P. Kane was arrested for treason, the Police Commissioners superseded, and John R. Kenly appointed Provost-marshal of the city. The Board of Police protested againt the arrest of Kane, but without avail; they were arrested July 1, and confined, with their chief, in Fort Henry. During the rebel invasion of Pennsylvania, martial law was proclaimed in the city, June 30, 1863.

Banks, N. P., was appointed Major-General of volunteers, May 30, 1861, and on June 10 he was detailed to, and assumed command of, the Department of Annapolis. On July 19 he was assigned to command the forces on the Upper Potomac, which position he assumed July 25. The various actions in this department will be found under their appropriate headings.

Banks's expedition (with sealed orders) sailed from New York December 4, 1862. It encountered a severe storm, and two of the vessels, in distress, put into Port Royal on the 11th, and one into Philadelphia on the 15th. The expedition arrived at New Orleans December 14, on which day General Banks relieved General Butler of the command of the Department of the Gulf. The formalities of General Butler's leave-taking, and of General Banks's assuming command, occurred the next day.

General Banks published the President's Emancipation Proclamation to the people of Louisiana February 6, 1863. The secessionists were highly incensed at this, and made an attempt to assassinate the General on his way to the opera, on the evening of the 11th. He continued in command of this department until General Canby relieved him, May 21, 1864. This command General Banks resumed December 1 of the same year. (The movements of his army, etc., will be found under their appropriate heads.)

Barbarities.—Mention will be made of only a few of the many instances.

German farmers massacred by a rebel mob in Western Texas, January 10, 1863.

Five Union men shot, in cold blood, by the rebels, at Little Rock, Ark., Jan. 23, 1863.

Attempt to assassinate General Banks, February 11, 1863.

Captain Dwight, *after surrender*, is murdered by the rebels, at Washington, La., May 4, 1863.

The rebel authorities refused to receive supplies for Union prisoners starving in the South, December 12, 1863.

A Union soldier was found hung at Smith's Mills, Va., with a placard calling it "retaliation," January 14, 1864.

A company of colored troops were surprised and captured near Grand Lake, Miss., by guerrillas, February 14, 1864. After surrendering, all but two were killed.

Rev. Dr. Cox, Chaplain 25th régiment Corps d'Afrique, was captured near Donaldsonville, La., by guerillas, and hanged, February 20, 1864.

The rebels at Kingston, N. C., hung 23 Union prisoners of war, one a drummer-boy 15 years old, March 6, 1864.

Five Union generals and 45 other officers were placed under fire at Charleston, June 15, 1864, and kept thero until retaliation compelled the rebels to end their unchristian course.

During a tacit truce, the rebels treacherously opened fire upon the Union soldiers outside their works, killing and wounding many, September 1, 1864.

An attempt was made, through rebel emissaries, on Nov. 25, 1864, to fire New York city by means of preparations of phosphorus left simultaneously in rooms, hired by the incendiaries, in fifteen of the chief hotels; Barnum's Museum and several ships were also fired; some of the fires caught, but none gained much headway. (See Fort Pillow, Mobs, New York Riots, Prisoners.)

Barbour, Va., was the scene of a skirmish between the cavalry forces under Pleasanton (U.) and Stewart (R.) Nov. 5, 1862. Rebels driven with considerable loss.

Barboursville, Va., was the scene of a skirmish, July 12, 1861, without any definite result. Four days later the rebels were defeated at the same place. A battle commenced here September 17, without loss to either side. It was resumed next day, and the rebels whipped. Union loss 1 killed and 1 wounded; rebel loss 15 killed and wounded. The place was occupied by Union forces without opposition November 4, 1861.

Bardstown, Ky., was the scene of a skirmish September 19, 1861. The Unionists coming up in force, the rebels evacuated the town, which the Unionists occupied October 4, 1862. Morgan's guerrillas captured the place July 7, 1863. It was again similarly captured and plundered June 18, 1864; and on January 17, 1865, another band of guerrillas attempted to burn the town. After a heavy fight, the Union garrison drove them out.

Barnsville, Ark.—Rebels routed at this place August 26, 1863.

Barnwell C. H., S. C., was burned by Sherman's troops February 5, 1865.

Bates, Attorney-General, resigned November 30, 1864.

Batesville, Ark., was dashed into on February 4, 1863, by a party of Union cavalry, who drove Marmaduke's forces out of the place, killing, wounding, and capturing a great many.

Bath, Va.—On January 4, 1862, General Jackson, with a large rebel force, attacked about 1,000 Union troops at Bath. Being overpowered by superior numbers, the Unionists fell back to Hancock. There was a cavalry skirmish at this place September 8, 1863.

Baton Rouge, La., battle of, Aug. 5, 1862. The Union troops were first driven from their position, but rallied and routed the rebels, who left their dead and wounded. Union loss 60 killed, (including General Williams, who commanded the Union forces,) 161 wounded, and 29 missing. The Confederates lost about 600 killed, and a large number wounded and prisoners. An expedition left New Orleans for Baton Rouge December 16, 1862, and the place was occupied by Union troops the next day. The capitol building was destroyed by fire about ten days later.

Baylor's Farm, battle of, June 15, 1864. Union victory, the rebels losing 16 guns and 300 prisoners.

Bayou Cache, battle of, June 7, 1862. The advance of General Curtis's army encountered 1,500 rebels, and after a desperate fight of two hours, put them to flight leaving 110 dead on the field. Union loss, 7 killed and 57 wounded.

Bayou Coteau, battle of, November 3, 1863. The rebels, 7,000, having received information from deserters of the strength and position of the Union forces, 1,600, attacked in force at 12 o'clock to-day. The Unionists were compelled to yield to superior numbers, and were driven about a mile, when a new line was formed. Being reinforced by General McGinnis's division, the Unionists advanced again. The rebels fled, first plundering and burning the captured camp. The Unionists occupied their old camping ground. Rebel loss, about 120 in killed and wounded, and 200 prisoners. Union loss, 26 killed, 124 wounded, and 566 missing.

Bayou Metaire Bridge, Ark., battle of, August 27, 1863. General Davidson, with 8,000 men of all arms, met the rebels, 7,000 strong, strongly posted at Bayou Metaire Bridge, and skirmished with them till dark.

Bayou Plaquemine, La.—The rebels burned 400 bales of cotton at this place, belonging to poor citizens in the vicinity, April 14, 1864.

Bayou Sara, La.—On July 9, 1863, the Unionists were here defeated, losing 210 prisoners. The rebels made a raid on this place, November 9, 1863. (See Port Hudson.)

Bay St. Louis, Miss.—A Union raid was made on this place, October 23, 1863, and a number of prisoners retaken from the enemy.

Beal, John Yates, of Virginia, was sentenced, on February 14, 1865, at Fort Lafayette, to be hung as a spy and violator of the laws of war. He was one of the Lake Erie pirates, and concerned in other rebel raids on the Northern frontier. He was hung ten days later.

Bealington, Va.—Skirmish and rebel rout, July 8, 1861.

Bealston Station, Va.—Mosby's guerrillas, in Union uniform, attempted to capture the forces at Bealston Station, but were discovered in time to frustrate their designs, November 20, 1863.

Bean Station, Tenn.—Longstreet turned upon his pursuers, under Shackleford, at this point, December 14, 1863, and a sharp fight ensued, lasting from 2 P. M. until dark; the Federal forces fell back to Tazewell. Union loss reported at 700 killed and wounded and prisoners; rebel loss admitted by General Gracie, who was wounded and captured, at 900. (See Saltville.)

Bear Creek, Mo.—The rebels were routed near this place, February 5, and also on April 17, 1863.

Beaufort, S. C., was found deserted by Commodore Dupont, who arrived there November 8, 1861. The place was occupied by Union forces December 6. There was an indecisive skirmish near this place February 5, 1862; also on January 7, 1863. A colored regiment, sent out from this place, returned May 3, 1863, having captured 800 slaves and destroyed $2,000,000 worth of rebel property. Sherman's head-quarters was at this point January 23, 1865.

Beaufort, N. C. General Terry's force in the transport fleet, after a boisterous passage, arrived at this place January 8, 1865, and arranged with Rear-Admiral Porter the attack on Fort Fisher.

Beauregard, General, assumed command of the rebels at Charleston, March 4, 1861. (See Anderson.) He relinquished this command May 27, and assumed command of the rebel army at Manassas Junction June 2. He was promoted to the rank of General in the rebel army July 21, 1861. He assumed command of the rebel army in Mississippi March 5, 1862, and three days later made his celebrated "bell call," begging of the planters to send in their bells for conversion into cannon. On January 31, 1863, he issued a proclamation declaring the blockade of Charleston legally raised. On February 18 he issued a proclamation to the people of Charleston and Savannah, stating the apprehensions of an early attack, and calling upon all able-bodied men to rally, with arms, pikes, scythes, spades, and shovels, for the defense of their homes and families. He protested against shelling Charleston August 22, 1863. And February 6, 1864, he paid a United States tax on property in Memphis. He assumed supreme command of the rebel "Army of the West" October 17, 1864, and was superseded by General J. E. Johnson February 25, 1865.

Beauregard, a privateer, was captured November 12, 1861.

Beaver Dam, Va., was occupied by Union cavalry, May 3, 1863, and again by Sheridan's forces, May 9, 1864, who destroyed three long trains of cars, the depot, two locomotives, eight miles of railroad and bridges, and an immense amount of supplies, estimated at 1,500,000 rations; 378 Union wounded and prisoners, about to leave for Richmond, were re-captured.

Beaver Dam Creek, Va.—A body of Union cavalry from Fredericksburg made a descent on the Virginia Central Railroad, at this place, July 20, 1862, destroyed the railroad and telegraph for several miles, and burned the depot, which contained large quantities of commissary and ordnance stores.

Beckwith, Mo., was the scene of a brisk skirmish October 13, 1861.

Bedford, Pa., was occupied by Milroy's rebel forces June 18, 1863.

Belle Boyd, a notorious rebel spy, was captured near Martinsburg, Va., August 29, 1863, and sent to Old Capitol Prison.

Belle Plain, La.—The rebels were defeated in a fight at this place May 21, 1863.

Belle Station, Tenn., was occupied by Burnside in his retreat on Knoxville, November 16, 1863.

Belmont, Mo., battle of, November 7, 1861. Generals Grant and McClernand, who left Cairo with a force of 2,850 men, landed at Belmont at 8 A. M. Immediately forming in line of battle, they advanced on the enemy's camp, and succeeded, after a stubborn resistance, in driving them for some distance and burning their camp. The Confederates being reinforced, General Grant withdrew his army to the boats. The advance and retreat were covered by the gun-boats Lexington and Tyler.

Benjamin, J. P., Senator from Louisiana, made a strong secession speech in the Senate December 31, 1860, from which body he withdrew February 5, 1861. He was appointed Attorney-General for the Rebel Government, and July 12 of the same year issued his "retaliatory circular."

Bennett's Mills was the scene of a skirmish September 1, 1861; casualties slight.

Bentonville, Ark., was occupied by Union troops February 20, 1862.

Bentonsville, N. C.—The 20th Corps, General Sherman's army, met the enemy at this place, 26 miles south-west of Goldsboro, March 19, 1865, where their advance was checked until the arrival of the 14th Corps, which held the enemy at bay, when the 17th Corps arrived and flanked the enemy, who left in confusion for Raleigh.

Berlin, Md.—An important bridge was burned by the rebels at this place June 8, 1861. Colonel Geary, with a part of the 28th Pennsylvania volunteers, took possession of the place, and shelled the rebels from their positions September 30.

Berlin, Ohio. (See John Morgan.)

Bermuda Hundred.—General Butler, moving by water from Yorktown, seized this place and intrenched himself May 5, 1864. June 2, a rebel charge was repulsed with severe loss. A short skirmish on February 17, 1865, resulted in a route of the rebels. (See Butler, Grant's report, etc.)

Berrett, Mayor of Washington, D. C., was arrested August 24, 1861, on a charge of treason. He was sent to Fort Lafayette. Upon taking the oath of allegiance, was released September 12.

Berry's Ferry, Va.—In a skirmish at this place May 16, 1863, 16 men of the 1st New York cavalry defeated 22 rebel cavalry, killing 2, wounding 5, and capturing 10 men.

Berryville, Va., was the scene of a skirmish with and capture of a few rebels April 21, 1863. The place was occupied by rebels June 13, after driving out McReynolds. General Wright arrived here July 19, 1864, in his pursuit after Early, and August 10, after some skirmishing, Sheridan encamped here.

Bertie, N. C.—A party, under Lieutenant-Colonel Maxwell, destroyed at this place, Feb. 26, 1864, over $200,000 worth of tobacco, cotton, pork, etc., and brought away many horses, mules, cattle, and wagons.

Bertrand, Mo., was the scene of a skirmish December 11, 1861.

Berwick Bay, La.—At a skirmish near this place March 18, 1863, the rebels were repulsed, with a loss of 12 killed and 20 wounded.

Beverly, Va.—By a forced march, General McClellan captured Colonel Pegram and 600 men at this place

2

July 12, 1861. The Union forces were defeated at the same point April 24, 1863.

Beverly Ford, Va.—There was a cavalry fight at this place June 9, 1863, between 15,000 of Stuart's cavalry and the Union cavalry, 9,000 strong, under General Pleasanton. It lasted from 5 A. M. to 3 P. M., when the rebels being heavily reinforced, Pleasanton withdrew, carrying off his wounded and 200 prisoners; also the bodies of his dead officers. The rebels had been driven back from three to five miles. This action frustrated, for a time, the intended invasion of Pennsylvania.

Big Bethel, Va., battle of.—Three regiments of Union troops from Hampton, Va., under General Pierce, moved about midnight of June 9, 1861, to attack the rebels at Big Bethel. At Little Bethel the advance and main body mistook each other for enemies, and fired, killing 2 and wounding 19. This alarmed the rebels, and the intended surprise was foiled. They then pushed on to Big Bethel, attacked the rebels, and after a fight of two hours' duration, the Union forces were compelled to withdraw. Union loss, 15 killed, 28 wounded, several missing; rebel loss, unknown. This place was occupied by Union forces January 3, 1862, and soon abandoned to the rebels, who again evacuated at the approach of the Unionists March 27, 1862.

Big Black River, Miss., was reached by Union forces May 2, 1863, and the battle of the Big Black occurred on the 16th. Grant again advanced toward Vicksburg, met Pemberton, and drove him into Vicksburg, with the loss of 2,600 men and 17 pieces of artillery. The rebels burned the bridge on their retreat. A brisk skirmish was fought near the bridge, without decided result, June 17, and six days later Gen. Osterhaus was attacked at the same place by Johnston's army. After a long engagement, Johnston went back again, his army having suffered terribly. The guerrilla Johnson was hotly pursued a few miles below the bridge July 6, and the Union forces captured nearly 2,000 men from the rebels at the same place two days later. There was a skirmish on the Big Black, 18 miles below Vicksburg, October 13. Rebels defeated, with a loss of 15 killed and wounded; Union loss 1 killed.

General Sherman's forces, consisting of 25,000 infantry, 1,200 cavalry, and 40 guns, commenced crossing the Big Black February 3, 1864, and the rear guard crossed it on the 7th. The Mississippi Central Railroad bridge over the Big Black was destroyed November 27, 1864. Major Crook and the 3d colored cavalry charged across the bridge on the ties, under rebel fire, and carried the defenses.

Big Creek, Miss.—The rebels were defeated in a brisk skirmish at this place July 11, 1863.

Big Hurricane Creek, Mo.—There was a battle at this place October 19, 1861, between 220 Federal soldiers and 400 rebels; the Confederates were completely routed.

Big Mulberry Creek, Ala., battle of, April 1, 1865. General Wilson defeated the rebels under Forrest (commanding), Chalmers, Rhoddy, and Lyon, taking 4 guns and over 200 prisoners.

Big Shanty, Ga., was occupied by McPherson's forces June 8, 1864, the rebels falling back on his approach. Quite a battle, in which the rebels were defeated, occurred here June 25. Hood made an attack upon this place October 5, 1864, and captured most of the garrison, but was soon driven out with heavy loss.

Biloxi, Miss., and its defenses surrendered to the Union fleet December 31, 1861.

Birds Point, Mo., was the scene of a brisk skirmish July 8, 1861. The rebels at this point were routed and dispersed February 28, 1862. The Union forces took 45 prisoners and six guns.

Birds Gap, Tenn.—The rebels attacked General Rosecrans at this place September 13, 1863.

Birney, Major General, died at Philadelphia, October 18, 1864.

Black Bayou, La., was the scene of brisk skirmishes March 5 and April 5, 1863.

Blackburn Ford, Va.—An engagement occurred at this place July 18, 1861, between a reconnoitering party of General McDowell's army and the Confederates. After a fight of a few hours, the Federals were ordered to withdraw, having accomplished their object.

Black Jack Forest, Tenn., was the scene of a brisk skirmish March 17, 1862.

Black River, Mo., was the scene of a skirmish September 12, 1861.

Blackville, S. C., was occupied by General William's corps February 9, 1861.

Black Walnut Creek, Mo., was the scene of a brisk action November 27, 1861.

Blackwater Bridge, Va.—The Union force at this point was overwhelmed by numbers and forced to retire, with a loss of 15 killed and wounded, December 11, 1862. An indecisive skirmish took place on the 26th. Skirmishes occurred March 8 and 17, also June 17, 1863, all resulting in Union victories.

A cavalry force from Grant's army made the passage of the river at this point March 18, 1865, destroying a large amount of cotton and other stores.

Blackwell, N. C., was occupied by Kilpatrick February 7, 1865.

Blair, jr., F. P., was ordered under arrest by the Provost-marshal of St. Louis, September 15, 1861. He offered his resignation as Major-General, to date from January 1, 1864. This he recalled April 20, and on the 23d assumed command of the 17th Army Corps. (His military history beyond this will be found under the appropriate battle headings.)

Blair, sen., F. P., together with Montgomery Blair, arrived at General Grant's head-quarters December 30, 1864, on their way to Richmond. General Grant refused to pass them through his lines, and they returned. Mr. F. P. Blair, sen., however, within a day or two set out for Richmond, returning on the 6th of January, 1865, and on the 8th again repeated the journey, accompanied by General Singleton. It was supposed that this time he carried informal peace propositions. He returned on the 18th, having accomplished nothing. His third trip he commenced on the 20th, and on the 26th returned. The result of these several trips was nothing.

Blakeley, Ala., and the entire line of works for the defense of Mobile were captured April 9, 1865, including 3,000 prisoners, 2 general officers, 20 guns, and much ammunition.

Blandville, Ky., was surprised and plundered by guerrillas November 7, 1863.

Blockade.—The President of the United States, April 19, 1861, issued a proclamation, declaring a blockade of the ports of the seceded States, viz.: South Carolina, Georgia, Alabama, Florida, Mississippi, Louisiana, and Texas; and the Secretary of the Treasury ordered that no clearances should be granted to vessels bound south of Maryland. The blockade was actually established as follows: Charleston, S. C., May 11; Mississippi River, at Cairo, May 13; New Orleans, May 26; Savannah, May 28.

The rebels blockaded the Mississippi River, at Memphis, May 26, 1861.

The blockade of New Orleans was modified, and a collector appointed, May 3, 1862.

The rebel authorities declared the blockade of Charleston legally raised January 31, 1863, and the blockade of Galveston and Sabine Pass raised February 7. These declarations were promptly denied by the authorities at Washington.

The blockade, except as to contraband of war, of Norfolk, Va., Pensacola and Ferdinanda, Fla., was raised by proclamation November 19, 1864.

A proclamation was issued April 11, 1865, substituting for the blockade a legal closure of all the Southern ports to trade except so far as some had already been partially and conditionally opened. The following is from the report of the Secretary of the Navy:

PROPERTY CAPTURED AND DESTROYED.

Naval men, while animated with the noblest feelings of patriotism, and ready to sacrifice their lives for their country, whose integrity was imperiled, were impressed at first with the conviction that to them, professionally, the war would offer but limited opportunity; for the rebels were not a commercial people, nor addicted to maritime pursuits. No naval conflicts were anticipated, and it was supposed very few captures would be made; but the efforts of the insurgents, cut off from foreign supplies, and the attempts of unscrupulous foreign adventurers to violate the blockade, have rewarded naval vigilance and fidelity with a large number of prizes, many of them of great value. It is a gratifying circumstance that these prize captures have inured to the benefit of the naval service instead of privateers—differing in this respect from previous wars.

The number of vessels captured and sent to the courts for adjudication, from May 1, 1861, to the close of the rebellion, is 1,149, of which there were: steamers, 210; schooners, 569; sloops, 139; ships, 13; brigs and brigantines, 29; barks, 25; yachts, 2; small boats, 139; rebel rams and iron-clads, 6; rebel gun-boats, torpedo-boats, and armed schooners and sloops, 10; class unknown, 7—making a total of 1,149. The number of vessels burned, wrecked, sunk, and otherwise destroyed, during the same time, were: steamers, 85; schooners, 114; sloops, 32; ships, 2; brigs, 2; barks, 4; small boats, 96; rebel rams, 5; rebel iron-clads, 4; rebel gun-boats, torpedo boats, and armed schooners and sloops, 11; total 355; making the whole number of vessels captured and destroyed 1,504. During the war of 1812 the naval vessels, of which there were 301 in the service at the close, made but 291 captures. There were 517 commissioned privateers, and their captures numbered 1,428. That war was with a nation having the greatest commerce on the globe. During the recent war we had no privateers afloat, and the rebels had but a limited commerce from which the prizes of the navy could be made. Nearly all the captures of value were vessels built in so-called neutral ports, and fitted out and freighted in the ports of a government with which we had treaties and were on friendly terms, which had publicly pledged itself to a strict neutrality, and manifested its sincerity, so far as we were concerned, by withdrawing hospitality to our national vessels.

The gross proceeds of property captured since the blockade was instituted, and condemned as prizes prior to the 1st of November, amounts to $21,829,543.96; costs and expenses, $1,616,223.96; net proceeds for distribution, $20,501,927.69. There are a number of important cases still before the courts, which will largely increase these amounts.

The value of the 1,149 captured vessels will not be less than $24,500,000, and of the 355 vessels destroyed at least $7,000,000, making a total valuation of not less than $31,500,000, much of which was British property, engaged in unneutral commerce, and so justly captured and condemned.

Bloomfield, Mo., was occupied by the Union forces January 24, 1862. Rebel loss, 80 men, including 12 officers. A battle was fought between this place and Cape Girardeau Aug. 24, in which the rebels were routed, with the loss of 30 killed, 50 wounded, and 16 prisoners; also arms, ammunition, equipage, etc. The town was attacked by the rebels and abandoned by the Unionists September 11, 1862, who, in turn, drove out the rebels January 27, 1863, and soon left it again to the Confederates, who were again dislodged March 1, with a loss of 20 men, including their Provost-marshal. The place was occupied by Price September 23, 1864, but his stay was short.

Bloomingdale, Ga., 16 miles from Savannah, was occupied by Sherman's advance December 10, 1864.

Blooming Gap, Va., was captured February 14, 1862, by General Lander, who captured a large number of prisoners and destroyed a large amount of stores.

Blount Ridge, N. C., was occupied by rebels April 9, 1863, after driving out the Union forces.

Blountsville, Ala., was the scene of a cavalry skirmish May 1, 1863.

Blountsville, East Tenn., was occupied by the Union forces October 14, 1863. The rebels were defeated and driven toward Saltville. Three locomotives and 34 cars were captured. Rebel loss, 8 killed, 26 wounded, and 10 captured; Union loss, 5 wounded.

Blue's Gap, Va., was the scene of a rebel route January 7, 1862. They lost 15 killed, 20 prisoners, 2 cannon, wagons, tents, etc.

Blue's Mills Landing, Mo., was the scene of two skirmishes September 17, 1861.

Blue Springs, Mo., was the scene of a Union defeat March 22, 1863.

Blue Springs, Tenn., was the scene of a brisk but undecisive engagement October 5, 1863. Five days later the fight was renewed. The rebels, 6,000 strong, were defeated and driven from the field at sundown. Union loss, 100 killed and wounded; 150 rebels were captured.

An engagement at this place August [illegible] 1864, between

Gillem's forces and Wheeler's, resulted in the rout of the latter.

Bluff Point, Va., (See Booth.)

Bluffton, S. C., was occupied by General Stevens (Union) December 21, 1861. The place was burned by the Union forces June 4, 1863.

Boat Burning was one of the means resorted to by the rebels to carry out their purpose; a few of the instances are given:

Three steamers were set on fire at St. Louis, September 29, 1863. The conflagration among the hay barges in New York harbor December 9, 1863, by which $500,000 worth of property was destroyed, was the work of the same class of men. Eight steamers were fired at New Orleans May 21, 1864, and six steamers burned at St. Louis July 15.

The United States Steamer "Roanoke," Captain Drew, from Havana for New York, when just out of Havana, took on board three boat-loads of persons claiming to be passengers. The same evening the gang captured the vessel, killing the carpenter and taking possession "for the Confederate States." Their leader was Braine, of the Chesapeake affair. He put the passengers aboard a vessel, went to Bermuda, and burned the steamer, going ashore in the boats.

Boca Chica, Texas, was captured and occupied by General Banks November 2, 1863. The last engagement of the war was fought at this place May 12, 1865.

Bogus Proclamation.—Joseph Howard, with a view to speculate in gold, put forth a forged proclamation, purporting to emanate from President Lincoln, calling for 400,000 men by immediate and peremptory draft. It was published in the New York *World* and *Journal of Commerce*, May 18, 1864. The military authorities seized these papers and temporarily silenced them, but released them on investigation. Howard was sent to Fort Lafayette.

Bolivar, Tenn.—A severe fight occurred at this place August 30, 1862; the engagement lasted seven hours, when, the Union troops being reinforced, the Confederates withdrew. The Union loss was 25 killed and wounded. Confederate loss not known.

Brisk skirmishes, in each of which the rebels were beaten, occurred at this place February 12 and 13, and March 9, 1863.

Near this place, on May 2, 1864, General Sturges routed General Forrest, who retreated burning bridges, etc.

Bolivar Heights, Va., was the scene of brisk skirmishes, in both of which the rebels were driven back, October 16, 1861, and November 26, 1862.

This place was abandoned by Mulligan's forces July 4, 1864.

Bolivar Point, Galveston Harbor, Texas, was attacked and the fortifications destroyed, by the United States frigate "Santee," December 3, 1861.

Bollinger's Mills, Mo., was the scene of a rebel rout, July 29, 1862.

Bolton, Miss., was occupied by the rebel guerrilla Johnson, July 6, 1863. General Sherman occupied the place February 3, 1864.

Boone, N. C., was occupied by General Stoneman's command March 27, 1865. The rebels were driven out, with a loss of 10 killed and 65 wounded and prisoners.

Boone C. H., Va., was occupied by Union forces, after routing the rebels, September 1, 1861. The town was burned next day.

Boone County, Ind., was, for the time, rendered notorious on account of a body of citizens there resisting the enrollment, about June 15, 1863.

Booneville, Mo.—General Lyon attacked and defeated the rebels, under Governor Jackson, at this place, and captured large quantities of military stores, June 17, 1861. Losses not known. Union troops held the town until July 3, when they left it on an expedition toward the south-west part of the State. A brisk but undecisive skirmish occurred here September 13, 1861.

Price made a speech at this place October 14, 1864, in which he said he had come to redeem the State, and if the people did not rally to his standard they would not have another chance. They were not redeemed, as he understood the term.

Booneville, Miss., battle of, July 1, 1862.—Colonel Sheridan, of the 2d Michigan Cavalry, with a body of Union troops, defeated 4,700 rebels after seven hours' hard fighting. They left 65 dead on the field. The Union loss was 41 killed, wounded, and missing.

Boonesboro, Md., was occupied by the Union cavalry, under Kilpatrick, after driving out the rebel Stuart, July 9, 1863.

Booth, J. Wilkes, assassinated President Abraham Lincoln, in his private box, at Ford's Theater, in Washington, about 10 o'clock on the evening of April 14, 1865. Booth entered the box unobserved by any of the party, and shot the President, the ball taking effect at the base of the brain, and almost coming through at the right temple. The report of the pistol alarming the party, they sprang to their feet. Major Rathbone tried to arrest Booth, who now had a large knife in his hands, and who, after severely cutting the Major in the right arm, rushed to the front of the box and sprang to the stage, some ten feet below, still holding the knife. In jumping down, one of his spurs caught in the folds of a flag adorning the front of the box, which threw him on his knees as he reached the stage, breaking one of his leg bones; gaining his feet, he flourished his knife over his head, saying, "*Sic Semper Tyrannis*"—the motto of Virginia—and ran across the stage to the rear, making his escape through the private door to the alley, mounting a horse, previously placed there by himself, and riding off at full speed. So quickly was it all done, and the audience not seeing into the box, and Booth's jumping on the stage being taken for a part of the performance, no one was quick enough to detain him, although several pursued him across the stage and into the alley, but were only in time to see him riding for life up the street. Booth had his leg dressed next day by Dr. Mudd, a violent secessionist, living in Maryland, about twenty miles below Washington. After lying concealed for several days in St. Mary's County, Maryland, Booth and Herold—an accomplice in the assassination—crossed the Potomac, into Virginia, at Bluff Point. They made their way southward, but were discovered by Lieutenant Docherty and a party of soldiers, in the barn of one Garrett, three miles from Port Royal. They were surrounded, and summoned to surrender, but refused. Herold, after a time, surrendered, but Booth continued to refuse, and to jeer Herold for so doing. The barn was finally fired, and the assassin shot in the head by Corporal Boston Corbett. He died, after about four hours of the most intense suffering, April 26. *His burial-place no man knoweth.*

Border State Convention, met at Frankfort, Ky., June 3, 1861, and adjourned without accomplishing any thing.

Boileau, A. D., proprietor of the Philadelphia *Evening Journal*, was arrested, under orders from Washington, for treasonable articles in his paper, January 27, 1863. He was released four days later.

Boston, Ky., was the scene of skirmishes, each of which resulted favorably for the Unionists, November 5, 1861, and June 13, 1863.

Bottoms Bridge, Va., was reached by the Army of the Potomac, and the rebels driven across the Chickahominy River at this point, May 17, 1862. One week later, another battle was fought at the same place, resulting in the rebels being repulsed. An indecisive skirmish occurred here, July 2, 1863. Butler held the position February 6, 1864, and Sheridan again May 13.

Bowling Green, Ky., was the scene of a skirmish February 1, 1862. Rebel loss, 5 killed and wounded. No Union loss. The town was evacuated by the rebels, and occupied by the advance of General Buell's army, under General Mitchell, February 15. The Unionists soon left the place, and again occupied the town September 7. The Union forces for the relief of Nashville passed through this place October 31.

Bradyville, Tenn.—A force of 1,000 cavalry and 1,000 infantry encountered a division of Morgan's cavalry at this place, and, after a severe engagement, drove them from the town, with the loss of 8 killed, 30 wounded, and 9 officers and 80 privates captured; 300 saddles and a collection of official papers were captured. The Union loss was about half that of the rebels.

Bramlette, Governor of Kentucky, on January 1, 1864, ordered that five rebel sympathizers be arrested for every loyal man taken by the guerrillas. His proclamation protecting fugitive slaves from rebel owners was issued February 13. On March 16 he remonstrated against the employment of slaves by the United States.

Brandon, Miss, was occupied by Johnson, in his retreat, July 21, 1863. Sherman, after a brisk skirmish, occupied the place March 7, 1864.

Brandon Farms, Va., was captured January 23, 1864, by Union raiders, who also captured 30 rebels, 100 negroes and 30,000 pounds of pork, all without losing a man.

Brandy Station, Va., battle of, August 4, 1863, between 6,000 of Stuart's cavalry and three brigades of Union cavalry and Major Brockhaus's artillery. The fight lasted from 2 o'clock till night, when Stuart retreated. He stated his loss at 6 killed, 18 wounded. (See Beverly Ford.)

Branchville, S. C., was evacuated by the rebels February 11, 1865, and occupied by Sherman's forces next day.

Brasher City, La., was captured June 22, 1863, by the Unionists, who were driven out two days later; but again reoccupied it, routing the rebels, July 22.

Brazos Island, Texas, was occupied by General Banks's "Texas Expedition" November 2, 1863.

Breckenridge, J. C., was expelled from the United States Senate December 4, 1861. He openly joined the rebels October 21.

Brentwood, Tenn. (See Nashville.)

Briar Forks, Mo. (See Carthage, Mo.)

Bridge Burning was extensively carried on during the entire continuance of the rebellion. Some instances were as follows: Baltimore mobs burned all bridges east, north and north-east of and near that city, April 19 and 20, 1861; an attempt to burn the Monocacy bridge (iron) May 12; Baltimore and Ohio Railroad bridge burned by the rebels May 16; Alexandria and Loudon Railroad bridges destroyed May 25; and at about this rate for over four years.

Bridgeport, Ala., was occupied by General Mitchell's forces April 29, 1862. The rebels, in their retreat, abandoned their arms, stores, etc., losing 72 killed and 350 prisoners.

Bridgeport, Tenn.—Near this place, on October 2, 1863, occurred a terrific explosion of a train-load of ammunition.

Bridgetown, Tenn., was occupied, and the bridge destroyed, July 7, 1863, by Bragg, in his retreat before Rosecrans.

Bright, Jesse D., of Indiana, was expelled from the United States Senate February 5, 1862.

Bristol, Tenn., was occupied by Morgan's guerrillas December 13, 1864. (See Saltville.)

Bristow's Station, Va., was captured by guerrillas March 9, 1864. They also captured 40 of the 30th Pennsylvania cavalry.

Britton's Lane, Tenn.—On September 1, 1862, a small force of Union troops defeated a large force of rebels at this place after a fight of four hours, the rebels leaving 175 dead on the field. Union loss, 5 killed and 51 wounded.

Broad Run, near Drainsville, Va., was the scene of a skirmish April 1, 1863. Unionists defeated.

Brookville, Md., was occupied by the rebels June 28, 1863.

Brown's Ferry, (Tennessee River, near Chattanooga,) battle of, October 27, 1863.—The rebels attacked General Hooker's force at 12 midnight, and a severe fight ensued, which continued two hours with lighter work, until 4 A. M. Every attack was repulsed, and the rebels driven from every position they assailed. The result was important, as it removed from this point the obstructions to steamboat navigation, and secured the way for army supplies. Hood's army—consisting of about 20,000 men and 10 guns—escaped across the Tennessee River near this place, December 28, 1864.

Brownsville, Mo., was captured and partially burned by guerrillas, October 16, 1863.

Brownsville, Tenn., was the scene of brisk skirmishes, all resulting favorably for the Unionists, December 5, 1861, July 29 and October 24, 1862, and September 1, 1863.

Brownsville, Texas, was captured by General Banks, and occupied by his Texas expedition November 3, 1863. The place was opened to commerce not "contraband of war" February 18, 1864.

Brownell, F. E. (See Ellsworth.)

Bruinsburg, Miss., was occupied by Union forces April 30, 1863.

Brunswick, Ga., was captured by Commodore Dupont's fleet March 2, 1862. It was made a port of entry July 1, 1862.

Buchanan, James, in his message December 3, 1860, upon the opening of the second session of the XXXVI Congress, denied the right of any State to secede, and also denied the right of the General Government to prevent secession. December 4, he sent Mr. Trescott to Charleston to "*request a postponement*" of hostile action until Congress could decide upon remedies in the case. At an extra session of the Cabinet, December 13, President Buchanan opposed the reinforcement of the forts in Charleston harbor. On the 30th of December, in reply to the application of the South Carolina Commissioners, he refused to receive them in an official capacity. We leave him here, simply remarking that he retired from the Presidential chair an object of detestation and pity to almost every citizen.

Buckhannon, Va., was the scene of a rebel rout, July 1, 1861. The guerrillas captured the town, burning the public stores, August 30, 1862.

Buckner, General. (See Fort Donaldson.)

Buel, General Don Carlos, was assigned to the command of the Department of Kentucky November 9, 1861, and was relieved from the command October 24, 1862.

Buffalo Hill, Ky., was the scene of a skirmish October 3, 1861. Union loss, 18. Rebel loss, 60.

Buffalo Mills, Mo., was captured by Union forces, and the rebel camp there broken up, October 22, 1861.

Buffington, Ohio. (See John Morgan.)

Bull's Bay, S. C., was held by General Potter's Union force operating in concert with General Sherman, February 13, 1865.

Bull's Gap, Tenn., was fortified and occupied January 10, 1864, by General Longstreet's force, numbering about 35,000 infantry and 12,000 cavalry. The rebels advanced from this position, but were forced to retreat to it February 20, with the loss of much camp equipage. They retreated toward Virginia March 31. (See Saltville.)

Bull Run, Va.—At 5 o'clock on the morning of July 21, 1861, the Federal army broke camp at Centerville and moved upon the rebel works in five divisions, commanded respectively by General Tyler and Colonels Hunter, Heintzelman, Runyan, and Miles. Richardson's brigade of Tyler's division was ordered to make a feint by way of Blackburn Ford, while the remainder of that division moved by way of Stone Bridge, strongly defended by the rebels with artillery. Heintzleman's division, by cutting a road through the woods, took position on the run about midway between Tyler and Hunter. Miles's division was held in reserve at Centerville, and to check any attempt of the rebels to turn our left flank, and Runyan's was seven miles nearer Washington. Both Tyler and Heintzleman, by making feint attacks, engaged the enemy's attention, while the main body, under Hunter, made a detour to the right. After passing Cub Run, and crossing Bull Run at Sudley's Springs, three miles above, they attempted to turn the enemy's left flank. This had, in a measure, been accomplished, when the enemy, finding the attack on his right was only a feint, commenced to strengthen his left. This being perceived, Heintzleman was ordered to press his attack to prevent this movement of troops. He succeeded in driving back the enemy from the bridge far enough to allow Sherman and Keys's brigades of Tyler's division to cross over and drive the enemy's right. This being accomplished, the balance of Tyler s division crossed, and the engagement became general along the whole line. After a severe fight of over six hours, when the Federals had nearly won the field, and the enemy almost disheartened, the rebels were reinforced by Johnston's army from Winchester. The suddenness and strength of this onset, and in the midst of the security felt on a field so nearly won, was sufficient to create disorder, which, in spite of all the efforts of the officers, resulted finally in a panic. The Union force engaged did not exceed 20,000; while that of the rebels was, according to their own accounts, 40,000 on the field and about 25,000 in reserve at Manassas Junction. Union loss, in killed, wounded, and missing, was 2,708; that of the enemy, 1,902. After the battle, Colonel Enstein, with the 27th Pennsylvania, brought off six pieces of artillery which had been abandoned in the retreat.

A battle was fought at Groveton, near Bull Run, on August 29, 1862, which lasted from daylight until dark, resulting in a Union victory. The battle was renewed next day, and is usually designated as "the second battle of Bull Run." General Pope's forces, having fallen back, were attacked by the Confederates under General Lee, on the old field of Bull Run. The fight raged fiercely all day, and with great slaughter. The Union left wing had been pressed back half a mile, but the right still held its ground. After the battle, the whole army fell back to Centerville.

The Army of the Potomac occupied the old battle-field June 15, 1863, and there occurred a brisk skirmish there four months later.

Bunker Hill, near Martinsburg, Va. was, on July 15, 1863, the scene of a skirmish approaching a battle, between General Patterson's advance and the rebel cavalry under Stuart. The Confederates were defeated and driven two miles. The place was occupied by Union forces March 5, 1862.

Burbridge, Brevet Major-General S. G., was appointed August 7, 1864, to command the Military District of Kentucky. (See Saltville.)

Burk's Station, Va., was occupied by Wilson and Kautz June 23, 1864. They destroyed the railroads in each direction, and repulsed the rebels twice.

Burksville, Va., was held by General Sheridan April 5, 1865, thus effectually preventing Lee from retreating in that direction.

Burley, the Lake Erie pirate, was, on January 20, 1865, committed by Recorder Duggan, at Toronto, for surrender to the United States. After a hearing and argument of the case, he was so surrendered, at Suspension Bridge, February 3.

Burnside, General A. E., was appointed to the command of the Army of the Potomac November 7, 1862. On the 14th he divided his forces into three corps, under Generals Sumner, Franklin, and Hooker, with the 11th Corps as a reserve, and the next day took up his march toward Fredericksburg. He occupied Falmouth on the

17th, and on the 21st General Sumner demanded the surrender of Fredericksburg. He threatened to burn the town in case of refusal, and allowed sixteen hours to remove non-combatants. The Mayor asked for a longer time. General Sumner acceded. Active hostilities were again resumed December 11, by the Union forces shelling Fredericksburg. Having laid their pontoons, the Federals passed the river under a terrific fire. The crossing continued on the 12th, when the city was taken. The next day General Burnside moved on the rebel works south of the city. The ground here is in the form of plateaus, from a quarter to half a mile wide, on the first of which stands the city; on the third or upper one was the rebel position, fortified with great skill and strength, and commanding every approach. The middle one was the principal battle-ground. Franklin moved against the rebel right, while Hooker attacked the center. Several charges were made by the Union troops, but they failed to make any impression, and night found the two armies in the same position as in the morning. The Union losses were 1,512 killed, about 6,000 wounded, and about 700 prisoners. Skirmishing continued on the 14th and 15th, and during the night of the 15th and the morning of the 16th the Unionists recrossed to the north bank of the river before the rebels were aware of the movement. Every man and all property was removed. General Burnside, on the 19th, in a letter to the President, assumed the responsibility of the defeat at Fredericksburg, and asked to be relieved from his command. His resignation was not accepted, however. He renewed it, however, and on January 24, 1863, was relieved by Major-General Joseph Hooker. His further military history will be found under the appropriate headings.

Burnside's Expedition, consisting of about 125 vessels of various sizes and descriptions, many of them collected from the merchant service for the occasion, sailed from Fortress Monroe January 11, 1862. After encountering a heavy storm, the advance of the expedition arrived at Hatteras Inlet, N. C., on the 19th. Some two weeks were occupied in getting ready for active operations, which commenced February 7, between the Union fleet and the rebel batteries on Roanoke Island, assisted by their gun-boats stationed behind a row of sunken ships. By nightfall several of the gun-boats had been disabled, and several of their guns dismounted. During the night General Burnside landed his troops, about 4,000 strong. In the morning about 1,000 additional were landed. The position was so well chosen, and the attack so stubbornly resisted, that several of the stronger works had to be carried at the point of the bayonet. Toward the close of the day, both flanks of the rebel works being turned, they surrendered. Union loss, 30 killed and 200 wounded. Rebel loss, 16 killed, 40 wounded, about 3,000 prisoners, six forts, mounting forty-two guns, 3,000 stand of small arms, and immense quantities of military stores.

About 9 o'clock on the morning of the 10th, Commander Rowan, with fourteen gun-boats, engaged the Confederate fleet which had escaped from Roanoke, off Cobb's point, N. C., and before 10 o'clock, two batteries on shore were silenced. Five of the rebel vessels were burned by their own crews, two were abandoned, one was captured, and Elizabeth City surrendered and was occupied by the Union forces next day. (See Newbern.)

Burnt Ordinary, Va., was the scene of a cavalry skirmish, January 19, 1863.

Burton's Ford, four miles from Charlottesville, Va., was captured by General Custar, February 29, 1864. At two o'clock A. M., he surprised a cavalry camp, blew up six caissons, and destroyed the camp equipage and captured 20 prisoners.

Bushy Creek, Indian Territory, 180 miles from Fort Smith, Ark., was the scene of a brisk engagement on December 9, 1861, between the Union Indians and the Confederates.

Butler, Benjamin F., was appointed Brigadier-General of volunteers from Massachusetts, April 17, 1861, and the same day started for Washington. Baltimore being in the hands of the secession mob, and the railroads destroyed, rendered passing directly through it impracticable. On the morning of the 20th, his command left Philadelphia and reached Annapolis, *via* Havre de Grace at midnight. His forces were next morning landed, and, repairing the railroad as they went, commenced their march to Annapolis Junction, and thence to the Relay House, which he occupied May 5. Moving from this place on the evening of the 13th, apparently for Harper's Ferry, he planted himself on Federal Hill, thus commanding the city of Baltimore, awing into quiet the secession mobocrats there, and reopening a safe transit for troops and citizens through "My Maryland." He received his commission as Major-General May 16, was assigned to the command of Fortress Monroe on the 20th, and two days later assumed that position. On the 27th, he declared in relation to fugitive slaves coming within the Union lines:

"These men are contraband of war; set them at work."

General Butler was relieved of his command by General Wool, August 16. He assumed command of the forces in the Department of Virginia—exclusive of those in Fortress Monroe—on the 22d, and, co-operating with Commodore Stringham, captured the forts at Hatteras Inlet on the 29th.

On February 22, 1862, he was assigned to the command of the land forces to co-operate with the navy in the attack on New Orleans. Sailing from Hampton Roads February 24, he reached Ship Island March 21, and four days later his troops joined him at that point. He landed at New Orleans May 1, and in a few days transformed the city from a "mob-ridden community" to a peaceable, if not a contented city. He found the city without supplies, and the poorer classes, and many of those in moderate circumstances, on the verge of starvation. This he, in some measure, remedied by gathering stores from the country, and levying an assessment upon those who had previously subscribed to the $1,250,000 loan for the defense of New Orleans against the United States. These measures brought in the produce and money which was mainly expended in cleansing the city, then in a very filthy condition. May 13, he forbid the observance of "Jeff. Davis's fast-day." The famous order concerning the women of New Orleans, which caused so much stir, was issued May 15. General Butler says its success was immediate and perfect. $800,000 was seized in the office of the Netherlands' Consul May 10. The city officials were suspended June 2, and new ones appointed two days later. For a full account of his action in New Orleans see Parton's "Butler in New Orleans." General Butler was relieved, December 4, of his command, and turned the same over to General Banks on the 15th. On his return North, he was received with hearty enthusiasm in Philadelphia, New York, Boston, Baltimore, and other places. November 11, 1863, he assumed command of the Department of Eastern Virginia and North Carolina, with head-quarters at Fortress Monroe. The War Department relieved him of this command, but General Grant, on July 19, 1864, rescinded the order and added the 19th Corps to his former force. November 5, General Butler assumed command of the "forces in New York City, arriving and to arrive, to meet existing emergencies." The troubles there settled, he resumed his command before Richmond on the 15th. General Grant relieved him of this command January 6, 1865, General Ord succeeding. On the 8th, in his farewell order to his troops, he made an attempt to show the injustice of his removal. (See Grant's Report.)

Butte a' la Rose, La., was occupied, and the rebel fort there captured by the Union gun-boats, April 20, 1863.

Buzzard's Roost Pass, Ga., was attacked by General Sherman May 8, 1864. The Union forces under General Thomas attacked in front, while McPherson made a flank movement. The rebels evacuated and retreated to Resaca. Union loss, about 700 killed, wounded, and missing, there being an unusually large number of slightly wounded.

Cabin Creek, Kansas.—The rebels 1,500 strong, under Sturdevant, on September 19, 1864, captured a train worth $1,000,000 at this place.

Cainsville, Tenn., was the scene of a cavalry skirmish February 15, 1863, resulting in a Union victory.

Cairo, Ills.—General Grant, with a force of 3,500, left this place November 6, 1861. They landed three miles above Columbus, Ky.

A reconnoitering expedition, 5,000 strong, under Generals Grant and McClernand, left this place January 10, 1862, for the vicinity of Columbus, Ky. The expedition was highly successful, penetrating to within three miles of Columbus and returned to Cairo on the 21st.

A great naval expedition left this place March 15, 1862.

Cairo, a United States gun-boat, was destroyed by a rebel torpedo on the Yazoo River December 18, 1862.

Caleb Cushing, a United States revenue cutter, was, on June 26, 1863, cut out of Portland (Maine) harbor by a rebel crew. Two steamers, the Forest City and Chesapeake, were started in pursuit, and pressed the cutter so hard that the rebels next day burned her and took to their boats to escape, but were all captured and taken to Fort Preble.

Calhoun, Fort, on the Rip Raps, Hampton Roads, was changed in name to Fort Wool March 18, 1862.

Calhoun, Ga., was attacked by the rebel General Wheeler August 15, 1864. He had previously cut the railroads at that point. The demand to surrender was refused, and the rebels driven by a charge of the colored troops, then holding the place.

Call for Troops. (See Conscription.)

Camden, Ark., was the scene of a brisk skirmish, April 2, 1864, between the rebel General Shelby, and Steele's rear guard. The rebels were repulsed, with a loss of about 100. Another battle ensued on the 19th, when the place was held by General Steele until the 26th, when he retreated to Little Rock.

Camden, N. C., was, on April 19, 1862, occupied by General Reno, after a sharp skirmish with the rebels. The Union troops afterward retired to the main army at Newbern. The rebels lost 60 men; the Nationals, 12 killed and 48 wounded.

Cameron, Simon, was called into Mr. Lincoln's Cabinet, as Secretary of War, March 5, 1861. In October of that year, he, in company with Adjutant-General Thomas and suit, made a tour of observation and inspection through the Western military departments. His rumored loose way of making contracts and disbursing money was very unsatisfactory to the people, and he resigned his place in the Cabinet January 11, 1862, and was afterward appointed Minister to Russia.

Camp Alleghany. (See Alleghany.)

Camp Dick Robinson, Ky., was occupied by the rebels, under Bragg, October 12, 1862, but evacuated next day. A lively skirmish occurred here March 26, 1863.

Camp Finnegan, Fla.—General Seymour's advance, under Colonel Guy V. Henry, pushed forward into the interior of Florida on the night of February 9, 1864, passed the rebel line of battle at Camp Finnegan, surprised and captured a battery three miles in the rear, took 100 prisoners, 8 pieces of artillery, and valuable property to a large amount, and reached Baldwin, Florida, at sunrise next morning, without loss; the rebels at Camp Finnegan, 500 strong, hastily retreated on the passing of the cavalry column, and the infantry coming up, took possession of the camp. The rebels on March 2 retook the camp from the Federals, driving them to within three miles of Jacksonville. The rebels lost 30 killed and wounded.

Campbell's Station, Texas.—A fight occurred here November 17, 1863, resulting in a rebel victory, and lasting from late in the morning until dark; Union loss, about 250 killed and wounded.

Campti, La., was the scene of an engagement between the forces under Colonel Gooding and Harrison's guerrillas, April 4, 1864. Unionists repulsed.

Canada Raids.—During the summer and fall of 1863, rumors of rebels in Canada planning raids upon our frontier were numerous and apparently authentic. November 11, Lord Lyons, the British Minister at Washington, officially informed Government that the Governor-General of Canada had informed him of a rebel plot to invade the United States, destroy the city of Buffalo, and to liberate the rebel prisoners at Johnson's Island, near Sandusky, Ohio.

January 17, 1864, 3,000 rebels were reported at Point Pelee, Canada, preparing for an attack on Johnson's Island.

July 18, a band of rebel refugees from St. John's, N. B., made a bold attempt to rob the City Bank at Calais, Maine, but were handsomely repulsed and driven out of the town by the home-guards.

Great excitement was caused upon the northern frontier of New York by rumors of an extensive raid about August 10 to 15.

Detroit was several times threatened, and it was only saved by the promptness with which the loyal citizens took up arms against the rebel invaders and their resident sympathizers. The citizens patrolled the streets, and on the night of December 7 nearly the whole city was under arms.

On September 19, a body of rebels, disguised as travelers, took passage on the merchant steamers "Island Queen" and "Parsons," with the plan of capturing both of them, and then, with the help of another party down the river, capture the United States gun-boat "Michigan." The "Michigan," however, captured most of the party, after they had sunk the "Island Queen," and abandoned the "Parsons." A number of accomplices, citizens of Sandusky, were concerned in the plot. They were arrested. Numerous rumors were circulated of raids planned and about to be executed; many, no doubt, truthful, but the vigilance of our people prevented any very large depredations. (See Beal, and St. Alban Raid.)

Canby, General, assumed command of New York July 17, 1863, *vice* General Brown, relieved. He relieved General Banks of the command of the Department of the Gulf May 21, 1864. He was severely wounded, November 6, by a rifle shot through the thigh, in White River, Arkansas.

Cane Hill, Ark.—General Blunt, by a forced march, met and attacked Marmaduke's rebel forces at this place November 28, 1862. The fight raged over twelve miles of ground. The Confederates retreated, with heavy loss, toward Van Buren.

The rebels attempted to drive out our forces December 6, but were themselves driven back.

Cane River, La., was the scene of a brilliant Union victory March 28, 1864. The Unionists, 8,000 strong, under Mower and Dudley, defeated the rebel force of 12,000, under Taylor.

A spirited engagement took place at this point April 24. The fight lasted three hours. The rebels lost 500 men and 9 pieces of artillery; Union loss, about 400 killed and wounded.

Canon de Chelle was occupied by Kit Karson January 31, 1861. He drove out the Navajos, killing 23 and taking 150 prisoners.

Canton, Miss., was captured by Union forces February 4, 1864. Sherman's army encamped here March 26.

Canton, Ky., was captured by the Union forces August 22, 1864.

Cape Girardeau, Mo., was attacked by the rebels, 8,000 strong, under Marmaduke, at 11.20 A. M., April 26, 1863; after two hours' fighting they were repulsed, and retreated toward Bloomfield. Their loss was about 60 killed, 200 wounded, and a large number of prisoners; the Union loss was 20 killed and wounded.

Carlisle, Pa. (See Pennsylvania Invasion.)

Carmel Church, Va.—A Union cavalry expedition, July 23, 1862, met and defeated a body of rebel cavalry stationed near this place, burned their camps, etc. An hour later a large body of Stuart's cavalry came up to attack them, and these, too, were defeated, driven across the North Anna River, and pursued till within sight of Hanover Junction.

Carnifex Ferry, near Summerville, Va.—A battle was fought at this place September 10, 1861. The engagement commenced at 3 o'clock A. M., between the Confederate army, under General Floyd, and the Union forces, under General Rosecrans. The rebels had 5,000 men and 16 guns in position, in intrenchments, almost inaccessible. The advance, under Colonel Lytle, drove a strong detachment into the inside fortifications. The fight soon became general. Colonel Smith's 13th Ohio attacked the enemy's left, (his weakest point,) while Colonel Lowe's 12th Ohio engaged the front. Colonel Lowe was killed at the first discharge. As night approached, the fight grew more furious, when Colonel McCook led in his German brigade. Night coming on, the men were withdrawn, and slept on their arms. During the night Floyed evacuated his intrenchments precipitately, and retreated over the Gauley River, destroying the bridge and sinking the boats. The Federal forces were too much exhausted to pursue. The Union loss was 15 killed and 70 wounded; 25 prisoners, taken by the rebels at Cross Lanes, were recaptured.

Carolina Iron Works, near Winchester, Va., were destroyed April 16, 1865. These works were furnishing the rebels from 75 to 100 tons of iron per day.

Carrick Ford, Va., was the scene of a brisk engagement July 14, 1861. Rebel General Garnett was killed and his troops scattered. The Union loss was 13 killed and 40 wounded.

Carrington, General, commanding in Indiana, reported to Governor Morton the existence of a secret military organization in that State, opposed to the Administration, June 28, 1864.

Carrol Station, Tenn., was captured September 30, 1864, by General Gillem, after driving out the rebels under Vaughan.

Carrolton, Miss., was captured by the Union forces, and the grain, mills, and stores there destroyed, March 8, 1864.

Carrsville, Va., was the scene of a skirmish, May 15, 1863.

Carter's Creek.—On April 27, 1863, Colonel Walker, with a force of Union cavalry, surprised a rebel camp on Carter's Creek Pike, near Franklin, Tenn., and routed them, killing 2 and wounding 10, and capturing 138 men, 150 horses, and 100 mules. The Unionists suffered no loss.

Carthage, Mo., battle of, July 5, 1861.—The Confederate troops, under Governor Jackson, marching toward Carthage, were met by Colonel Sigel, at the head of 1,500 men, at Briers' Forks, seven miles north of that place. A fight ensued. After two hours' fighting, the Confederate ranks were broken and their artillery silenced. Rallying again, they attempted to outflank Sigel, who, discovering it feigned a retreat, which drew the enemy into a compact mass, when Sigel opened fire right and left, with great slaughter. Sigel finally fell back to Carthage. The Confederate loss estimated from 300 to 500. Union loss, 13 killed and 31 wounded.

Carthage, Tenn., was the scene of brisk skirmishes March 26 and May 30, 1863, both resulting in favor of the National forces.

Cass, Hon. Lewis, Secretary of State in Buchanan's Cabinet, resigned December 14, 1860. The cause of

General Cass's resignation was the refusal of the President to reinforce Fort Moultrie.

Cassville, Ga., was occupied by Sherman's forces, May 19, 1864.

Catawba Indians offered their services to Governor Pickens, of South Carolina, January 24, 1861.

Catlett's Station, Va.—The rebels attacked a train of sick and wounded soldiers at this place August 22, 1862.

A brisk cavalry skirmish occurred here January 10, 1863. Mosby's guerrillas made an attack on this place, but were handsomely repulsed, May 30.

Cave City, Ky., was occupied by the rebels, May 11, 1862, who destroyed two trains of cars, including the locomotives.

Cedar Creek, Va., was occupied by Sheridan's cavalry August 12, 1864, the place having been just evacuated by Early's forces. (See Grant's Report.)

Cedar Keys, Fla., was captured by the Union forces January 17, 1862.

Cedar Mountain, Va., battle of, August 9, 1862.—The Confederates, under Jackson, advanced across the Rapidan, and marched against the Unionists, under General Banks. General Banks advanced to meet them, and at 6 o'clock P. M. the battle opened. It raged severely for about two hours, when the Confederates fell back under cover of the darkness. The Union loss was 1,500 killed, wounded, and missing. The Confederate loss not known, but supposed to be about 2,500.

Cedar Point was occupied by Colonel Moore's brigade March 18, 1865.

Celina, Tenn., was captured, and the rebel camp there broken up April 18, 1863.

Centralia, Mo., was the scene of a shocking barbarity on September 27, 1864. A band of guerrillas captured a train on which were between 40 and 50 veteran Union soldiers; these were taken out and murdered in cold blood, except about 10, who escaped. The next day they ambushed Major Johnson's militia, 150 men, who were in pursuit, killing about 100 of them, including the commanding officer.

Centerville, Va., was evacuated by the rebels March

7, 1862, and occupied by the Unionists three days later. A battle was fought near this place August 28, between the Federals under McDowell and Sigel, and the rebels under Jackson. The enemy was completely routed, with the loss of 1,000 prisoners, many arms, and one gun. The place was held until September 3, when it was abandoned, the Union forces falling back toward Washington. It was many times taken and retaken during the rebellion.

Centerville, La., was evacuated by the rebels April 13, 1863.

Chalmette Batteries, on Lake Ponchartrain, in the rear of New Orleans, were evacuated by the rebels April 25, 1862.

Chambersburg, Pa. (See Maryland and Pennsylvania Invasion.)

Chambersburg, Md. (See Maryland and Pennsylvania Invasion.)

Champion Hill. (See Baker's Creek.)

Chancellorsville, Va., was occupied by General Meade's force April 30, 1863. The rebels attacked him next day, when an engagement of an hour and a half ensued, without decided result, to be renewed with more fierceness the next day. The rebels, 40,000 strong, under Jackson, attacked Hooker's right, but were only partially successful. The 11th Corps, which received the first shock, broke, but reinforcements being promptly supplied, the rebels were checked; they captured, however, 12 pieces of artillery. General Sickles penetrated the rebel column, completely cutting it, but the retreat of the 11th Corps compelled his recall. Finding the communications with General Sickles interrupted, General Hooker ordered a night attack, at 11 o'clock. The rebels were driven back and communications restored. General Sickles brought off 400 prisoners. The battle again opened on the morning of the 3d, at five and half o'clock, and raged with terrible slaughter till eleven and a half. The rebels made several ineffectual attempts to break the Union lines. Over 2,000 prisoners were taken. General Sedgwick stormed and carried Marye's Hill and the heights of Fredericksburg, and drove the rebels back on to the rear of Lee, and bringing the rebel army between Sedgwick and Hooker. Lee afterward recovered Chancellorsville, and drove Hooker a mile and a half toward United States Ford. "Stonewall" Jackson was severely wounded in this fight. The day following (the 4th) the rebels retook Fredericksburg, forcing Sedgwick to retire. He crossed the river and rejoined Hooker.

On the morning of the 5th, General Lee, being heavily reinforced, attacked Hooker, and a fierce battle ensued. Hooker was driven back, and forced to recross the Rappahannock. The Union loss in these battles was 1,720 killed, 9,518 wounded, and about 2,500 missing. The rebel loss unknown, but supposed to be 15,000 men.

Chantilly, Va., battle of, September 1, 1862.—The battle lasted nearly an hour, and the rebels were driven back at all points. Major-General Kearney and Brigadier-General Stevens were killed in this action. This was the last of the battles fought by the Army of Virginia on their retreat. The losses on both sides were heavy; that of the Unionists was set down at 1,000 killed, 6,000 wounded, and 2,000 prisoners; Confederate loss not known definitely. The army fell back toward Washington.

Chapel Hill, Tenn., was the scene of a Union victory March 4, 1863. Rebel loss, 12 killed, 72 captured; Union loss, 10 wounded.

Chaplin Hill, near Perryville, Ky., battle of, October 8, 1862.—The rebels under Bragg, Buckner, and Marshall attacked the Union forces under Rousseau. The battle lasted several hours without a definite decision. It was renewed next morning, and before night the enemy had been driven nearly ten miles, with great slaughter, and completely routed. Union loss, 490 killed, 1,560 wounded, and 150 missing. Rebel loss known to have far exceeded that of the Federals; 640 dead rebels were buried by the Union troops. The Federals captured 17 guns, 500 prisoners, and 100,000 rounds of ammunition.

Chapmansville, Va., was the scene of skirmishes September 25 and October 2, 1861. The latter was a brisk engagement. Both resulted favorably to the Unionists.

Charles City Cross-roads, near White Oak Swamp,

Va., the battle of, June 30, 1862.—This fight lasted nearly the whole day. As the troops neared the James River, the gun-boats opened fire and caused great havoc in the rebel ranks; they were again checked, and night closed the battle. Losses heavy on both sides.

Charleston, Ill. (See Mattoon.)

Charleston, Mo., was the scene of a brisk but undecisive skirmish August 18, 1861. The following day the battle was renewed with considerable loss to each side, and on the 20th resulted in a rout of the rebels. Union loss, 1 killed, 8 wounded; rebel loss, 40 killed and 17 prisoners.

The place was abandoned by the Union forces, and soon again occupied by the rebels. A rebel camp was dispersed October 2. The same operation was repeated August 19, 1862, with a rebel loss of 4 killed, and 19 prisoners, 27 horses, and 100 stand of arms captured.

Charleston, S. C.—The authorities seized the Custom-house, Post-office, and Arsenal in this city, raising over them the Palmetto flag, December 28, 1860. Fort Moultrie, Castle Pinckney, and the batteries previously erected, were manned the same day. The work of building batteries (on shore and floating) progressed until the attack on Fort Sumter. (See Anderson.)

Notice was given April 8, that no United States vessel would be allowed to enter the harbor. Nearly half the city was burned December 11. The "stone fleet" was sunk in the harbor on the 19th and 20th, and a second one January 23, 1862.

The blockade of this port commenced May 11, 1861. Two gun-boats and three smaller vessels attacked the blockaders January 31, 1863, and for a short time dispersed the inner line, whereupon General Beauregard issued a proclamation that the blockade was legally raised. This was promptly denied by the Washington authorities. A fleet of seven iron-clads, under command of Commodore Dupont, arrived off Charleston April 5, crossed the bar next day, and on the 7th made an attack on Fort Sumter; but, after an action of 30 minutes, in which several of the fleet were disabled, they were compelled to withdraw. In this action the rebels had 300 guns, while the fleet had but 34. The

Keokuk was so badly injured that she sunk soon afterward, and fell a prey to the rebels. The rebel loss in the action was 6 wounded; the fleet lost 2 or 3 killed and 10 wounded.

On July 10 a fleet of 27 iron-clads and 25 transports made an attack on the rebel works on Morris Island. After a fight of three and a half hours, General Gilmore effected a landing, and immediately commenced the erection of batteries against Forts Wagner and Gregg, on the north end of the island, and which commanded the approaches to the city. About 150 Unionists were killed, wounded, and captured in this action. Eleven heavy guns were captured from the rebels. The Union flag was raised over Fort Wagner next day, but the Unionists were again driven out, with a loss of 350 men. The siege, by regular approaches, was then commenced. The Unionists took 500 prisoners on Folly Island August 2. The rear wall of Fort Sumter was breached August 12, and it was bombarded by 200-pound Parrots on the 14th, and an attack in force was commenced on the 17th, at daylight, the shore batteries bombarding Sumter, while the fleet engaged Wagner and Gregg, silencing Wagner and nearly silencing Gregg. The fleet retired at 2 P. M., but the shore batteries kept up a cannonading all day and night. The attack continued, and General Gilmore on the 21st demanded the surrender of Sumter and Morris Island, with the alternative of shelling Charleston in 4 hours. He opened fire upon the city at midnight of the 23d, and next day reported Sumter practically demolished. He occupied Wagner and Gregg September 7, the rebels having evacuated in the night, leaving 75 men, 36 guns, and some ammunition. An attempt was made to occupy Sumter, but the party was repulsed, on the 8th, losing 110 men. The magazine of Moultrie was exploded the same day. The rebels lost 700 men on the 15th, in the struggle for Morris Island. Then, for months, the two parties looked at each other, with occasional bombardment. June 15, 1864, 50 Union Generals were placed under fire at Charleston, but retaliation occasioned their removal. The rebels, on the approach of Sherman, evacuated the place February 17, 1865, and the Unionists next morning marched in to find the lower part of the city in ruins, and take possession of 450 guns. On April 14 General Anderson, aided by Sergeant Hart, raised upon Fort Sumter the same flag the Sergeant lowered there when the fort surrendered four years before, thus symbolically fulfilling Mr. Lincoln's promise to repossess the forts and places belonging to the United States. An oration was delivered in the fort by Rev. H. W. Beecher, with other appropriate ceremonies.

Charleston, Va., was occupied by the Union troops February 28, 1862. 64 men of the 7th Illinois Cavalry charged upon 90 rebel cavalry and a battery of artillery, under Jeff. Thompson, and captured four guns, and put the rebels to flight, losing only one man, who was taken prisoner.

The town was soon abandoned by the Union forces, and again occupied by them October 16. Skirmishes occurred here November 20, 24 and 26.

A squad of Union cavalry was captured at this place May 15, 1863, but recaptured the following day, bringing with them 50 prisoners.

The rebels surprised and captured the garrison at this place October 18, 1863. Five hundred men, besides a quantity of supplies, were taken. The rebels lost 5 killed and 20 wounded.

Charlotte, N. C., was the location of the Branch U. S. Mint. This was seized by the rebel State authorities April 21, 1861.

Charlottesville, Va., was occupied by Sheridan March 3, 1865. He here captured a large number of prisoners.

Chartres, Duc de, and Count de Paris, "the French princes," entered the United States service, as aids to General McClellan, September 24, 1861.

Chase, Hon. Salmon P., was called into Mr. Lincoln's Cabinet as Secretary of the Treasury, March 5, 1861. To him is due the development and practical working of the financial policy of the Government during the rebellion. He tendered his resignation—rumor said on account of the people's dissatisfaction with the Cabinet—December 19, 1862. The President declined accepting it, and he continued in his position until June 30, 1864, when his resignation was accepted, Hon. W. P. Fessenden, of Maine, succeeding him.

He was appointed Chief Justice of the Supreme Court of the United States December 6, 1864. This is the highest and most honorable office in our Government which can be filled by appointment, and was tendered to Mr. Chase by the President, and heartily indorsed by the people, as a fitting tribute to a man able, upright, and patriotic—the man for the place.

Chattanooga, Tenn.—The rebel batteries at this place were silenced June 17, 1862, and the town occupied by Bragg July 13, 1863.

The place was shelled by the Union forces under Colonel Wilder—Rosecrans's advance—August 21, and the investment proper commenced ten days later. The place was shelled almost continually until September 7, when the rebels evacuated, and the Union forces took possession. General Rosecrans thus gained a most important and almost bloodless victory. In about 23 days the Army of the Cumberland had marched 300 miles, carrying 45 days' rations, and captured one of the most powerful natural strongholds in the United States. The Union loss in this was six men, four of these being killed accidentally. The Union troops cautiously followed the rebels, with daily fighting, until the rebels, being heavily reinforced, they, on the 16th, with a force of 16,000 men, attacked Negley's division, 5,300 strong, at Bird's Gap, Northern Georgia, and drove them three and a half miles. Negley lost 35 men, killed, wounded, and missing; he afterward recovered his ground.

Rosecrans concentrated his army on the west of Chickamauga River, 12 miles from Lafayette, Georgia; Bragg, strongly reinforced by Longstreet's corps, from the Rappahannock, being in position on the east side of that river.

Chickamauga, the battle of, was commenced September 19.

About 11 o'clock Bragg attempted to flank the left of Rosecrans's army. General Thomas's corps moved from the center to the left to counteract this movement. Longstreet's corps was opposed to Thomas. The left wavered a little, but rallied, and, the whole corps advancing, the rebels retreated, and were driven a mile and a half, when Thomas was compelled to halt by the center not advancing. At 2 P. M., Polk's and Hill's corps, of the rebel army, were hurled against McCook and Crittenden, which they succeeded in breaking and driving back; but the Federals being reinforced, the rebels were driven back, and the Union army occupied its original ground.

The battle was reopened the next day at 8:30 A. M., by a fierce attack on the left of the line under Thomas, but the attack was unsuccessful. Thomas's men had constructed a breastwork of rails and logs, and maintained their ground against the repeated assaults of the enemy. The right and center, being vigorously attacked, broke in confusion. Thomas, finding himself alone, retreated to the base of a spur of the Mission Ridge, and here, being reinforced by two brigades of the reserve and portions of the other corps, he repulsed the rebels, and maintained his position till dark, saving the army. At night he fell back to Rossville. The Union losses in the two days' battles were 1,644 killed, 9,262 wounded, and 4,945 missing; total, 15,851. The rebel reports place their loss at 16,499, killed and wounded, and 1,500 prisoners.

On the afternoon of the 21st the rebels made another attack on General Thomas, holding the rear of the army in its retreat, but they were repulsed, and the army fell back without interruption to near Chattanooga, which they, within a few days, occupied. Fighting was a daily occurrence until the army moved toward Lookout Mountain, which see.

Chattahoochie River, Ga., was reached by Sherman's forces July 1, 1864; they were all across on the 16th.

Cheat Mountain, Va., was attacked by the rebels September 12, 1861, but were repulsed. The attack being renewed the next day, they were again repulsed with heavy loss.

Cheraw, S. C., was occupied by Sherman's forces, under Howard and Mower, March 3, 1865. The bridge at this place, and a train of cars with some military stores, were destroyed.

Cherokee Indians.—A large proportion of them seceded and joined the Confederates, August 23, 1861. The National Council, however, met, and on February 26, 1863, repealed their secession ordinance, abolished slavery, and disqualified those who continued disloyal.

Cherokee Station, Ala.—2,500 men of the 15th Corps, under General Osterhaus, encountered 5,000 rebels, under Loring and S. D. Lee, at this place, October 21, 1863; the fight lasted an hour and a half, when the rebels fled, and were driven into their intrenchments at Tuscumbia.

Chesapeake, a merchant steamer, was seized about 1 o'clock A. M. of December 7, 1863, by Henry Osborne, a coast pilot of St. Johns, New Brunswick, and 15 others, 20 miles north-north-east of Cape Cod; they had shipped at New York as passengers; the second engineer, Mr. Shaffer, was killed, the captain and crew placed in irons, and the pirates took the vessel toward St. Johns, where they landed on the 9th. She was recaptured in Sambro Harbor, near Halifax, on the 17th, by the U. S. gun-boat "Ella and Anna." The capture having taken place in a British harbor called forth an explanatory correspondence between Lord Lyons and Secretary Seward, the result of which was that the Chesapeake and her piratical captors were handed over to the British authorities at Halifax for adjudication. The pirates, on landing, were received with acclamations by the sympathizing citizens, who rescued them from the Government officers; they were again taken and, after a hearing, were by a police magistrate committed for surrender to the United States authorities. This committal was, on March 10, 1864, overruled by a judge of the higher court. The pirates were then liberated.

Chester Gap, Va., was the scene of cavalry skirmishes November 5, 1862, and July 22, 1863.

Chickahominy River, Va., was crossed by the retreating rebels at Coles Ford May 7, 1862, and at Bottom's Bridge on the 17th, followed by McClellan in pursuit on the 23d.

McClellan in his retreat crossed it August 18. (For further items, see appropriate headings.)

Chickasaw, Miss.—The rebel boats Muscle and Sallie Wood were captured at this place February 8, 1862.

Chickamauga. (See Chattanooga.)

Chickasaw, Ala., was occupied March 21, 1865, by General Wilson's cavalry on a raid to the central portion of the State.

Chickamacomico, near Hatteras Inlet, N. C., battle of, October 5, 1861.—The battle was opened by an attack of 4,000 rebels driving the 20th Indiana from their camp. The Union troops retreated to that part of the island where the light is situated. The gun-boat Monticello hastened to their relief, and shelled the rebels for four hours, while they were attempting to embark in their boats. The slaughter is represented as terrible. Night coming on, the Confederates made their escape.

Chuckatuck, Va., was the scene of a skirmish April 23, 1863.

Cincinnati, O., was threatened by the approach of Kirby Smith; and September 2, 1862, martial law was proclaimed and the Ohio "Squirrel Hunters" invited out. The city was fortified, and all put in readiness for an attack, which on the 10th was seemingly imminent. A reconnoisance in force on the 12th found the enemy had fallen back.

Martial law was again proclaimed July 11, 1863, on the approach of John Morgan, which see.

Cincinnati, Union gun-boat, was sunk opposite Vicksburg, May 26, 1863.

City Point, Va., was shelled August 3, 1862, and entirely destroyed on the 28th.

Sheridan occupied the place March 26, 1865, and the day following President Lincoln, Generals Grant, Sherman, Sheridan, and others, held there a consultation preparatory to a move of Grant's army.

Clarksville, Tenn., surrendered, without an engagement, to Flag-officer Foote, February 19, 1862. The place, with large amounts of Federal property, was, on August 20, surrendered to the rebels, without resistance. Colonel Mason, the commander, had been previously denounced as a coward by General Sherman. The Union forces again captured it January 4, 1863.

Cleveland, Tenn., was the scene of a brilliant skirmish November 27, 1863, in which Wheeler's cavalry were put to flight. They returned, however, as soon as the Union forces were gone, and January 9, 1864, conscripted nearly every man in the place.

Clinch River, Tenn., was the scene of a skirmish December 2, 1863. Rebels defeated.

Clinton, La., with the rebel provost-marshal, 30 men, stores, and ammunition, was captured by the Unionists October 6, 1864.

Clinton, Miss., was captured by the Union forces May 6, 1863. It was again captured August 24, 1864, the rebels losing 30 men, including a colonel, killed; 150, including a major, wounded, and $500,000 worth of property.

Clinton, Mo., was the scene of a skirmish March 30, 1862.

Clinton, N. C., was the scene of a brisk skirmish May 19, 1862.

Clinton, Tenn., was destroyed by Union troops February 18, 1863.

Cloyd Mountain, Va.—A battle was fought at this place May 9, 1864. The rebels were defeated, with a loss of three guns, 1,000 men, killed, wounded, and missing, including General Jenkins, killed. Union loss, nearly 500.

Cobb, Howell, Buchanan's Secretary of War, robbed the Government, resigned his position December 10, 1860, and left for the South February 4, 1861. He was elected President of the Montgomery Convention.

Cochran's Cross-roads, Miss., was the scene of a rebel defeat September 8, 1862. Union force, 380; rebels, 750. The rebels were driven nearly three miles.

Cockpit Point, on the Potomac, was the scene of an engagement January 2, 1862, between the rebel batteries at this place and the U. S. gun-boats "Anacosta" and "Yankee." The place was captured by the Potomac flotilla March 9.

Cockspur Roads, Ga., was the scene of an attack upon the Federal fleet November 26, 1861.

Coffeville, Miss., was the scene of a cavalry engagement December 5, 1862.

Cold Harbor, near New Bridge, Va., was the scene

of a cavalry skirmish May 24, 1862. Rebel loss, 65 killed, 15 wounded, 40 prisoners. Union loss, 45 killed and wounded. One wing of Grant's army occupied the place May 30, 1864.

Cold Knob, Va., was the scene of a rebel surprise November 26, 1862. Union loss, none. Rebel loss, about 100 prisoners.

Coldwater, Miss.—On September 9, 1862, Colonel Grierson's cavalry skirmished with the enemy at Cochran's Cross-roads and Coldwater Bridge, Miss., killing 4 and taking 70 or 80 prisoners. And on February 19, 1863, a reconnoitering party from Yazoo Pass surprised 200 rebel cavalry at Coldwater, and routed them, killing 6, wounding 3, and capturing 15, without loss to the Federals.

Cole, Camp, Mo., was the scene of a brisk battle between the secessionists and the Union Home-guards January 19, 1861. The Unionists were victorious.

Cole's Island, nine miles from Charleston, S. C., was occupied by Union troops March 27 and 28, 1863.

Colliersville, Tenn., was captured by Union forces, and General Geary, commanding the rebels, was taken prisoner, November 3, 1863.

Colored Soldiers.—The subject of enlisting colored men into the United States army called forth much discussion, for and against it, in both military and political circles. The first regiment, composed of freedmen, was organized at Port Royal, S. C., on January 25, 1863. An act authorizing the enlistment and providing for the payment of colored troops soon after became a law, and recruiting went briskly on. As this act first read, the colored men received less bounty and less pay than the whites, but April 29 they were, in these respects, put upon the same footing.

The rebels were very much excited upon this question. They talked about the indignity, the insult, and the "Southern heart being fired," and so on; and the authorities threatened instant execution of the officers of colored regiments, and the execution or enslavement of the troops when taken prisoners. General Hunter, commanding at Port Royal, S. C., addressed a letter upon this subject, threatening "retaliation" in kind, to

Jeff. Davis, April 23, and President Lincoln, on July 30, proclaimed retaliation upon rebel prisoners if the barbarous proceedings were enacted.

The valor and fighting qualities of the colored troops was demonstrated first at Milikin's Bend, June 6, and afterward confirmed on many a battle-field.

A remarkable revolution of sentiment was observed upon this subject, both at the North and South. The enlistment of colored troops was opposed, ridiculed, and denounced by many at the North, who, before the close of the year, were but too well satisfied to pay a poor negro man a large bounty to "go as substitute" for them. The rebels, too, who were so violently shocked at the idea when first broached, were converted to the belief that "niggers would, could, and should fight;" and February 18, 1865, General Lee urged upon the Confederate authorities and Congress the benefit, expediency, and absolute necessity of conscripting the negroes to help establish their own bondage.

Columbia, Ark.—On June 6, 1864, General A. J. Smith, of Red River celebrity, met Marmaduke near this place, with two regiments, and drove them back. His forces advanced to the enemy's second position, and a brisk artillery duel was kept up, until, under heavy fire, his men ceased using their guns, and dashed into the enemy's lines and drove him back. Loss, about 125 on each side.

Columbia, Ky., was the scene of a brisk skirmish January 18, 1865; the rebels were defeated with a loss of 8 men; Union loss, one slightly wounded.

Columbia, Pa. (See Pennsylvania Invasion.)

Columbia, S. C.—One of the rebel prisons, in which were stowed brave Union soldiers, was located at this place.

The place was evacuated by Beauregard, upon the approach of Sherman, February 17, 1865. The place was occupied by the Union troops for three days, and then evacuated as they continued northward.

Columbia, Tenn., was the scene of a brisk engagement, October 22, 1863; Captain Bunch, with 60 men defeated 200 of Hawkins's guerrillas, killing 9, wounding several, and taking 12 prisoners.

The rebels were also defeated here in skirmishes on October 29 and November 3.

Columbia, Va., was occupied by Union cavalry, and the James River Canal destroyed, May 3, 1863.

Columbia, a United States war vessel of 44 guns, was, in anticipation of a rebel attack, destroyed at Gosport Navy-yard April 20, 1861.

Columbia, a United States gun-boat, was stranded at Masonboro Inlet, N. C., January 15, 1863. She was destroyed by the rebels next day.

Columbine, a United States gun-boat, was captured by the rebels, on St. John's River, Fla., May 23, 1864.

Columbus, Ga., was captured by the Unionists April 12, 1865.

Columbus, Ky., was occupied by 7,000 rebels, under Generals Pillow and Polk, September 7, 1861. There was a gun-boat action near this place January 11, 1862, and three days later the gun-boats made a reconnoissance to the town. After some fighting for several days, the rebels commenced its evacuation, the Union troops occupying the place March 3. It was found entirely deserted, and almost totally destroyed. Several guns and a large quantity of military stores, abandoned by the Confederates, fell into Union hands.

Columbus, Ohio, was not during the rebellion exempt from those who sympathized with secession. On October 31, 1863, a conspiracy to release the prisoners in the Ohio Penitentiary and Camp Chase and McLean Barracks came to light. Six of the leaders were arrested.

Columbus, a United States war vessel of 94 guns, was, in anticipation of a rebel attack, destroyed at Gosport Navy-yard, April 20, 1861.

Commerce, Mo., which had been captured by the rebels, was recaptured by the Unionists August 19, 1861. It was soon afterward abandoned, and about December 24 was again occupied by the rebels.

Concordia, Ark., was burned December 7, 1862, in retaliation for the burning of the U. S. Steamer Lake City, by guerrillas at that place the day previous.

Confederate Congress.—The South Carolina State Convention, on December 27, 1860, called a convention of such slaveholding States as in the mean time should have seceded from the Union, to meet at Montgomery, Ala., February 4, 1861. The Convention met, and on the 9th adopted a provisional frame-work of government for the "Confederate States of America." This provisional constitution was, on March 11, superseded by the permanent (?) Constitution. (See Confederate Constitution.) The Convention, after adopting the provisional Constitution, elected Jefferson Davis and Alexander H. Stevens as "Provisional President and Vice-President," to hold office until their successors were elected and inaugurated. The Convention, on February 12, took charge of all questions pending between the seceded States and the United States.

The Congress met at Montgomery, and after providing for the establishment of the "Army of the Confederate States of America," March 9, ratifying President Davis's Cabinet appointments, and some similar work, adjourned. They reassembled at the same place April 29, and May 21 adjourned to meet at Richmond, July 20, having, in the mean time, among many other things, authorized Jeff. Davis to accept all the volunteers that offered, and authorizing the issue of $50,000,000 in C. S. A. bonds, running 20 years and bearing 8 per cent. interest.

The first *regular* Congress of the C. S. A. convened at Richmond February 18, 1862. Representatives from all the slaveholding States, except Maryland and Delaware, were present. The adjournment of this session, upon the approach of the Federal army and threatened capture of Richmond, April 22, was hasty, informal, and exciting in the extreme.

To attempt any extended history of the enactments of this body is beyond the province of this work. Their last, and to the country their most pleasing enactment, (to adjourn *sine die,*) passed unanimously, March 15, 1865.

Confederate Constitution.—This document, which was adopted by the Montgomery Convention March 11, 1861, was substantially a copy of the Federal Constitution, except in the following particulars:

The President and Vice-President were to be elected for a term of six years, and the former not eligible to re-election while he was in office. He could not remove appointed officials, except members of his Cabinet, without the consent of the Senate. The heads of Departments might each be accorded a seat on the floor of each house, with the right to discuss any measure pertaining to his department. The more important differences will be seen from the following extracts.

"No, bounties shall be granted from the Treasury; nor shall any duties or taxes on importations from foreign nations be laid to promote or foster any branch of industry.

"The citizens of each State * * * * shall have the right of transit and sojourn in any State of this Confederacy, with their slaves and other property; and the right of property in said slaves shall not be thereby impaired.

"No slave or other person held to service or labor in any State or Territory of the Confederate States, under the laws thereof, escaping or unlawfully carried into another, shall, in consequence of any law or regulation therein, be discharged from such service or labor; but shall be delivered up on claim of the party to whom such slave belongs, or to whom such service or labor may be due.

"The Confederate States may acquire new territory. * * * * In all such territory, the institution of negro slavery, as it now exists in the Confederate States, shall be recognized and protected by Congress and by the Territorial Government; and the inhabitants of the several Confederate States and Territories shall have the right to take to such territory any slaves lawfully held by them in any of the States or Territories of the Confederate States.

"The importation of negroes of the African race, from any foreign country, other than the slaveholding States or Territories of the United States of America, is hereby forbidden, and Congress is required to pass such laws as shall effectually prevent the same.

"Congress shall also have power to prohibit the introduction of slaves from any State not a member of, or Territory not belonging to, this Confederacy.

"No clause contained in the Constitution shall be

construed to delegate the power to Congress to appropriate money for any internal improvement intended to facilitate commerce, except for the purpose of furnishing lights, beacons, and buoys and other aids to navigation upon the coasts, and the improvement of harbors, and the removing of obstructions in river navigation, in all which cases such duties shall be laid on the navigation facilitated thereby as may be necessary to pay the costs and expenses thereof."

Confiscation.—The subject of confiscating the property of those in rebellion was warmly discussed both in and out of Congress. A bill "to confiscate property used for insurrectionary purposes," etc., approved August 6, 1861, providing for the immediate confiscation of all property belonging to office-holders under the Confederate Government, and confiscation within sixty days after the President's Amnesty Proclamation (which see), of all property belonging to disloyal citizens, or privates in the Confederate army, was passed the House July 11, 1862, and the Senate the next day; and after a slight modification, suggested by the President in his veto of the same, on constitutional grounds, it was again passed by both houses on the 16th, and approved, becoming a law the next day.

On July 22 the President issued an order that property needed for the support of the armies of the United States should be seized, an account being kept of the same.

Congree River was crossed by Sherman's forces February 16, 1865.

Congress met, pursuant to the call of the President, in extra session July 4, 1861. The principal acts passed were the confiscation, war tax, tariff, and military bills. The latter authorized the raising of 500,000 men and $500,000,000 in money. The action of this body upon confiscation, conscription, currency, amendment to the Constitution, etc., will be found under these and other appropriate heads.

Conscription.—The first draft was ordered August 4, 1862, and was for 300,000 men for 9 months. This order made a great commotion in many places—was applauded and denounced. Four days after the order for the draft, the War Department ordered the arrest of all persons discouraging enlistments, and passports were denied to persons liable to draft, until the order was filled.

On September 8 the restrictions on travel were rescinded, and arrests for disloyalty forbidden, except by direction of the Judge-Advocate at Washington.

On May 8, 1863, the President issued a proclamation declaring what shall constitute the national forces, and declaring also that no plea of alienage will be received from any foreign-born citizen after 65 days from the date of the proclamation.

June 15 100,000 men were called out for six months, to repel rebel invasions.

October 17 a call was made for 300,000 men, to be drafted January 5, if not sooner raised by volunteering.

On February 1, 1864, the President ordered a draft for 500,000 men, to take place the 10th of March, if not raised by voluntary enlistments by the 1st of March. This order included a former call for 300,000.

A call for 200,000 men to supply deficiencies and form a reserve for the draft, to be made on the 15th of April, was made March 14.

July 18 a call was made for 500,000 men, to be raised by volunteering within 50 days; otherwise the deficiency to be drafted September 5.

The last call was made December 19, for 300,000 men, the deficiency to be drafted February 15, 1865.

The enforcement of the draft was the occasion of mobs in many places. (See mobs.)

Constitutional Amendment. (See Appendix.)

Contraband, a term for fugitive slaves who came within the Union lines, and soon became a slang or distinguishing term for all negroes. Was first used by General Butler, May 27, 1861.

Coosa River, S. C., was crossed in a captured ferryboat by General Rousseau, July 13, 1864. He was immediately attacked by about 5,000 rebels, whom he defeated, driving them southward.

Corbin and Graw, convicted of recruiting for the

rebels within the Union lines, were executed at Sandusky, May 15, 1864.

Corcoran, Michael, was taken prisoner by the rebels, and on November 10, 1861, was held by them as hostage for the pirate Smith, convicted at Philadelphia. He was, with other officers, held until August, 1862, reaching Fortress Monroe on the 16th, and New York on the 22d, where he was received with great enthusiasm.

He shot Colonel Kimbal, April 30, 1863, for refusing to give the countersign. A court of inquiry exonerated him from all blame for so doing. He did gallant service during the war, and met an untimely death by a fall from his horse, December 22, 1863, from the effects of which he expired in convulsions soon after.

Corinth, Miss., was, during the war, the scene of many a conflict, ranging in importance from small to great. Brisk skirmishes were fought April 24 and 29, 1862, and on the 30th the railroad communications north were cut by the Union forces.

On May 8, four companies of the 7th Illinois Cavalry, reconnoitering, charged upon two regiments of rebel infantry near this place. The rebels lost 30 killed and wounded, and 4 prisoners; Union loss, about 20 killed and 50 prisoners. On the 16th and 17th, the two armies were maneuvering, their pickets skirmishing, and a Union loss of 44 killed, wounded, and missing; rebel loss, 40 dead left on the field, and 100 wounded. Skirmishing continued, with approaches to battles, on the 21st, 24th, 26th and 27th, in which the Unionists were uniformly successful. On the 28th, the rebels were driven back, with considerable loss. They left 30 dead on the field; Union loss was 25 killed and wounded. The day following, Beauregard, who commanded the rebels, evacuated the place, and the next day it was occupied by the Union forces, under General Halleck. The rebels had destroyed every thing they could not carry away, and for five miles along their route the roads were filled with arms, equipments, and stores. The Unionists took over 2,000 prisoners. The victory was followed up, and June 4 General Halleck reported that General Pope was thirty miles south of Florence, Ala., with 40,000 men, and pushing the enemy hard. He had captured 10,000 prisoners, and 15,000 stand of arms and 9 locomotives. Early on the morning of October 4, the combined rebel forces, under Van Dorn, Price, and Lovell, attacked the Union lines at Corinth. The fight lasted until night closed the contest. The Unionists were driven back into the town. The battle was renewed early next morning, by the Confederates advancing to the attack. The battle raged fiercely till noon, when the rebels, being repulsed, broke and fled The Confederates numbered in this fight 38,000 men; while General Rosecrans, who commanded in person, had not over 20,000. The Union loss was 315 killed, including General Hackleman, 1,812 wounded, and 232 missing. The Confederate loss was 1,423 killed; wounded estimated at 5,692; 2,248, including 137 officers, taken prisoners; 3,300 stand of arms, 14 stand of colors, together with vast quantities of stores of all kinds. The rebels were pursued forty miles in force, and sixty miles with cavalry. On the 5th, Generals Ord and Hurlbut overtook the retreating rebels at the Hatchie River, where they made a stand. After seven hours' hard fighting, the rebels fled in great disorder, leaving their dead and wounded and 400 prisoners. Nearly 1,000 stand of arms were taken here. The Union loss, 500 killed and wounded. January 25, 1864, Corinth was evacuated, and the Memphis and Charleston Railroad abandoned by the Federal troops, who concentrated at Memphis, preparatory to a movement forward.

Corpus Christi Pass, Texas, was captured by Union forces under Banks, November 15, 1863.

Cortez, General, reviewed the Army of the Potomac, September 28, 1863.

Corydon, Ind. (See Morgan's raid.)

Cottage Grove, Tenn.—This place is near Bradyville, which see.

Cotton.—The export of this staple was prohibited by the rebels May 26, 1861.

Cotton Burning was extensively done by both parties, in which way it is estimated that one-half of all the cotton in the South was consumed.

Cotton Hill, Va., was besieged from October 30 to November 7, 1861.

Count de Paris. (See Chartres.)

Courier, the, of Louisville, was denied the mails September 18, 1861, on account of its alleged sympathy with the rebels.

Cove Station, Va., was reached and occupied by Sheridan March 6, 1865, on his way to Lynchburg.

Covington, Ky., was in great commotion during the threatened attack upon Cincinnati in September 1862, and slight skirmishing occurred near it on the 12th of that month.

Covington, Tenn.—On March 10, 1863, Colonel Grierson, with the 6th and 7th Illinois Cavalry, surrounded Richardson's guerrillas, near Covington, and captured them; 25 were killed.

Another haul of guerrillas was made near the same place on the 16th.

Cox's Mills, Va., was the scene of a skirmish August 2, 1862.

Crab Orchard, Ky., was reached by the Federals October 15, 1862, in their pursuit of Bragg. The rebels were about 45,000 strong; Union forces less than 20,000. Union loss, 600 killed, 2,000 wounded. Rebel loss, 1,350 killed and 2,100 wounded.

Crany Island, Va., was bombarded by the Union forces May 8 and 9, 1862, and abandoned by the rebels on the 10th.

Cripple Creek, Tenn., was the scene of a brisk skirmish May 16, 1863, in which 18 rebels were taken prisoners.

Crittenden Compromise.—This measure was introduced into the United States Senate December 18, 1860, and its author, John J. Crittenden, Senator from Kentucky, in its defense, made a very strong Union speech on the 22d. A committee of 13, appointed to devise a means of settlement between the North and South, voted down this measure on the 20th. It was virtually killed in the Senate January 16, 1861, by the adoption of "Clark's substitute," "that the Constitution is good enough and secession ought to be put down." The following is the material portion of the measure:

"To renew the Missouri line of 36° 30′; prohibit slavery north and permit it south of that line; admit new States with or without slavery, as their constitutions provide; prohibit Congress from abolishing slavery in States, and in the District of Columbia so long as it exists in Maryland and Virginia; permit free transmission of slaves by land or water in any State; pay for fugitive slaves rescued after arrest; repeal the inequality of commissioners' fees in the Fugitive Slave Act, and ask the repeal of Personal Liberty Bills in the Northern States. These concessions to be submitted to the people as amendments to the Constitution, and, if adopted, never to be changed."

Cromwell, Ky., was the scene of a brisk skirmish October 28, 1861.

Cross Keys, Va., battle of, June 8, 1862.—General Fremont attacked Stonewall Jackson at Cross Keys, 7 miles from Harrisonburg, Va., at 8:30 o'clock in the morning, and drove him out after a severe fight. The Union loss was about 600 killed, wounded, and missing; rebel loss unknown.

Cross Lanes, Va., was the scence of a skirmish August 21, 1861.

Crump Hill, near Natchitoches, La., was the scene of a cavalry skirmish and rebel defeat March 30, 1864.

Crystal Springs, Miss., was burned by the Federal forces May 11, 1863.

Culpepper, Va., was the head-quarters of General Pope August 8, 1862. There was a cavalry skirmish here August 1, 1863; and on September 13, General Pleasanton's cavalry drove the rebels through the place, and captured 5 guns and 104 men; the 2d Army Corps afterward occupied the place.

The Union Army fell back to this place October 9, and on November 9, 700 rebels were taken prisoners, about a mile from the town.

Culpepper C. H., Va., was captured by the Unionists May 2, 1863.

Culp's Farm, Ga., was the scene of a hard battle June 22, 1864. The rebels attacked Sherman's forces, while the latter were crossing Moses Creek, but were repulsed several times with great loss.

Cumberland, Md. (See Pennsylvania Invasion.)

Cumberland, Va., was the head-quarters of General McClellan, and the scene of a brisk skirmish May 13, 1862. On August 2, 1864, General Kelly was attacked at Cumberland, by the rebel raiders under Bradley Johnson and McCausland. The rebels were routed, after a severe fight, losing caissons, wagons, and a large quantity of their plunder. General Kelly pursued them toward Old Town.

Cumberland Gap, Tenn., near the Virginia and Kentucky line, is a place about which clusters many a war incident. It was occupied by Zollicoffer in his retreat November 13, 1861. On March 22, 1862, a reconnoissance in force was made from Cumberland Ford to this place. The rebel pickets were driven in, and firing commenced early in the morning, which continued all day, without any definite results.

The Gap was occupied by the Union forces under General Morgan June 18. Skirmishing was of almost daily occurrence. In an engagement August 7, the rebels lost, in killed and wounded, 125 men; Union loss, 3 killed, 15 wounded, and 50 prisoners, large quantities of forage, tobacco, stores, horses and mules.

General Morgan destroyed every thing of value as war material, and evacuated the place September 17, and, though surrounded by the enemy, he succeeded in saving his command, which reached Greenupsburg on the 3d of October.

It was occupied by General Bragg October 22.

On September 8, 1863, the place, with 2,000 men and 14 pieces of artillery, under rebel General Frazer, surrendered, without firing a gun, to General Shackelford; 40 wagons, 200 mules, and a large quantity of commissary stores were captured.

A three hours' skirmish occurred January 29, 1864, on the Virginia road, 13 miles from this place. Colonel Love, with 1,600 cavalry, 400 only of whom were mounted, with no artillery, held his position till dark, and then fell back 3 miles to camp.

Nine hundred rebels surrendered, and were paroled at Cumberland Gap April 28, 1865.

Cummings Point. (See Charleston, S. C.)

Curlew, a steamer, ran aground in the Arkansas River and was attacked by guerrillas April 25, 1864. The guerrillas and Tom Keenan, "the Wild Irishman," their leader, was killed.

Cushing, Lieutenant, of the "Monticello," performed some very heroic deeds during his connection with the navy. March 20, 1864, with two boat-loads of men, he made his passage by the rebel guards, into Smithville, N. C., where he entered a house opposite the rebel camp and carried off a rebel captain as prisoner. On February 4, 1865, with four boats and a force of fifty men, he captured the town of All Saints, N. C., taking about 30 prisoners. He held the place one day, destroyed $15,000 worth of cotton, brought off about 20 bales, and returned to repeat a like experiment upon Charlotte, four days later.

His most daring feat, however, was performed October 28, 1864, in destroying the rebel ram "Albemarle," which was lying at Plymouth, protected by a log barricade.

Cynthiana, Ky., was captured, after a severe fight, by John Morgan, July 17, 1862. The place was again captured by Morgan June 11, 1864. General Burbridge, who had marched his men (cavalry) 90 miles in twenty-four hours, came up with the raiders at this place next day. The fight was fierce and sanguinary, lasting over an hour, and resulted in the complete rout of the guerrillas. His loss was 150; theirs, in killed, wounded, and prisoners, 500. They were compelled to leave behind them over 1,000 horses, and a large amount of their plunder. Over 100 of the troops which Morgan so easily captured were recovered.

Dahlgren, Colonel Ulrick, and his party, were, on March 3, 1864, ambushed at King and Queen Courthouse, when the Colonel and several others were instantly killed; many were taken prisoners. The corpse of Colonel Dahlgren was horribly mutilated, for which inhumanity the rebels attempted a justification, by forging an order which they pretended was found upon him.

Daily News, Day-Book, Journal of Commerce, and Free-man's Journal, were denied the use of the mails about August 21 and 25, 1861.

Dallas, Ga.—On the 25th of May, 1864, a portion of General Sherman's army secured a good position near this place, after some hard fighting; this was followed, on the 26th and 27th, by active assaults of the enemy on his slightly-intrenched position. On the 28th, the assaults were renewed with greater vehemence, and continued all day. McPherson closed the day by driving the enemy back.

Dalton, Ga., was evacuated by General Hood's forces January 31, 1864; pickets were, however, kept there by the rebels for some days, when they again occupied the place. A rebel regiment, on February 1, mutinied, rather than reënlist, many of them escaping to the Union lines. The Union forces under General Thomas commenced operations against the place early in March, skirmishing and fighting being almost of daily occurrence, until May 12, when the outer works of the place was carried. General McPherson next day cut off nine trains of military stores, leaving Dalton, while Howard was threatening their left wing. On the 14th the town was occupied by Sherman's 4th Corps, the rebels retreating to Resaca.

The place was threatened August 14, 1864, by the rebel General Wheeler, with 5,000 men, who demanded the surrender of the place. Colonel Sieboldt, commanding the garrison of 420 men, refused the demand, and being reinforced during the night by General Steedman's forces, drove Wheeler in confusion from the place.

Dam No. 4, on the Potomac, was the scene of a skirmish December 11, 1861.

Danby's Mills, on the east of Mobile Bay, was, on March 20, 1865, occupied by the Union forces under General A. J. Smith, from which point they operated against Mobile.

Danville, Ky., was taken by the rebels, but retaken by the Federals, March 28, 1863.

Danville, Tenn., was attacked by the rebels October 23, 1863, but they failed to capture it at that time. They, however, occupied it soon afterward, and were driven therefrom January 29, 1864.

Dardanelles, Ark., was captured May 30, 1864, by the rebels under General Shelby, who took about 200 prisoners. General Price, on his way to Missouri, crossed the Arkansas River at this point September 8, 1864.

Darksville. (See Perryville.)

Darleystown. (See New Market Heights.)

Darnstown, Md., was the scene of a battle and Union victory September 15, 1861. The town was plundered by the rebels July 10, 1864.

Dauphin's Island was occupied March 8, 1865, by Union troops, intended to operate against Mobile. The place was thus occupied until the 20th, when the troops were moved to Danby's Mills.

Davisboro, Ga., was evacuated by the rebels under Iverson, on November 27, 1864, and occupied by Sherman's advance the same day.

Davis, Jeff. C., killed Major-General Nelson at the Galt House, Louisville, Ky. The affair grew out of a personal quarrel. Nelson died in fifteen minutes after being shot. General Davis surrendered himself up, passed an examination, and was acquitted October 21.

Davis, Jefferson, Senator from Mississippi, withdrew from the United States Senate January 21, 1861. He was elected Provisional President of the "Confederate States" February 9, inaugurated on the 18th, appointed his Cabinet on the 21st, and exercised the veto power for the first time on the bill legalizing the African slave-trade on the 28th. His first requisition for Confederate troops was made April 9, and the first "letter of marque and reprisal in aid of the Confederacy" was by him granted on the 17th. On August 15 he ordered all Northern men to leave the Confederacy within 40 days. The Confederate Congress, February 19, 1862, declared him elected President, and Alexander H. Stephens Vice-President of the Confederate States, having received all the electoral votes cast. They were inaugurated three days later.

January 12, 1863, on the meeting of the Confederate Congress, he transmitted to that body a message strongly urging retaliatory measures against the Emancipation Proclamation. On February 10, he issued an address to the rebel army, thanking them, for himself and the Government, for the esteem and regard manifested in their voluntary (?) re-enlistment. He closed with a presage of success to the Confederate and downfall of the Union cause. He "dismissed from his court" the Consuls of England and Austria June 14, 1863. His call for "all white men between the ages of 18 and 45 was made July 15. He issued a proclamation of amnesty and entreaty to all deserters and malcontents August 1, and during September and October made a tour of observation to cheer his constituents, and refire the now desponding Southern heart. Several attempts were made to burn his residence in Richmond, and one, on January 19, 1864, was nearly a success.

At the outbreak of the rebellion, no one was more popular in the South than "Jeff. Davis," but, as the rebels began to see the result of their effort, his popularity rapidly declined. First the soldiers, then the citizens, and soon the rebel Congress denounced his administration and policy. His last proclamation from Richmond was issued January 25, 1865, appointing March 10 as a day of public fasting and prayer.

While attending church on the morning of April 2, he received a dispatch from General Lee that the rebel lines were broken, and Richmond in danger. Davis, with his family and a few friends, immediately left the city, fleeing toward North Carolina, reaching Danville next day. His last proclamation was issued from this place on the 4th, declaring the rebel cause yet hopeful, and urging continued and renewed resistance. The party continued their flight toward the coast until May 10, when the whole number, including Jeff. Davis, his wife, sisters, and brother, his Postmaster-General, Reagan, his Private Secretary, Colonel Harrison, Colonel Johnson, Aide-de-Camp on Davis's staff, Colonels Morris and Lubbick, Lieutenant Hathaway, and others, also a train of five wagons and three ambulances, were captured at Irwinsville, Wilkinson County, Georgia, by Lieutenant-Colonel Pritchard, commanding the 4th Michigan Cavalry, of Minty's 2d Division. The honor and reward of this splendid achievement had narrowly escaped falling to another battalion, Lieutenant-Colonel Harden, 1st Wisconsin Cavalry, of Lagrange's brigade, McCook's (1st) division, of Wilson's corps. Minty's division had been distributed all along the south banks of the Ocmulgee and Altamaha. Harden's forces had struck the trail of Davis at Dublin, Lawrence County, on the evening of the 7th, and followed him closely night and day, through the pine wilderness of Alligator Creek and Green Swamp, *via* Cumberlandsville, to Irwinsville. At Cumberlandsville, Colonel Harden met Colonel Pritchard, with one hundred and fifty picked men and horses of the 4th Michigan. Harden followed the trail directly south, while Pritchard, having fresh horses, pushed down the Ocmulgee toward Hopewell, and thence toward House Creek to Irwinsville, arriving there at midnight of the 9th. Jeff. Davis had not yet arrived. From a citizen Pritchard learned that his party were encamped two miles out of the town. He made dispositions of his men and surrounded the camp before day. The captors report that he hastily put on one of his wife's dresses and started for the woods, closely followed by our men, who at first thought him a woman, but seeing his boots while he was running, they suspected his sex at once. The race was a short one, and the rebel President was soon brought to bay. He was conveyed to Fortress Monroe, where he has since been, and is now (January 1, 1866) a prisoner.

Petitions to President Johnson in his case have been many, numerously signed, and for all sorts of sentences, reprieves, and pardons.

Davis's Mills, Miss.—6,000 rebels, under Van Dorn, made an attack on 200 infantry and 50 cavalry, under Colonel Morgan, 25th Indiana, protected by earth-works and block-houses, at this place, December 25, 1863, and, after a desperate fight of three and a half hours, during which they made three distinct charges, were repulsed. Van Dorn lost 22 killed, 60 wounded, 20 prisoners, and 100 stand of arms; Union loss, 3 wounded.

Dawson. (See Dryersburg.)

Day-book. (See Daily News.)

Day's Gap, Ala.—Colonel Streight's command, on April 30, 1863, had a skirmish with the rebels at this place, in which they repulsed the rebels, killing and wounding about 70 of them; their loss was 1 killed and 20 wounded. He captured the rebel artillery. At 3

P. M. they had another fight, which lasted till dark; two Unionists were killed and several wounded. Colonel Streight spiked the captured pieces and moved off under cover of the darkness.

Decatur, Ala., was the scene of a brisk engagement July 26, 1862.

A regiment of rebel soldiers mutinied at this place February 8, 1864, rather than re-enlist. The place was occupied by the Union forces on the 14th. Rousseau, with 3,000 men, left this place for the south July 10.

October 28 a sortie was made from the garrison at this place on the enemy's rifle-pits, which cleared them out, capturing 120 prisoners, besides killing and wounding a number. Colonel Morgan, with the 14th U. S. colored troops, carried one of the enemy's batteries just above the town. He spiked the guns and returned in safety. General Hood, the same day, with a large force, attempted to take the place, then garrisoned by a small force under General Granger, but was repulsed, with a loss of 134 men and 6 guns. Decatur was besieged by Beauregard, but November 26 he was attacked, and on the 29th repulsed, with a loss of over 500 men. General Steedman, in pursuit of Hood's retreating forces, crossed the Tennessee River at this point December 27.

Dechard, Tenn., was occupied by Union forces, after driving out the rebels, June 29, 1863.

Deep Gully, N. C., was the scene of heavy skirmishing March 13 and 14, 1863.

Deep Run, Va., was the scene of a brisk though undecisive battle—sometimes called "Battle of White Tavern"—on August 16, 1864. The rebel Generals Gheiardi and Chambliss were killed. Loss nearly 1,400 on each side.

Deer Creek, Miss., was captured by a Union raiding party April 26, 1863. Much rebel property, including 32 cotton-mills and 400,000 bushels of corn, was destroyed.

Delaware Legislature passed a resolution opposing secession January 2, 1861.

Demara's Ferry was used by the Union forces in crossing the Savannah River November 27, 1864.

Dennison, Hon. William, ex-Governor of Ohio, succeeded Montgomery Blair in the position of Postmaster-General October 1, 1864.

Denver City, Colorado Territory.—At this place, on March 26, 1862, the advance of a body of Union troops, under Colonel J. P. Slough, *en route* for New Mexico, met and attacked a force of 250 Confederate cavalry, and, after a short engagement, took 57 of them prisoners.

Des-Ark, Ark., was taken by the Federals without opposition, January 17, 1863.

Detroit, Mich. (See Canada Raids.)

Diana, United States gun-boat, was captured by the rebels, on the Atchafalaya River, La., March 28, 1863.

Dinwiddie C. H., Va.—Near this place, March 31, 1865, Sheridan was furiously attacked by one cavalry and two infantry divisions of rebels, and driven four miles, when Custer's troops checked the pursuit.

Dismal Swamp Canal, N. C., was destroyed April 24, 1862.

Dix, General John A., was called into President Buchanan's Cabinet as Secretary of the Treasury. His celebrated order, which sent a thrill of delight and encouragement through the great loyal heart, was issued to the United States special agent at New Orleans, January 29, 1861, as follows:

"**If any person attempts to haul down the American flag, shoot him on the spot.**"

He was, May 6, commissioned as Major-General of volunteers, from New Jersey, and June 14, to the same grade in the regular army. He was assigned to the command of the Middle Department, March 28, 1862. He was ordered to New York in the riotous times of 1863. He was arrested July 1, 1864, for his suppression of the New York Journal of Commerce, and other like papers; waiving the benefit of the suppression of the "*habeas corpus*," he passed an examination, and was discharged.

In consequence of the incendiary attempts to burn New York city on the night of November 25, he ordered all persons in the city from the rebel States to register themselves at General Peck's office; also declaring the incendiaries to be spies, and ordering that if caught, they should be "immediately tried, and, if found guilty, instantly executed."

Dodge, a United States revenue cutter, was seized by the State authorities, in Galveston Bay, Texas, March 2, 1861.

Donaldsonvile, La., was the scene of a brisk but undecisive engagement September 24, 1862. General Weitzel's forces, from New Orleans, arrived at this place November 26, and the next day met the Confederates, when half an hour's fight ensued, which resulted in the rout of the rebels, with a loss of 6 killed, 15 wounded, and 268 prisoners; Union loss, 18 killed and 68 wounded. The rebels attacked the place, June 28, 1863, but were repulsed with considerable loss. They being reinforced, occupied the place a few days later, but were driven out September 25. The town was surrounded by a band of guerrillas under one Scott, and the surrender of the Union forces demanded, August 5, 1864. This was refused, when the garrison (the 11th New York Cavalry) cut their way out, leaving their sick in camp.

Doniphan, Mo., was the scene of a severe skirmish and Union defeat, May 28, 1863. The Unionists lost 80 men.

Douglas, Stephen A., United States Senator for Illinois, died at the Tremont House, Chicago, at ten minutes past 9 A. M., June 13, 1861. His last words were a message to his children, telling them to "obey the laws and support the Constitution of the United States."

Dover, Tenn., was attacked by rebels February 3, 1863. They were, by the aid of the gun-boats, repulsed with heavy loss.

Drainesville, Va.—An engagement occurred near this place December 20, 1861, between a foraging party, under Gen. Ord, and the rebels, under Gen. Stuart. After a severe fight of about two hours, the rebels retreated, leaving from fifty to seventy-five dead on the field, and a great many wounded, besides large quantities of war material. Union loss, 8 killed and 50 wounded. A detachment of 150 of the 2d Massachusetts Cavalry, under Captain Reed, while scouting near this place, February 22, 1864, was attacked by 200 or 300 of Mosby's guerrillas in ambush; the Unionists fell back; 7 men were killed, and a number captured.

Draft. (See Conscription.)

Dryersburg, Tenn., was occupied for some time by guerrillas, who were driven out January 30, 1863. February 7, there was a severe skirmish near the town with Dawson's guerrillas; 7 killed and the balance captured, except Dawson, who escaped.

Duck River, Tenn., was reached and crossed by the rebels, who were attacked and driven back March 19, 1863.

Duck River Shoals, Tenn., was, on April 25, 1863, the scene of a severe bombardment between the Union gun-boats and the rebel shore batteries. The batteries were silenced, with a rebel loss of 25 men killed and wounded. Union loss none.

Duffield's Station, on the B. and O. R. R., was occupied, and the track there destroyed by Mosby's guerrillas, January 19, 1865. A train was thrown from the track the same day.

Dug Springs, Mo.—On August 2, 1861, Gen. Lyon's forces had a fight with the rebels under Ben McCulloch, at Dug Springs, nineteen miles south-west of Springfield, Missouri, and defeated them with artillery and cavalry. Union loss, nine killed and thirty wounded; Confederate loss heavy.

Duguidsville, Va.—The rebels destroyed the bridge over James River, at this place, March 8, 1865.

Duke, Basil, and a few of Morgan's guerrillas, under his command, were captured near Pomeroy, Ohio, July 30, 1863. (See John Morgan.)

Dumfries, Va., was, on December 23, 1862, the scene of a battle between General Sigel's forces and 4,000 Confederate cavalry under Stuart. After several repulses the rebels retired; but being reinforced, he, three days later, made another attack with 6,000 men and 6 pieces of artillery. The place was defended by three companies of infantry, 400 cavalry, and 4 pieces of artillery; after a fight of six hours the rebels retired, defeated, losing 10 killed, 16 wounded, and 30 prisoners. Union loss, 4 killed, 8 wounded, and 20 men captured on patrol duty. One week later the attack was again renewed, the place captured, and the Federal depot and stores destroyed.

Durham Station, 25 miles north-west of Raleigh, N. C., was, on April 18, 1865, the meeting-place between Sherman and Johnson, for settlement of the terms of surrender.

Dutch Gap Canal. (See Grant's Report.)

Duval's Bluff, Ark., was, on July 6, 1862, the scene of a sharp contest between 200 of the 24th Indiana and 450 rebel cavalry. The cavalry were defeated. Their loss was 84 killed, wounded, and missing; Union loss, 1 killed and 21 wounded. The Unionists pursued the rebels, and the following day again won a victory, capturing the rebel stores, camp equipage, etc.

The place was captured January 16, 1863, by the Union forces under General Gorman. 150 prisoners, 2 columbiads, 300 small arms, and a large quantity of ammunition were taken. Nearly all the 54th Illinois Infantry were captured near this place, by the rebel General Shelby, August 23, 1864.

Early. (See Grant's Report.)

East Bay, Fla., was occupied, and nearly 20 salt-kettles destroyed, by a party from the U. S. bark "Restless," February 18, 1864.

East Point, Ga., was for a time the head-quarters of the rebel General Wheeler. He finally evacuated the place August 10, 1864.

Eastport, Miss., was General Thomas's head-quarters January 9, 1865.

Eastport, Tenn., was thrown into great excitement March 24, 1862, by the near approach of the Union gunboats. The town was occupied by Union forces April 19, 1863. They burned the town and abandoned it ten days later.

Edenton, N. C., was occupied by an expedition under Lieutenant Maury, U. S. N., February 12, 1862.

Edward's Ferry, on the Potomac, was the scene of a skirmish June 17, 1861. An artillery engagement took place here October 25, in which the rebel batteries were silenced. A rebel raiding party crossed the Potomac at this point into Maryland November 13, 1863.

Edwards Station, Miss. (See Baker's Creek.)

Egypt, Miss., was occupied by the Union forces from

February 14 till the 19th, 1864. Immense quantities of corn and provisions were destroyed.

Elizabeth City, N. C. (See Burnside's Expedition.)

Elizabethtown, Ky., was captured by the guerrillas, under John Morgan, December 27, 1862. The rebels occupied the town June 13, 1863, capturing a train of 200 Government horses and other valuable stores.

Elk Creek, Indian Territory, was the scene of a rebel defeat July 16, 1863.

Elk Fork, Ky.—250 men of the 10th Kentucky Cavalry, under Major Foley, surprised a body of 350 Confederates at this place December 27, 1862. They killed and wounded 47, and captured 57 men and 80 horses, and burned their camp. No loss to the Unionists.

Elk River, Va., was, on September 12, 1862, the scene of a desperate fight which lasted nearly all day and resulted in a drawn battle.

Elkwater, Va., was the scene of a rebel defeat September 11, 1861. John A. Washington, former proprietor of Mount Vernon, was killed while reconnoitering near Elkwater next day.

Ellsworth, Elmer E., was commissioned as Colonel at the outbreak of the rebellion. May 2, 1861, his regiment—the New York fire Zouaves—arrived in Washington, and moved to Alexandria on the 24th. Colonel Ellsworth, seeing a secession flag flying from the "Marshall House," stepped in, and with four others took it down. As he was returning from the roof he was shot and instantly killed by the landlord, one James Jackson. Jackson was almost as instantly killed by Corporal Brownell, of the Colonel's party. Jackson's deed, which was at the North shudderingly regarded as assassination, was at the South exulted over as heroic patriotism, and a subscription set on foot for the benefit of his family.

Emancipation.—General Fremont, on August 31, 1861, issued a proclamation, which, among other things, declared that the slaves of rebels should be free. President Lincoln disapproved of that portion of the proclamation September 11. On December 4, General Phelps issued his emancipation order.

President Lincoln, on February 6, 1862, sent to Congress a message, recommending gradual emancipation.

These resolutions passed the House March 14, and the Senate April 2.

General Hunter issued his emancipation order May 9, which the President repudiated the 19th.

In a message, July 14, President Lincoln recommended to Congress the abolition of slavery, and providing compensation to owners.

The Emancipation Proclamation was issued September 22, 1862, and the extent of its application defined January 1, 1863. (For these documents see appendix.)

The number of slaves emancipated by this proclamation was, taking the census of 1860 as a basis, as follows:

Alabama	435,080
Arkansas	111,115
Florida	61,745
Georgia	462,198
Louisiana, (part,)	247,715
Mississippi	436,631
North Carolina	331,059
South Carolina	402,406
Texas	182,566
Virginia, (part,) about	450,000
Total	3,120,515

The number of slaves not affected by its provisions was about 832,000. (See Adams, Davis, Maryland, Missouri, Tennessee, etc.)

Eminence, Ky., was the scene of a brisk skirmish, and the capture of the guerrilla "Jessy," and 28 of his men, April 25, 1865.

England. (See Mason and Slidell, and Neutrality.)

Eureka, Mo., was captured by the Federals September 13, 1862.

Fairfax C. H., Va.—Forty-seven men, under Lieutenant Tompkins, of the 2d United States Cavalry, surprised the rebels at Fairfax Court-house June 1, 1861. Result indecisive. The town was occupied by the Union forces July 17, from which they moved next day in the direction of Centerville. A sharp skirmish occurred near this place November 27, and also on February 7, 1862.

Brisk skirmishing occurred between this place and Washington September 2, 1862. The rear guard consisted of Hooker's and Porter's commands, and did effectual service in keeping the rebels in check as the Union troops were moving into the fortifications protecting Washington on the Virginia side.

The rebels were dispersed at this point May 14, 1863. Mosby's gang surprised and occupied the place March 8, 1863, capturing General Stoughton, the Provost-marshal, patrols, and all the men, with 110 horses.

Fairfax Station, Va., was unsuccessfully attacked by Stuart's cavalry December 28, 1862. A band of guerrillas were dispersed near this place June 4, 1863, and, on the 27th, the Union cavalry were defeated on the same field. A skirmish, without loss or decided results, occured near the Station August 24. On September 25, Mosby's guerrillas tore up the track, and committed other depredations, near the town.

Fairmount, Va., was the scene of a gallant defense April 29, 1863. A heavy force of rebel cavalry, under Imboden and Jones, attacked this place, defended by 350 men, under Colonel Mulligan. After fighting nearly all day, the garrison were obliged to surrender. The rebels admitted a loss of 100; the Union loss was 1 killed and 4 wounded. The rebels then plundered the place.

Fair Gardens, near Sevierville, Tenn.—Two divisions of rebel cavalry, under General Martin, the advance of Longstreet's army, attacked General Sturgis at this place January 28, 1864. Sturgis fell back to a commanding position, and next morning opened the fight. After a stubborn contest, lasting from daylight till 4 P. M., the rebels were defeated; 65 rebels were killed and wounded. Two steel rifle-guns and 100 prisoners were left in the hands of the Union troops.

Fair Oaks, Va.—On May 31, 1862, at 10 o'clock A. M., taking advantage of a heavy storm which had flooded the valley, the main body of the rebels, under General Joe Johnston, attacked the Union advance which had crossed the river at Fair Oaks and Seven Pines. General Casey's division was overpowered, and fell back. General Couch's division came to the rescue, and checked the further advance of the rebels. The fight was desperate, and lasted until night. The rebels occupied the ground they had won. The battle was resumed next morning at daylight, and continued all day. In one of the brilliant bayonet charges made by the Union troops, the rebels were driven back toward Richmond. Union loss, 890 killed, 3,627 wounded, and 1,217 missing; rebel loss, 8,000, including five Generals. They left 1,200 dead on the field.

The rebels made an attempt June 17, to flank a portion of the Union forces at Fair Oaks, but they were repulsed.

Falling Waters, Va., was the scene of an unimportant skirmish July 1, 1861. Lee crossed the Potomac at this point July 14, 1863.

Falls Church, Va., was the scene of a skirmish June 29, 1861.

On September 29, Colonel Baker's California regiment and Colonel Owen's Irish regiment, of Pennsylvania, mistaking each other for secessionists, fired into each other near this place, and, before the mistake was discovered, some 9 men were killed, and 25, including three officers, were wounded.

On the morning of November 16 a foraging party of the 30th New York were betrayed near Upton's Hill, Virginia, by a man named Doolin, at whose farm the men were collecting forage. Doolin, who was previously supposed to be a Union man, was arrested.

Falmouth. (See Fredericksburg and Burnside.)

Farmington, Miss., was the scene of a short but desperate action April 2, 1862. A battalion of the 2d Illinois Cavalry were surrounded by a body of Confederate troops, but cut their way out, inflicting a loss on the rebels of 49, killed, wounded, and missing. The cavalry lost 1 killed and four wounded. The rebels being reinforced, the Unionists were forced to retire on the 4th. Skirmishing was renewed May 3, when the rebels were defeated, with a loss of 30 killed and a large amount of camp equipage. Union loss, 2 killed and 12 wounded.

The most important action at this place occurred on May 9, 1862. The rebel army, under Bragg, was held in check for five hours, but being heavily reinforced, the Unionists, under General Paine, retired across the Tennessee River. Union loss, 21 killed and 140 wounded; rebel loss, 420 killed and wounded.

Farmington, Mo., was the scene of a brisk, though undecisive skirmish, July 1, 1861.

Farmington, Tenn.—General Crook defeated General Wheeler at this place October 8, 1863. Union loss, 30 killed, 150 wounded; rebel loss, 300 killed, wounded, and prisoners.

Farnden's Creek, three miles from Raymond, Mississippi, was the scene of a hotly contested battle May 12, 1863. The rebels were under Gregg, the Unionists commanded by Logan; each about 5,000 strong. After two hours' hard fighting, the rebels were routed, with a loss of 70 killed and 185 prisoners; wounded unknown. Union loss, 52 killed, 104 wounded.

Farragut, Commodore D. G., though well known as a true man and sailor before, came more prominently before the public when he assumed command of the naval forces for the capture of New Orleans. The fleet under his command at this time was twenty mortar-vessels and eight war steamers, besides schooners, store-ships, etc., with officers and seamen numbering about 2,000. The expedition, including Butler's land force, left Ship Island April 15, 1862, and on the 17th the bombardment of Forts Jackson and St. Philip, on the Mississippi, below New Orleans, was commenced. A furious cannonade was kept up by both parties until the 24th, when it was decided to run the gauntlet with his fleet. They started early in the morning, and succeeded in passing the forts with very little damage. They were then attacked by the rebel fleet, and a desperate fight ensued. Thirteen Confederate gun-boats and three transports were destroyed, and one Union vessel was sunk. The fleet came to anchor within twenty miles of New Orleans. Confederate loss, 185 killed, 197 wounded, and 400 prisoners; Union loss, 30 killed and 119 wounded.

On the 28th, Forts Jackson and St. Philip, finding themselves surrounded and cut off, surrendered to Commodore Porter, commanding the mortar fleet. The city of New Orleans was also surrendered to Commodore Farragut on the 29th, General Lovell, with 20,000 men, having previously evacuated the city, which was turned over to General Butler May 1.

While preparing for the ascent of the river, the officers of some British and French men-of-war, lying there, made very discouraging representations to him of the difficulties to be overcome, and the opposition to be met in his undertaking. His reply was worthy the man: "You may be right; but I was sent here to make the attempt. I came here to reduce or pass the forts, and to take New Orleans, and *I shall try it on*."

Almost immediately the fleet was ordered "up the river." (The history will be found under the appropriate headings, Mobile, Vicksburg, Port Hudson, etc.)

He was appointed Rear-Admiral July 30, 1862, ranking first on the active list; and by his achievements won the rank of Vice-Admiral (corresponding with Lieutenant-General in the army), which was conferred upon him December 21, 1864.

Fayetteville, Ark., was captured by General Curtis February 23, 1862. The rebels fled, in great confusion, across the Boston Mountain; not, however, before poisoning a quantity of bread and meat, which was eaten by the Federal troops. Forty-two officers and men were poisoned, some of whom died.

On July 14, the Unionists, 600 strong, under Major Miller, attacked the combined rebel forces of Rains, Coffee, Hunter, Tracy, and Hawthorne, about 1,600, nearly eight miles west of this place, defeating them. The enemy's main body was pursued for twelve miles.

The place was, on April 18, 1863, attacked by 3,000 rebels. The garrison numbered about 2,000, many unarmed. The rebels were repulsed with considerable loss; Union loss, 5 killed and 17 wounded. The place was shelled by the rebels November 3, 1864. (See Prairie Grove.)

Fayetteville, Ga., was occupied by Union forces under General McCook July 28, 1864. He destroyed six miles of railroad, and all the rebel stores found there.

Fayetteville, N. C., was occupied by General Howard's forces, March 10, 1865. They remained there until the 14th, when they moved toward Goldsboro.

Fayetteville, Va., was the scene of an artillery duel November 15, 1862, and of a brisk cavalry skirmish October 22, 1863.

Fessenden, Wm. P., was called into President Lincoln's cabinet, as Secretary of the Treasury, July 1, 1864. He resigned March 6, 1865, and was succeeded by Hugh McCulloch, of Indiana.

Fish, Hon. Hamilton. (See Ames.)

Fisher's Hill, Va., was, on September 22, 1864, the scene of a desperate battle and rebel defeat. Sheridan here met the rebel forces under Early. After hard fighting nearly all day, the rebels were flanked on both sides, and about 5 P. M. charges were made upon their center and both flanks. The rebels were routed, with a loss of about 1,500 killed and wounded, 2,500 prisoners, 21 cannon, and a great quantity of small arms. Union loss, 700. Sheridan then advanced toward Woodstock.

Flemington, Ky., was the scene of a skirmish between the rebels and home-guards, October 6, 1861. Rebels defeated.

Flint Hill, Va., was the scene of a skirmish and rebel defeat January 18, 1864.

Florence, Ala.—Three rebel steamboats were burned at this place February 8, 1862. On July 22, a body of guerrillas burned the commissary and quartermaster's warehouses, and all the cotton, at this place; they took also the steamer Colonna, and robbed and burned her. An engagement occurred here May 27, 1863; rebels defeated. The great Union raid into Northern Alabama arrived at Florence, November 1. Forrest crossed the Tennessee River on flatboats, at this place, October 6, 1864, thus escaping from Rousseau, while the latter was detained by high water at Elk River and Shoal Creek.

Florida Legislature, on December 1, 1860, provided for holding a State Convention, to consider the question of secession, and ordered an election for delegates thereto. The Convention met at Tallahasse, January 3, 1861, and on the 7th passed an ordinance of secession. (62 *v.* 7.)

Florida, Mo., was the scene of a skirmish, and the breaking up of a rebel camp, July 8, 1861.

Florida, the Anglo-Confederate cruiser, *alias* **"Oreto,"** ran the blockade, into Mobile, January 13, 1863, and four days later captured and destroyed the brig "Estella." The authorities of Nassau, N. P., showed their sympathy with the Confederates by giving the captain (Maffit) and officers of this pirate a public reception on January 31, she having arrived there the day previous. Many ships were captured by this crusier, which were bonded or destroyed. About the 8th and 10th of July, 1864, she made several very daring captures near the coast of Delaware. She was captured by the U. S. Steamer "Wachusett," Captain Cillius commanding, at Bahia, Brazil. She was, together with 12 officers and 58 men of her crew, her papers, records, and valuables, among her captures, sent to the United States. Her officers and crew were for a time confined at Fort Warren, but were released February 1, 1865, when they immediately sailed for Halifax.

Floyd, John B., Secretary of War in Buchanan's Cabinet, was, on December 23, 1860, discovered as the principal agent in robbing the Indian Trust Fund at Washington. He resigned his seat in the Cabinet on the 29th, charging the President, by refusing to withdraw Major Anderson, with trying to provoke civil war. The real cause, however, was probably his fear of prosecution for robbing the Indian Trust Fund. On January 30, 1861, the Grand Jury of the District of Columbia presented charges against him for maladministration in office and conspiracy against the Government. He figured to a considerable extent in the rebellion, and died at Abington, Va., August 27, 1863.

Floyd's Fork, Ky., was on October 1, 1862, the scene of a brisk engagement between the advance of General Sill's division and a body of rebel cavalry; the rebels were finally defeated, and pursued several miles.

Folly Island. (See Charleston.)

Foote, Andrew H., was, on August 26, 1861, assigned to the command of the naval forces on the Western waters, then ranking as Captain. He was soon promoted to Commodore, and for gallant service was, on July 16, 1862, promoted to the rank of Rear-Admiral, ranking fourth on the active list. He relieved Admiral

Dupont, commanding the forces operating against Charleston, June 3, 1863, and on the 26th of the same month died at the Astor House, New York. The history of his prominent movements will be found under their appropriate headings.

Ford's Station, Va., was occupied by Union cavalry, under Wilson and Kautz, June 22, 1864. The railroad track, two trains, etc., were destroyed.

Foreigners.—On July 22, 1862, President Lincoln issued an order that foreigners should not be required to take the oath of allegiance.

Forsythe, Mo., was the scene of a brisk engagement July 22, 1861. The rebels were defeated and the place occupied by Union forces.

Forsyth, Ga., was occupied by Sherman's cavalry, cutting the railroad to Macon, November 18, 1864.

Fort Anderson, N. C., was, on February 19, 1865, evacuated just before dawn, the rebels taking with them some light artillery, and all else movable and of value. After daylight some Union troops, who were near by, went in and hoisted their flag on the ramparts, when the firing ceased from the vessels, which had been kept up at intervals all night. 10 heavy guns, some ammunition, and 50 prisoners were taken. Loss in killed and wounded small on either side.

Fort Armstrong, N. C., was taken by the Unionists February 21, 1865.

Fort Barrancas and the United States Navy-yard at Pensacola were surrendered to the Florida and Alabama State troops January 12, 1861.

A heavy bombardment between this fort and Fort Pickens, held by the Union troops, occurred November 22 and 23, 1861.

Fort Brown, Texas, was surrendered by General Twiggs to the rebels, February 26, 1861, but was, for the time, held by the Unionists under Captain Hill, who refused to obey Twiggs's order. It was, on March 6, actually surrendered, under special agreement.

Forts Caswell and **Johnson,** N. C., were taken possession of by the State authorities January 8, 1861.

Forts Clark and **Hatteras,** on the coast of North Carolina, were, early in the rebellion, taken possession of by the rebels. On August 29, 1861, after a cannonading of two days, the expedition, under General Butler and Flag-officer Stringham, succeeded in capturing both forts, with their garrisons, who surrendered as prisoners of war, together with large quantities of commissary and ordnance stores, and 765 prisoners and 1,000 stand of arms.

Fort Clinch, Ga., was captured by Commodore Dupont, March 7, 1862.

Fort Craig, near Valverde, New Mexico, was, on February 21, 1862, the scene of an engagement between the rebel forces, under Colonel Steele, and the Federals, under Colonel Canby. The battle lasted all day, when Colonel Canby was obliged to retreat to the fort, with a loss of 62 killed and 162 wounded.

Fort Darling, on James River, near Richmond, for a long time commanded the river, and was the scene of frequent engagements. (See Richmond.)

Fort De Russey, on the Red River, near Alexandria, was captured by Admiral Porter, May 5, 1863, but it soon after fell into rebel possession, and they set about obstructing the river navigation, and, for a time, succeeded. Operations were commenced by the Union forces for its reduction. On March 14, 1864, at 4 o'clock, a portion of General A. J. Smith's troops (the 3d and 9th Indiana Batteries) opened on the fort, and one hour later General Mower's brigade charged the rifle-pits and stormed the works, and in twenty minutes the colors of the 58th Indiana were upon the ramparts. Previous to Smith's taking the fort, General Dick Taylor endeavored to flank him and cut him off from the fort; then commenced a most extraordinary race between the Union and Confederate troops, which resulted, however, in Smith arriving at the fort three hours before his opponent. During the siege the gun-boat Benton participated with great success.

By the possession of these works, the obstructions in Red River, which occupied the rebels five months to construct, were rendered entirely useless to them. They lost 300 prisoners, 8 guns, a quantity of gunpowder, small arms, ammunition, and commissary stores.

The fort was blown up and abandoned on the 17th.

Fort Donaldson, on the Cumberland River, was invested by the Union forces, numbering 40,000 strong, under General Grant, February 12, 1862. The rebels in and about the fort numbered about 20,000 under Floyd, Buckner, and Bushrod R. Johnson, the former being first in command.

The attack commenced on the 13th by the Union advance, under McClernand, driving in the rebel pickets. Skirmishing continued all day, but as the gun-boats had not arrived, no general engagement took place beyond 200 shells from the Carondelet thrown into the fort.

At 2 o'clock on the 14th, the gun-boats moved to the attack, and one hour later the St. Louis opened fire. The firing was kept up vigorously for an hour and a half, the water-batteries being silenced; but the St. Louis having received a "plunging shot" in the pilot-house, disabling her wheel, and the other vessels having also suffered, Commodore Foote directed the fleet to drop down the river, and the contest ceased for the day.

Early next morning the extreme right of the Union line was attacked by a heavy body of the Confederates, who attempted to cut their way through. The attack was promptly met; but the rebels, being reinforced, were successful in pushing back the Unionists. Being reinforced in turn, the Federals drove them back again. So the battle wavered during the day, until, in the afternoon, an assault at the point of the bayonet was made on the left of the line, (rebel right,) which was gallantly executed, and night found the Union troops in possession of the outer line of fortifications.

During that night Generals Floyd and Pillow, with about 5,000 men, made their escape. Daylight of the 16th revealed the white flag on the ramparts in token of surrender. Union loss, during the three days' fighting, 446 killed, 1,735 wounded, and 150 prisoners. Rebel loss, 237 killed, 1,007 wounded, and 13,300 prisoners, including General Buckner, 3,000 horses, 48 field-pieces, 17 heavy guns, 20,000 small arms, and an immense amount of stores.

Two regiments of rebel Tennesseeans, 1,470 men, unaware of the surrender of the fort, and intended as a reinforcement, marched into it on the 17th, and were added to the list of prisoners.

The fort was attacked by the rebels August 6. The Unionists repulsed them, and following, came up with them on the Clarksville road, about 7 miles from the fort. The rebels were strongly posted in ambush, but after half an hour's engagement, were defeated with heavy loss. Union loss, 2 killed, 18 wounded.

On August 25, the rebel Colonel Woodward attacked the fort with 775 men, but was repulsed therefrom by Major Hart and four companies of the 71st Ohio; the rebels lost 30 killed and wounded; the garrison did not receive a scratch.

The fort was invested, and an attack made on February 3, 1863, by General Wheeler, with between 3,000 and 4,000 men; but, after a severe fight, lasting till night, they were repulsed, with a loss of 200 killed, 500 wounded, and 50 prisoners. The Unionists lost 12 killed and 14 wounded and missing. The garrison had fired their last shot as the gun-boats arrived and dispersed the rebels.

Fort Esperawza, commanding Pass Cavallo and the defenses of Matagorda Bay, Texas, was captured by Unionists, November 30, 1863; this capture cleared the entrance to Matagorda Bay, and gave command of Saluria, Port Lavacco, Matagorda, and Victoria.

Fort Fillmore, N. M., was traitorously surrendered to the rebels by Major Lynde, August 2, 1861.

Fort Fisher, near Wilmington, N. C., was bombarded August 23, 1863, but no result achieved.

A combined land (under General Butler) and naval (under Rear-Admiral Porter) force was sent against Fort Fisher in December, 1864, and on the 24th the gun-boats opened fire and the torpedo boat Louisiana was exploded near the fort, without effect. The land forces did not co-operate. The bombardment continued all the next day, and, under cover of the fire, a portion of the troops landed and captured the outer fort, but were soon forced to abandon it. The whole force then withdrew, having accomplished nothing. The removal of General Butler, immediately after, would indicate that he was to blame in the matter.

Rear-Admiral Porter, having gathered a fleet of 52 vessels of all classes, 531 guns, sailing in three columns, left Beaufort, North Carolina, for Fort Fisher, arriving off Half Moon Battery on the night of January 12, 1865.

Next morning at dawn the fleet was in line of battle. Line No. 1 took position near the beach to land troops, and lines Nos. 2 and 3, anchoring just outside the reserves, taking charge of the provision vessels. At 8 A. M., the iron-clads, five in number, got into position about 1,000 yards from the fort, and opened fire deliberately; the troops landed before 3 P. M. Lines Nos. 1 and 2 went in on the attack at 4 P. M., and bombarded the fort until after dark, when the wooden vessels were ordered to haul out and anchor. The monitors and ironsides kept up firing, at intervals, all night. The enemy had ceased to fire before dark, and kept in his bomb-proofs; most of his guns on the sea-front were dismounted or destroyed, and the greater portion of the fort, at that point, was reduced to a crumbling condition.

Next morning, (the 14th,) all the small gun-boats carrying 11-inch guns, were ordered in to try to dismount all the guns on the face of the work where the assault was to be made by the sailors. The attack lasted from 1 P. M. until after dark, and one vessel fired at intervals all night. Two thousand sailors were landed to assault the sea-face, armed with cutlasses and revolvers, and some with Sharp's rifles. Admiral Porter and General Terry spent part of the night in arranging and perfecting plans for contest.

The squadron reached a position for attack in three lines, at 11 A. M., and opened fire as soon as anchored; the upper batteries were silenced. At three P. M. the vessels changed their fire to the upper batteries, and the troops and sailors dashed ahead, each trying to gain the parapets first. The mariners were to have held the rifle-pits, to cover the boarding party of the sailors, which they failed to do, so that the head of their column received a murderous fire of grape and canister, and were forced to retreat, with severe loss; in the mean time, the troops were successful on their side. The enemy, seeing so large a body of men coming at them from the sea side, supposed that it was the main attack, and concentrated the largest part of their forces at that point; but when the rebels were giving three cheers, thinking they had gained the day, they received a volley in their rear from the troops who had gained the highest parapet, who went in on a hand-to-hand fight, and gained, in one hour, five or six traverses, which are immense bomb-proofs; the fighting lasted until 10 P. M. The vessels prevented reinforcements reaching the fort by throwing shells. Success after success was followed up, carrying the whole line of works and batteries, capturing some 400 prisoners. About 12 o'clock, midnight, General Whiting and Colonel Lamb, both wounded, surrendered with the balance of the garrison, about 1,400 men, to Captain R. W. Dawson, Assistant Inspector-General. The fort was garrisoned by Union troops, of whom 300 were killed on the 16th, by an explosion of the magazine. The Union loss, killed, wounded, and missing, including the explosion, was about 300 in the navy and 900 in the army. So fell the most formidable fort ever taken in the world; and the conquerors proceeded to operate against Wilmington.

Fort Gains. (See Mobile.)

Fort Gibson, Ark., was on May 20, 1863, the scene of a fight between the advance of Price's army, under Steele, Cooper, and McIntosh, and the Union forces under Colonel Phillips. The rebels were driven back with great loss; Union loss, 30 killed.

Fort Gregg, S. C. (See Charleston.)

Fort Henry, on the Tennessee River, was captured by the Union naval forces, under Commodore Foote, on February 6, 1862. About 10 o'clock the signal to move was given at the rendezvous, nine miles below the fort. At 12:30 o'clock Commodore Foote opened fire from his fleet, then about one mile below the rebels. The fire was replied to by the fort, and severe cannonading kept up till a quarter before 2 o'clock, when the fort surrendered. The fort and prisoners were handed over to General Grant, when he arrived, which was about an hour afterward. By this surrender the rebels lost 19 killed and 8 wounded, twenty guns, seventeen mortars, and vast quantities of stores, besides sixty or seventy prisoners, (the main body having escaped,) among whom was General Tilghman, commanding officer. Union loss, 17 killed, 31 wounded. Immediately after this capture, operations for the reduction of Fort Donaldson were commenced.

Fort Hill, near Cairo, Ill., was the scene of a brisk engagement September 20, 1861.

Fort Hindman, Ark. (See Arkansas Post.)

Fort Huger. (See Mobile.)

Fort Jackson. (See Farragut.)

Fort Johnson. (See Fort Caswell.)

Fort Kearney, in Kansas, was taken by the secessionists February 19 1861, but soon after retaken.

Fort Kelly, at New Creek, Va., was captured by General Rosser November 28, 1864.

Fort Lyon.—Five hundred Indians were killed near this place, by Colonel Livingston's force, December 9, 1864.

Fort Macon, N. C., was invested by the Unionists, and summoned to surrender March 23, 1862. The bombardment from the fleet and three batteries commenced on the morning of April 25, continuing all day, and was renewed next morning, when the fort, at 10 o'clock, surrendered.

Fort McAllister, near Savannah, Ga., was stormed by Wagner's division of Sherman's army, at 4:30 o'clock A. M., December 13, 1864. After an assault of half an hour, the fort and the garrison of 200 men, all the armament, stores, etc., were taken. This opened safe communication with the fleet and General Sherman's army.

Fort McRae. (See Fort Pickens.)

Fort Morgan, at the entrance of Mobile Bay, was taken possession of by the State authorities January 4, 1861. The peculiar course of the channel here, and the great strength of the fort, together with the obstructions, (sunken hulls, torpedoes, etc.,) enabled the rebels to hold the place, and make Mobile one of the great headquarters for blockade-runners. For the capture, etc., see Mobile.

Fort Morgan, at Okracoke, was abandoned by the rebels August 30, 1861.

Fort Moultrie. (See Charleston.)

Fort Nelson, five miles below Fort Donaldson, was, on October 11, 1864, the scene of a brisk and bloody engagement between 90 colored troops, under Colonel Weaver, and 200 rebels. The rebels were repulsed with a loss of 29 killed and wounded.

Fort Pemberton, at the mouth of the Tallahatchie, Miss., was, on March 11, 1863, attacked by the Union gun-boat Chillicothe. After exchanging a few rounds the gun-boat withdrew. The gun-boat De Kalb came up two days later, when the bombardment was renewed throughout the day. After several severe contests, the gun-boats withdrew and the rebels held their position commanding the river until the Federal forces had gained the Yazoo, by way of Steele's and Black Bayous and Rolling Fork and Sunflower Rivers.

Fort Pickens, on the end of Santa Rosa Island, at the entrance of Pensacola Bay, Fla., was occupied by Lieutenant Slemmer in much the same manner and for the same reason that Anderson took possession of Fort Sumter. When the rebels demanded of him the surrender of the fort, he replied: "I have orders from the Government to defend this fort, and I shall do so to the last extremity." Supplies to the fort were cut off by the rebels, March 18, 1861, leaving the garrison of about eighty men in a very critical position. The reinforcements brought by the Brooklyn (which was generally supposed to be for Fort Sumter) arrived there April 12. The rebels, at a very early date in the rebellion, commenced operations for the capture or destruction of the fort, and an attack was expected almost any day during the summer.

On August 31, Colonel Brown, commanding the fort, suspecting that the rebels intended sinking the United States Dry-dock, in Warrenton Navy-yard, in the channel (where it is very narrow) opposite Fort McRae, laid plans for its destruction. Awaiting a dark night, (it came September 2,) a boat's crew of eleven men, provided with combustibles, and three loaded columbiad shells, proceeded to the dock, and, luckily for them, found it unguarded. The shells they put in the boilers, arranged their combustibles, fired the pile, and escaped.

The dock was soon in flames and the bursting shells shivered it to atoms; thus the channel was kept unobstructed.

On the night of September 8, the rebels landed a force of about 1,500 men on the island, and about nine o'clock surprised the Wilson Zouaves, numbering about 400 strong. The Unionists were driven in confusion, but, being reinforced and reformed, and "knowing the ground," the rebels were in turn driven, and, in the darkness, suffered heavy loss. Arriving at their boats, they found them stuck in the mud, and many were lost in the endeavor to get them off. The rebel loss is not known, but was very heavy, partially from one party mistaking friends for foes, and thus killing more than the Unionists. Union loss, 14 killed, 30 wounded, 1 (Major Voges) prisoner.

On November 22, according to an arrangement with the fleet, Fort Pickens opened fire on the rebel steamer Time, as she was entering the harbor, which called out a return from Forts Barrancas and McRae. The firing continued all day, and was vigorously renewed next morning. Fort McRae was silenced. Fort Barrancas and the navy-yard was much injured. The town of Warrington was burned. Union loss, one killed, and six wounded; rebel loss, unknown. The war vessels "Niagara," and "Richmond" took part in the engagement on the first day, but were prevented on the second, on account of the lowness of the water.

A period of comparative quiet now ensued, until January 1, 1862, when Fort Pickens again opened on the rebels, as a "New Year salute." Fort Barrancas was breached, and Warrenton burned. Again a time of waiting and watching until May 9, when the rebels destroyed all they could not carry away, and abandoned their position.

Fort Pillow, or Wright, on the Mississippi, 80 miles above Memphis, which had for some time been held by the rebels, blockading the river, was invested by Commodore Foote's flotilla April 13, 1862. Fire was opened next morning, and continued for some days. On the 15th the rebels cut the levee on the Arkansas side, and thus frustrated the erection of Union works, also causing immense destruction of property. Not taking the fort by assault, the Unionists, on the 17th, commenced the siege.

A desperate naval engagement between eight rebel and six Union gun-boats took place just above the fort May 10. The Confederates lost one of their boats by explosion, another by fire, and a third by sinking. The five remaining boats took refuge under the guns of the fort. Only one of the Union gun-boats was damaged.

The fort being no longer tenable, was evacuated by the rebels on the night of June 4. The Unionists occupied it next morning, while the fleet proceeded to Memphis.

A skirmish occurred near the fort March 16, 1864, between a small party of the 12th Tennessee Cavalry and some rebels, resulting in the rout of the latter, with a loss of about 50 killed and wounded.

Fort Pillow was attacked on the morning of April 12, 1864, by 5,000 rebels under General Forrest. They assaulted the works for a long time, but made no sensible impression, being kept at bay by the gallant little fortress. Forrest sent flags of truce, demanding a surrender, which was promptly refused; meanwhile, he stealthily disposed his forces to advantage, within stonethrow of the works. At 2 P. M. the rebels stormed the works and drove the men from their guns down to the river. An indiscriminate slaughter was then commenced; black and white, alike, were ruthlessly butchered. The garrison consisted of 400 of the 13th Tennessee Cavalry and 200 of the 6th United States Heavy Artillery, colored, all under command of Majors Bradford and Booth. After killing the negroes, the most fiendish atrocities were perpetrated; some were found horribly mutilated and burned; 5 were buried alive; only about 200 of the garrison escaped, by hiding and swimming. 53 of the white troops were killed and 100 wounded; 300 negroes butchered in cold blood. The rebels burned every building and blew up a portion of the works. They lost only 25 killed and 50 wounded. The inhuman wretches killed a number of women and children; many of the wounded were burned, and then thrown into the river; the inner fort fairly ran with blood. Forrest retired just as the steamer Platte Valley hove in sight. The survivors hailed this vessel, when men were sent ashore to bury the dead and carry off some of the wounded. The rebels did not leave until they perfected their horrible work. They carried away 6 guns and all the stores of the garrison; next day they visited the scene of their exploits, and bayoneted some unfortunates whom they found still alive. Every officer commanding colored troops they shot, even after they surrendered. Forrest fell back to Brownsville.

The committee appointed by Congress to investigate this horrible affair, reported upon it, and substantiated all above stated, and, in some points, even more.

Fort Powell. (See Mobile.)

Fort Powhatan, on James River, below Richmond, was captured by the Union forces under Admiral Lee, July 14, 1863.

Fort Pulaski. (See Savannah.)

Fort Scott, Kansas.—On October 6, 1863, General Blunt's staff and body-guard were attacked near this place by 300 of Quantrell's men, in Federal uniform; the escort broke, and 78 out of 100 men were captured and afterward killed. General Blunt escaped, and meeting reinforcements, took command, and started in pursuit of the rebels.

General Price, on October 25, 1864, was attacked and defeated near the fort, losing camp equipage, 20 wagons of plunder, 1 gun, and a large number of cattle. He was again defeated next day, losing 1,500 prisoners, 1,000 stand of arms, 10 guns, 200 wagons, etc. Generals Marmaduke and Cabell, and a number of colonels, were among the prisoners.

Fort Smith, Ark., was taken possession of by the State troops, under Senator Borland, April 25, 1861. Captain Sturgis made his escape with two companies of cavalry, with horses, equipments, and provisions. It was held by the Confederates until September 1, 1863, when a detachment of General Blunt's army, under Colonel Cloud, took possession of it, defeating a rebel force of 4,000 men.

Fort Steedman, near Petersburg, Va., was assaulted and captured by the rebels under General Gordon, March

25, 1865. General McLaughlin and 500 men were taken prisoners. The Union troops rallied, and, after a short but vigorous contest, the fort was recaptured, with 2,700 prisoners.

Fort Sumter. (See Major Anderson, and Charleston.)

Fort Wagner. (See Charleston.)

Fort Walker. (See Port Royal.)

Fort White, at Georgetown, was captured by Admiral Dahlgren February 25, 1865.

Fort Williams. (See Plymouth, N. C.)

Fort Wright. (See Fort Pillow.)

Four Mile Creek, north of the James River, was, on July 28, 1864, the scene of a desperate struggle. The Union cavalry, under Generals Gregg and Sheridan, was attacked by the rebel infantry. Gregg's forces fell back, but Sheridan held his own, and, after a vigorous contest, defeated the attacking party. Rebel loss, 600; Union loss, 240.

Fourteen Mile Creek, near Vicksburg, was the scene of a brisk battle May 6, 1863. Rebels defeated.

Frankfort, Ky.—The Border State Convention met at this place June 3, 1861. On June 10, 1864, the place was visited by John Morgan, and the garrison was demanded to surrender. This demand was refused. Some brisk firing took place, when the guerrillas withdrew with loss.

Frankfort, Va.—The rebels were defeated near this place November 27, 1863, losing about 100 prisoners.

Franklin, Major-General, was taken prisoner at Gunpowder Bridge, while in a railway train, July 11, 1864. He escaped next day, and, after lying concealed in the woods two days, arrived at Baltimore.

Franklin, Ky., was, on October 9, 1863, the scene of a cavalry skirmish and rebel defeat.

Franklin, La., was captured and occupied by the Union forces April 15, 1863.

Franklin, Tenn., was occupied by the Federal troops January 31, 1863. A skirmish occurred near the town March 4, brought on by Van Dorn's advance. The Union army came out to meet the rebels, and drove them back six miles. Thirteen rebels killed; 2 Unionists wounded.

Van Dorn being reinforced until his force numbered 18,000 men, two days later, attacked Colonel Coburn's force, consisting of three regiments of infantry, 500 cavalry, and one battery, at Thompson's Station, 10 miles south of Franklin. The fight lasted all day, when the infantry were either killed or captured, their ammunition being exhausted. The Federal loss was 65 killed, 250 wounded, and over 1,000 prisoners; the cavalry and artillery escaped. Rebel loss, 25 killed and 400 wounded. The rebels immediately marched into and took possession of Franklin. After holding the place a few days, Van Dorn left it, retreating toward Shelbyville, when the town was occupied by the Union forces, under General Granger. Van Dorn returned, and again attacked the place, April 10. After severe fighting for two hours, the rebels retreated, leaving their dead on the field. . Union loss, 100 killed, wounded, and missing; rebel loss estimated at 300.

The Texan rebel legion was captured near this place April 27. The Union garrison here was attacked June 4, by 1,200 rebel cavalry. The rebels were repulsed with considerable loss.

A sharp battle was fought here November 30, 1864. Hood attacked at 4 P. M., in a very obstinate charge, broke and drove back the first Union line; in another, still bloodier one, broke their second, but was then repulsed after a sharp hand-to-hand fight. Subsequent rebel attacks were altogether in vain, and at 9 P. M., the fight was over. Thomas's loss was about 3,000; Hood's, at least twice as much, including 13 generals killed or wounded. At night Thomas continued his retreat to Nashville.

Frederick City, Md., was occupied by the rebels September 6, 1862. The citizens made no demonstration of enthusiasm. The rebels evacuated the place on the 12th, upon the arrival of General Burnside, who was received with acclamation and the display of Union banners. (See Maryland Invasion.)

Fredericksburg, Md. (See Maryland Invasion.)

Fredericksburg, Va.—A part of McDowell's forces left Warrenton April 17, 1862, and marched upon Fredericksburg, arriving at Falmouth the same evening.

A rebel force here made a slight resistance, but were driven across the river, the town being occupied by Union forces next day. Fredericksburg, was, the day following, occupied by the Federal forces. General Burnside's forces occupied the city August 14. He evacuated the place August 31, destroying the bridges, quartermaster's stores, etc., when the city was immediately occupied by the rebels, who in a scare, commenced to leave on the 9th, but being informed of the true state of affairs remained there. Captain Dahlgren, with a small cavalry force, made a daring dash into the city November 10, and captured two wagon-loads of gray cloth. The Confederate loss was 3 killed, several wounded, and 39 prisoners; Union loss, 1 killed and 4 missing. (See Burnside and Hooker.)

The city was occupied by General Sedgwick May 2, 1863. He abandoned it on the 4th.

Frederickaham, Va., was occupied by General Sheridan's forces March 11, 1865. Early's forces had passed through toward Richmond about four hours earlier.

Fredericktown, Md., was occupied by a rebel force, who encamped in the suburbs. The Unionists attacked them, breaking up the camp, August 16, 1861.

Fredericktown, Mo., being occupied by a large force of rebels, under Jeff. Thompson and Lowe, was attacked and captured October 21, 1861, by the Federal troops, under Colonel Plummer, of Indiana. After a fight of two hours, the Confederates fled in disorder, and were pursued a distance of 22 miles. General Lowe was killed, besides 200 others, and a large number wounded. Union loss, 6 killed and 40 wounded.

The town was occupied by Shelby's rebel cavalry September 24, 1864.

Freeman's Journal. (See Daily News.)

Freestone Point Batteries, on the Potomac, were attacked by the Union forces September 25, 1861, but without capturing them. They were destroyed by the Union flotilla December 9.

Free Territory bill was signed by the President June 20, 1862.

Fremont, J. C., arrived at Boston from Europe, bringing a large assortment of Arms for the Government

June 27, 1861. He had been, while in Europe (May 1), appointed Major-General in the regular army, and was, on July 9, appointed to the command of the Western District, including the States of Illinois, Kentucky, Missouri, Kansas, and the territories west of these States.

He arrived at St. Louis and assumed command of his department July 25, and immediately commenced to unravel the difficulties surrounding him. He declared the city under martial law August 14, and on the 31st extended it over the State of Missouri, at the same time and in the same order declaring as follows:

"The property real and personal, of all persons in the State of Missouri, who shall take up arms against the United States, or shall be directly proven to have taken active part with their enemies in the field is declared to be confiscated to the public use; *and their slaves, if they have any, are hereby declared free men.*"

With an expedition of 12,500 men, on 15 transports, he left St. Louis September 27, and started up the Missouri. (See Jefferson City, Lexington, Wilson's Creek, etc.)

He was relieved of his command, being succeeded by General Hunter, November 2, and on the 26th left St. Louis for Washington. General Fremont was assigned to the command of the Mountain Department March 11, 1862, and, at his own request, was relieved June 27.

On May 31, 1864, the Cleveland Convention (Radical Democratic) nominated him as their candidate for President, upon a platform of which the following were the essential points:

"The restoration of the Union; the suppression of the rebellion, without compromise; a free press; the *habeas corpus;* abolition of slavery; the Monroe doctrine; one-term presidency; confiscation of rebel lands, and their division among the soldiers of the army and sailors."

His acceptance of this nomination cost him much of the political power and influence which he had until this time held in the Republican party. Many who were until that time his warm political friends discarded him. He withdrew from the canvass September 21, and, having resigned his commission, retired to private life.

Fremont's Orchard was the scene of a brisk engagement April 12, 1864, in which a party of the 1st Colorado Cavalry defeated the Cheyennes.

French Lady, *alias* a man in woman's clothes, which disguise he assumed the better to aid the rebels, with his Confederate associates, on the night of June 29, 1861, captured the steamer St. Nicholas, on the Potomac. He was captured by the Baltimore police July 8.

Front Royal, Va., was the scene of a brisk engagement May 15, 1862, between the Unionists guarding the railroad there and a party of mounted guerrillas. The Union party was defeated, with a loss of 1 killed and 11 wounded.

Colonel Kenley, commanding the place, was, on May 23, driven thence by a large force of rebels under Ewell; the Union loss was very heavy. The Unionists returned in force, and, driving out the rebels, reoccupied the town on the 30th, capturing a large amount of rebel stores and a number of wagons. Brisk but undecisive skirmishes occurred near this place July 20 and 23, 1863.

Fugitive Slave Law was repealed in June, 1864. (For particulars, including analytical vote, see Appendix.)

Fulton, Mo., was the scene of a slight skirmish July 17, 1861.

Funkstown, Md. (See Pennsylvania Invasion.)

Gadsden, Ala. (See Streight.)

Gains's Cross Roads was the scene of a cavalry dash on the rebels, but without decided result, November 8, 1862.

Gains's Mills, near Richmond, Va., is noted as being the scene of many balloon ascensions during the summer of 1862.

The battle of Gains's Mills was fought June 27, 1862. The Union forces made a stand here, and were attacked by greatly superior forces of the rebels, who attempted, by massing them in various places, to break the Federal lines, but they were checked in every instance; until, finally, they broke the Union left wing, when the troops, finding themselves outflanked, fell back, but the advance of the rebels was checked by the arrival of reinforcements. Night closed the battle, and the Union troops crossed to the south side of the river. Both sides lost very heavily. The Union dead were estimated at 300, and the wounded were very numerous; the prisoners were reported at 4,000.

The place was occupied by General Sheridan, during his raid, May 12, 1864.

Gainsville, Fla., was surprised and occupied by Captain Marshall, with about 50 of the 40th Massachusetts regiment, February 14, 1862. He held it over two days against a force twice his, repulsing them several times. He captured there, and distributed to the people, over $1,500,000 worth of rebel supplies.

Gallatin, Tenn., was occupied by the Union troops under General Buell, February 23, 1862.

On August 12, the town was surrendered to Morgan's guerrillas, who captured four companies of Federals, a train loaded with forage, and 60 horses. During the night the town was retaken by a force from Nashville, under Colonel Miller.

After a sharp and vigorous contest, the town was surrendered to the rebels on the 21st. Union loss, 26 killed, 35 wounded, and 200 prisoners; rebel loss, 13 killed and 50 wounded. The Federal prisoners were released upon parole. Rosecrans occupied the place November 8, 1862.

Galveston, Texas, was startled, August 3, 1861, by a few shells from the Union fleet, which was the occasion of a protest from the neutral (?) foreign consuls there stationed.

A demand for the surrender of the place was made, and refused, May 17, 1862.

The advance of a fleet, for the capture of the place, arrived in the bay September 21, and, on October 4, all the forces had arrived, when a demand was made for its surrender, allowing four days' time for an answer. The place was surrendered and occupied the next day. The formal possession and flag-raising occurred on the 9th. Comparative quiet prevailed until January 1, 1863, when General Magruder, with 5,000 men and 5 steamers, made an attack on the city, then defended by about 500 men, under Colonel Burrill, and two or three steamers. Barricades were erected in the streets.

After sustaining an unequal contest for four hours, during which they repulsed the rebels several times, the Unionists were compelled to surrender to overpowering numbers. The Harriet Lane was captured by boarding; 2 officers and 8 men were killed, 10 men wounded, and 110 taken prisoners. The Westfield ran aground, and was blown up by her commander, to prevent her capture by the rebels; by a premature explosion, Commander Renshaw and several officers were blown up with the vessel. The rebel loss in the engagement was very heavy. The rebels captured 30,000 rifle-cartridges, 5,000 picks, and 500 shovels.

On the 4th, General Magruder issued his proclamation, declaring the port open to the commerce of the world. The blockading squadron, however, in the bay, showed the falsity of the statement.

Generals Kirby Smith and Magruder surrendered their forces at Galveston, June 2, 1865, and the city was occupied by the Union forces on the 5th.

Garrettsburg, Ky., was the scene of some severe but undecisive fighting November 6, 1862.

On the 11th, General Ransom overtook the rebel General Woodward near this place, and completely routed him, and drove the whole force out of Kentucky. The rebels lost 16 killed, 40 wounded, 25 prisoners, and a large lot of stores, etc.

Gauley, Va., was attacked by the rebels September 10, 1862, but without advantage to either party. The next day, the Unionists being hard pressed, burned the public buildings and all the Government property, and evacuated the town, to prevent being surrounded.

Gauley Bridge, Va., was the scene of an artillery fight November 1, 1861. The rebels, under Floyd, attempted to captured Rosecrans's army, but failed, and Floyd only saved himself by flight. He encamped a few miles distant, where he remained until the 20th, when he made a hasty retreat, burning 300 tents and destroying a large amount of equipage.

General Lyon, a transport steamer, was burned at sea, off Hatteras, March 31, 1865. About 500 soldiers were lost.

George Creek, O. (See John Morgan.)

Georgia.—The Legislature, on November 18, 1860, voted $1,000,000 for the purpose of arming the State, and ordered an election for delegates to State Convention.

The Convention assembled at Milledgeville, January 16, 1861, passed an ordinance of secession, by a vote of 208 ayes to 89 nays, on the 19th, and on the 29th adjourned, to meet at Savannah upon the call of its President. The Convention reassembled at Savannah March 7, ratified the Confederate States Constitution on the 16th, and adjourned, *sine die*, on the 23d.

On February 8, Governor Brown seized five New York vessels in Savannah harbor, in retaliation for the seizure of arms in New York. The vessels were released on the 10th. He again, on the 21st, seized two other New York vessels, which were released March 19.

On April 26 he issued a proclamation prohibiting the payment of debts due to Northern men. He called out the reserve State militia (from 16 to 55) to aid Johnston, July 9, 1864, and on September 14, by proclamation, withdrew the "Georgia militia," 15,000 strong, from Hood's army.

Georgetown, Mo., was the scene of a brisk skirmish, and the capture of a rebel company, April 11, 1861.

Georgetown, S. C., was captured, without serious resistance, by Admiral Dahlgren, February 22, 1865.

Germania Ford, Va., was the scene of a skirmish November 18, 1863.

Germantown, Ky., was the scene of a rebel defeat April 10, 1863.

Germantown, Tenn., was occupied, and the railroad destroyed by the rebels, October 11, 1863.

Germantown, Va., was the scene of a skirmish January 7, 1862.

Gettysburg, Penn.—The battle-field at this place was, on November 19, 1863, consecrated as a national cemetery for the Union soldiers who fell in the July battles. Edward Everett, President Lincoln, and others, made eloquent speeches. (For a history of the battle, see Pennsylvaniania Invasion.)

Gilmore. (See Jaques.)

Gillmore, General Q. A., left New York June 4, 1863, to relieve General Hunter of the command of the Department of the South, and assumed the actual command on the 12th. (For the history of his operations during 1863, see Charleston, S. C.)

Glasgow, Ky., was captured by the Union forces September 17, 1862; 450 rebels were taken prisoners. The town was soon abandoned by the Unionists, and the rebels occupied it Christmas day. A band of guerrillas visited the place October 3, 1863. A passenger train on the Louisville and Nashville Railroad was robbed by Harper's guerrillas, near this place, March 21, 1865.

Glasgow, Mo., was the scene of a short, sharp struggle December 7, 1861. A band of guerrillas, under Captain (?) Sweeny, was captured.

Glendale. (See White Oak Swamp.)

Gloucester, opposite Yorktown, Va., was shelled by the Union forces April 15, 1862, and occupied by them May 4.

Gloucester County, suffered from Union raids April 7 and May 22, 1863.

Gloucester Point, Va., was the scene of a skirmish April 12, 1863.

Goldsboro, N. C., was, on December 17, 1862, occupied by the Union forces under General Foster, who drove out the rebels, burned the railroad bridge, destroyed the track, and then returned to Newbern. The city was occupied March 21, 1865, by the Union forces under General Schofield, who there effected a junction with Terry and Sherman, when the whole army rested to reclothe and refit, before entering upon a new movement in concert with the armies before Richmond.

Gonzales, a rebel camp for conscripts in Florida, was captured by General Asboth July 20, 1864.

Goochland, Va., was captured by Union cavalry twice—May 3, 1863, and March 11, 1865—and large quantities of rebel stores destroyed each time.

Gordon, Nathaniel P., convicted as a slave-trader, was hung in New York February 21, 1862. This was the first execution for this offense under the laws of the United States.

Gordonsville, Va., one of the most important strategic points between Washington and Richmond, was, until a comparatively late period in the rebellion, held by the rebels. Sheridan on November 21, 1864, made an attempt to capture it, but was forced to retire over the North Anna.

Gosport (Va.) Navy-yard, was, on April 20, 1861, with all its contents, destroyed by Commander McCauley, to prevent their use by the secessionists. The sloop-of-war Cumberland was saved to the Government. The loss to the Government was about $50,000,000. The rebels held the place until May 10, 1862, when they burned or destroyed all that remained.

Grafton, Va., was the scene of an engagement August 13, 1861. A company of Unionists surprised and drove 200 rebels, killing 21 men.

Grahamsville, S. C., was the scene of an engagement November 30, 1864.

Grand Coteau, La.—The Union camp at this place was attacked November 3, 1863. The Unionists were compelled to yield to superior numbers, and were driven about a mile, when a new line was formed. Being reinforced, the Unionists advanced again, when the rebels fled, first plundering and burning the captured camp. The Unionists occupied their old camping-ground. The rebel force was 7,000 strong, under Dick Taylor and Greene, and lost about 120 killed and wounded, and 200 prisoners. The Union force was 1,600, under General Burbridge, and lost 26 killed, 124 wounded, and 566 missing.

Grand Ecore, La. (See Mansfield, La.)

Grand Gulf, Miss., was the scene of a brisk skirmish June 18, 1862. The rebel batteries at this place were attacked by the forces under Admiral Farragut, March 31, 1863, and frequent shelling and bombarding occurred from that time until May 3, when the place surrendered to the land and naval forces under Grant and Porter; 500 prisoners and immense quantities of stores were taken. A cavalry engagement, resulting in a rebel defeat, took place here July 17, 1864.

Grand Lake, La., was, on February 14, 1864, the scene of a most shocking barbarity; about 60 well-mounted guerrillas, in Federal uniforms, surprised and brutally murdered a company of colored troops, the escort of a foraging party, one and one-half miles distant. The foragers afterward destroyed the house where the escort was posted.

On July 26, 1864, an expedition from Brasher City arrived at this place, and destroyed a large number of new flat-boats, completed, and others building; also twc saw-mills, and brought away with them a steamboat-load of lumber. This loss was a serious one to the rebels as it frustrated their plans of a movement from thence

Granny White Hills, Tenn., were occupied and fortified by General Hood, in his retreat, December 13, 1864

Grant, Ulysses S., was born at Mount Pleasant, Clermont County, Ohio, April 27, 1822. He had the advantage of a common-school education, and early in lifc exhibited energy, industry, and will as prominent characteristics. He entered West Point Military Academy in 1839, from which he graduated—No. 21 in a class of 38—June 30, 1843. He entered the regular army as Brevet Second-Lieutenant of infantry, attached to the 4th Regiment. He soon after joined General Taylor in Texas, where he received his full commission as Second-Lieutenant of infantry, dating September 30, 1845. Immediately after the battle of Vera Cruz, (March 29, 1847,) he was made quartermaster of his regiment. September 8, 1847, he was promoted to First-Lieutenant for distinguished service at the battle of Molino del Rey. For gallant service at Chepultepec he was, the following day, September 13, 1847, made Brevet Captain, which was made full Captain in August, 1853. He resigned his position in the army July 31, 1854, and lived upon a farm near St. Louis. In 1859 he embarked in the leather business, at which he remained until the outbreak of the rebellion. He was appointed Commander-in-chief of the Illinois forces, as mustering officer. This he resigned to accept the Colonelcy of the 21st Illinois Regiment, his commission dating June 15, 1861. In the latter part of August he was promoted to Brigadier-General, his commission dating May 17, 1861. He was made Major-General of volunteers February 16, 1862. Immediately after the fall of Vicksburg, he was appointed Major-General in the regular army, his commission dating July 4, 1863. Then followed the Tennessee and Georgia campaign. Upon the successful termination of this movement, Congress, without opposition, resolved "to provide that a medal be struck for General Grant, and that a vote of thanks be given him and the officers of his army."

The bill reviving the grade of Lieutenant-General having been introduced, and being slightly amended, came up before the House of Representatives on February 1, 1864, and debate ensued upon it. Mr. Ross submitted an amendment, recommending Major-General U. S. Grant for the position of Lieutenant-General. The amendment was carried by a vote of 117 to 19, and the bill, thus amended, was finally passed, and sent to the Senate. The Senate having passed the bill, so far as it revived the grade of Lieutenant-General, it became a law, and the President nominated General Grant for the position. On the 2d of March the nomination was confirmed by the Senate, in Executive Session.

As soon as General Grant's appointment as Lieutenant-General was confirmed in the Senate, he was ordered to report at Washington. There he arrived, *incognito*, on the 8th of March, 1864, in the evening. He went to Willard's Hotel, and was quietly eating his dinner, when he was recognized, and his health proposed, all the guests rising to their feet with cheers. In the evening he was obliged to undergo the ordeal of a "reception" at the White House. On the afternoon of March 9, President Lincoln formally presented him with the commission as Lieutenant-General, addressing him as follows:

"GENERAL GRANT: The nation's appreciation of what you have done, and its reliance upon you for what still remains to be accomplished in the existing great struggle, are now presented with this commission, constituting you Lieutenant-General in the army of the United States. With this high honor devolves upon you, also, a corresponding responsibility. As the country here trusts you, so, under God, it will sustain you. I scarcely need to add, that with what I here speak for the nation, goes my own hearty personal concurrence."

General Grant replied—a long speech for him—as follows:

"MR. PRESIDENT: I accept the commission with gratitude, for the high honor conferred. With the aid of the noble armies that have fought on so many fields for our common country, it will be my earnest endeavor not to disappoint your expectation. I feel the full weight of the responsibilities now devolving upon me, and I know that if they are met, it will be due to those armies, and, above all, to the favor of that Providence which leads both nations and men."

General Grant was assigned to the command of the armies of the United States March 12, which position he immediately assumed. His superior rank set at rest all questions of precedence, while his achievements inspired both officers and men with that confidence which ever is the presage of victory. A few quiet changes were made in division and corps commanders; tried and accomplished men were placed in positions of trust; reorganization and consolidation followed, and, by May 1, the country was astonished with the intelligence that once more, the "on to Richmond" campaign was to open.

May 11, the Lieutenant-General telegraphed his gradual advance, and added, with his characteristic sincerity:

"*I propose to fight it out on this line, if it takes all summer.*"

Struggle after struggle rapidly followed; blood dyed every stream flowing to the east, and crimsoned almost every hill-top from Spottsylvania to Hanover. May 29, Grant forced the passage of the Pamunky. On the 30th, Lee attacked his foe with desperate fury, to retain the line of the Chickahominy. But slowly the tide rolled southward, each day entered on the crimson calendar with a bloody signet. Every art of war, every resource of valor availed nothing; Lee was pressed back, until, by a master movement across the James, June 14, Grant placed Richmond and Petersburg under a state of siege.

From that moment up to the momentous first week of April, the generalship of the two commanders was the chief point of interest. Lee's policy evidently was to worry out his foe as McClellan was discomfited; Grant's aim seemed solely to hold his own until those wonderful combinations which he had inaugurated were complete, for the capture not only of the rebel capital, but of the entire insurgent force. It is fair to assume that the world never witnessed a more truly Titanic labor, or a more skillfully-wrought campaign. Although every event is yet fresh in our minds, we can even now perceive, in the sublime patience of the man, that rare quality of greatness which is equal to all emergencies, and master of events. When the discerning mind comes to investigate the *processes* of Grant's procedure—to understand the relations of *all* his correlative movements which Sherman, Thomas, Sheridan, Foster, Terry, Schofield, and Gillmore executed—it will not fail to pronounce our subject the greatest captain which modern times has produced.

Grant's Pass. (See Mobile.)

Gravelly Run, Va., was reached December 9, 1864, by the Union forces under General Miles, who bivouacked there for the night. (See General Grant's Report.)

Graw. (See Corbin.)

Great Bethel. (See Big Bethel.)

Greek Fire. (See Charleston.)

Greenbrier, Va.—October 3, 1861, General Reynolds made a reconnoisance in force from his position at Cheat Mountain, and met the Confederate forces, under General Lee, at Greenbrier. After a fight of an hour the Confederates were driven from the ground, with the loss of 300 killed and wounded, and 13 prisoners. The Union loss was 8 killed and 32 wounded.

Greencastle, Penn. (See Pennsylvania Invasion.)

Greenland Gap, Va., was the scene of a rebel defeat April 25, 1863.

Green Hill, Tenn.—The rebel camp at this place was broken up March 6, 1863. The Unionists abandoning the place, it was occupied by rebels, who were again, April 6, dispersed, with a loss of 5 killed and 15 prisoners.

Green River Bridge, Ky., was the scene of skirmishes on October 15 and December 12, 1861, and on July 4, 1863; the two former undecided; the latter resulted in the defeat of the guerrilla Morgan.

Greensboro, 84 miles west of Augusta, Ga., was occupied by Sherman's left wing November 20, 1864.

This was one of the halting places for Jeff. Davis and escort, after their flight from Richmond.

The arms and military effects of General Johnston's

army were formally transferred to the United States authorities, at this place, April 29, and the paroling of the troops commenced there next day.

Greenville, Miss., was the scene of a brisk skirmish and Union repulse, in which one Federal major was killed, February 23, 1863.

Greenville, Mo., was the scene of a brisk but undecisive skirmish October 25, 1862.

Greenville, Tenn., was, on September 4, 1864, the scene of a battle between the Union forces under General Gillam, and the guerrilla chief John Morgan. Morgan was killed, his staff captured, and his forces badly cut up and routed.

Greenwich, Va., was, on May 30, 1863, the scene of a short skirmish, in which a gang of Mosby's cavalry were defeated. Loss light on both sides.

Grenada, Miss.—General Hurlbut, learning that the rebels had collected a great quantity of stores at Grenada, resolved to destroy them. Accordingly, on the 13th of August, 1863, a force, under Lieutenant-Colonel Phillips, of the 9th Illinois, left La Grange, Tenn., and reached Grenada on the 17th. The rebels, 2,000 strong, with 3 pieces of artillery, under General Skinner, were driven from the town. He destroyed 57 locomotives, and over 400 cars, depot buildings, machine-shops, and a large quantity of ordnance and commissary stores.

Greytown, Mo., was occupied by Union troops, who captured 25 rebels, August 29, 1861.

Grierson's Raid, through Mississippi, consisting of a newly-organized division of cavalry, commanded by Colonel Grierson, set out from La Grange, Tenn., April 17, 1863, reached Ripley, Miss., the next day, capturing a rebel camp and dispersing a small rebel force at Pontatoc on the 19th. The 21st he destroyed a tannery, and a large quantity of leather, saddles, harness, etc., intended for the rebels. A detachment from his command, on the 22d, captured Mayhew, 12 miles from Columbus, Miss., and tore up 20 miles of the Central Mississippi Railroad. His main force, on the 23d, reached Philadelphia, Miss., after a fatiguing and perilous march through swamps and rivers from Starkville. He reached Newton Mills on the 24th. At this place he destroyed

38 car-loads of quartermaster and commissary stores. About this date, Central Mississippi was in a great excitement over "Grierson's Cavalry Raid," and great efforts were made to "head him off." The next day he reached a point seven miles west of Montrose, burning and destroying the bridges and trestle-work of the railroads on his route; and on the 26th his advance, under Colonel Prince, captured and destroyed a train of 40 cars, loaded with all kinds of military stores, at Hazelhurst, his main force arriving there the next day, and immediately set out for Bahala. On the route there, a large portion of the N. O., J. and G. N. Railroad was destroyed, together with a great amount of other property, inflicting great damage on the rebels. On the 27th he entered Brookhaven, where he captured and paroled 200 prisoners, and destroyed a large camp of instruction, with its equipage; he then moved along the railroad to Bogue Chitto Station, destroying the track, bridges, and cars on the route. At Wassita, on the Tickfau, they had an engagement with a regiment of cavalry, who were put to flight, with a considerable loss in killed and wounded. At Edwards's Depot they dispersed another regiment, and then cut their way through a regiment of infantry drawn up to check their advance, and rode off in the direction of Baton Rouge. Continuing his course, on May 2 he and his brave command arrived at Baton Rouge amid great enthusiasm, having traveled over 800 miles in the heart of rebeldom, fought and dispersed the rebels wherever they met them, and captured 1,000 prisoners, 1,200 horses. and destroyed over $4,000,000 worth of property.

Grimball's. (See Charleston.)

Griswoldsville, Ga., was the scene of slight skirmishes on November 20 and 23, 1864; loss small in each case.

Ground Squirrel Bridge, Va., was taken and held by General Sheridan on March 14, 1865, after a brisk engagement with Early. Early was so badly defeated that he jumped from his horse and ran into the woods with only one orderly as company, and made his escape by aid of the darkness.

Grovetown, Va. (See Bull Run.)

Guerrillas were, by the United States Circuit Court, at

Louisville, Ky., declared to be common enemies, and hence carriers could not at law recover goods stolen by such parties. They were recognized as a part of the Confederate army by the Richmond authorities, July 16, 1862. (See John Morgan and Sue Munday.)

Gum Swamp, N. C., was the scene of a battle, commenced on May 22, 1863, and renewed next morning, about noon. The rebels were driven from their intrenchments, and the works destroyed; 195 prisoners, 1 gun, and 50 horses and mules were captured; 7 rebels were wounded; 1 Unionist killed and 7 wounded.

Guntown, Miss.—About June 10, 1864, a battle occurred near this place. The Union force was 3,000 cavalry and 5,000 infantry, with 18 pieces of artillery, under General Sturgis. With an equal force, Forrest, Roddy, and Lee suddenly attacked and thoroughly defeated them, capturing nearly or quite all the artillery and ammunition, and the entire wagon train. The Union loss in men was reported at more than a thousand.

Guyandotte, Va., on the Ohio River, near the Kentucky line, was, on November 10, 1861, captured by a force of rebel cavalry under Colonel Jenkins, who took over one hundred prisoners. Every Union soldier who made the least resistance was killed. The rebel force, who had been for some time carrying on a guerrilla warfare, left next morning, taking with them all the plunder they could carry. Colonel Zeigler, of the 5th (loyal) Virginia, who arrived next morning, ordered the houses of the leading secessionists to be burned, on the assumption that they had furnished the information which rendered safe and successful the guerrilla raid of the rebels. The leading citizens being mostly secessionists, the town was mainly consumed.

Habeas Corpus.—The first refusal to obey this writ, after the opening of the rebellion, was by General Cadwallader, May 27, 1861, on a writ issued in the case of John Merryman, confined in Fort McHenry. President Lincoln suspended the writ in the District of Columbia October 24, 1861.

On August 8, 1862, the Secretary of War issued an order to prevent the evasion of military duty, and suspending the writ of *habeas corpus* in respect to all persons arrested and detained under its provisions; also for the arrest and imprisonment of persons who, by act, speech, or writing, discourage volunteer enlistments, etc.

President Lincoln, October 24, 1862, issued a proclamation suspending the writ of *habeas corpus* in respect to all persons arrested and imprisoned in any fort, camp, arsenal, military prison, or other place, by any military authority, or by sentence of court-martial, etc.

An act relating to *habeas corpus*, and regulating judicial proceedings in connection therewith, was approved March 3, 1863. The following is a synopsis of the bill:

"When the President deems it necessary, and required for public safety, during the present rebellion, he is authorized to suspend the privilege of the writ of *habeas corpus* in any case throughout the United States, or any part thereof. And whenever suspended, upon the certificate, under oath, of the officer having charge of any one detained, that such person is detained by him as a prisoner under authority of the President, further proceedings under the writ shall be suspended. Government is to furnish Federal judges the names of all per sons, citizens of States in which the administration of the laws has continued unimpaired in Federal courts, who are or may be state or political prisoners. Should no indictment be found against such person by a grand jury, the judge shall have him brought before the court for discharge, should such prisoner desire it, and any officer refusing to obey the judge is guilty of misdemeanor; but no person shall be discharged without having taken an oath of allegiance; and the court, at discretion, may compel the prisoner to give bonds. Prisoners indicted may be bailed if the offense be bailable. Any order of the President, or under his authority, made during the present rebellion, shall be a defense, in all courts, to any action or prosecution, civil or criminal, pending or to be commenced, for any search, seizure, arrest, or imprisonment, made, done, or committed, or acts omitted to be done, under and by virtue of such order, or under color of any law of Congress, and such defense may be made by special plea, or under the general issue. The act provides for the removal of actions against officers for torts in arrest, to the United States Circuit Courts, whereon the State courts can go no further; if final judgment has been given in a State court, the case goes to the United States court on appeal, and is tried as if originally begun there. Such appeals are not allowed in criminal cases when judgment has been given for the defendant. Appealed cases may be carried to the Supreme Court. No party shall be debarred by this act until two years after its passage; suits must be brought within that period."

Hagerstown, Md., was occupied by the rebels September 11, 1862. (See Pennsylvania Invasion and Maryland Invasion.)

Haines's Bluff, Ark. (See Vicksburg.)

Half Mountain, Ky.—On April 14, 1864, 400 men of the 14th and 20th Kentucky, surprised a rebel camp at Half Mountain, on Licking River, Ky., and defeated them, capturing 70 prisoners, 200 horses, 300 stand of arms, and a wagon train; 85 of the rebels were killed and wounded.

Halleck, General H. W., assumed command of the Department of the West November 10, 1861, and on the 19th assumed command of the Department of Missouri. On December 5, he issued an order for the arrest of every man found in arms against the Union in Missouri, those found guilty of aiding the rebels to be shot.

General Halleck was assigned to the command of the Army of the Mississippi March 11, 1862, and two days later assumed that position with head-quarters at St. Louis. He left that place April 9, and assumed command in the field at Pittsburg Landing on the 11th. He was appointed General-in-chief of the Armies of the United States July 11, took leave of the Army of the Mississippi on the 16th, left St. Louis on the 20th, and arrived at Washington for duty on the 22d. A very characteristic correspondence occurred between Generals Halleck and McClellan August 29 and 30. The point was Halleck advising, urging, and finally ordering a movement, and McClellan giving reasons for not moving, and finally refusing to move, or rather not moving without refusing. Again, on October 1, General Halleck urged General McClellan to cross the Potomac, and on the 6th peremptorily ordered him "to cross the Potomac, and give battle to the enemy or drive him south. Your army must move now, while the roads are good."

General Halleck's order thanking Rosecrans and his army for their gallant conduct and victory over the rebels at Murfreesboro, Tenn., was issued January 9, 1863. His military history will be found under the appropriate headings.

Halltown, Va., was occupied by the Union troops October 28, 1862.

Hamburg, S. C., was occupied, and the railroad there destroyed, by Union troops, February 7, 1865.

Hamburg, Tenn., was occupied and destroyed by the Union forces April 29, 1863.

Hamilton, N. C., was occupied by the 9th New York Zouaves July 9, 1862. The rebel batteries were captured and their forces routed; two or three steamers and schooners, with supplies, fell into the hands of the Federals. The rebels left 30 or 40 dead on the field; the Unionists lost 2 killed and 8 or 10 wounded.

Hammond, Surgeon-General, of the United States Army, was charged with gross violation of duty, and a court-martial ordered for his trial January 8, 1864. He was dishonorably dismissed the service August 4.

Hammond Station, La., was attacked, and the railroad bridge there destroyed by Union forces, May 12, 1863, and the place captured and occupied two days later.

Hampton, Va.—A reconnoisance from Fortress Monroe to this place, was made May 23, 1861. The rebels attacked the Unionists, and attempted to cut them off by destroying an important bridge. The town was nearly all destroyed by a party of Confederate troops, under General Magruder, on August 7. The advance of General McClellan's army, on its way to Richmond, occupied this place August 17, 1862.

Hampton Roads, at the mouth of James River, Va., was, during the war, the scene of many important events. Here it was that the first trial of iron-clads or monitors took place. The rebel steamer "Merrimac," or "Virginia," accompanied by four or five gun-boats, came out from Norfolk, and on March 8, 1862, attacked the Union fleet. The "Merrimac" steamed directly for the United States frigates Cumberland and Congress. The fire from the Cumberland had no effect on her adversary. She was struck amidships by the ram, and her sides laid open. She immediately sunk. The ram started for the Congress, which surrendered, and was burned. The Minnesota, in endeavoring to escape the ram, got aground, and the gun-boats "Oregon" and "Zouave," were badly damaged. The rebel ships returned to Elizabeth River.

The rebel steamers again appeared the next morning, to continue operations. The United States iron-clad battery "Monitor," had arrived from New York, at 10 o'clock the previous evening, and was immediately sent to aid the Minnesota. The fight between these two iron-clads was a terrific one, and lasted nearly four hours, the two vessels touching each other part of the time. The "Merrimac" at last gave up the contest, badly damaged, and so much disabled as to require the aid of tugs to get her away. The "Monitor" was uninjured. As the first encounter of iron-clad vessels, this contest created much interest with maritime nations.

Hancock, Md., was shelled by the rebels from the opposite side of the Potomac, January 5, 1862. They were driven off, however, by the Union artillery. (See Pennsylvania Invasion and Maryland Invasion.)

Hanover, Penn. (See Pennsylvania Invasion.)

Hanover, Va. (See Pennsylvania Invasion.)

Hanover C. H., Va., was captured by the Union forces under Fitz John Porter, after defeating the rebels, who lost 100 killed and 500 prisoners, May 27, 1862. The place was again captured by the Union cavalry May 3, 1863.

Hanovertown, Va. (See Grant's Report.)

Hardy County, Va.—The Unionists in this county were defeated, with a loss of about 40 men, January 5, 1863.

Harper's Ferry, Va.—Lieutenant Roger Jones, of the United States Army, destroyed the Government buildings at Harper's Ferry, and their contents, to prevent their falling into the hands of the Confederate forces, April 18, 1861.

This important point was soon occupied by the rebels, who, by the middle of May, had it fortified, and on the 19th received reinforcements to help hold it. The Unionists made a demonstration against it May 29, and the rebels left it, retiring toward Martinsburg, but soon returned and reoccupied it. On June 14, however, they evacuated the place, destroyed the railroad bridge, and took the armory machinery to Richmond. Skirmishes occurred at this point, across the river, July 4.

On July 28 the rebels made an attack upon Harper's Ferry, and General Banks, who had assumed command on the 25th, withdrew his forces to the Maryland side of the Potomac. The rebels occupied the place three days, when they retired toward Leesburg, August 1. An artillery duel was fought here, without injury to either party, November 29. On February 7, 1862, twelve houses, including three hotels, the railroad depots, etc., were fired by Colonel Geary, for harboring rebel murderers, who used a flag of truce to cover their designs. The place was occupied by General Banks on the 24th, who, after some skirmishing, crossed the Potomac. The rebels invested the place September 12, and continued the fight until the 14th, when they gained possession of Maryland and Louden Heights. The Union cavalry, under Lieutenant-Colonel Davis, of the 12th Illinois Cavalry, cut their way out, and arrived at Greencastle, Penn., capturing 100 prisoners and General Longstreet's wagon train. The attack was renewed next morning, and the place surrendered to Stonewall Jackson; 80 Federals (including Colonel Miles) had been killed, 120 wounded, while 10,500 surrendered; 47 pieces of artillery and a vast amount of stores were captured by the rebels. The rebel loss in this fight was not known. The rebels held the place four days, when, after burning all the Government property, they retired southward. An immense quantity of quartermaster and commissary stores was burned in a great fire which occurred here October 29. (See Maryland Invasion.)

Harris, Benjamin G. (See Alexander Long.)

Harrison, 12 miles from Chattanooga, Tenn., was attacked by the rebels, December 3, 1863. The rebels were repulsed.

Harrisonburg, Va., was the scene of a brisk skirmish May 6, 1862. The place was captured by the Union troops under General Fremont, after driving the rebels, who lost their camp equipage, stores, etc., June 6. Sheridan also captured the place September 25, 1864.

Harrison's Landing, on James River, was occupied by Union troops, who were fired upon by the rebels, from their batteries on the opposite side of the river, on the night of August 1, 1862. The fire was returned, and before morning their batteries silenced. Union loss, 6 killed and 8 wounded. General McClellan, in his advance, left this place on the 16th.

Harrisonville, Mo., was the scene of a four hours' skirmish July 18, 1861.

Harrodsburg, Ky., was occupied by the rebels, under General Bragg, October 9, 1862.

Hartford, Ky., was the scene of a skirmish May 25, 1863.

Hartsville, Ky., was the scene of an engagement between a Union force and the rebel General Morgan December 7, 1862. Union loss, 55 killed, and the 104th Illinois, 106th and 108th Ohio, and part of the 2d Indiana Cavalry taken prisoners.

Hartsville, Mo., was the scene of an undecisive skirmish January 11, 1863.

Hartwood, Va., was occupied by a large body of rebel cavalry, who crossed the Potomac near that point, and made a descent upon two companies of the 3d Pennsylvania Cavalry, capturing nearly the whole force, November 28, 1862.

Harvest Moon, Admiral Dahlgren's flag-ship, was blown up by a torpedo, on his return from Georgetown, March 1, 1865. One man was killed and a few slightly wounded. The vessel was sunk.

Harwood Church, Va., was the scene of a cavalry fight February 25, 1863. The rebels were repulsed, with a loss of many killed and 200 prisoners, when they retreated across Kelley's Ford. Union loss, 40 killed and wounded.

Hatchie River.—On October 5, 1862, Generals Ord and Hurlbut overtook the retreating rebels from Corinth at the Hatchie River, where they made a stand. After seven hours' hard fighting, the rebels fled in great disorder, leaving their dead and wounded, and 400 prisoners. Nearly 1,000 stand of arms were taken here. The Union loss, 500 killed and wounded.

Hatteras Inlet.—On August 28, 1861, after a cannonading of two days, the expedition, under General Butler and Flag-officer Stringham, succeeded in capturing Forts Clark and Hatteras, with their garrisons, who surrendered as prisoners of war.

The advance of Burnside's expedition, after encountering heavy gales, arrived at this place January 17, 1862. (See Chickamacomico.)

Hawk's Nest, in the Kanawha Valley, Va., being barricaded and occupied by the 11th Ohio Regiment, was, on August 20, 1861, attacked by a Confederate force 4,000 strong. The rebels were driven back, with heavy loss.

Haysville, Va., was the scene of an engagement July 1, 1861.

Hazel Run, Va., was the scene of a cavalry skirmish November 8, 1863.

Helena, Ark., was reached by General Curtis's advance, under General Washburn, after a forced march of 65 miles in a day and night, July 12, 1862. A combined naval and military force, under General Curtis and Commodore Davis, after an extensive raid, returned to this point August 26. The expedition captured the rebel transport steamer "Fair Play," containing 1,200 Enfield rifles, 4,000 muskets, a large quantity of ammunition, four field-guns, etc. Colonel Woods captured one rebel encampment with all their arms, etc., and another with tents, baggage, and provisions. The expedition proceeded up the Yazoo River, where it captured a battery of four guns, with 7,000 pounds of powder, and 1,000 rounds of shot, shell, and grape.

Fifteen Union couriers were captured near this place January 15, 1863.

A skirmish occurred here April 20, and on July 4 Generals Holmes, Price, and Marmaduke, with 8,000 or

10,000 rebels, attacked the Union forces at this place. The battle lasted from 4 to 10 A. M., and was very severe. The rebel loss was estimated at 1,500 killed and wounded, 1,130 prisoners, and 2 pieces of artillery; Federal loss, about 230 wounded.

Henderson, Ky., was attacked by a force of 400 Confederate troops July 21, 1864. They were repulsed.

Henderson Hill, near Nachitoches, La., was the scene of a brisk engagement March 21, 1864, in which the rebels were whipped, losing 4 pieces of artillery and 270 prisoners, after a spirited engagement. General Mower flanked them, got in their rear, and compelled a retreat.

Hernando, Miss., was the scene of cavalry skirmishing April 19, 1863, and of a Union defeat June 18.

Herold, Payne, Atzerodt, and Mrs. Surratt, condemned as conspirators with and accomplices of Booth, the assassin, were executed July 7, 1865.

Hickman, Ky., was attacked by rebels, who were repulsed, July 16, 1863.

Hickory Hill, S. C., was occupied by the commands of Slocum and Howard, who here formed a junction, February 3, 1865.

Hicksford, Va., was unsuccessfully attacked by the Union forces under Warren December 9, 1864. Failing in their attack on the town, they destroyed about 12 miles of railroad.

Hillsboro, Miss., was occupied by Sherman's forces March 9, 1864, the rebels retiring toward Meridian.

Hilton Head, S. C.—Expeditions from this place left on October 1 and 21, 1862. The rebels made a raid, resulting in damage to the Unionists, March 12, 1863.

Hindman, Fort. (See Arkansas Post.)

Holly Springs, Miss., was occupied by Sherman's forces June 20, 1862. The rebels had previously removed their armory to Atlanta, Georgia. The Unionists soon gave up the place, and the rebels held it until November 13, when it was occupied by General Grant's advance. On December 20, Van Dorn's cavalry captured the place, with 1,500 prisoners, whom they paroled; they destroyed about $6,000,000 of property, of which $1,000,000 was cotton. They burned a new hospital, containing 2,000 bunks, and attempted to destroy the general hospital, by piling ordnance stores against it and firing them; 20 men were wounded by the exploding shells. The town was nearly destroyed. They held it but a short time. They made a raid upon it January 12, 1863, but without advantage to either party.

Holmes County, Ohio, was the scene of a riotous resistance of the enrollment in June, 1863. The resistants assembled to the number of nearly 3,000, on the Black Hills, in the western part of the county, but a company of troops quickly dispersed them on the 17th. Several were killed and wounded.

Holston, Tenn.—Longstreet crossed the Tennessee at Loudon, and advanced against Burnside, at Holston, who fell back to Lenoir's, toward Knoxville; considerable skirmishing all day. Losses, about 250 on each side.

Holt, Joseph, of Kentucky, was appointed Secretary of War in Buchanan's Cabinet January 17, 1861, and on February 18 wrote his noble patriotic letter which encouraged so many in the then dark hours.

Honey Springs, Ark.—General Blunt, with 2,500 men and 2 batteries, attacked and defeated 6,000 rebels and 4 pieces of artillery, under Cooper, at this place, July 15, 1863. The fight lasted from 9:30 A. M. to 1:45 P. M., when the rebels retreated, contesting the ground. Their loss was fully 300 men; Union loss, 50. 400 stand of arms and one 12-pound howitzer were captured.

Hooker, Joseph, was confirmed as Brigadier-General in the United States service August 3, 1861, and by his daring and soldierly qualities, soon earned and received the name of "Fighting Joe," by which appellation the boys in blue loved to call him. He was soon made a Major-General and given an important position. When Burnside, at his own request, was, on January 26, 1863, relieved of the command of the Army of the Potomac, General Hooker was appointed as his successor, and assumed the place next day. Having, in consultations with the authorities at Washington, determined upon the plan, he on the 29th reorganized the Army into grand divisions. His campaign against Fredericksburg was commenced April 27, by sending out cavalry scouting expeditions from Fairfax Court-house, and Warrenton Junction. On the 29th his forces commenced crossing the Rappahannock; the rebel pickets were surprised, and 400 prisoners captured; 20 men were wounded in the *mêlée*. The left wing, 35,000 strong, crossed four miles below Fredericksburg, engaged the rebels 12 hours, and drove them out of their rifle-pits and a distance of eight miles.

On June 28, General Hooker was succeeded by General Meade. He was subsequently transferred to Sherman's Army. In the fall of 1865 he was stricken with palsy, rendering nearly one half of his body useless. (See Chancellorsville, Lookout Mountain, Shell Mound, etc.)

Hoovers Gap, Tenn., was the scene of a severe skirmish between the rebels and General Rosecrans's forces June 24, 1863; the rebels were defeated.

Hopefield, Ark., opposite Memphis, was destroyed under orders from General Hurlbut, February 19, 1863, for harboring guerrillas, who had been firing upon and capturing transport vessels.

Horse Shoe Bend, Tenn., was the scene of a heavy skirmish, and a brilliant Union Victory, May 9, 1863.

Houston, Texas County, Mo., was taken posession of November 4, 1861, by Federal forces, under Colonel Dodge, who captured a large amount of rebel property, a number of rebel soldiers and secessionists, and a large mail for the rebel army.

Houston, Sam.—On March 26, 1861, the Texas State Convention passed an ordinance, and the Legislature approved the act, deposing Sam Houston from the Executive chair, in consequence of his refusal to take the new oath of allegiance to the Confederate States.

Howard Co., Mo., was the scene of a spirited engagement January 6, 1862. A rebel encampment of 1,000 men, under Poindexter, was attacked and completely routed by 500 Union cavalry, under Major Hubbard.

Howard, Oliver O., was born in Leeds, Maine, November 8, 1830. He graduated at West Point in 1854, served in the Ordnance Department of Florida for a time, and became then an Assistant Professor of Mathematics at West Point, where he was found when the civil war broke out. He then asked leave of the War Department to command a regiment from his native State, but the request was not granted, and he resigned.

Not long after he became Colonel of the 3d Maine Volunteers, and commanded a brigade in the first battle at Bull Run. He was thereupon made Brigadier-General, and commanded the 1st Brigade of the Second Army Corps, and followed the fortunes of General McClellan till the battle of Fair Oaks, where he lost his right arm. The next day he started for his home in Maine, and spent two months visiting various parts of that State, stirring up the people to sustain the Government. He returned to the army in time to command a brigade in the second battle of Bull Run. At Antietam, after General Sedgwick was wounded, he assumed command of the division, in which capacity he acted at the battle of Fredericksburg, in December, 1862, having been made Major-General of volunteers. He was assigned to the Eleventh Army Corps, and took part in the battles of Chancellorsville and Gettysburg. In September, 1863, he, with his corps, went to the assistance of General Rosecrans in Tennessee. Here he led his men in the hard-fought battles at Wauhatchie, Lookout Mountain, Mission Ridge, and Ringgold; went to the relief of Burnside at Knoxville, and thence accompanied Sherman to the taking of Atlanta, having been put in command of the Fourth Corps. On the fall of General McPherson, at Atlanta, General Sherman appointed Howard to command the Army of the Tennessee, which post he filled with marked ability and success.

General Howard was commissioned Brigadier-General in the regular army on the 13th of December, 1864. At this time, January 1, 1866, he is at the head of the Freedmen's Bureau. His fidelity and Christian fortitude is most conspicuous. He is emphatically the soldier's friend, and does not lose sight of the fact that all heroes do not wear shoulder-straps or lead regiments. He prayed with his command and fought with them alternately. His unostentatious piety commanded the respect of all. Men loved him because of his humility as a Christian and his bravery as a soldier.

Hudson, Mo., was the scene of an exciting but undecisive engagement December 21, 1861.

Hudsonville, Miss., was reached, and Forrest's cavalry there defeated, by General Grierson, April 21, 1864.

Hughes, Alf. John. (See N. Y. Riots.)

Hunter, Mo., was the scene of a skirmish September 22, 1861.

Hunter, General, arrived at Springfield, Mo., and assumed command of General Fremont's army November 3, 1861. He was on the 19th assigned to the command of the Department of Kansas. He declared martial law throughout that State February 8, 1862. He assumed command of the Department of the South March 31. On April 12 he declared free all the slaves in Fort Pulaski and Cockspur Island, and on May 9 issued a proclamation declaring free all the slaves in South Carolina, Georgia, and Florida. This order the President repudiated on the 19th. He, after being relieved, again assumed the same command January 20, 1863, and February 9 issued an order conscripting all able-bodied negroes in his department, and, one week later, placed Brigadier-General Stephenson under arrest for refusing to fight in company with negroes. He ordered the drafting of negroes in his department March 6. The Confederate authorities having threatened the enslavement of negro soldiers, and the execution of the officers captured from the Unionists, General Hunter, on April 23, addressed a letter to Jeff. Davis, threatening retaliation on Confederate prisoners if the barbarous order was carried out. He was relieved of his command June 12. He was assigned to the command of West Virginia May 20, 1864, and relieved August 29.

Hunter's Mills.—On January 8, 1863, Captain Moore, with 100 men, surprised a party of 300 rebels at Hunter's Mills, 35 miles east of Fort Pillow, and killed 16, wounded 40, and captured 46 men, with their horses and a lot of small arms. Two Federals were wounded.

Huntersville, Va., was occupied by the Union forces January 4, 1862, and $80,000 worth of supplies, intended for the rebels, captured and destroyed.

Huntsville, Ala, was occupied by General Mitchell's forces April 11, 1862. The town was surprised, and two trains, just starting eastward, were stopped; 17 locomotives, 150 cars, and 170 prisoners were captured.

The rebels made an attack on the place April 30, and succeeded in cutting the telegraph wire. The

Unionists soon abandoned the place, but reoccupied it July 17, 1863.

Huntsville, Mo., was taken by a band of guerrillas July 26, 1864, who robbed the citizens of $100,000.

Hurricane Creek, Miss., was fortified by Forrest. General A. J. Smith attacked him there August 13, 1864, driving him out of his works, with a loss of about 25 men to each party.

Independence, Mo.—A band of rebels, at this place, December 7, 1861, captured and paroled several Union citizens, and took the Lexington stage, but afterward released it.

On February 18, 1862, at the same place, a band of rebels, under the notorious Quantrell and Parker, were routed, with a loss of three killed, and many wounded and prisoners. Federal loss, one killed and three wounded. A brisk but undecisive fight occurred here March 1. The town was surrendered to the rebels August 11.

Indians.—The Indians made considerable trouble during the rebellion, but have been generally brought back to allegiance to the Union.

On September 8, 1862, there was an Indian fight at the lower agency in Minnesota, in which the red-skins were repulsed, with considerable loss. The whites lost 14 killed and 45 wounded.

The Indians in that State continuing to create trouble, murdering many of the whites, 38 of them were arrested. These were of the Sioux tribe. They were found guilty of murder, and sentenced to be hung. The sentence was approved, and the execution took place December 8, 1862.

Indianola, Texas, was, on March 13, 1864, evacuated by the Union forces, who took the land route, and, in crossing the bayous, 30 men were drowned.

Iron Banks, above Columbus, Ky., were occupied by rebel batteries, which, on October 7, 1861, attacked the Union gun-boats Tyler and Lexington. The boats returned the fire with shell, and did considerable execution in the rebel quarters; the gun-boats finally returned to Cairo, Illinois.

Iron Mountain Railroad.—The rebels attempted,

April 24, 1863, to burn the bridges on this road, but were repulsed, with a loss of five killed and twenty wounded.

Ironton, Mo., was the scene of a sharp skirmish October 16, 1861.

Irwinville, Ga. (See Jeff. Davis.)

Isaac Smith, a Federal gun-boat, with 11 guns and 180 men, surrendered to the rebels, after a smart engagement, in Stono River, January 30, 1863. The Smith had 8 killed and 15 wounded.

Island Ford.—After the Union forces had crossed this ford, July 18, 1864, the rebels, under Breckinridge, charged with great violence, and drove them back over the river, inflicting some loss.

Island No. 10.—The attack for the reduction of this stronghold was commenced by the Unionists March 16, 1862. The bombardment was very heavy on the 18th. A gun burst on the St. Louis, killing two men and wounding twelve. General Pope allowed a rebel gun-boat to approach within fifty yards of a masked battery, and then sunk her, killing fifteen of those on board. He then had five steamers between his batteries, unable to escape.

Colonel Roberts, with fifty men of the 42d Illinois and fifty men from the boats, spiked the six guns in the upper fort of Island No. 10 on the morning of April 1, thus very much impairing the rebels' strength. On the evening of the 6th the gun-boat Pittsburg ran the blockade, and four steam transports and five barges were got through the canal, which had been cut opposite the island, by Colonel Bissell's engineer corps. At 11 o'clock of the 7th, General Paine's division crossed; afterward the divisions of Generals Stanley, Hamilton, and Granger, and prepared to attack the island in the rear. After a bombardment of twenty-three days, the garrison, finding themselves thus surrounded, surrendered the island to Commodore Foote. Part of the garrison escaped to the main land.

The main army of the rebels was overtaken on the 8th, in their retreat, at Tiptonville, and forced to surrender their entire numbers. The whole force captured was 233 officers (including four Generals) and over 6,000 privates; 10,000 stand of arms, 2,000 horses and mules, 1,000 wagons, and $40,000 worth of provisions, were taken.

A very brilliant and spirited engagement occurred in Arkansas, near this place, October 17, between a Union force from the Island and 300 rebel cavalry. During the engagement, two parties of rebels, by mistake, fired into each other, and thus aided the Federals in subduing both. 2,000 rebels, with 3 pieces of artillery, attacked the gun-boat New Era, at this point, on the night of February 1, 1863. The fight lasted till daylight, when the rebels retreated.

Island Queen. (See Canada Raids.)

Iuka, Miss.—A battle at this place was fought September 19, 1862, between the Union forces, under Rosecrans, and the rebels, commanded by Price. It lasted about two hours, just before dark. Rebel loss, 385 killed, 692 wounded, and 361 prisoners; Union loss, 144 killed, 565 wounded, and 40 missing. The Federals captured 1,629 stand of small arms and 13,000 rounds of ammunition.

Jackson Mills, N. C.—A battle occurred near this place, March 8, 1865, between Cox's advance and the rebels, under Bragg. The rebels turned the left of the Union position, cutting off and capturing 1,500 men and 3 guns, and drove the whole line back nearly five miles.

Jackson, Miss.—The rebel General Joe Johnston arrived at this place, and assumed command of the Confederate forces, May 13, 1863. Next day, over miry roads and through torrents of rain, but in good order and fine spirits, Sherman's and McPherson's forces marched from Clinton, and met the enemy at noon, three miles from Jackson. Johnston finding himself unable to hold the city, had marched out, with the view of delaying the advance and gaining time to remove the public property. The bulk of his force engaged McPherson on the Clinton road, and a small body of artillery and infantry opposed Sherman. McPherson was held at bay on the Clinton road, until Sherman flanked the enemy on the right, when the rebels were found to have retreated. Their infantry had escaped to the north by the Clinton road; but about 250 prisoners, with all their artillery (eighteen guns) and much ammunition and valuable stores, fell into the hands of the victors. The total Union loss, in killed, wounded and missing, was 286. The Union forces evacuated the place on the night of the 16th, destroying all the public property, and took up their advance (Johnston called it a retreat) upon Vicksburg. When the Union troops left Jackson, the rebels re-entered it, and, for nearly two months, worked day and night to fortify the city. Immediately after the surrender of Vicksburg, General Grant ordered Sherman to move against Johnson, and July 6 found the latter investing Jackson, where the former had made a stand. After a few days' skirmishing, he had invested the city on the north, south, and west, cutting off one hundred cars from the rebels. On the morning of the 16th, it was suspected that the rebels were evacuating, and a charge was ordered as a feint, but they were still found in force. During the night, however, they evacuated, and hastily retreated toward the east, after destroying most of the business part of the city. Not much of value fell into the hands of the Union troops, except the cotton used in the fortifications, and a large quantity of ammunition.

Jackson, Mo., was the scene of a skirmish, and the defeat of Marmaduke's forces, April 28, 1863.

Jackson, Thomas J., better known as "Stonewall," was wounded at the battle of Chancellorsville, May 2, from the combined effects of which and pneumonia he died on the 10th.

Jackson, Tenn., was the scene of a rebel defeat September 1, 1862. They retreated, leaving 110 dead upon the field; their wounded was estimated at about 250. The rebels destroyed the railroad near this place December 19. Colonel Hatch dispersed the rebels at this place July 13, 1863, releasing 500 conscripts. All their artillery and 250 horses taken, and 200 men killed, wounded, and captured. Two companies of rebels, with the ammunition train, to which they were an escort, were captured here six days later.

Jacksonport, Ark., was the scene of an engagement June 13, 1862. The rebels were defeated, losing 28 killed, wounded, and prisoners. Union loss, 1 killed and 12 wounded.

Jacksonville, Fla., was occupied by Union forces March 12, 1862. It was soon abandoned to be retaken March 10, 1863, by the First South Carolina (colored) regiment. The place was held twenty-one days, when it was burned and abandoned. (See Camp Finnegan.)

James Island, S. C. (See Charleston.)

Jacques, Rev., (and Colonel,) and Mr. J. R. Gilmore, started on an unauthorized mission to Richmond, where they arrived July 11, 1864. In their interview with the rebel leaders, they were informed that terms of peace other than the independence of the Confederate States, could not and would not be considered.

Jefferson City, Mo., was evacuated by the rebels, under Governor Jackson, June 14, 1861, and occupied by General Lyon's forces next day. General Price, with his main body of troops, crossed the Osage near this place October 7, 1864, his plan being to seize the capital, and hold a bogus State election there. He was frustrated by the timely arrival of the Union troops, who had, by forced marches, arrived just in season to hold the town. Price made an attack next day, but, upon being repulsed, retired westward, followed by about 4,000 Union cavalry, under General Sanburn.

Jessie, a notorious guerrilla chief, was captured September 8, 1864, at Ghent, Ky., and again, April 25, 1865, at Eminence, Ky.

John's Island. (See Charleston.)

Johnson, Andrew, United States Senator from Tennessee, at the outbreak of the rebellion took strong Union ground. He denounced secession as treason, both in and out of Congress. This subjected him to many insults and indignities from Southerners, who had counted upon him as "going with his State." Instead of that, however, he, by the aid of Union men there, kept the State with him. His course was so acceptable to the Union party, that they made him their candidate as Vice-President, to which place he was elected November 8, 1864. Upon the assassination of Mr. Lincoln, he was sworn in as President of the United States, on April 15, 1865. He retained Mr. Lincoln's Cabinet and subordinate officers, avowing his intention of carrying out the policy of his lamented predecessor. (See Proclamation.)

Johnson, Waldo P., of Missouri, was expelled from the United States Senate as a traitor, January 10, 1862.

Johnson, S. C., was occupied by Kilpatrick February 10, 1865.

Johnsonville, Ky., was shelled, and 3 tin-clads and 7 transports destroyed by the rebels, under Forrest, November 5, 1864.

Jonesborough, Ga.—On September 1, 1864, the 14th Corps assaulted and carried the enemy's works at Jonesborough, capturing 10 guns and 2,000 prisoners, among them Brigadier-General Gorman. The rebels again occupied the town when the Unionists had abandoned it. Sherman's right wing took the town, driving out Wheeler and Cobb, November 18, 1864.

Jonesville, Tenn.—On January 3, 1864, Sam. Jones, with 4,000 men, made a descent on a small body of Union troops, numbering 280 Illinoisans and 18 of Neil's Ohio battery, stationed near Jonesville. A desperate resistance was made, lasting from 7 A. M. to 3 P. M., when the Unionists surrendered, having 30 killed, and about the same number wounded.

Journal of Commerce. (See Bogus Proclamation and Daily News.)

J. P. Elliott.—The rebel privateer Retribution captured, in lat. 28° 12′ N., long. 68° 55′ W., the brigantine J. P. Elliott, and put a prize crew on board, January 10, 1863. The wife of the mate, who was left on board, succeeded in getting the officers drunk, and ironed them, and, with the aid of the crew, most of whom were negroes, took the vessel to St. Thomas, and delivered it to the United States Consul.

Kansas City.—On November 11, 1861, 110 Kansas troops broke up a large rebel camp on the Little Blue, near Kansas City, Missouri.

Kearney, Philip, was appointed Brigadier-General of volunteers July 25, 1861. Before this, he had fought the Indians, the Arabs, and the Mexicans, having lost his left arm at the storming of the city of Mexico. In 1859, Major Kearney acted as volunteer aid to Marshal

Maurice. For his gallantry at Magenta and Solferino, the Emperor Napoleon bestowed upon him the Cross of the Legion of Honor. Throughout the bloody and disastrous campaign of the Peninsula, his division was generally in the hottest of the fight. In recognition of his great service in this campaign, he was commissioned as Major-General of volunteers. While in advance of his aids and orderlies during the battle of Chantilley September 1, 1862, a ball ended his earthly career. His body rests at Trinity Church, New York city, near that of the illustrious Montgomery.

The Kearney medal was presented to the 3d Army Corps, May 27, 1863.

Kearneysville.—A party of 30 or 40 guerrillas, under Major Harry Gillmore, February 12, 1864, stopped the western express train on the Baltimore and Ohio Railroad, at Kearneysville, 8 miles west of Harper's Ferry, and robbed the passengers and express of 35 or 40 watches, and about $35,000 in money; no lives were lost. Several of the robbers were afterward taken by General Kelly's command.

Kearsarge. (See the Alabama.)

Kelley's Ford.—On March 27, 1863, about 200 of General Averill's cavalry, on a reconnoissance, crossed the Rappahannock at Kelley's Ford, where the ford was so narrow that they were compelled to cross singly, and, in the face of a galling fire, they charged the rebel rifle-pits and intrenchments, capturing nearly the whole force. They then encountered and whipped Fitzhugh Lee's cavalry (who were hastening to reinforce the rifle-pits) in several hand-to-hand fights, and drove them four miles. General Averill then withdrew, bringing in 80 prisoners.

A brisk skirmish occurred here April 14. Hooker, in his advance upon Fredericksburg, crossed the Rappahannock at this place April 29. On August 1, General Buford drove Stuart's rebels one and a half miles from Kelley's Ford, when the rebels were reinforced and Buford was compelled to withdraw. He brought away over 100 prisoners; his loss was 4 killed and 60 wounded.

The 3d and 6th Corps of Meade's army, in their forward movement, crossed the Rappahannock, at Rappahannock Station and Kelley's Ford, November 7, and, after a spirited engagement, took the rebel rifle-pits and 480 prisoners and 600 Enfield rifles. The rebels lost besides 100 killed and 300 wounded. Federal loss, 370. Over 1,900 prisoners, 4 guns, and 8 battle-flags were taken in this forward movement.

Kelley's Ford, Tenn. (See Bean Station.)

Kenesaw Mountain, Ga., was occupied by the rebels, in their retreat before Sherman, June 8, 1864, and the 13th found that General preparing for the attack. The rebel works were very extensive, including Kenesaw, Lost, and Pine Mountains. General Hooker, on the 15th, after a severe fight, obtained possession of *Pine Mountain*. After this, heavy skirmishing was experienced, on the 16th, 17th, and 18th, in front of the rebel position, which was one complete net-work of fortifications. The army advanced, closing in on the enemy's intrenchments, under a murderous fire. All day long, on the 18th, the fighting continued, and, also, with little intermission during the night. Works were constructed immediately under the enemy's sharp-shooters, but with great sacrifice of lite. The rebel cavalry tried to disturb General Sherman's movements by raiding on his communications. After the engagement of the 18th, General Sherman pressed the rebels so hard they were compelled to draw in their lines on the left from Lost Mountain, concentrating all at Kenesaw.

On the 23d they assaulted Schofield and Hooker, but were promptly repulsed.

On the 27th an advance was ordered along the entire line, with the purpose of covering an attempt to force the rebels from Kenesaw Mountain. The position to be attempted was one which offered but a desperate chance of success. On the summit of the rugged mountain peak, covered with a dense growth of underbrush, the rebels had stationed a battery of twelve guns, from which they maintained a withering cross-fire on the troops engaged in forcing a passage up the steep sides of the mountain, and over the abatis and rifle-pits, behind which the enemy lay sheltered. The Union commander made two fierce assaults, in the hope of dislodging the enemy, but without success. General McPherson's three corps, under Logan, Dodge, and Blair, as well as Palmer, Hooker, and Schofield's columns, exhibited extraordinary valor and endurance; but, after fighting two hours, were withdrawn.

The Union loss in general officers was very heavy, besides about 2,500 men killed and wounded, many of whom were injured by huge rocks hurled down upon them from a high cliff. Rebel loss unknown. They kept clear behind their breastworks all through the assault. An armistice was agreed upon, on the 28th, for the purpose of burying the dead.

After the unsuccessful assault of the 27th, General Schofield forced the enemy to evacuate the place, which he did on the 30th. He did this by executing a flank movement. On the 1st of July, the Union forces followed quickly in pursuit, and took a large number of prisoners, probably 1,000. On the 3d, Joe Johnston commenced crossing the Chattahoochee, still retreating.

Kennedy, R. C., one of the New York hotel burners, was arrested, tried, and condemned. He was hung at Fort Lafayette March 25, 1865.

Kentucky.—The State Legislature, on May 17, 1861, authorized the suspension of specie payment by the banks. Three days later, Governor Magoffin issued a proclamation declaring the neutrality of the State, and forbidding the march of troops from either section across it.

The new Legislature met September 2, and on the 11th, by a vote of 71 yeas to 26 nays, ordered the Confederate troops to leave the State. Fearing rebel raids, the Legislature was, September 1, 1862, adjourned from Frankfort to Louisville.

Kettle Run.—General Hooker came upon the rebels at Kettle Run, near Manassas, on August 27, 1862, and, after a sharp engagement, completely routed them, capturing a large number of arms, etc.

On May 30, 1863, the rebel cavalry destroyed a locomotive and 16 cars, loaded with forage, on the Alexandria Railroad, near Kettle Run. They were routed by a detachment of cavalry, who captured their artillery, and wounded a great many. Union loss, 4 killed and 14 wounded.

Kickapoo Bottom, Ark., was the scene of an engagement May 8, 1862.

Kilpatrick, Judson, was, during the rebellion, one of the most daring, dashing, and successful cavalry Generals in the service; some of his exploits seemed almost wonderful. He was loved by his men, esteemed by his brother officers, and praised by the people. During the Gubernatorial campaign in New Jersey, in the fall of 1865, he proved himself a power on the stump as well as in the saddle. At the close of the rebellion he was appointed Minister to Chili. The history of his doings will be found in connection with the places he visited.

Kinderhook, near Columbia, Tenn., was, on August 11, 1862, the scene of a four hours' skirmish, resulting in a rebel discomfiture.

King George's C. H., was surprised and captured by a party of Union cavalry, December 2, 1862.

Kingsport, Tenn., was invested on December 13, 1862, by General Stoneman, who captured or killed about one hundred of Morgan and Duke's rebel brigade, they retreating toward Bristol.

Kingston, Ga., was occupied by a portion of General Sherman's army May 18, 1864.

Kingston, Tenn., was the scene of a repulse of the rebel cavalry November 25, 1863.

Kingston Springs, Tenn., was the scene of a skirmish October 22, 1863.

Kinston, N. C., was occupied by the retreating rebels December 12, 1862. They were next morning attacked by Foster's forces; they held out for five hours, when they were driven from the place, with the loss of 400 prisoners and 11 guns. The rebels were defeated near this place April 27 and 28, 1863. On March 6, 1864, twenty-three soldiers of C. H. Foster's North Carolina Regiment of Union troops were hung at Kinston, N. C., by the rebels, as deserters from the conscription. They met their fate like heroes. On March 11, 1865, Kinston was occupied by General Schofield, after heavy fighting since the first assault, General Bragg and army retreating. Battle severe; loss about 2,500 on each side

Kirksville, Mo., was the scene of a guerrilla defeat, August 7, 1862.

Knoxville, Tenn.—During the raising of a United States flag in this place, May 7, 1861, there commenced a serious riot, in which two men were killed and several injured. The city was for some time held by the rebels. The advance of Burnside's army captured the city Septemper 1, 1863, and the main army occupied it on the 4th, amid great enthusiasm. When Rosecrans moved on southward, General Burnside established his headquarters at Knoxville. The attempts of the rebels to break his communications was frequent, and hence skirmishing was of almost daily occurrence. About the middle of November, Burnside having retreated to this place, Longstreet besieged it, and on the 17th made an attack which was repulsed. Part of the city was burned on the 22d. A sortie was made by the Unionists on the 24th, when the rebels were driven to their original besieging position, losing their advance works, which were destroyed. The next day, Longstreet, with three brigades, attacked one of Burnside's brigades, in a strong position; after a hard fight the rebels were repulsed, with a loss of 150 men. On the 29th, two of Longstreet's brigades made a desperate assault on Fort Sanders, one of the defenses of Knoxville, but were repulsed with a loss of 1,000 killed, wounded, and prisoners, and 3 battle-flags. Union loss at the assault, 4 killed and 7 wounded. The siege was abandoned on December 4, Longstreet marching toward Virginia.

General Gillem's retreating forces reached this place November 20, 1864.

Labadieville, La., was the scene of a battle October 27, 1862. The rebels were put to flight after a short resistance. Rebel loss, 6 killed, 15 wounded, and 208 prisoners; Union loss, 18 killed and 74 wounded.

Ladies' National League, to disuse imported articles, was formed at Washington May 1, 1864.

Lafayette, Ga., then occupied by Union forces, was attacked on June 24, 1864, by Pillow, who was repulsed. Hood, in his retreat, left the town October 17, and Sherman's forces occupied it the same day.

La Fourche, La.—The rebels, on June 20, 1863,

attacked the railroad bridge at this place, but were repulsed, leaving their dead and wounded.

La Grange, Ark., was the scene of a skirmish and rebel repulse October 11, 1862. The rebel camp here situated was surprised and captured January 3, 1863. The Unionists were here defeated May 1, 1863, with a loss of 41 men.

La Grange, Tenn., was occupied by General Grant November 9, 1862. Union raids were organised and started from this place April 17, May 1, and August 13, 1863. General A. J. Smith left this place July 5, 1864, on a raid southward, returning on the 20th, having inflicted upon the rebels a loss of 2,500 men.

Lake Phelps, N. C.—A Union raid upon this place January 23, 1864, captured and destroyed 200,000 pounds of pork, together with tobacco, cotton, horses, and mules.

Lancaster, Ky., was occupied by the retreating rebels July 31, 1863.

Lancaster, Mo., was the scene of a skirmish November 24, 1861.

Lane's Prairie, Mo., was the scene of a skirmish July 26, 1861.

Languella River, Texas.—An action occurred at "the bend" July 31, 1862. A regiment of Texas rangers surrounded a company of Union troops, and killed, wounded, and captured all but 20, who escaped.

Laurel Hill, N. C., was occupied March 8, 1865, by Sherman's advance.

Laurel Hill, Va., was the scene of a fight July 10, 1861. General McClellan attacked General Pegram, drove him from his rifle-pits, and, with the loss of 1 killed and 3 wounded, completely routed the whole rebel force.

Lavergne, Tenn., was the scene of a battle October 7, 1862. General Negley dispatched a force from Nashville to break up the rebel camp at this place. The expedition was successful, the rebels retreating after thirty minutes' fighting. Their loss was 80 killed and wounded; the Union loss was 14 killed and wounded.

A sharp fight occurred here December 9, and the town was occupied by Rosecrans on the 20th.

Lawrence, Kansas.—On the evening of August 20, 1863, Quantrell, with about 800 guerrillas, crossed from Missouri into Kansas, about 60 miles below Lawrence, and immediately marched on that place, where they arrived at 4 o'clock next morning. The citizens being entirely surprised, and unarmed, made no defense. The guerrillas committed great atrocities, killing and burning the bodies, robbing houses of all money and valuables, even to the jewelry from women's fingers. One hundred and ninety persons were killed, many of them women and children; nearly 600 were more or less wounded. Over $2,000,000 worth of property was destroyed, among which were 182 houses. General James H. Lane, who was in the town, escaped on horseback, and, rallying about 200 men, followed and fought Quantrell 12 miles south of Lawrence. Quantrell fled, closely pursued by the infuriated Kansans.

Lawton, N. C., was occupied by Kilpatrick February 4, 1865.

Leavenworth, Mo., was the scene of a skirmish and rebel defeat November 2, 1861.

Lebanon, Ky., was the scene of a cavalry fight September 21, 1862.

On January 1, 1863, Colonel Hoskins, commanding the Union forces, attacked Morgan's forces six miles south of this place, and defeated him. Several rebels were killed and wounded, and 60 taken prisoners; their caissons and provisions were taken. Morgan fled in the direction of Columbia.

Lebanon, Mo.—Three hundred Confederates were surprised and defeated at this place October 13, 1861, by two companies of cavalry, under Major Wright. Rebel loss, 20 killed and 30 prisoners; Union loss, one man killed. The town was occupied by the rebels November 25.

The rebels were repulsed here March 12, 1862, with a loss of 13 killed, 5 wounded, and 13—including General Campbell—taken prisoners.

Lebanon, Tenn., was, on February 8, 1863, occupied by the Unionists, who captured over 600 of Morgan's command.

Lee, Robert E., formerly of the U. S. Army, went

with his State, and was appointed commander of the "Virginia forces" April 22, 1861, and assumed command on May 10. Having assumed command of the rebel forces, he made incursions into Maryland, and, September 8, 1862, issued his celebrated proclamation, in which he urged the citizens of Maryland to cast off the yoke which bound them to the Union, promising his aid and support. There was but little, if any, response to this document.

His history will be found closely identified with the Confederacy. A few points only is added here. April 2, 1865, he telegraphed to Jeff. Davis that his lines were broken, and that the latter must fly. After surrendering his army he issued an address, in which he thanked them for "*duty faithfully performed, constancy and devotion to their country.*" He, of course, applied for pardon.

Leesburg, Va., was taken possession of by Union forces March 7, 1862. The rebels were also defeated in a skirmish September 17.

Lee's Mills, Va.—The Union position on the Warwick River, near Yorktown, was attacked April 16, 1862. The rebels were repulsed; but, in the end, the Unionists were compelled to retire. Losses—Union, 35 killed, 120 wounded, and 9 prisoners; rebels, 20 killed, 75 wounded, and 50 prisoners.

Lewinsville, Va.—On September 11, 1861, a reconnoitering party, under Colonel Stevens, of the New York Highlanders, returning to their camp at Chain Bridge from Lewinsville, were attacked by a strong Confederate force from Falls Church. The rebel battery was soon silenced by Griffin's battery, and the other forces were scattered. The Federals then returned to the bridge. Union loss, 7 killed and 9 wounded. The town was occupied by the Unionists October 9.

Lewisburg, Va.—On May 23, 1862, 3,000 Confederates, under General Heath, attacked two regiments, under Colonel Crook. After a spirited fight of an hour, the rebels were routed in utter confusion; 38 dead and 66 wounded were left on the field; 100 prisoners, 300 stand of arms, and four pieces of artillery were captured. Union loss, 10 killed and 40 wounded.

November 5, 1863, a detachment of General Averill's

cavalry, under General Duffie, attacked the rebels, under General Patton, and defeated them, capturing 3 guns, 100 prisoners, and a large number of small arms, etc. Rebel loss, in killed and wounded, estimated at 350.

Lexington, Ky., was occupied August 30, 1862, by the retreating Unionists, who left it September 1, when it was taken by Kirby Smith, who held it until October 7. The rebels, under Morgan, made a dash into the town October 18, killing 6, and capturing about 120 Unionists. The same party, on June 10, 1864, robbed the city.

Lexington, Mo., was, on August 29, 1861, attacked by 2,000 rebels. The place was defended by 250 men, who successfully beat off their assailants.

The Confederates, under General Price, on September 16, commenced the siege of Lexington, which post was held by a small force of Unionists, under Colonel Mulligan. The assault by the Confederates was repulsed, with great loss. After holding out for 4 days—fifty-nine hours of which the supply of water had been cut off—and reinforcements failing to come, Mulligan was compelled to surrender, which he did on the 20th. He had previously offered to meet the enemy in the open field—4 to 1—which General Price declined. A quarter of a million in gold fell into the hands of the Confederates. The garrison of Lexington was 3,000 men; the attacking party, 20,000. Union loss, 39 killed and 120 wounded. The Confederate loss was not far from 1,200 killed and wounded. Price held the place until the 29th, when he moved on, leaving a garrison of 300 men. This garrison was surprised by Major White, with 150 men, October 16. They threw away their arms and escaped. The town was again occupied by Price October 17, 1864, but he was speedily routed by General Blunt.

Lexington, Tenn., was occupied by the rebels December 18, 1862. In the fight the Federals lost 7 killed, 10 wounded, and 110 prisoners, and rebels 35 killed and wounded. The rebels were defeated here July 16, 1863.

Liberty, La., was the scene of a rebel defeat November 21, 1864. They lost 3 guns and 200 prisoners.

Liberty, Tenn., was the scene of a guerrilla rout June 5, 1863.

Liberty Gap, Tenn., was the scene of a fight June 25, 1863, between Cleburne's division and Willich, Wilder, and Carter's brigades. After an hour's fight the rebels were defeated, with heavy loss; Union loss, 40 killed and 100 wounded.

Lickingtown, Ky., was the scene of a skirmish and rebel repulse February 25, 1863.

Lincoln, Abraham, was born on February 12, 1809, in Hardin County, Ky. His father, Thomas Lincoln, was one of the "poor whites" of the South, who, seeing no chance for his children to rise in a slave State, removed, when Abraham was seven years old, to Spencer County, Indiana, where he built a cabin, in which the family lived until 1830, when they removed to near Decatur, Illinois.

His mother died when he was ten years old, but had previously taught him to read, to which, under great disadvantages, was afterward added some knowledge of arithmetic and the art of writing. Thus began the career of one who, subsequently, held the most exalted official positions, and wielded an influence second to few in the world's history.

At the age of nineteen, he was employed, at ten dollars per month, to make a trip to New Orleans, upon a flat-boat. Though twenty-one years of age, Abraham, before beginning an independent life, aided his father in *fencing* his new farm in Illinois, and the RAILS which he split have passed into "song and story." He used, while President, a cane made from one of them, and portions of them are to be found in every State of the Union.

When Abraham began life for himself, he was entirely dependent upon his own exertions. He worked as a farm-hand and as a clerk in a store. His sagacity, force of character, and sterling integrity gained him the confidence of acquaintances. As a captain of a volunteer company in the Black Hawk war, he won the reputation of a faithful, courageous, and efficient officer.

After his return, he ran for the Legislature, and met his first and last defeat before the people. He studied surveying, and won a fine reputation for his skill in the art. In 1834 he was elected to the Legislature, and at the close of the session, being twenty-five years of age, he began the study of the law, and so rapid was his progress, that in 1836 he was licensed, and the next year removed to Springfield, the State capital. He was three times elected to the Legislature, where his acquaintance with Stephen A. Douglas was first formed. His law practice was large, and very successful, and his interest in politics was active and constant. He "stumped" his State in the presidential contest of 1844, and was elected to Congress in 1847, the only Whig member from his State.

He canvassed his State, in 1848, for General Taylor. In the intervening period, until 1854, he was actively engaged in the practice of his profession. In that year, the proposition to repeal the Missouri Compromise led to a most exciting canvass, in which he engaged, having for a competitor, before the same auditors, the Hon. Stephen A. Douglas. The result was the defeat of the Democrats. In 1858, he held the very memorable discussions, before the people of his State, with Senator Douglas. Seven joint debates were had, and the topics discussed embraced all the great questions then dividing the country. His competitor was confessedly one of the most ingenious debaters in the country, and the interest which centered in the discussions drew large and enthusiastic audiences. The debaters were rival candidates for United States Senator, and the contest became one of national interest. In the election which followed, Douglas was defeated by over 5,000 majority in the popular vote; yet the legislative districts had been so arranged, that he secured a majority of the votes in that body, and was elected to the U. S. Senate.

This notable discussion had brought Mr. Lincoln prominently before the country, and doubtless had much influence in securing his nomination for the presidency, by the National Republican Convention, in May, 1860. The exciting canvass, the disorganization and disintegration of the opposing parties, his election, and the active movements for secession which followed, with the subsequent official career of the subject of this sketch, is simply the history of our country since that time until his death.

The following is a brief epitome of his history as

President. He was nominated by the National Republican Convention, at Chicago, May 18, 1860, and elected by the people November 6. The electoral vote was counted in Congress February 13, 1861, resulting, Lincoln, 180; Breckenridge, 72; Bell, 39; Douglas, 12. Of the popular vote, Lincoln had received 1,857,610; Douglas, 1,365,976; Breckenridge, 847,953; and Bell, 590,631. He was inaugurated March 4, 1861. April 15 he issued his proclamation calling for 75,000 volunteers, and commanding the rebels to return to peace within 30 days. An extra session of Congress was called the same day, to meet July 4. On April 19 he declared the States of South Carolina, Georgia, Alabama, Florida, Mississippi, Louisiana, and Texas to be in insurrection, and on the 19th ordered the ports of Virginia and North Carolina to be blockaded. On May 3 he called for 42,000 additional three-years' volunteers, 22,714 additional regulars, and 18,000 additional seamen, to be mustered into the service of the Government, and on the 10th declared martial law upon the islands of Key West, the Tortugas, and Santa Rosa, Florida.

He acknowledged the Wheeling Government as the government of Virginia, June 26. His first message to Congress was read July 5; in it he called for 400,000 men and $400,000,000 to aid in putting down the rebellion, and on the 11th he approved the resolution of Congress remitting the duties on arms imported by States to be used in suppressing the rebellion. August 16 he declared the States of Virginia, North Carolina, Tennessee, and Arkansas in insurrection, and ordered all commercial intercourse between the North and seceded States to cease. September 11, in a letter to General Fremont, he directed him to modify the confiscation clause in his proclamation. January 20, 1862, he issued his order for the appointment of commissioners to visit Richmond, to provide for the welfare of the Union troops imprisoned at that place.

February 14 the Secretary of War ordered the release of all political prisoners, on the condition of their taking the oath of allegiance. The President proclaimed a general amnesty to all such as complied. March 6 he asked Congress to declare, by resolution, that the United States ought to co-operate with any State which may adopt a gradual abolition of slavery, giving to such State pecuniary aid as indemnity. He signed the bill for the abolition of slavery in the District of Columbia April 16. May 12 he declared that the blockaded ports of Beaufort, North Carolina, Port Royal, South Carolina, and New Orleans, Louisiana, should be open on and after the 1st of June, for commercial intercourse. On the 19th he repudiated the manifesto of General Hunter, liberating the slaves in his department. On the 26th he, by proclamation, took military possession of all the railroads, for the transportation of troops and munitions of war.

His call for 600,000 volunteers was issued July 1. On the 22d he issued an order for the seizure of supplies necessary for army use, in all the rebel States, and directing that persons of African descent should be employed as laborers, giving wages for their labor. The same day his order that foreigners should not be required to take the oath of allegiance was issued. On the 25th he issued a proclamation warning the rebels of the provisions of the confiscation act.

August 4 he ordered a draft for 300,000 militia, to serve in the army of the United States for nine months; also a special draft from the militia in States whose quota of volunteers, under the last call, shall not be filled by the 15th of August. A third article of this order relates to promotions for meritorious and distinguished services, the prevention of the appointment of incompetent and unworthy officers, and the expulsion from the service of such incompetent persons as now hold commissions.

The Emancipation Proclamation, declaring the slaves in any State in rebellion on the 1st of January, 1863, thenceforward and forever free, was issued September 22. On the 24th he issued a proclamation suspending the writ of *habeas corpus*. The bill admitting West Virginia as a State of the Union was signed December 31. The Emancipation Proclamation, defining the States and parts of States where it was operative, was issued January 1, 1863.

On May 8 he issued a proclamation declaring what shall constitute the national forces, and declaring also that no plea of alienage will be received from any foreign-born citizen after sixty-five days from the date of the proclamation.

On April 20 he issued his proclamation reciting that West Virginia, having complied with the provisions of the act of Congress, approved 31st December, 1862, the said act shall take effect and be in force from and after sixty days from date.

June 4 he revoked General Burnside's order in relation to the Chicago *Times* and New York *World*. His letter to the Albany Committee of Constitutional Union Democrats was dated June 13. He called for 100,000 men for six months, to repel invasion, June 15.

July 30 he proclaimed a retaliation policy in favor of negro soldiers. August 7 he wrote to Governor Seymour, of New York, that the draft would be enforced. His letter to Springfield, Illinois, and Syracuse, New York, Conventions, is dated August 26.

October 17 he called for 300,000 more men, to be drafted January 5, if not sooner raised by volunteering. December 8 he issued a proclamation of amnesty to rebels who would lay down their arms.

February 1, 1864, he ordered a draft for 500,000 men, to take place the 10th of March, if not raised by voluntary enlistments by the 1st of March (this order included a former call for 300,000); and on March 14 called for 200,000 men to supply deficiencies and form a reserve for the draft, to be made on the 15th of April.

On March 26 he explains his Amnesty Proclamation. He ordained that all those insurgents who are at large, but not those who are at present in the custody of the military or civil authorities of the United States, are eligible for the advantages to be derived from this measure.

The Jewett and Greeley peace affair, during July, called forth from the President the following, as his *ultimatum*:

"*To whom it may concern:*

"Any proposition which embraces the restoration of peace, the integrity of the whole Union, and the abandonment of slavery, and which comes by and with an authority that can control the armies now at war against the United States, will be received and considered by the Executive government of the United States, and will be met by liberal terms on substantial and collateral points, and the bearer or bearers thereof shall have safe conduct both ways.

[Signed] "ABRAHAM LINCOLN."

The same day a call was made for 500,000 men within fifty days, and any deficiency to be made up by drafting on September 5.

In his message to Congress, December 6, he asserted that the nation is fixed in the resolution to put down the rebellion and establish legal authority, and is well able to do so; that apparently this object must be attained by pushing the war through; that the rebels can have peace at once by laying down their arms and submitting to the laws; and that he will not retract or modify the Emancipation Proclamation, nor return to slavery any one freed by it or by acts of Congress.

A conference was had between Mr. Lincoln and some of his advisers, and rebel commissioners, February 3, 1865, but without result.

Mr. Lincoln was nominated June 9, 1864, by the Baltimore Convention, for re-election. The nomination was almost unanimous on the first ballot, and was immediately made so upon motion of a delegate from Missouri, the only State that cast a vote adverse to him in the convention, the delegates voting, under instructions, for General Grant.

The 10th of November came, and that nomination was overwhelmingly ratified. Mr. Lincoln's popular majority, in a vote of 4,015,902, was 411,428, and he received 212 of the 233 electoral votes. He was re-inaugurated March 4, 1865, and entered upon his duties with a prospect of soon seeing the rebellion crushed and peace restored. (See his Inaugural Address in the Appendix.)

The agonies of war was passed, the Stars and Stripes were again floating in supremacy over the whole land; the Union was preserved and re-established. President Lincoln shared the common joy of loyal hearts at this glorious result, but with an intensity of feeling doubtless that none other felt. His friends were reassured, his enemies silenced; the purity of his motives and the honesty of his purpose vindicated. Those who knew him best, knew he had no resentment to gratify, no revenge to inflict, no malicious passion to clamor for indulgence. The thought that of now proving to the people of the South that love for his country, and not any ill will to them, prompted his course, and the determination to deal with them as gently as safety to the country would allow, filled his noble heart with the sweetest and noblest satisfaction.

The President, Mrs. Lincoln, Miss Harris, and Major Rathbone, on the evening of April 14, occupied the President's private box at Ford's Theater. About 10 o'clock, Booth entered, unobserved, and shot the President, the ball taking effect at the base of the brain, and almost coming through at the right temple. (See Booth.) Mrs. Lincoln, who was sitting by the side of the President, noticed, as she was startled by the pistol-shot, the President's head fall against the back of the large cushioned arm-chair in which he was sitting. She, seeming to understand at once what had happened, shrieked, and bent over him just as Booth ran past them to get over the front of the box. As soon as it was ascertained by the audience and the theater people what had occurred, the play stopped, and many rushed into the President's box. The house was soon cleared, and the wounded President was carried upon a litter to a dwelling-house opposite the theater, where, at twenty-two minutes past seven o'clock next morning, amid a few of his personal friends and his family, the Christian patriot-martyr died. The body was embalmed, and lay in state at Washington and the principal cities between there and Springfield, Ill., where it was interred in Oak Ridge Cemetery, May 4. Nothing that the ingenuity of grief could desire was left undone to make the passage an imposing testimonial to the memory of the dead. The whole country seemed to flock to the railroad stations to witness the passage of the car bearing the remains; business was suspended, and we were a nation in tears; bells were tolled, bands breathed plaintive dirges, mottoes were displayed, and at the cities where the coffin was opened, tens of thousands flocked to take a farewell look upon the features they loved so well.

The Hon. W. H. Herndon of Springfield, Illinois, who was for twenty years the law partner of Abraham Lincoln, gave a lecture on the life and character of his illustrious companion, prefacing it with the following description:

"Abraham Lincoln was about six feet four inches high, and when he left the city, was fifty-one years old, having good health, and no gray hairs, or but few, in his head. He was thin, wiry, sinewy, raw-boned, thin across the breast to the back, and narrow across the shoulders; standing, he leant forward—was, what may be called stoop-shouldered, inclining to the consumptive by build. His usual weight was about one hundred and sixty pounds. His organization—rather his structure and function—worked slowly. His blood had to run a long distance from his heart to the extremeties of his frame, and his nerve force had to travel through dry ground a long distance before his muscles were obedient to his will. His structure was loose and leathery; his body was shrunk and shriveled, having dark skin, dark hair, looking woe-struck. The whole man, body and mind, worked slowly, creakingly, as if it needed oiling. Physically he was a very powerful man, lifting with ease four hundred or six hundred pounds.

"His mind was like his body—it worked slowly but strongly. When he walked, he moved cautiously but firmly; his long arms, and hands on them like giant's hands, swung down by his side. He walked with even tread; the inner sides of his feet were parallel. He put the whole foot flat down on the ground at once, not landing on the heel; he likewise lifted his foot all at once, not raising from the toes, and hence had no spring in his walk. He had the economy of fall and lift of foot, though he had no spring or apparent ease of motion to his tread. He walked undulatory, up and down, catching and pocketing tire, weariness, and pain, all up and down his person, preventing them from locating. The first opinion of a stranger, or a man who did not observe closely, was that his walk implied shrewdness, cunning, a tricky man; but his walk was the walk of caution and firmness. In sitting down in a common chair, he was no taller than ordinary men. His legs and arms were abnormally, unnaturally long, and in undue proportion to the rest of his body. It was only when he stood up that he loomed above other men.

"Mr. Lincoln's head was long and tall from the base of the brain and from the eyebrows—the perceptive faculties. His head ran backward, his forehead rising as it ran back at a low angle, like Clay's, and, unlike Webster's, almost perpendicular. The size of the hat, measured on the hatter's block, was 7⅛, his head being, from ear to ear, 6½ inches, and from the front to the back of the brain, 8 inches. Thus measured, it was not below the medium size. His forehead was narrow, but high; his hair was dark, almost black, and lay floating where his fingers or the wind left it, piled up at random; his cheek-bones very high, sharp, and prominent; his eyebrows heavy and jutting out; his jaws were long, up-curved and heavy; his nose was large, long, and blunt, having the tip glowing in red, and a little awry toward the right eye; his chin was long, sharp, and up-curved; his eyebrows cropped out like a huge rock on the brow of a hill; his face was long, sallow, cadaverous, shrunk, shriveled, wrinkled, and dry, having, here and there, a hair on the surface; his cheeks were leathery; his ears were large, and ran out almost at right angles from his head, caused by heavy hats, and partly by nature; his lower lip was thick, hanging, and undercurved, while his chin reached for the lip, up-curved; his neck was neat and trim, his head being well-balanced on it; there was the lower mole on the right cheek, and Adam's-apple on the throat.

"Thus stood, walked, acted, and looked Abraham Lincoln. He was not a pretty man by any means, nor was he an ugly one. He was a homely man, careless of his looks, plain-looking and plain-acting. He had no pomp, display, or dignity, so-called. He appeared simple in his carriage and bearing. He was a sad-looking man; his melancholy dripped from him as he walked. His apparent gloom impressed his friends, and created a sympathy for him—one means of his great success. He was gloomy, abstracted, and joyous; rather humorous, by turns. I do not think he knew what real joy was for more than twenty-three years. Mr. Lincoln sometimes walked our streets cheerily, good-humoredly, perhaps joyously, and then it was on meeting a friend, he cried, 'Howd'y,' clasping one of his friend's hands in both of his, giving a good, hearty soul-welcome.

"Sometimes he might be seen wending his way to his office, to the court-room, or railroad depot, with his baggage, looking like a rail in broadcloth. Of a winter's morning he might be seen stalking and stilting it to the market-house, basket on arm, his old gray shawl wrapped around his neck, his little Willie or Tad running along at his heels, asking a thousand little, quick questions, which his father heard not—not then even knowing that little Willie or Tad was there, so abstracted was the father. When he thus met a friend, he said that something put him in mind of a story which he heard in Indiana, and tell it he would, and there was no alternative but listen.

"Thus, I say, stood and walked this singular man. He was old, but when that gray eye and face, and every feature, were lit up by the inward soul in fires of emotion, then it was that all these apparently ugly features sprang into organs of beauty, or sunk themselves in a sea of inspiration that sometimes flooded the face."

Lincoln County, Mo., was the scene of a skirmish and Union defeat May 31, 1863.

Linn Creek, Mo.—Major Wright, with one company of cavalry, made prisoners of the notorious Bill Robbins and 45 guerrillas, at this place, October 14, 1861.

Lithonia, Ga., was occupied by Kilpatrick October 21, 1864.

Little Bethel. (See Big Bethel.)

Little Blue, Mo. (See Kansas City.)

Little River, N. C.—The fort here was captured June 5, 1863.

Little Rock, Ark.—The U. S. Arsenal at this place was surrendered February 8, 1861. Steele occupied the place September 10, 1863; the rebels retreated south, pursued by General Davidson. General Steele's loss was 20 killed and wounded. At a Union meeting here, October 30, it was resolved that Arkansas should be a free State after the war. On January 6, 1864, Colonel Hall and a squad of rebels attacked Lieutenent Grebel and a detachment of the 3d Arkansas Cavalry, *en route* to Fort Smith, near this place. The rebels were routed, and Colonel Hall and 9 men captured.

Little Santa Fe, Mo., was captured by 500 rebels November 6, 1861. The Union garrison, of 120 men, were all made prisoners.

Little Washington, Va., was the scene of a skirmish November 8, 1862.

Little Washington, N. C., was evacuated by the Unionists April 28, 1864.

Logan, John A., was born in Jackson County, Illinois, February 9, 1826. He entered the army in 1846 as Second-Lieutenant of the 1st Illinois Volunteers, and served with credit in Mexico, returning home in 1848. He was the next year elected County Clerk, and admitted to the bar in 1851, being elected the year following to the post of Prosecuting Attorney for the 3d Judicial District, and later in the same year sent to the State Legislature. He was a Democratic elector in 1856, and cast his vote for Buchanan and the same year returned to the Legislature. In 1858 he was elected to Congress from the 9th District, and returned, in 1860, as a Douglas Democrat. He left the House during the Battle of Bull Run, and fought as a private with the 2d Michigan Regiment. He was appointed Colonel of the 31st Illinois Regiment September 18, 1861, was promoted to Brigadier-General March 5, 1862, and to Major-General, dating November 29 of the same year. He assumed command of the 3d Division of the 17th Army Corps in December. He was assigned to the command of the 15th Army Corps October 27, 1863, and to the Army of Tennessee July 22, 1864. He was brave in the army, powerful on the stump or rostrum, and loyal always; and no general was more loved than "John A." At the close of the rebellion he entered the diplomatic service.

Logan's Cross Roads, Ky. (See Mill Spring.)

Lone Lack, Mo.—At this place, 20 miles west of Lexington, on August 16, 1862, 800 Missouri militia, under Major Foster, were attacked by Colonel Coffee's guerrillas, numbering between 3,000 and 4,000. After a fight of four hours, the Federal forces were defeated, with a loss of 60 killed, and 100 wounded and missing; the rebels lost 110 killed and wounded.

Long, Alexander, member of Congress from Ohio, in the course of debate, April 8, 1864, used language upon the floor of the House upon which the Speaker, Mr. Colfax, on the next morning, offered the following resolution:

Resolved, That Alexander Long, a Representative from the Second District of Ohio, having, on the 8th of April, 1864, declared himself in favor of recognizing the independence and nationality of the so-called Confederacy, now in arms against the Union, and thereby "given aid, countenance, and encouragement to persons engaged in armed hostility to the United States," *is hereby expelled.*

This resolution was freely discussed. During its pendency, **Benjamin G. Harris,** a member from Maryland, in his defense of Mr. Long, used language, upon which, the same day, Mr. Washburn, of Illinois, rising to a privileged question, offered the following resolution:

WHEREAS, Hon. Benjamin G. Harris, a member of the House of Representatives of the United States, from the State of Maryland, has, on this day, used the following language, to-wit: "The South asked you to let them go in peace. But no, you said you would bring them into subjection. That is not done yet, and God Almighty grant that it never may be. I hope that you may never subjugate the South." And whereas, such language is treasonable, and is a gross disrespect of this House; therefore, be it

Resolved, That the said Benjamin G. Harris be expelled from this House.

The vote was taken, and resulted yeas, 81; nays, 58. As it requires a two-thirds vote to expel a member, the resolution was lost.

Mr. Schenck, of Ohio, then offered the following:

Resolved, That Benjamin G. Harris, * * * having spoken words this day, in debate, manifestly tending and designed to encourage the existing rebellion, and the enemies of this Union, is declared to be an unworthy member of this House, and is hereby severely censured.

This resolution was adopted—yeas, 93 ; nays, 18.

The resolution of Speaker Colfax was modified to read as follows:

Resolved, That said Alexander Long * * * be, and he is hereby, declared to be an unworthy member of the House of Representatives.

It was then adopted—yeas, 80; nays, 69. The preamble was adopted—yeas, 78; nays, 63.

Longview and Mt. Elba, Ark., were attacked by a small force under Colonel Clayton. The bridge over the Washita River was destroyed, 320 rebels taken prisoners, and a large amount of stores captured and destroyed.

Lookout Mountain, on the Tennessee and Georgia line, was the scene of a vigorous contest October 29, 1863. The rebels attacked General Hooker's position, at Wauhatchie, near Lookout Mountain, at 2 A. M., but, after two hours' severe fighting, were repulsed, and driven across Lookout Creek. Hooker lost 350 officers and men, killed and wounded, and took many prisoners and 1,000 Enfield rifles. The position was abandoned by the Unionists on the 30th, and soon reoccupied by the rebels, who held it until November 25.

General Grant directed an attack on the 24th, Bragg commanding the rebels. General Sherman, at daylight, crossed the Tennessee, at the mouth of the South Chickamauga, and carried the north end of Mission Ridge; General Hooker moved up Lookout Valley, and turned the rebel left, formed line of battle, three miles in the rear, and moved to the assault; the fight lasted from 8 A. M. to 5 P. M.; the rebels were driven into their works at the summit of the mountain. Part of this battle was fought "above the clouds." 700 prisoners were captured.

Next day Bragg abandoned Lookout Mountain, and General Hooker took possession. General Sherman made two unsuccessful assaults upon the rebel position in front; the rebels, massing heavily against him, weakened the center, perceiving which, General Grant, at 3 o'clock, started two columns against the rebel center and broke it; the main body was driven toward Sherman, who opened on them, when they broke again, and fled in confusion toward Ringgold. In this battle, the divisions of Wood and Sheridan were ordered to carry the rifle-pits on the slope of the ridge, at all hazards, but so elated were they that they rushed on and carried the crest of the ridge, without orders. At 5 P. M. the battle was closed. The Union losses in the capture of Lookout Mountain and Mission Ridge were about 500 killed and 2,500 wounded; rebel loss, 2,000 killed and wounded, and 7,000 prisoners, 62 pieces of artillery, and 7,000 small arms.

The rebels evacuated Mission Ridge in the night, retreating easterly, closely pursued by the victorious Unionists.

Lost Mountain. (See Kenesaw.)

Louisiana.—The Governor of Louisiana, on November 19, 1860, ordered an extra session of the State Legislature, which convened at Baton Rouge December 10. They appropriated $500,000 to arm the State, and ordered the election of a State Convention, which met at the same place January 23, following, and on the 26th adopted—113 yeas to 17 nays—an ordinance of secession, which was submitted to the people and ratified—20,448 for, and 17,296 against. The Confederate Constitution was ratified March 21—101 ayes, 7 nays.

January 11, 1864, General Banks issued a proclamation, under the President's plan—one-tenth or more—for an election of civil officers of the State of Louisiana, to take place February 22, and for a convention to amend the Constitution of the State, to be held March 28. The convention met April 6, adjourning July 25, meanwhile having framed a free State Constitution, which was submitted to the people, and by them, on September 5, adopted—6,836 for, and 1,566 against it.

Lovettsville, Va., was the scene of a rebel repulse August 8, 1861.

Low Creek, Va., was the scene of a rebel defeat June 21, 1863.

Lucas Bend, Mo., was, on September 10, 1861, the scene of a naval engagement between the United States gun-boats Connestoga and Lexington and two Confederate gun-boats, assisted by a sixteen-gun battery on shore. The battery was silenced, and the gun-boat Yankee escaped capture by running under the guns of the battery at Columbus.

Lucas Bend, Ky., was the scene of a spirited affair and Union victory September 26, 1861.

Luray, Va., was occupied by Union troops, June 30, 1862. Skirmishes occurred here September 21 and 24, 1864.

Lynchburg, Va., on April 11, 1865, surrendered to a lieutenant of Griffin's forces. Mackensie's brigade of cavalry were ordered to occupy the town.

Lyon, Nathahiel, was, at the breaking out of the war, a captain in the regular army, commanding the arsenal at St. Louis, and May 6 refused the demand of the police commissioners to remove the United States soldiers to the arsenal. May 10 he captured a body of rebels at Camp Jackson, near the city. Being, by the removal of his superior officer, left in command of his department, he commenced operations against the "State troops" at Jefferson City. Governor Jackson fled at his approach, and he marched into the city June 15. General Lyon now moved on after the fleeing rebels, and on the 17th came up with and defeated them, occupying Booneville the same day. This place he left for the southwest July 3. (See Dug Spring.) He fell back to Springfield, before an advancing foe thrice his own numbers. On the 9th of August, having ascertained that Ben McCullock, with about 22,000 Confederates was encamped on Wilson's Creek, nine miles from Springfield, he moved against them with only 5,200 Union troops, mostly volunteers; one column, under Colonel Sigel, marched fifteen miles in a southerly direction, for the purpose of turning the enemy's right flank. At 6 o'clock the next morning, the battle commenced by an attack of the First Missouri Infantry on the Confederate camp. Fighting soon became general, and the enemy were driven back. At 9 o'clock they returned to the attack, and General Lyon, placing himself at the head of the 1st Iowa, whose officers had been disabled, was instantly killed by a rifle-ball in the breast. Major Sturgis now assumed command. Sigel's attack was progressing successfully; but supposing a rebel regiment, which was advancing, were reinforcements, he allowed it to approach too close, when its fire threw his advance into disorder, and he was driven back, losing five guns. At noon the enemy's camp was discovered on fire, supposed to be his own act. Major Sturgis finally fell back, in good order, to Springfield. The rebels made no pursuit. The Union loss was 1,235 killed, wounded, and missing. The Confederate loss was officially stated at 421 killed and 1,300 wounded.

Madison, Ga., was captured by General Sherman, and the depots and public buildings burned, November 19, 1864.

Madison C. H., Va.—On September 21, 1863, General Buford and Kilpatrick occupied Madison C. H. and Orange C. H., driving the rebels toward Gordonsville. The losses were 1 killed and 21 wounded; 45 rebels were captured, and two days later the forces of Hampton and Jones were defeated near Madison C. H. Union loss small; rebel loss, 50 killed and 85 prisoners. A spirited cavalry fight came off at the same place October 9.

Madisonville, Ky., was, on November 12, 1862, the scene of a rebel defeat, they losing 24 killed and 60 prisoners.

Madisonville, La., was captured by the Unionists January 11, 1864.

Mail.—The St. Louis and Memphis mail contract was annulled, and the mails stopped, May 14, 1861; all mail steamships on the coasts and rivers having any connection with the rebel States were stopped on the 20th, and on the 24th all Southern mails were discontinued.

Malvern Hill, Va.—After the battle of White Oak Swamp, the Unionists fell back to Malvern Hill, on July 1, 1862, where they were assailed, while under cover of the gun-boats on James River. The Confederates were repulsed at all points. The loss in these battles is set down at 1,565 killed, 7,701 wounded, and 5,958 missing; total, 15,224. The rebel loss was never fully known, but was supposed to be fully 20,000. This was the last of the "seven days' fighting before Richmond." General Hooker made a reconnoissance to Malvern Hill August 5, and had a fight of two hours with the rebels, when the latter took their artillery and left, the former occupying the position, which he on the next night abandoned.

Manassas, Va., was, early in the war, occupied by rebels, Beauregard assuming command there June 2, 1861. Union scouts, on March 10, 1862, ascertained that the rebels had evacuated the place, which was next day occupied by the Union forces under McClellan. The rebel cavalry occupied the place August 26. They scattered the guard and destroyed the railway train and a large quantity of Government stores. From there, they advanced nearly to within cannon-shot of Washington, and retired again, leaving Manassas in Union hands. A slight skirmish occurred here October 25.

Manassas Gap, Va.—On July 23, 1863, 800 men of General Spinola's Excelsior Brigade had an engagement with Longstreet's rebels, with 17 pieces of artillery, near this place, and drove them from their position at the point of the bayonet. The rebel loss was about 500.

Manchester, Tenn., was the scene of a skirmish June 3, 1863. General Rosecrans occupied the place on the 27th.

Manitee, Fla., was occupied by Unionists August 4, 1864.

Mansfield, La.—A disastrous affair came off at Sabine Cross-roads, near this place, April 8, 1864. A heavy cavalry train of over 300 wagons, followed by a slender force of cavalry, which, contrary to all precedent, formed the advance of General Banks's expedition to Shreveport, La., and far away from any infantry support, encountered and were surrounded and easily captured by the rebels under General Dick Taylor. The Union force at this time numbered about 5,000. The rebels concentrated their whole strength, numbering 10,000 men, and fairly hemmed them in, cutting them up very badly. The Union troops fell back quickly, and a shameful retreat, rapidly quickened to a rout, was apparent; soon batteries and teams became deserted, and the utmost confusion and panic reigned, all rushing, helter-skelter, along the narrow roads to the rear, some mounted on artillery horses, some on wagon mules, with and without saddles or bridles. Most of the 13th Army Corps was, by this time, terribly disorganised; and when driven some four miles, they encountered the 19th Corps, 7,000 strong, headed by Banks and Franklin, who personally exerted themselves to stem the current, but without avail. The presence of this force somewhat checked the impetuosity of the victors, and enabled part of the train to be got off. It was then deemed expedient to fall back to Pleasant Hills, a distance of 12 miles, which was done in tolerable order. This continued all through the night. Twenty-four pieces of artillery, and several hundred dead and wounded, were left in the hands of the foe. It was charged that the Union Generals concerned in this affair paid too much attention to cotton, sugar, and politics, and too little to strategy and fighting. (See Pleasant Hills, La.)

Maple Leaf.—On June 12, 1863, 90 rebel officers—prisoners—*en route* for Fort Delaware, in the steamer Maple Leaf, overpowered the crew and sent them below; they then steamed for the Virginia shore, 65 miles below Fortress Monroe, and made their escape. The vessel was secured by those below, after the escape of the rebels.

Marais des Cygnes was the scene of a rebel defeat October 27, 1864.

Mariatown, Mo., was the scene of a skirmish and rebel defeat September 17, 1861.

Marietta, Ga., was invested by General McPherson May 30, 1864, who that day, after a three hours' skirmish, captured 400 prisoners, some guns, small arms, and a train-load of rebel sick and wounded. Hooker and Schofield came up June 2. The place was occupied by the Unionists July 3.

Marion, Va. (See Saltville Raid.)

Markham, Va., was the scene of an engagement November 4, 1862.

Marque and Reprisal.—Orders were given by the Navy Department, April 21, 1861, to treat as pirates all persons sailing under letters of marque and reprisal from Jeff. Davis.

Martinsburg, Va.—Forty-eight locomotives, valued at $400,000, belonging to the Baltimore and Ohio Railroad Company, were destroyed at this place, by the rebels, June 23, 1861. The rebels were defeated in a skirmish near this place July 2. General Banks occupied Martinsburg, without opposition, March 3, 1862, and in his retreat he reoccupied it May 25. The rebel cavalry were here defeated September 6. The rebels entered the town October 19, destroying the railroad, etc. (See Maryland and Pennsylvania Invasion.)

Maryland.—Governor Hicks refused to receive the Mississippi Commissioner December 19, 1860, and January 6, 1861, published a strong Union address to the people, refusing to call a convention. May 15 he issued a call for four regiments of volunteers, in response to the President's demand. The Legislature, April 29, repudiated secession—the Senate unanimously, and the House by a vote of 53 to 15.

The new Legislature was to have met September 17, and, from indications, were likely to aid secession. On the 13th, 13 of the members, two editors of secession newspapers, one member of Congress, and the Gubernatorial candidate of the secession party were arrested in Baltimore. This prevented their meeting, and, on the 18th, 18 members, the Speaker, and Clerk were arrested at Frederick and sent to Fort McHenry.

It was, on April 6, 1864, determined, by a large majority, to call a constitutional convention on emancipation. The convention met, and June 24 submitted an emancipation clause, which was ratified—31,174 yeas, 29,199 nays—by the people, October 11.

Maryland Heights. (See Maryland and Pennsylvania Invasion.)

Maryland Invasion.—The beginning of September, 1862, found Washington threatened, and the rebels pushing toward the Upper Potomac. General Lee, with a large force, crossed into Maryland on the night of the 4th, fording the Potomac near the mouth of the Monocacy and at two or three other points. Frederick City was occupied on the 6th, the citizens making no demonstrations either of joy or grief. Hagerstown, Md., and Chambersburg, Penn., were threatened on the 7th, great excitement prevailing in both States. The rebels were defeated at Poolesville, Md., on the 8th, and the same day General Lee issued his celebrated proclamation to the people of Maryland, stating they had come to "assist them in regaining their rights." Governor Bradford called out the militia of Maryland. The excitement in Pennsylvania increased. The militia turned out in many places and prepared to resist the rebels. On the 9th, the 8th Illinois Cavalry and the 3d Indiana Cavalry, on their march to the Upper Potomac, had fights with the rebels at Monocacy Church and Barnesville. The rebels lost 8 killed and 15 prisoners; the Unionist had lost but one man, wounded. The same day, Middletown, Md., was occupied by the rebels, who conscripted the citizens for the rebel army. The rebels made an unsuccessful attempts on Williamsburg, Va. Stuart's cavalry were repulsed at Edwards's Ferry by General Keyes, with the loss of 90 men.

General Lee evacuated Fredericksburg on the 10th. Westminster and Hagerstown were occupied by the rebels on the 11th, and Sugar Loaf Mountain and New Market by the Union forces. General Burnside occupied Fredericksburg, amid great enthusiasm, on the 12th. The position on Maryland Heights, opposite Harper's Ferry, held by the Unionists, was attacked on the afternoon of the 12th; the fighting lasted till sundown. It was resumed next morning, and continued till 3 o'clock, when an order was received to spike the guns and remove to the Ferry. (See Harper's Ferry, South Mountain, and Antietam.)

For the invasion of 1863, see Pennsylvania Invasion. Early's invasion occurred in July, 1864.

Early, after defeating Hunter, at Lynchburg, on the 18th of June, and being largely reinforced by Breckinridge and Rhodes, penetrated, unmolested, up the Shenandoah Valley, with about 20,000 troops. He came within sight of Martinsburg, July 2, which General Sigel abandoned on the 3d, without firing a gun. He retreated to Sharpsburg, Md. Vast quantities of quartermaster's and commissaries' stores were left behind in the flight. At Leetown a slight skirmish took place, when some 30 of Sigel's men were wounded, and the rest sent flying toward the Potomac. On the 4th, Early had possession of all the country between Winchester and Williamsport. At 9 P. M., Sigel held Maryland

Heights, Harper's Ferry having been evacuated by Colonel Mulligan's forces, who burned the iron trestle bridge over the Potomac. The roads were filled with pedestrians, on their way to Baltimore, with droves of cattle and wagons, carrying such goods and valuables as the owners had dared to pick up. The terror of the fugitives was humiliating, and their stories, of what they had seen and heard, extravagant. The panic was universal, and the region, for miles, became depopulated.

On the 5th, President Lincoln made a call for 12,000 Pennsylvania militia, 12,000 from New York, and 5,000 from Massachusetts. General Couch's head-quarters were at Chambersburg, Pennsylvania, whither many of the Pennsylvania troops repaired, and General Wallace's at Baltimore. Hunter's forces were approaching the scene of action. The enemy were scattering in various directions, crossing the Potomac at several points, both below and above Harper's Ferry. A portion of Early's cavalry, under McCausland, accompanied by a battery, took possession of Hagerstown, on the 6th, and plundered the stores. They made a demand on the people for $20,000 and some outfits, all of which was quickly furnished. The Union forces had previously retired, and had marched to Chambersburg, Pennsylvania, without once halting. Bands of the enemy occupied Williamsport, Sharpsburg, and Boonsboro, Md., sweeping every thing before them, without resistance.

On the 8th, another party of the enemy, under Imboden, again entered Hagerstown, and plundered the citizens, exacting contributions. Several buildings were burned.

On the 9th, at sunrise, the rebels entered Frederick, General Lew. Wallace having evacuated the place the previous night. Early at once levied contributions on the authorities to tho enormous amount of $200,000, which was immediately paid. He then moved out to give battle to Wallace, at **Monocacy**, four miles distant. At 9 o'clock the engagement commenced. Ricketts's veteran division of the 6th Corps, who had just arrived from Petersburg, held the left of the Union line, where the brunt of the battle was most severely felt. Early's infantry forded the stream which lay between the Unionists and his main forces, drove back Ricketts, and, by the aid of his heavy batteries, got in the rear of the Union right, where the hundred-days' men were posted. He here captured 600 raw troops. Wallace, thus outflanked, fell back rapidly toward Ellicott's Mills, Early pursuing for several miles. Small portions of the rebels raided upon Westminster and Reisterstown, 16 miles from Baltimore. Both of these places were plundered.

The excitement in Baltimore and Washington, on receipt of the news of the defeat of Wallace at Monocacy, was intense. In the former place the alarm-bells were rung, at 6 o'clock, on the morning of the 10th, and the citizens were mustered for the defense of the city. A battalion of rebel cavalry dashed into Darnestown, 20 miles from Washington, making a raid on the stables and stores, and again leaving for Frederick. The enemy continued to gather up horses, hogs, and sheep, sending all live stock across the Potomac, whose various fords they held by small cavalry forces. At Washington preparation was made by General Augur to resist attack, and, in addition to the ordinary forces, the marines, the home-guards, and a large body of Department employes were called out. Meantime, the Union forces began to close in on the enemy's rear. General Couch's cavalry occupied Hagerstown on Saturday, and a part of Hunter's command took possession of Martinsburg. Small detachments of rebel cavalry operated, during Sunday, on the railroads and in the country from 10 to 20 miles above Baltimore, but the main body moved down toward Washington. On the 11th, the enemy was chiefly occupied in plunder. Bridges were burned on the Northern Central road; two trains were captured on the Philadelphia road, in one of which was Major-General Franklin, who was taken prisoner, but who afterward succeeded in effecting his escape; and railroad communication was suspended between Washington and the North. A large body of the rebels menaced Washington, and, toward evening, threatened Fort Stevens, on the Seventh Street road, about 7 miles from the capital. The rebel forces continued to invest Washington, moving nearer to the city than on the 11th. Toward evening, on the 12th, the rebel sharp-shooters had become so annoying, and the fact of their presence at the National Capital so humiliating, that an attempt was made by General Augur to dislodge them. A brigade of veteran infantry was detached along the Seventh street road, and attacked and completely routed the enemy, who left about a hundred of their dead and wounded on the field, near Silver Spring. The Union loss was reported at about 200. This attack and success virtually ended the invasion.

On the morning of the 13th there was no enemy to be seen in the vicinity. The body of the enemy's troops moved in force toward Edwards's Ferry. A large part of the Army of the Potomac moved toward the borders of Virginia, to give pursuit. Generals Wright, Ricketts, and Crook, with Averill's cavalry, commenced the pursuit (or, more properly speaking, the escorting) of the raiders, crossing the Potomac at Edwards's Ferry. On the 14th they leisurely marched to Leesburg; the cavalry, coming upon their rear on the 17th, at Snicker's Gap, captured a small part of their plunder, the rebels burning a portion, which they could not save. At this place there was a sharp skirmish, which resulted in the enemy flying southward. On the 18th they were found, holding the Shenandoah River, with two guns.

After the Union infantry had crossed, at Island Ford, the rebels, under Breckenridge, charged with great violence, and drove them back over the river, inflicting some loss. At Ashley's Gap the cavalry met with a similar repulse. The Union loss, in both engagements, was about 500, killed, wounded, and prisoners. Many of the wounded were left in the hands of the enemy, in the retreat. After this, Crook's command returned to Harper's Ferry, and Wright's went in the direction of Washington. On the 20th, Averill came up with Early, with 5,000 troops, near Winchester, where he gave them battle. The engagement lasted three hours, ending in the enemy withdrawing to his old intrenchments. Rebel loss, 300 killed and wounded; Union loss, about 250, killed, wounded, and missing. Here the Federal pursuit ended.

Early's second invasion gave rise to a similar scare and panic as in the early part of the month, with a repetition of the stories that 50,000 rebels had crossed the Potomac, that Washington was taken, and Philadelphia destroyed. In Maryland and Southern Pennsylvania a general exodus, of the most disorderly and hasty character, set in, and continued for a week. However, all the stories of a vast force, under Breckenridge, about to menace Pittsburg and Philadelphia, and being already in Maryland, were found to be exaggerations. On the 23d, Averill having been joined by Crook, after the disaster of the 18th, followed by the more fortunate affair on the 20th, was attacked by the enemy at Kernstown, near Winchester, and was driven back. On the 24th the rebels repeated their tactics, and pressed the Union cavalry to the rear, in great confusion, capturing a number of prisoners. General Crook had 8,000 men under his command, but the desertion of the cavalry obliged him to retreat. The force dispatched by Early was, undoubtedly, larger. The Unionists lost about 1,300, in killed, wounded, and prisoners. The brave Colonel Mulligan, of Lexington (Missouri) celebrity, was killed. Some of the Union officers behaved in a very cowardly manner. General Hunter, a few days afterward, dismissed thirteen for deserting their commands, and going to the rear with false reports.

Early's cavalry followed the retreating army up to Martinsburg, where a brisk cannonading ensued, with some loss. He soon occupied the town. General Crook, who had succeeded, by this time, in getting most of his stores across the Potomac, fell back to Hagerstown, Maryland.

The Union troops, rallying again on the 28th, at Maryland Heights, where they had concentrated in their retreat, ventured down to Harper's Ferry, and General Kelly reoccupied Martinsburg the same day.

On the 30th a party of rebel cavalry, under McCausland, numbering about 230, crossed the Potomac at Williamsport, and, having driven off some Union troops, visited Chambersburg, Pennsylvania, and demanded $500,000, with the alternative of burning the town. Their demands not being complied with, they quickly reduced three-fourths of the place to ashes. Nearly 300 houses fell a prey to the flames. About two million dollars' worth of property was destroyed, and nearly 3,000 people rendered homeless. At noon McCausland left the town, and succeeded in making his way back to his reserves, without hindrance. The same day Mosby, with 60 men, visited Adamstown, Maryland, drove off the cavalry pickets, robbed the stores, and retired. This adventure gave rise to the story of Early having been seen, with 50,000 men, menacing Baltimore and Philadelphia. The fact is that no important leader of the rebels took part in this "second invasion of Maryland," and only about 2,000 cavalry were known to be detailed for the expedition. Crook's command made forced marches to reach the scene of action, but only arrived to find this small force far away in the Shenandoah Valley.

The following is an estimate of the damage inflicted by the great raid, led by Breckenridge and Early, commencing on the 2d of July also by McCausland, with his few troopers, on the 28th and 30th: Philadelphia, Wilmington, and Baltimore Railroad, $107,000; Northern Central Railroad, $100,000; Baltimore and Ohio Railroad (this road being longest occupied), say, $400,000; telegraph lines, $4,000; Chesapeake and Ohio Canal, $150,000; Hartford County, $15,000; Baltimore County, $42,000; Carroll County, $10,000; Frederick County, $372,000; Washington County, $85,000; estimated value of supplies consumed and wasted, $100,000; food for horses, $25,000; damage to fences and farms (small), $250,000; four thousand cattle, at $30 each, $120,000; five thousand horses and mules, $600,000; sheep and hogs, $50,000; cash contributions levied, $230,000; burning of Chambersburg, Pennsylvania, $2,000,000; miscellaneous plunder from stores, $300,000. Total, $4,960,000.

Marysville, Tenn., was visited by guerrillas March 2, 1864.

Marysville, Va., was the scene of a skirmish October 31, 1862.

Mason, James M., of Va., and John Slidell, of La., the former Confederate envoy to Great Britain, the latter to France, on their way to Europe, in the British mail-steamer Trent, was taken therefrom, November 8, 1861, by Captain Wilkes, of the United States steamer San Jacinto. They were placed in Fort Warren, Boston Harbor. England demanded the unconditional surrender of these men, which was acceded to, and they were, December 30, delivered to the British minister.

Mattoon, Ill.—A Copperhead riot broke out at Charleston, Ill., March 29, 1864. Several men of the 54th Illinois, who were there on a furlough, organized to resist the rioters and quell the disturbance. The roads were picketed; Charleston and Mattoon were garrisoned. The Copperheads were pursued, and about 30 prisoners taken. The next day the rioters mustered in a force estimated at 1,000 strong. Martial law was proclaimed, and the greatest excitement reigned. Four soldiers were killed, and 6 wounded; 3 citizens were killed, 4 wounded, and 40 taken prisoners.

Mayfield, Ky., was occupied by the Unionists September 20, 1861. The rebels entered the town November 2, 1863, robbed the citizens, plundered the stores, and destroyed the railroad.

Maysville, Ark.—On October 22, 1862, General Blunt's command attacked 5,000 rebels at this place, and, after an hour's fight, completely routed them, with the loss of all their artillery and a portion of their equipage, and 150 killed and wounded. Union loss, 5 killed and 9 wounded.

Maysville, Ky., was captured by the rebels September 11, 1862. On June 14, 1862, 300 rebel cavalry made a raid into the town, and took about $16,000 worth of goods, paying therefor in Confederate money; they took also about $4,000 worth of Government property. They were pursued, and next day defeated, losing all their plunder and 107 prisoners.

McClellan, George B., was appointed Major-General May 16, 1861, and assumed command of the Federal forces in West Virginia June 20. July 22 he relinquished this command to assume that of the forces on the Potomac, which he did August 20. He was, on November 1, placed as chief in command of the armies of the United States, in place of General Scott, retired.

He was relieved of this command, and appointed to that of the Army of the Potomac, March 11, 1862. On July 4 he issued an address to his army, congratulating them on their valor and endurance in having succeeded in changing their base of operations to James River, and promising them that they should enter the capital of the South, etc.

He was, September 2, placed in command of the fortifications at Washington, and all the troops for the defense of the National Capital. On the 7th he left Washington, under orders to drive the rebels from Maryland, most of his force having preceded him, and on the 11th called for reinforcements. On the 16th and 17th he fought the battle of Antietam (which see). Not moving fast enough to suit Halleck, the latter urged him, October 1, to cross the Potomac at once, and give battle to the enemy. The urging not being complied with, on the 6th he peremptorily ordered him to do so. (See Halleck.) He was removed from his command November 7, and arrived at Trenton, N. J., on the 12th. He had an enthusiastic reception at Boston February 2, 1863, and at other places thereafter. The Chicago Convention nominated him as their candidate for President, August 29, 1864. The rebels in front of Petersburg cheered this nomination September 2. He resigned his commission November 8.

McCook, General Robert L., while riding in an ambulance, sick, and in advance of his troops, was brutally murdered, near New Market, Ala., by a band of guerrillas, 100 or 200 strong.

McConnelsburg, Pa. (See Pennsylvania Invasion.)

McCoy's Mills was the scene of a rebel defeat November 14, 1861.

McDonough, Ga., was occupied by Sherman November 17, 1864.

McDowell, Va.—Generals Milroy and Schenck, with nine regiments of Federal troops, had a battle with 14,000 rebel troops, under General Jackson, at this place, May 8, 1862. The fight lasted from 6 to 9 P. M., when the Union troops fell back to Franklin, in good order. Union loss, 30 killed and 216 wounded; that of the rebels very heavy, but not definitely known.

McMinnville, Tenn., was captured by the Unionists, under General Reynolds, April 21, 1863. He took 130 prisoners, and destroyed the depot buildings and a large quantity of military stores. Breckenridge's forces were defeated, with considerable loss, near this place, May 26. Wheeler, with 4,000 rebel cavalry, made an attack here, October 3, capturing the 4th Tennessee (Union) infantry, burning a train of cars and escaping.

McPherson, Major-General James B., commanding the Army of the Tennessee, one of the ablest and most valorous of the Union commanders, was killed by a rebel sharp-shooter, July 22, 1864. He was shot through the lungs.

Meade, Major-General J. G., succeeded General Hooker in the command of the Army of the Potomac June 28, 1863. (See Pennsylvania Invasion, and Grant's Report.)

Meadow Bridge, on the Chickahominy was destroyed by Kilpatrick May 4, 1863, and rebuilt May 12, 1864, by General Sheridan.

Meagher, Brigadier-General Francis, formally took command of the "Irish Brigade," amid great enthusiasm February 5, 1862. He resigned his commission May 8, 1863, taking leave of his command on the 19th, and on June 16 received the honor of the "hospitalities of New York. His history will be found in connection with many a battle, and always shows him brave and true.

Mechanicsburg, Pa. (See Pennsylvania Invasion.)

Mechanicsville, Va., was occupied a few hours, May 23, 1862, by General Banks, in his retreat. A battle was fought here June 26, commencing at noon, by an attack of the rebel forces, commanded by General Lee, on General McCall's division. It lasted till night, increasing in fury as it progressed, and was one of the hardest and most terrific battles of the campaign. The Union loss was 80 killed and about 150 wounded; the rebel loss was reported at 1,000. The Unionists fell back to Gaines's Mills.

Medway, Ky., was captured February 2, 1865, by 26 guerrillas, who burned the telegraph office, robbed the stores, citizens, etc.

Memphis, Mo.—On July 18, 1862, 400 Unionists,

under Major Clopper, defeated 600 rebels near this place; losses heavy on both sides.

Memphis, Tenn.—Part of the citizens held an enthusiastic meeting December 20, 1860, to ratify the secession of South Carolina. On the 28th there was held an equally enthusiastic Union meeting. At a large gathering, on April 21, the American Flag was buried, with solemn ceremonies.

A severe gun-boat fight occurred before the city June 6, 1862. The firing commenced at daylight, and in less that two hours 4 of the enemy's gun-boats were disabled, and the other 4 in full retreat, followed by the Union boats, which captured 3 of them. The rebel flag-ship alone escaped. After the battle, the city was unconditionally surrendered to the victors.

Important expeditions left this place November 26 and December 21. On August 21, 1864, a portion of General Forrest's raiders entered Memphis, on a dash, robbed a few stores, took a few prisoners, and as hastily fled.

Meridian, Miss., was captured by Hurlbut's corps of Sherman's army February 14, 1864.

Merrimac, a rebel iron-clad (see Hampton Roads), was blown up by her commander, off Crany Island, May 11, 1863.

Messella, N. M., was the scene of a skirmish and Union victory, August 3, 1861.

Metley's Ford, Tenn., was the scene of a skirmish November 5, 1863.

Metropolis, Ill.—A band of guerrillas attempted to cross the river at this point, January 16, 1865, but were dispersed by a gun-boat.

Middlebury, Va., was occupied by Colonel Geary, the rebels retreating precipitately after a short skirmish. There was a cavalry skirmish near this place January 27, 1863, and also on June 17; the rebels defeated both times.

Middle Fork Bridge, near Buchannon, Va., was the scene of a Union defeat, July 6, 1861.

Middleton, Tenn.—Stokes's cavalry surprised a rebel camp at this place, 15 miles from Murfreesboro, killing 10 of them, and capturing 100 prisoners, with all their camp and equipage, February 2, 1863. The Unionists made a raid upon the town April 22, and a rebel camp was again broken up May 21.

Middletown, Md., was occupied by the Unionists, after driving out the rebels, September 13, 1862.

Middletown, Va., was the scene of skirmishing, and a rebel defeat, June 12, 1863, and of Meade's flanking Lee, July 7.

Milford, Mo.—General Pope's forces surprised the enemy's camps near this place December 18, 1861, and succeeded in capturing many prisoners and large amounts of stores, ammunition, etc. About 2,500 prisoners were taken in three days.

Mill Creek, Va. (See Romney.)

Milledgeville, Ga., was occupied by General Howard November 20, 1864. The State Legislature had fled two days before.

Millerstown, Penn. (See Pennsylvania Invasion.)

Milliken's Bend. (See Vicksburg.)

Mill Spring. (See Somerset, Ky.)

Millsville, Mo., was the scene of a skirmish July 16, 1861.

Milton, Fla., including the extensive salt-works there, was destroyed, and a number of prisoners captured, by the Federals, October 26, 1864.

Milton, Tenn., was the scene of a battle March 20, 1863. The Union forces, 1,323 strong, with 2 pieces of artillery, under Colonel Hall, were attacked by 3,800 rebels, under John Morgan. Hall fell back to a commanding position on Vaught's Hill. After a furious fight of four hours, the rebels retreated in confusion, leaving their dead and wounded. Rebel loss, 50 killed, 150 wounded, and 100 prisoners. Colonel Hall lost 7 killed and 31 wounded.

Mingo Swamp, Mo., was the rendezvous of a band of guerrillas, of whom 9 were killed and 29 wounded in an action February 3, 1863.

Missionary Ridge. (See Lookout Mountain.)

Mississippi.—The Legislature, on November 29, 1860, voted to send commissioners to confer with the authorities of the other slaveholding States on the question of secession. A State Convention assembled at Jackson January 7, 1861, and, two days later, passed a secession ordinance—84 ayes, 15 nays. Her Representatives withdrew from the House on the 12th.

The Governor, on March 22, called for the organized militia of the State, and the Convention, on the 30th, ratified the Confederate Constitution.

Mississippi Springs, Miss., was captured by General Grant May 13, 1863.

Missouri.—The Legislature, January 16, 1861, ordered a State Convention.

Governor Jackson refused, April 18, to furnish troops for coercion, and, August 5, issued a paper declaring the independence of Missouri.

A Provisional Government was established by the Union authorities June 18. A Union State Convention met at Jefferson City July 22, and on the 30th declared vacant the offices of Governor, Lietenant-Governor, and Secretary of State, by a vote of 56 to 25. The seats of the members of the Legislature were also declared vacant. The State officers and a majority of the Legislature were secessionists. The next day they elected Hamilton R. Gamble, Governor; Willard P. Hall, Lieutenant-Governor, and Mordecai Oliver, Secretary of State—all Union men. August 30 the State was declared under martial law. General Rosecrans, on June 29, 1864, ordered the raising of enrolled militia to put down the guerrillas in the State.

A Free State Constitution was adopted January 11, 1865.

Mitchell's Fork was the scene of a brisk action and rebel defeat March 27, 1865.

Mobile, Ala., was blockaded May 27, 1861; notwithstanding which, it was a place of resort for contraband trade during the rebellion, especially before the capture of Fort Morgan. August 22, 1864, the bombardment of this fort was opened from the fleet and the land batteries; next morning it surrendered, with 600 men, 60 guns, ammunition, etc.

Operations were commenced against the city March 8, 1865. On the 11th two rebel shore batteries were silenced, and the day following General Maury issued a proclamation announcing the attack upon the city, and calling upon "every body to help defend it." On the 18th Colonel Moore's brigade landed at Cedar Point,

General Benton's division at Mobile Point, and the day following A. J. Smith's corps occupied Danby's Mills, on the east of the bay. The fleet continued the bombardment. Spanish Fort was captured by assault April 8. With it was taken 25 officers, 540 men, 5 mortars, and 24 guns. Blakely, near the city, with 2,500 prisoners and 20 guns, was next day surrendered. The rebels began to evacuate Mobile on the 10th. Forts Huger and Tracy were abandoned on the 11th, and the day following Canby's troops occupied the city, without resistance.

Mobs were of frequent occurrence, both North and South, during the rebellion. Newspaper offices at the North, conceived to be in sympathy with secession, or, at the South, with Union, were very frequently destroyed Drafting for the rebel army at Nashville caused a serious riot December 6, 1861. A mob at Elizabethtown, N. J., attempted to "shut up" Beecher during a lecture January 6, 1863; they did not do it. A serious bread riot occurred at Richmond, Va., April 2, 1863; one at Mobile September 4, and one at Savannah April 17, 1864. (See Boone County, Holmes County, Mattoon, Morgan County, New York Riots, Vallandigham.)

Monitor, the iron-clad gunboat from which the general name originated, was launched at New York January 30, 1862, from whence she sailed February 27, (see Hampton Roads,) and foundered south of Cape Hatteras December 31.

Monocacy. (See Maryland Invasion.)

Monroe Station, Mo., was the scene of a skirmish July 10, 1861.

Monteith, Ga., was occupied by Sherman's left wing December 11, 1864.

Monterey, Tenn., was the scene of a slight engagement April 29, 1862.

Monterey, Va., was the scene of a skirmish April 12, 1862.

Montgomery, Ala. (See Alabama.)

Monticello, Ark.—A force of Union troops belonging to Steele's army engaged the rebels, numbering 1,000, at this point, March 30, 1864, and routed them, capturing a quantity of arms, wagons, and horses.

Monticello, Ky., was captured by General Carter, after driving out the rebels, May 1, 1863. A brisk skirmish was fought here May 31, in which the rebels lost 16 prisoners. Near this place, on June 10, after two hours' fighting, the rebels were defeated. Union loss, 30 killed and wounded; rebel loss unknown.

Moore, La., was captured, the rebel camp and depot destroyed, and the rebels routed, May 15, 1863.

Moorefield, Va., was occupied by Unionists, and a guerrilla camp there broken up, February 12, 1862. The rebels were defeated near this place November 9. Imboden and Jenkins's rebel cavalry attacked Colonel Washburne at this place January 3, 1863; the fighting continued all day, and was renewed next morning, when the rebels were driven six miles. Imboden, with 12,000 men, attacked Major Stevens, with 300 men, at this place September 5. Stevens fell back to Cumberland, without loss. In a skirmish near Moorefield, on the 11th, the rebels were repulsed, with a loss of 15 killed and 150 captured. Colonel Mulligan overtook Early's rebel forces at Moorefield February 4, 1864, and, after six hours' fighting, drove them from the town. Harry Gilmore's camp of guerrillas was broken up, and the leader captured, at this place, February 5, 1865.

Morehead City, N. C., was taken possession of by General Parke April 23, 1862.

Morgan County, Ind., was the scene of an anti-draft riot January 31, 1863. It was speedily quelled.

Morgan, G. W. (See Cumberland Gap.)

Morgan, John, a noted rebel cavalry General and guerrilla, whose daring, dashing raids, and extreme cruelty, was the terror of all within his power. His invasion of Indiana and Ohio was, perhaps, his most noted raid. On July 7, 1863, he was reported at Bardstown, Ky., moving toward Louisville, where the excitement was intense, and the defenses against him limited. On the 8th, with 4,800 men, 5,000 horses, and 4 guns, he crossed the Ohio in two captured steamers, one of which was burned, the other released. The Home-guards of Leavenworth disputed his passage, but were overpowered by superior numbers. They lost 2 killed, and 15 prisoners; the rebels lost 2 killed and several wounded.

Corydon, Ind., surrendered to him on the 9th, when he marched upon *Seymour*, burning the depot and destroying the railroad there. He occupied *Selem* on the 10th. He burned the depot, tanks, etc., and destroyed the railroad. A portion of his forces occupied Greenville and Paoli, then Vienna, where he burned the railroad bridge and tore up a portion of the track. Lexington and Paris were also captured. The excitement extended throughout the State. The stores at Indianapolis were closed, and the militia ordered out. On the 11th, 20,000 armed men paraded the streets. A portion of the rebel force on the 12th demanded the surrender of North Vernon, which was refused. General Love, of the Indiana Legion, marched to its relief, when Morgan decamped. Colonel Gavin's militia regiment overtook Basil Duke's detachment at Sunman's, when a fight ensued, which resulted in Duke's retreat; losses unknown. On the 13th he made his way into Ohio, burning and destroying bridges and railroads in his way. He crossed the Big Miami and burned the bridge. Fearing the rebels, martial law was declared in Cincinnati, Covington, and Newport. He reached Williamsburg and Batavia, Ohio, on the 14th. At Miamiville he destroyed the Little Miami Railroad, and fired into an accommodation train and burned the cars. At Loveland he destroyed 50 Government wagons. He occupied Georgetown, Ohio, on the 15th, on which day the State militia was pouring into Camp Chase. He captured Piketon on the 16th. He was closely pursued by Union forces under Generals Judah, Shackelford, and Hobson. He was, on the 17th, surrounded near Gallipolis, but managed to cut his way through with a small portion of his force. Colonel Runkle had a three hours' fight with him near Berlin, Ohio; three rebels were killed.

The day following he retreated toward Bealesville, where about 300 of his men managed to cross the river before the arrival of the gun-boats. More infantry coming down the river, he was immediately surrounded. About 1,500 managed to escape to near Buffington Island, a few miles above Pomeroy, Ohio, where Generals Hobson and Judah came up with him, about 9 o'clock. They immediately commenced an attack.

Morgan made two attempts to cross the river, but was prevented by the gun-boats. In the fight which ensued the rebels lost 40 men killed and their artillery; the balance escaped. Basil Duke and a brother of Morgan were captured.

On the 20th, General Shackleford, near George's Creek, brought Morgan to a stand, and had a fight of an hour, when Morgan and a small squad fled, the balance surrendering. He was checked by the militia, near the Muskingum, on the 23d, but managed to escape, with loss of 15 killed and several wounded. General Shackleford captured him and the balance of his force, near New Lisbon, Ohio, at 3 P. M., on the 26th. Morgan previously had a fight with Major Way and 250 of the 9th Michigan Cavalry, and lost 240 men. Seeing his hour had come, he surrendered to Captain Beckwith, of the militia, on condition of his parole; but General Shackleford coming up, refused to acknowledge the condition, and took Morgan into custody.

Morgan and Duke, with 28 others, were confined in the Ohio Penitentiary, from which Morgan and six of his officers escaped, on the night of November 28, by undermining the walls. They were received by their sympathizers, and Morgan finally made his escape southward.

He crossed the Tennessee River at Gillespie's Landing, 60 miles from Chattanooga, December 12.

Morgan was killed, his staff captured, and his forces badly cut up and routed, by General Gillem, at Greenville, East Tennessee, September 4, 1864.

Morgan Raid. (See John Morgan.)

Morgantown, Ky.—The rebels attacked the Union camp at this place October 31, 1861, but were repulsed, with considerable loss. In a skirmish here October 24, 1862, 16 rebels were captured.

Morgan's Bend, on the Mississippi, was the scene of a brisk engagement September 29, 1863; General Dana attacked the rebels, but fell back, losing several hundred killed and wounded, and 1,500 prisoners. The rebels then assumed the offensive, and the gun-boats had to be called in to check their advance.

Morris Island. (See Charleston.)

Morristown, Tenn., was the scene of a skirmish December 1, 1861.

Mound City, Ark., was burned by the Union forces January 15, 1863.

Mount Airy. (See Saltville Raid.)

Mount Crawford, near Piedmont, Virginia, was the scene of a battle between General Hunter and Confederate General W. E. Jones, which resulted in a Union success, June 5, 1864. The rebels lost Jones, killed, 1,300 prisoners, three pieces of artillery, and 3,000 stand of small arms. The balance were scattered toward Waynesboro and Charlottesville.

Mount Elba. (See Longview, Arkansas.)

Mount Gilead, Va., was attacked by rebel cavalry, and 35 Federals captured, November 10, 1862.

Mount Jackson, Va., was occupied by General Banks April 17, 1862.

Mount Sterling, Ky., was attacked by the rebels, who were repulsed by the home-guards, July 29, 1862. In their retreat they were met by a party of volunteers, who drove them back toward the town, where they were again beaten by the guards, who took all their horses and 48 prisoners.

The rebel Colonel Cluke, with 800 men, surrounded the town March 20, 1863. The Union garrison threw themselves into the houses and fought for four hours, but were finally compelled to surrender. Rebel loss, 22 killed and wounded; Union loss, 3 killed and wounded. The rebels held the town ten days, when they were driven out, burning most of the business houses before their retreat. General Burbridge defeated John Morgan at this place June 8, 1864.

Mount Zion, Mo., was the scene of an engagement December 28, 1861, between 450 troops, under General Prentiss, and 900 rebels, under Colonel Dorsey. 150 rebels killed and wounded, and 35 prisoners; Union loss, 3 killed and 11 wounded.

Mulligan, Colonel. (See Lexington, Missouri.)

Mumford, W. B., was executed at New Orleans, June 7, 1862, for hauling down the U. S. flag from the mint building, after it had been placed there by the Union soldiers.

Mumfordsville, Ky.—In a fight near this place December 17, 1861, the rebels lost 33 killed—including Colonel Terry, commanding—and 50 wounded. Unionists lost 9 killed and 16 wounded. The rebels attacked the town with artillery September 14, 1862. The engagement lasted seven hours, during which time they were repulsed five successive times. Fighting continued on the 15th and 16th, and it surrendered on the 17th. About 4,000 prisoners, 4,000 stand of arms, and a quantity of stores were surrendered to the rebels. The town was reoccupied by Union troops, the rebels being driven out on the 21st.

Murfreesboro, Tenn., was, on July 13, 1862, captured by General Forrest; $30,000 worth of property was destroyed. General Crittenden and Acting General Duffield were taken prisoners, together with the whole garrison. Loss heavy on both sides.

General Rosecrans, finding that the rebel army manifested a feeling of security, and had weakened their force somewhat by expeditions to various parts of the State, left Nashville December 26, in three columns, under Thomas, McCook, and Crittenden, and came up with the rebels on the 29th, near Stewart's Creek, and drove them back to their intrenchments, which was advantageously situated on Stone River, three miles from Murfreesboro. Supposing the rebels were retreating, Harker's brigade, of Wood's division, was ordered across the river, but were met by a heavy fire from a regiment in ambush. Harker held his fire until within short range, when he fired and charged, driving the rebels back upon their main body, Breckenridge's division. Finding the force in front too strong, the brigade was recalled. On the 30th there was considerable fighting and maneuvering for position, the Union forces pressing forward and constantly gaining ground. At dawn on the 31st, Hardee advanced noiselessly, in heavy columns, against the right wing, commanded by McCook. Kirk's and Willich's brigades first felt the shock, and stood their ground for awhile, but were finally compelled to yield to overpowering masses. Kirk was wounded and Willich taken prisoner. The rebel forces, in about an hour, routed the whole right wing, and drove them back nearly four miles, capturing 28 pieces of artillery. The plan of battle was defeated. The left wing, which had commenced its advance, was halted. Beatty's and Fyffe's brigades, with Rousseau's division from the reserve, were sent to reinforce the right. A new line was formed; and Rosecrans, massing the artillery in the center, completely checked them, when the rebels broke and fled. The battle raged fiercely for ten hours, General Rosecrans freely exposing himself during the whole fight. During the progress of this fight, Wheeler's rebel cavalry, 3,000 strong, with two guns, attacked Colonel Innis's regiment of Michigan engineers and mechanics, who had been posted at Lavergne to protect communications. They were repulsed in seven distinct charges, when they withdrew.

During the night, General Rosecrans, at Murfreesboro, readjusted his line of battle, preparatory to another attack next day. The army bivouacked on the field. During the day there was heavy skirmishing, but no general engagement, the enemy throwing out small bodies, as if to feel a weak point. On the 2d of January the rebels had massed their columns against the left, and, at 3 o'clock P. M., they advanced in three heavy columns, battalion front; advancing to within 100 yards, they were met by a heavy fire from the left, now reinforced, and the artillery being massed. In forty minutes the rebel column broke and fled, losing 2,000 men; General Rains among the killed. Skirmishing continued on the 3d, and became so annoying that General Rosecrans ordered the corps commanders to clear their fronts. Rousseau's division was ordered to dislodge the rebels, which they did. The rebels retreated in the night, abandoning the town, which General Thomas's corps advanced and occupied on the morning of the 5th. The Union loss in the whole fight was officially stated at 92 officers killed, 384 wounded; 1,441 men killed, 6,861 wounded, and 3,000 taken prisoners. The rebel loss is estimated at 14,560 killed and wounded. The Union force engaged was 43,400 men; the rebel force was estimated at 62,520. Altogether this was one of the most fierce and bloody battles of the war, and exhibited the superior generalship and tenacity of General Rosecrans. The victory effectually cleared Middle Tennessee of the rebels, and saved it and Kentucky from a formidable invasion. On the 9th General Halleck issued a special order "thanking General Rosecrans and his army for their gallant conduct and victory over the rebels at Murfreesboro. Several skirmishes occurred here during 1863, and the rebels were repulsed near this place September 1, December 5, 6, and 15, 1864.

Mustang Island, Texas, was captured by General Banks November 18, 1863, and with it a rebel fort, a company of artillery, and a squadron of cavalry. No Union loss; one rebel wounded.

Napoleon, Ark. (See Arsenal.)

Napoleon, Emperor. (See Neutrality.)

Nashville, Tenn., was evacuated by the rebels February 23, 1862. Before leaving, they destroyed both bridges across the Cumberland River, and committed great depredations on the property of the citizens. The town was occupied by the Union advance, under General Nelson, on the 25th. The Mayor, on March 3, issued a proclamation, calling upon all citizens to return and resume their business, under the protection of the Federal authorities.

The rebels invested the town October 11, and skirmishing continued until the 21st, when they were temporarily driven back. On December 10 they appeared in force, and drove in the Union pickets. Unimportant skirmishes were of occasional occurrence until November 30, 1864, when, after the battle of Franklin, the Union army fell back to Nashville, where Thomas was reinforced by General A. J. Smith's forces. Hood followed Thomas, and laid siege to the town, throwing up earthworks. After a number of skirmishes, a battle was fought on December 13, resulting in about 1,000 killed and wounded on each side; over 1,000 prisoners, 16 guns, and several battle-flags fell into Union hands. No ground positively gained or lost. Firing was kept up next day, and on the 15th the Unionists were formed ready for action by 6 A. M. The enemy was surprised at the offensive operations. The different commanders of corps made a simultaneous attack on the enemy's whole line, drove him from his position, capturing 1,200 prisoners, 16 pieces of artillery, several thousand small arms, and 40 wagons. The Union loss was unusually light. Hood's killed were left on the field. Next day General Thomas's forces continued in pursuit toward Franklin to Hood's lines, formed during the night, at Overton's Hill, about 5 miles south of Nashville. His lines were assaulted at 3 P. M., and, after some hard fighting, they were broken, and the enemy fled precipitately, losing about 3,500 prisoners—over 200 being officers—40 pieces of artillery, and thousands of small arms. Hood again abandoned all his dead and wounded. The pursuit was continued several days.

Natchez, Miss., surrendered to Commander Palmer, of the "Iroquois," May 13, 1862. Rebel attacks upon the place were repulsed December 6, 1863, and January 23, 1864. The rebels, on the latter date, captured 30 prisoners, 60 wagons and teams, 80 negroes, and a lot of cotton.

Natchitoches, La., was occupied March 30, 1864, by General A. L. Lee, the rebels retiring with a loss of 30 men.

Neosho, Mo.—A battle was fought at this place April 26, 1862, between Major Hubbard (Union) and 146 men of the 1st Missouri Cavalry, and 600 Indians, under Colonels Coffee and Stainwright, resulting in the defeat of the Indians. Thirty Indians were killed, 62 taken prisoners, and a large quantity of stores captured.

Neutrality.—Queen Victoria, May 13, 1861, issued a proclamation, enjoining neutrality in the contest between the North and South. December 4 she prohibited the exportation of gunpowder, niter, nitrate of soda, brimstone, lead, and fire-arms.

Emperor Napoleon's Neutrality Proclamation was received in the United States June 24.

January 31, 1862, Queen Victoria declared her purpose to adhere to the duties of neutrality. Notwithstanding the proclaimed neutrality, and the order forbidding the export of war materials, the rebels continued, from the first, to receive from British subjects all the arms, ammunition, clothing, accoutrements, guns, war-vessels, etc., that they could pay for, either in cotton or gold.

New Albany, Ark., was, on October 5, 1863, the scene of a brisk cavalry skirmish.

Newark, Mo., was surrendered to the rebels, after a three hours' fight, August 1, 1862. Union loss, 4 killed and 5 wounded; rebel loss, about 100 killed and wounded.

New Baltimore, Va., was occupied by the Unionists November 5, 1862, the rebels retreating toward Warrenton. In a skirmish June 20, 1863, the rebels were victorious.

Newbern, N. C., after a heavy fight, was evacuated by the rebels and occupied by the Federal forces, March 14, 1862. The rebels, 10,000 strong, were behind strong intrenchments, two miles in extent, defended by 21 guns in position, besides a large quantity of field artillery. The batteries were taken one after another; the rebels fled, taking cars in the direction of Goldsboro. 46 heavy siege-guns, 3 light batteries, and 3,000 stand of small arms were among the prizes which fell to the victors. The Union loss was 90 or 100 killed and about 400 wounded.

A severe but undecisive skirmish occurred here April 27. Important Union expeditions left this point, which was made a base of supplies, April 17, June 25, November 2, and December 10. The last one, under General Foster, was absent eight days, during which time, it lost between 200 and 300 men. It fought four battles, and had numerous skirmishes along the Neuse River and railroad track. The battles of Goldsboro and Whitehall were splendid victories. A body of 4,000 rebels attacked Newbern, November 25, but were forced to retreat in disorder. A like attack, with like result, occurred March 13, 1863. Important raids left this point March 8, April 5, July 3, and October 10. Early on the morning of February 1, 1864, the rebels, said to be 15,000 strong, attacked the Union outposts at Bachelor's Creek, 8 miles from Newbern; the Unionists fell back before superior numbers, destroying their camp, a few stores, and losing 20 or 30 killed, and 200 captured; a section of artillery, 300 small arms, and a quantity of material were also lost. At the same time the rebels advanced on the south side of the Trent River, but were handsomely repulsed, losing 35 killed and wounded. The rebels next morning followed up the attack, capturing and destroying the Union gun-boat Underwriter. Attacks were made upon the place, February 7, 29, and May 10, all of which were repulsed. The town was fired by incendiaries in several places April 1, 1865, but little harm was done.

Newburg, Ind., was entered July 18, 1862, by Johnson's band of guerrillas, who robbed the citizens and hospital, and committed other depredations.

New Creek Valley, Va., was the scene of an engagement February 1, 1864. The rebels were defeated and driven two miles.

New Iberia, La., was occupied, and the rebel camp there broken up, November 19, 1863.

New Lisbon, O. (See John Morgan.)

New Madrid, Mo. (See Island No. 10.)

New Market, Va., was the scene of skirmishes November 29 and December 22, 1861. The Unionists surprised and defeated on the latter date. The place was occupied by General Banks April 17, 1862.

General Sigel, with 5,000 men, was badly repulsed at Rood's Mills, near New Market, May 15, 1864. He acted contrary to orders, in moving against Imboden, Echols, and Breckenridge. The enemy had an equal number of men, and drove the Union commander, in much disorder from the field. He lost in the engagement, and in the retreat to Strasburg, 30 miles distant, 800 men, killed, wounded, and missing, besides 6 guns and 1,000 small arms; he burned the most part of his train to prevent it falling into the hands of the foe.

Newnan, was the scene of a defeat to McCook's forces July 30, 1864.

New Orleans, at an early stage of the rebellion, declared against the Union. December 21, 1860, 100 guns were fired, and the Pelican flag raised as an indorsement of the secession of South Carolina. The Branch Mint and Custom-house were seized by the State authorities January 31, 1861. The city was blockaded by the sloop of war "Brooklyn," May 26; and September 18, the banks suspended specie payments. (See Farragut and Butler.)

In the fall of 1863, the rebels held several secret meetings, with a view of handing the city over to the

Confederates, but no action was taken. On January 8, 1864, an immense mass-meeting was held to consider the propriety of a free State Constitution, and on March 28 the Convention to revise the State Constitution met in this city.

Newport News was the scene of brisk naval skirmishes June 5, July 12, and December 2, 1861. The great Sawyer gun burst at this point February 11, 1862, killing 2 and wounding 5 men.

Newtonia, Mo., was the scene of Price's last defeat in the State, October 28, 1864. Rebel loss, 450; Union, 120.

New York City was thrown into some commotion by a secession meeting January 15, 1861. The forts in the harbor were fully armed and manned March 12, 1862. The most fearful riot during the rebellion occurred in this city, commencing July 12, 1863. Drafting commenced on the 11th, which, being misunderstood by some and misrepresented by others, produced immense excitement. On the 13th, the mobs were triumphant, the Tribune office was assailed, the Colored Orphan Asylum and Provost-marshals' offices in the 8th and 9th district burned. The military were called out on the 14th, and all cars and omnibuses stopped running. Governor Seymour issued a proclamation and addressed the mob, which continued next day, when the military fired upon them with considerable slaughter. Many of the large stores were sacked. The excitement began to wane on the 16th, and by the timely arrival of military forces, and the advice of Governor Seymour and Archbishop Hughes, for their "friends to disperse and calm down," the mob grew rapidly less, and, on the 17th the police commenced their search for stolen property. A peculiar feature of the mob was their hatred and murder of negroes and of Abolitionists, and of the most prominent men in the city, or State, counseling with the rioters as their "friends."

Nolan's Ferry, on the Potomac, was the scene of a skirmish July 22, 1863.

Nolansville, Tenn., was occupied by General Rosecrans's army, in their march upon Murfreesboro, December 27, 1862.

Nonconna, Tenn., was occupied and the rebel cavalry there dispersed April 18, 1863.

Norfolk, Ky., was the scene of a brisk skirmish September 29, 1861.

Norfolk, Mo., was the scene of a skirmish September 10, 1861.

Norfolk, Va., was almost unanimously secession at the outbreak of the rebellion. The main entrance to the harbor was, by order of Governor Letcher, obstructed April 17, 1861. On the night of May 9, 1862, 5,000 Union troops landed at Willoughby Point and marched toward Norfolk. At 5 P. M. they were met by a delegation of citizens, who formally surrendered the city and also Portsmouth. The Navy-yard, at Gosport, was almost entirely destroyed by fire. The expedition was superintended by the President in person.

North, Colonel Samuel, and others, of the New York agents, collecting the military vote of the State, were arrested for forgery October 27, 1864. The plan, as it appeared at the trial, was briefly to make lists of the dead New York soldiers and make them vote the Democratic State and Presidential tickets.

North Carolina.—The State Legislature, on January 30, 1861, submitted the question of a State convention to the people. The election was held February 28, and resulted against holding a convention—46,409 ayes, 46,603 nays. The Governor, on April 16, refused to furnish troops in response to the President's call. The Legislature, on May 1, passed a State convention bill. The convention met at Raleigh on the 20th, and next day unanimously passed an ordinance of secession and ratified the Confederate Constitution. The State was declared in insurrection August 16. A convention of delegates, representing 42 counties, met at Hatteras November 18, and declared against the action of the State convention held at Raleigh, and appointed Marble Nash Taylor, Provisional Governor, with power to fill official vacancies by temporary appointments.

Oak Grove, Va., was, on June 25, 1862, the scene of a seven hours' fight between General Hooker's division of the Army of the Potomac and the rebels. The rebels were driven back; loss, about 200 killed and wounded on each side.

Occoquan, Va., was occupied, and 31 Union soldiers captured, December 19, 1862, and nearly the same thing, with like result, repeated on the 27th.

Ocean Queen, a California steamer, was the scene of a conflict, May 16, 1864, between some rebels, disguised as pirates, and the crew. The rebels made an attempt to capture the vessel. Their leader was shot by Commander Ammen, and the rest ironed.

Okolona, Miss., was occupied by the Unionists February 13, 1864.

Old Church, Va., near Richmond, was the scene of driving in the Union pickets June 13, 1862.

Olive Hill, Ky., was the scene of a defeat to John Morgan October 3, 1862.

Opelika, Ala., was occupied, great quantities of hardware, cotton, tobacco, etc., destroyed, and the public warehouses burned, by the Union forces, under Rousseau, July 19, 1864.

Opelousa, La., was occupied by Banks's forces April 20, 1863.

Orange C. H., Va., which was occupied by two regiments of rebel cavalry, was taken by a party from Pope's army, August 2, 1862. Rebel loss, 11 killed, 52 prisoners; Union loss, 2 killed and 3 wounded.

Orangeburg, S. C., was occupied by Sherman's forces February 8, 1865.

Orange Grove, Fla., was occupied by the Union colored troops March 26, 1863.

Orange Springs, Va., was occupied by Stoneman April 29, 1863.

Order of American Knights, *alias* **"O. A. K's."**—During the spring of 1864, many rumors concerning this body were circulated in the country. June 28, General Carrington, commanding in Indiana, reported to Governor Morton on the existence of such a body. About the latter part of July arrests were made at Indianapolis, St. Louis, New York, and some other places. Fire-arms were seized and confiscated, and three men, at Indianapolis, sentenced to be hung, which sentence was commuted to life imprisonment, in the Ohio Penitentiary.

Orleans, Ind. (See John Morgan.)

Osceola, Mo., was the scene of a skirmish September 25, 1861.

Owensboro, Ky., was attacked by guerrillas September 19, 1862. The Colonel commanding the Unionists was killed, when the forces retired. Next day the rebels were driven out by the Spencer (Indiana) Home-guards with great loss. The home-guards had two men killed and 18 wounded.

Ozark, Mo., was the scene of a skirmish August 2, 1862.

Paducah, Ky., was taken possession of by General Grant, with two regiments, in the face of 4,000 rebel troops, September 6, 1861. The city was attacked, March 25, 1864, by Forrest, who soon drove the small Union force holding the place to the fort below the town. Forrest then demanded its surrender, and threatening, in the event of his storming the works, that he would extend no quarter. Colonel Hicks refused, and successfully resisted four separate assaults. Later in the day, three Union gun-boats arrived in the river, and, after a warm contest, drove the rebels out of the town. During the shelling of the gun-boats, the cowardly Forrest collected a number of women and children, and placed them in an exposed position, immediately in front of his lines; several were killed and wounded. A portion of the town was burned by the fire from the gun-boats, in all about 50 buildings. Colonel Hicks burned some buildings within range of the little fort. The cannonading continued until 10 o'clock. Before the gun-boats arrived the rebels sacked the town. The Union loss, in killed and wounded, numbered 80; the rebels sustained a somewhat greater loss.

Palmetto Station, 25 miles south of Atlanta, was occupied by General McCook July 28, 1864. He destroyed five miles of railroad, cars, supplies, etc.

Palmyra, Mo., was burned by the Union gun-boats March 4, 1863.

Paintsville, Ky., was captured from the rebels, under Humphrey Marshall, by the Unionists, under General Garfield, January 7, 1862.

Panther Springs, Tenn.—A body of rebels, under Major Goforth, attacked a picket of 93 men of the 3d

Tennessee, at this place, March 4, 1864. A desperate running fight ensued, the rebels being repulsed; loss slight on both sides.

Papinsville, Mo., then held by a large force of Confederates, was attacked September 21, 1861. The rebels lost 40 killed, 100 prisoners, and all their camp equipage. The place was burned by the Kansas Volunteers December 13.

Paratta, N. M., was the scene of a rebel defeat April 23, 1862.

Paris, Ill. (See Mattoon.)

Paris, Ky., was the scene of a Union victory July 30, 1862. Six companies of the 9th Pennsylvania Cavalry, after a march of two days and nights, overtook Morgan's guerrillas, drove in his pickets, and captured the town. Rebel loss, 27 killed, 30 wounded, and 9 prisoners. The rebels were repulsed here July 29, 1863.

Paris, Tenn.—At this place, March 12, 1862, the Unionists defeated a body of rebels, and took possession of the town, but learning that a large force of rebels were within a short distance, they retired.

Paris, Va., was the scene of a skirmish October 29, 1862.

Parksville, Mo., was sacked by guerrillas July 8, 1864.

Parsons. (See Canada Raids.)

Pascagoula, Miss., was captured April 10, 1863, by Colonel Daniels, with 900 colored troops. They next day drove off a large force of rebels, killing 20 and wounding a large number.

Pass Christian, Miss., was held by Union forces April 4, 1863.

Passports.—On April 19, 1861, the Secretary of State ordered that all persons leaving or entering the United States shall be possessed of a passport. On August 8, 1862, notice was given that no passports would be issued until the quota of troops should be filled.

Patapsco. (See Charleston.)

Patterson, Mo., was the scene of an indecisive skirmish April 20, 1863.

Patterson Creek, Va.—On June 26, 1861, Corporal Hays, and 12 men of the 11th Indiana Zouaves, attacked and routed 40 Confederate cavalry near this place, killing 8 men and capturing 17 horses. The Confederates, being reinforced by about 70, resumed the attack, but were met with such firmness that 23 of them fell. Five hundred rebel cavalry captured a company of Union troops, near this place, January 2, 1862. The prisoners were retaken, and the cavalry routed, next day.

Pawpaw, Tenn., was the scene of the capture of a squad of Unionists November 10, 1861.

Payne. (See Herold.)

Peace Conference.—The rebel Vice-President, A. H. Stephens, Senator R. M. T. Hunter, and Judge Campbell came, as Peace Commissioners, within Grant's lines January 30, 1865. They were taken to Fortress Monroe, where they were met by President Lincoln and Secretary Seward. Their exchange of views was full and free, but no agreement was made, and the parties separated to continue hostilities.

Peace Resolutions were numerous during the war, especially in 1863, and during the campaign of 1864. They were, almost without exception, monopolized by those styling themselves Democrats. Some of the more prominent of them were those of the New Jersey Legislature, passed March 18, 1863—38 ayes, 13 nays; those of the New York Democracy, expressing sympathy with Vallandigham, passed May 15, 1863; those of the Philadelphia Democracy, for the same purpose, passed June 1, 1863; those of the Brooklyn "peace party," June 12, 1863; those of the Chicago Convention, August 29, 1864.

Peach Orchard.—The battle at this place and Savage Station was fought June 29, 1862. After the battle of the Chickahominy, the Confederates still pressed on the Union troops, who reserved their fire until the rebels were within close range, when they fired, with terrible effect. General Burns's brigade of Sumner's corps, bore the hottest of the fight. Sumner held the rebels in check until night.

Peach Tree Creek, Ga. (See Atlanta.)

Pea Ridge, Ark.—A battle was fought at this place, commencing March 6, 1862, between the rebels (about 35,000), under McCulloch, and the Federals (about 22,000), under Curtis. The rebels commenced the attack on the right wing of the Union army, pursuing General Sigel's rear guard to the main lines on Sugar Creek; but, about 4 o'clock in the afternoon, the Union reinforcements coming up, the rebels withdrew, and the action ceased. Both armies slept on their arms during the night. Next day, at 11 o'clock, the rebels attacked the right of the Union lines. The fight was heavy here during the day, and the losses severe; General McCulloch fell mortally wounded. On the morning of the 8th, at sunrise, firing was renewed by the center and right of General Curtis's forces. The fire was replied to with great energy by the whole rebel line. General Curtis ordered the center and left wing forward—the left turning the right of the enemy. A charge was then made by the whole line, which resulted in the complete rout of the rebel forces, and their flight through the deep defiles of Big Sugar Creek. The Union loss in this battle was 212 killed, 926 wounded, and 174 missing; rebel loss, 1,100 killed, 2,400 wounded, 1,600 prisoners, and 13 guns.

Pennsylvania Invasion.—Lee commenced his movement up the Rappahannock June 12, 1863, preparatory to his march into Pennsylvania. His forces were estimated at 90,000 to 100,000. The rebel rear left Fredericksburg on the 13th. The same day there was skirmishing at Edward's Ferry and Middleton, Pa. General Milroy, at Winchester, Va., was, on the 14th, nearly surrounded by 18,000 men, under General Ewell, who carried his outer works. The rebels advanced on Martinsburg, and demanded its surrender, which General Tyler refused. An artillery fight followed, after which General Tyler retreated to Harper's Ferry. General Milroy, at 1 o'clock P. M., on the 15th, evacuated Winchester, first spiking his guns; four miles out he was compelled to cut his way through. He lost about 2,000 men, 3 batteries of artillery, 6,000 muskets, 280 wagons, etc. The same day President Lincoln called out 100,000 men for six months. Governor Curtin, of Pennsylvania, called out 50,000 militia to repel the threatened invasion. Jenkins's rebel cavalry entered Chambersburg at 9 P. M.; they burned the railroad bridge at Scotland, six miles from Chambersburg. The rebels occupied Harper's Ferry. General Tyler retreated to Maryland Heights, and shelled them out, when they retreated to Williamsport. Colonel Smith was surrounded by the rebels at Hagerstown, and, after fighting an hour and a half, was compelled to surrender.

17th.—2,000 rebel cavalry advanced 11 miles beyond Chambersburg, in the direction of Harrisburg, and the Federals evacuated Frederick, Md.

18th.—Harrisburg, Penn., was fortified. Jenkins's cavalry evacuated Chambersburg at 1 P. M. The rebels captured and burned a train of 23 cars at Point of Rocks, Md., and carried off the passengers. Hagerstown was occupied by General Rhodes and 3,000 Confederates. General Lee occupied Thoroughfare Gap.

19th.—Jenkins plundered McConnellsburg, Penn., and drove off $12,000 worth of cattle.

20th.—General Schenck called on the citizens of Baltimore to rally to the defense of the city. Baltimore appropriated $100,000 for the defense of the city.

21st.—The rebels fortified Hagerstown, and a force of their cavalry reached Gettysburg.

23d.—Pittsburg was fortified.

24th.—The rebels occupied Chambersburg

25th.—There was a skirmish at McConnellsburg, Penn.; the Unionists retired before superior numbers. The Union forces, being insufficient to hold it, evacuated Carlisle.

26th.—Gettysburg was occupied by Early's division, and General Rhodes's division occupied Chambersburg.

27th.—General Meade succeeded General Hooker in command of the Army of the Potomac. The rebel army occupied Carlisle, Penn.; the advance of their army reached Kingstown, 13 miles from Harrisburg. General Lee at Chambersburg.

28th.—Great excitement throughout Pennsylvania on account of the rebel invasion. In Philadelphia all business was suspended, and drilling took its place. Mechanicsburg and York, Penn., occupied by rebels.

29th.—The rebel troops tore up the Baltimore and Ohio Railroad at Sykesville, and the Northern Central, from Galesboro to York, 16 miles. Fight at McConnellsburg; rebels defeated, losing 3 killed and 33 prisoners; Union loss, 2 wounded. General Lee and staff were at Carlisle. The 1st Delaware (Union) Cavalry were chased to within five miles of Baltimore. They fought with sabers and revolvers, until, overpowered by superior numbers, they were scattered; 15 out of 110 reported at Baltimore.

30th.—General Pleasanton's cavalry drove the rebels from Gettysburg and occupied the place. General Early issued an address to the people of York, saying that he abstained from firing the depot buildings, as it would endanger the whole town, and he did not wish to punish the innocent with the guilty. He afterward evacuated the place. The rebel army, 40,000 strong, with 40 pieces of artillery, left Carlisle for Gettysburg. The Army of the Potomac occupied York and Hanover, thus cutting the rebel lines. General Schenck declared martial law in Baltimore city and county, and the counties on the western shore of Maryland. The response to his appeal for public defense was prompt and enthusiastic.

July 1.—Fight at Carlisle, Penn. The rebels were gradually driven back, and our forces occupied the town. The rebels afterward returned and demanded the surrender of the town, which being refused, they commenced to shell it. During the fight they made a detour and burned the barracks, gas-works, several lumber yards, and private buildings. Union loss is stated at 10 wounded. Rebel loss, not known. Cavalry fight at Hanover, Penn., lasting nearly all the afternoon. Union loss, about 200. Rebel loss, 400 killed, wounded, and prisoners, and six pieces of artillery.

The battle of **Gettysburg** opened at 9 A. M. this morning by an attack on the 1st and 11th Corps, by the rebels under Longstreet and Hill; the 1st Corps being in advance, sustained the whole shock until the other came up. The fight was severe, and attended with heavy loss. Major-General Reynolds was mortally wounded.

Next day (the 2d) the rebels attacked the Union lines at 4 P. M., but, after a severe contest, were repulsed at all points; upward of 6,000 prisoners reported taken.

The 3d was the fiercest of the three days' fight. The

rebels attempted to turn Meade's left flank, but were repulsed, losing 3,000 prisoners. The fighting was most furious, and the slaughter terrible; the loss in officers on both sides was heavy. The rebel loss was estimated at 2,439 killed, 14,580 wounded, and 6,235 prisoners taken. The Union loss is set down at 14,000 killed and wounded. 20 battle-flags were taken by one corps.

The town was occupied by General Meade on the 4th. He issued a congratulatory letter to his army, thanking them for the glorious results of the recent operations, and telling them he looked to them for yet greater efforts. This virtually ended the invasion, General Lee now being in full retreat.

General Kilpatrick captured and burned, near Hagerstown, Md., nearly 300 wagons of Ewell's train, and ran off the horses.

5th.—The rebels retreated to Chambersburg and Greencastle, Penn., abandoning their dead and wounded. Jeff. Davis's dispatches to Lee intercepted. Davis said he could not reinforce Lee, and ordered his return to Richmond.

6th.—General Pleasanton occupied the mountain passes near Chambersburg, impeding Lee's retreat. Battle near Mercersburg, Penn., between Fitzhugh Lee and General Pierce. General Gregg, of Pleasanton's cavalry, had a fight with the rebels at Fayetteville, Penn., taking 4,000 prisoners. Lee retreated toward the Potomac, his army utterly routed; Meade in close pursuit. The Potomac commenced rising, damaging the rebel pontoon bridges. His army reached Hagerstown on the 7th. Up to the 9th he had lost over 500 wagons, and his losses were continual and heavy until the 14th, when he crossed the Potomac at Williamsport and Falling Waters. The Union cavalry, under Kilpatrick, captured 1,500 prisoners, 3 battle-flags, a section of artillery and a lot of small arms belonging to Lee's rear guard.

Pensacola. (See Fort Pickens.)

Perryville, Ky. (See Chaplin Hill.)

Petersburg, Va. (See Richmond and Grant's Report.)

Petty's Mills, N. C.—A rebel camp, near this place, was surprised May 5, 1863, and 14 men, 36 horses, and the whole camp captured, without loss.

Philadelphia, Tenn., was occupied by the rebels, and Colonel Woolford's wagon train and battery captured, October 21, 1863.

Philomont, Va.—General Pleasanton's cavalry overtook the rebels at this place November 1, 1862, and, after a short skirmish, the rebels fell back to Union. The fight was renewed next morning, when the rebels were compelled to abandon the ground in confusion, and with heavy loss. Union loss, 12 killed and wounded.

Phillippi, Va., was occupied, and the rebel camp there dispersed, June 19, 1861. A guerrilla band captured and burned 13 of a train of 26 wagons, on the road near this place, August 27, 1863, and ran off the horses and mules.

Piedmont, Va., was occupied by a rebel force June 20, 1861. The place was occupied by Union cavalry November 3, 1862. Major Cole's Maryland cavalry had a skirmish with Mosby's cavalry at Piedmont, February 20, 1864, and took 17 prisoners, including 3 officers; 5 were killed, and a number wounded; Union loss, 2 killed and 2 wounded.

Pikeville, Ky., was occupied, and 78 Union troops taken prisoners, April 15, 1863.

Pilatka, Fla., was occupied by Federal troops March 10, 1864.

Pilot Knob, Mo., was occupied, after driving out the rebels, October 16, 1861. On September 26, 1864, General Ewing repulsed a charge of the enemy at Pilot Knob, killing rebel General Cabell. General Ewing afterward blew up the fort and retreated.

Pine Bluff, Ark., was the scene of a rebel repulse October 28, 1863. Near this place, on April 25, 1864, a superior force of rebels, under Drake, attacked 200 wagons and 4 guns, a portion of General Steele's train, which, with the escort, nearly 2,000 men, were captured.

Pine Mountain. (See Kenesaw.)

Piney Factory, Tenn. Lieutenant-Colonel Shively, with the 1st Middle Tennessee Infantry, attacked Hawkins's guerrillas, at this place, October 30, 1863, and routed them, pursued them to Centerville, where they made a stand, and were again defeated. The rebel loss was 20 killed and 66 wounded.

Pittsburg Landing, Tenn.—Two gun-boats of Commodore Foote's fleet engaged the rebel batteries at this point March 1, 1862. The batteries were reinforced, and three regiments of infantry opened on the gun-boats, but were driven back with great slaughter. Union loss, 5 killed and missing, and 5 wounded; rebel loss, about 20 killed and 200 wounded. In a skirmish April 4, the rebels lost 40 killed and 10 prisoners; Union loss, 1 killed. (See Shiloh.)

Platte City, Mo., was the scene of a spirited engagement November 2, 1862. The town was fired, and the principal houses burned December 16. The city was taken by Thornton's guerrillas July 26, 1865. It was garrisoned by 70 "Pawpaw" militia, who surrendered without resistance; 55 of whom joined the enemy.

Plattsburg, Mo., was the scene of an undecisive skirmish, October 27, 1861.

Pleasant Hill, Mo., was the scene of an engagement between the State militia and a band of guerrillas July 11, 1862; guerrillas defeated.

Pleasant Hill, La.—After the engagement at Mansfield (which see), General A. J. Smith and the 16th Corps were formed in line of battle, at this place, April 9, 1864. The disorganized and more intact portions of the army had arrived the evening previous, after their severe repulse. At 4 o'clock, P. M., they received the onslaughts of Dick Taylor's forces, who, in the early part of the fray, gained ground, steadily driving the Union troops. General Smith, who showed undoubted evidence of personal bravery throughout the day, maneuvered into more favorable positions than he had previously held, and toward evening rallied his men, and succeeded, by some well-directed assaults, in routing the over-confident foe, with much loss. Their discomfiture was only a little less disastrous than that of the Unionists the day before. The Union Generals, however, did not consider themselves strong enough to hold the field, so fell back to Grand Ecore. General A. J. Smith covered himself with glory, and literally saved Banks from annihilation. There was over 6,000 men killed and wounded, on both sides, in the battles of the 8th and 9th. The rebels lost heavily in prisoners, besides Ex-Governor and General Moreton and Parsons killed.

Plymouth, N. C., was attacked September 2, 1862, by 1,400 rebels. After fighting about half an hour, the rebels fled, having lost 30 killed and 40 prisoners. The Unionists lost 3 killed. The town was nearly all destroyed by the rebels December 10. Five thousand rebels, with 15 guns, aided by the ram Albemarle and four gun-boats, made an attack on this place April 17, 1864. The ram sunk the United States gun-boat Whitehead, of 3 guns. At the same time, a land attack was made on Fort Gray; three assaults were repulsed, with some loss to the attacking party. The Federal gun-boat Miami, Captain Flusser, the Ceres, and the Bombshell, got under weigh for Fort Gray, but, before reaching there, they were attacked by the artillery, which they soon drove from their position. Next morning the ram Albemarle floated down the river, and was under the bows of the Miami before she was discovered. Captain Flusser fired his bow-gun, loaded with shell, which rebounded, killing him instantly. The Miami turned, ran down the river, and escaped. The ram then attacked and sunk the Southfield, captured the Bombshell, and dropped down to Plymouth, holding command of the river, and threatening the garrison holding Fort Gray. The 19th was a day of comparative quiet, but, on the morning of the 20th, the rebels assaulted Fort Williams, and, after a violent storm, it was captured. The rebel gun-boats rendered ample assistance in reducing the place. Union loss, 200 killed and wounded, and 1,500 prisoners; rebel loss, 100 killed and wounded.

The place was captured by the Unionists October 31. After a severe shelling from the fleet, 100 men were landed, and stormed Fort Bateman, capturing 200 prisoners, 40 pieces of heavy and 12 pieces of light artillery; a magazine was exploded by a shell, and the town fired by the explosion.

Pocahontas, Ark., was occupied, and 100 rebels, including Jeff. C. Thompson and staff, captured, April 22, 1863.

Pocotaligo, S. C., was the scene of a skirmish May 29, 1862. The Union forces attempted to gain possession of the Charleston and Savannah Railroad, at this point, October 22. The railroad bridge was destroyed, but the rebels being strongly reinforced, the position could not be held. Union loss, 30 killed, 180 wounded, and 3 missing. A grandson of J. C. Calhoun was killed by a scouting party at this place November 23, 1863. The town was occupied, and the rebels there driven out or captured, by Sherman's forces, January 15, 1865.

Pohick Church, Va., was occupied by 400 Unionists October 4, 1861.

Pohick Run, Va., was the scene of an indecisive skirmish January 9, 1862.

Point of Rocks, Md., was the scene of a skirmish August 5, 1861. The rebels attempted to build fortifications opposite this place, but were driven back, November 14. The Union forces were victorious in a brisk engagement here December 19.

Point Pleasant, Mo., was, on March 9, 1862, occupied by Federals, thus cutting the communication between New Madrid and the main Confederate army down the river.

Point Pleasant, Va., was captured by 100 rebels March 30, 1863. They were subsequently driven out, with a loss of 19 killed and 15 prisoners. Union loss, 2 killed and 3 wounded.

Polk, Trusten, of Mo., was expelled from the United States Senate January 10, 1862.

Pollard, Ala., was occupied by Union forces December 16, 1864, the railroad destroyed, and public buildings burned, etc. General Steele defeated a rebel force near this place March 25, 1865, mortally wounding and taking Clauton, their commander, capturing 250 prisoners, seizing two railway trains, and tearing up the Montgomery Railroad track.

Pollocksville, N. C.—An expedition from Newbern encountered 1,800 rebels at this place January 17, 1863, and drove them from the town and took possession. A number were wounded on both sides.

Pomeroy, Ohio. (See John Morgan.)

Pontachoula, La., was occupied by Union troops March 24, 1863. The combined forces of white and Indian rebels were defeated here May 13.

Pontotoc, Miss., was occupied by A. J. Smith's forces July 11, 1864.

Poolesville, Md., was the scene of a fight September 8, 1862. Rebels defeated, losing 7 killed; Union loss, 1 killed and 8 wounded. November 25, 60 Confederate cavalry crossed the Potomac and captured and paroled two telegraph operators at Poolesville. (See Pennsylvania Invasion.)

Pope, Major-General John, was assigned to the command of the Army of the Mississippi December 7, 1861, where he did gallant and noble service, clearing Missouri of Price and his forces. In connection with Foote, he invested and captured Island No. 10. While in pursuit of the rebels, after the battle of Shiloh, he was called to Washington, June 26, 1862, and July 14 assumed command of the Army of Virginia, and issued his famous orders, discarding the idea of maintaining lines of retreat and base of support. On the 23d he ordered the arrest of all disloyal male citizens within the lines of his command. A retaliatory order was issued by the rebel Government, August 1, and General Pope and his officers declared not to be entitled to the privileges of prisoners of war. His campaign was signally a failure, and September 8 he was relieved of his command, and assigned to that of the Army of the North-west.

Porter, D. D., was, soon after the outbreak of the rebellion, placed in command of the steam sloop-of-war, Powhatan, ranking No. 77 in the list of commanders. After a short time in the blockading service, he was called to take charge of the Mortar expedition. For a history of his service, see Forts Jackson and St. Phillip, Vicksburg, Port Hudson, etc. He now bears rank as Rear-Admiral.

Porter, Fitz John, by gallant service, won the rank of Major-General of volunteers. September 6, 1862, General Pope preferred against him charges of insubordination. He was dismissed the service January 22, 1863.

Port Gibson, Miss.—Early on the morning of May 1, 1863, Grant's forces met the rebels about four miles from Port Gibson. Here the roads branched and ran along narrow, elevated ridges, with deep ravines on either side, the rebels occupying both branches in strong positions. On the right the Unionists drove the enemy steadily all day. On the left the rebels held their ground until nearly night, when they retreated, to make no further stand south of Bayou Pierre. On the road leading to Port Gibson the rebels were pursued until nightfall, when the troops slept upon their arms until daylight.

This was called the battle of Port Gibson, or of Thompson's Hills. The rebel loss was very heavy, and the Union loss was about 850 in killed and wounded. The contest had been a bloody one, but the results assured the capture of Port Gibson and the evacuation of Grand Gulf.

The next morning McClernand's advance entered Port Gibson, the enemy having retreated, burning the bridge over Bayou Pierre.

Port Hudson, La., was bombarded March 14, 1863. Admiral Farragut passed the batteries with a portion of his fleet. The Mississippi was grounded and burned by the rebel batteries. Of her crew 22 were killed and 42 taken prisoners. Little more was done until May 8, when the bombardment was renewed; no reply was elicited until the 10th, when the rebel batteries were silenced. A division of General Banks's army, May 21, had a nine hours' fight with the rebels on the Bayou Sara road, four miles in rear of Port Hudson. The rebels were defeated, losing 1,000 prisoners and a large number of killed and wounded left on the field. They retired within their intrenchments. Union loss, 12 killed and 60 wounded. The place was invested May 26, and the attack made next morning, by an assault on the rebel works in rear, and the bombardment by the fleet in front. The outer line of works was taken, but with a loss of between 2,000 and 3,000 men. The 2d Louisiana (colored) Regiment lost 600 out of 900 men.

The bombardment continued, with frequent skirmishings, until June 14, when General Banks made a partially successful attack. He gained a position within 100 yards of the fortifications. He lost 700 men killed and wounded. Finally, after two months' siege, the place surrendered July 8. 5,500 prisoners, 2 steamers, 60 guns, 5,000 small arms, 150,000 rounds cartridges, and

44,800 pounds of cannon-powder were among the captures.

Port Republic, Va., was the scene of a battle June 9, 1862. After a severe engagement, the Federals were forced to retire, with the loss of 2 guns and a large number of killed and wounded.

Port Royal, S. C.—The Union fleet, after several days preparation and reconnoitering, made an attack on Forts Walker and Beauregard, commanding the entrance to Port Royal harbor, November 9, 1861, and after a five hours' fight the forts surrendered. The action is represented as most valorous, and the destruction by shells from the fleet terrible. The Union loss was 8 killed and 23 wounded. Rebel loss, heavy. The rebels fled, leaving behind them all their private property.

The islands adjacent were occupied by Union forces, and the work of cotton-picking on the plantations commenced December 11. Skirmishes occurred near here January 2, 5, 26, and August 29, 1862, in the last of which a rebel battery was captured. The rebels operating in 8 large flatboats attempted to capture the Union pickets at Jenkins Island, Port Royal harbor, March 19, 1864, but were driven off.

Port Royal, Va.—The Union gun-boats having been fired upon by the rebel batteries in front of Port Royal, Va., shelled the town, and destroyed a number of its best buildings, December 10, 1862; the batteries, after a two hours' engagement, were silenced. Union loss, 2 killed and 4 wounded. An artillery duel came off here September 1, 1863.

Potosi, Mo., was the scene of a skirmish and rebel defeat May 17, and August 9, 1861; but the result was different October 15, when Jeff. Thompson captured 50 Union troops.

Pound Gap, Tenn., was taken by General Garfield, March 16, 1862, after defeating a body of rebels posted there.

Prairie d'Anna, Ark., was abandoned by Price April 17, 1864, after being flanked by Steele.

Prairie Grove, near Fayetteville, Ark., was the scene of a hard-fought battle December 7, 1862, there having been, three days previous, skirmishing. The rebels made a feint in front of Blunt, and sent the main body to attack General Herron, who was advancing to reinforce Blunt. Blunt hastily moved forward, and arrived in time to prevent a flank movement on Herron's right; and, at 1:45 P. M., the engagement became general along the whole line. The battle raged fiercely and with great slaughter till dark, the contending armies alternately advancing and retiring. During the night the Confederates retreated over the Boston Mountains, abandoning their dead and wounded. The Union loss in the engagement was killed, 167; wounded, 798; missing, 1,148. Rebel loss estimated at 3,000 killed and wounded, of whom nearly 1,000 were buried on the field.

Prentiss, Miss., was shelled and burned by the Union forces September 18, 1862.

Prestonburg, Ky., was occupied by General Nelson, (Union) November 5, 1861. General Garfield overtaking Humphrey Marshall's forces at the forks of Middle Creek, near this place, January 10, 1862, a fight ensued, which resulted in the total defeat of the rebels.

Princeton, Ky., was the scene of a repulse to John Morgan, June 10, 1864.

Prisoners.—Nothing, during the war, more exasperated the Unionists of the nation than the starvation of Federal prisoners of war in the Confederate prison-pens. Andersonville, Libby, and Salisbury were, for some time at the North, considered as synonymous with murder and starvation. It was a common thing when Union soldiers were taken prisoners, for them to be stripped of their clothing, leaving them only their drawers, shirt, and mayhap a blanket. With this short allowance of clothing the men were kept, during the winter even, without any other shelter than they could contrive by excavating a pit, and covering it with their blankets. At Andersonville, for some time, the daily ration was eight ounces of Indian meal (kernel and cob ground together), and for sleeping apartments—they all had one—bounded by the prison walls, roofed by the vaulted arch of heaven, with mother earth for a bed. The result was, death to thousands, idocy to many, and the loss of feet and limbs to others.

On October 29, 1863, a boat-load of exchanged Union

prisoners arrived at Annapolis, Md., several having died on the way, the result of exposure and starvation while in rebel hands. Indignation meetings were held throughout the North, and supplies collected and forwarded for the relief of these suffering patriots. The Confederate authorities, for a time, allowed them to be delivered, but through their officers, on December 12, 1863, notified the Union authorities that no more supplies would be admitted within their lines. Colonel Ould (rebel commissioner of exchange) on March 17, 1863, in a report to his superiors, seemingly exulted over the result of this inhuman course, and added: "The arrangements I have made (for exchanging prisoners) works largely in our favor. We get rid of a set of miserable wretches, and receive some of the best material I ever saw." A portion of the rebel Congress remonstrated with Jeff. Davis against the treatment of Union prisoners of war, but obtained no change for the better. General Winder, when remonstrated with on the subject by one of his officers, replied, "the G—d d—d wretches are not dying half fast enough." Henry Wirz was a fit subordinate, too, for such a chief. May 2, 1864, of 400 exchanged prisoners, 150 had to be carried to hospital; many died on their way and after their arrival. It was, on May 15, 1865, estimated that there had been, during the past two years, *sixty-four thousand* Union soldiers starved to death in rebel prisons. As a contrast with this, out of 500 rebel prisoners confined at Camp Chase, Ohio, who were ordered exchanged, 260 voted to remain, preferring their place there to liberty in the so-called Confederacy.

Proclamations. (See Appendix.)

Public Debt. (See Appendix.)

Pulaski, Tenn., was occupied by the rebels, who captured 250 Union troops, May 2, 1862. The town was occupied by General Rousseau, September 26, 1864, after whipping Forrest, and driving him toward Lafayette. Thomas, in his retreat before Hood, occupied the town November 23, 1864.

Putnam's Ferry, Ark., was the scene of a skirmish, and rebel defeat, April 1, 1862.

Putnam's Ferry, Mo., was held by the Unionists October 27, 1862, after defeating a force of 1,500 rebels.

Quaker Church, Va., was, on June 17, 1864, the scene of an undecisive action between Hunter and Imboden.

Quallatown, N. C., was occupied by a Union expedition from Knoxville, February 7, 1864, after surprising Thomas and his white and Indian forces stationed there. Rebel loss, 215 killed and wounded, and 50 prisoners; Union loss, 8 killed and wounded.

Queen City, Union gun-boat, was attacked June 23, 1864, near Clarendon, Ark., by a large force with 4 guns, and, after a sharp fight of half an hour, surrendered. Her stores were hastily removed, when she was blown up by her captors. Three gun-boats arrived soon after, ran the batteries, drove off the rebels, and recaptured one of the Queen City's guns. Union loss, 40 men.

Queen of the West, Union ram, was captured by the rebels at Gordon's Landing, on Red River, February 14, 1863, through the treachery of the pilot, who ran her aground under the guns of the rebel batteries; 20 prisoners and 30 negroes were taken.

Raleigh, N. C., was occupied, without resistance, by the Union troops April 13, 1865.

Rappahannock River.—On August 21, 1862, the two armies faced each other on opposite sides of the Rappahannock. The rebels attempted to cross, but were driven back by General Reno. Cannonading continued next day. General Schurz crossed the river in the morning, and drove the rebels back, who rallied, and a severe fight ensued, which lasted till night, when the Union troops, not being strong enough to hold the advanced position, retired across the river. The battle was resumed on the 23d; the rebels succeeded in crossing the river in the vicinity of Sulphur Springs, upon which an engagement ensued, which resulted in the rebels being driven across Great Run. General Pope subsequently fell back to Warrenton and Sulphur Springs.

Raymond, Miss. (See Farnden's Creek.)

Readyville, Tenn., was captured September 7, 1864, by Colonel Jordan, with about 250 of the 9th Pennsylvania Cavalry, after defeating Dibrell's rebel brigade, 2,000 strong, killing and wounding many, and taking over 100 prisoners. Union loss, small.

Resaca, Ga., was occupied by Johnson, on his retreat

before Sherman, May 14, 1864, and the latter immediately attacked. After two days' hard fighting, Johnson was compelled to evacuate this strong position, and before night of the 15th Hooker was in vigorous pursuit. Nine railroad trains, loaded with rebel stores, designed for Dalton, were captured by McPherson near Resaca on the 13th. Hood demanded the surrender of the place October 12, which Colonel Weaver, commanding, refused. The summons threatened, if surrender was refused, to take no prisoners. After some fighting, the rebels withdrew.

Richland, Ky.—Morgan's guerrillas captured a train on the Louisville and Nashville Railroad near this place March 17, 1863, and were robbing it when they were dispersed by a detachment of Union soldiers, who killed several of them.

Richmond, Ky.—A battle commenced here August 29, 1862, by a portion of the Union forces attacking, to check the rebel advance on the town. Coming upon them, General Manson opened with his artillery, and in a few minutes the whole line was engaged. After a severe fight of an hour, the rebels were driven beyond Rogersville. Early next morning the Confederates advanced upon the Unionists and drove them back. The battle raged with varying success all day. The Unionists were finally compelled to retreat. The Union loss is set down at 400 killed, 1,100 wounded, and 3,000 prisoners; the rebel loss was 250 killed and 500 wounded.

The town was, on February 22, 1863, entered by a body of 700 cavalry, under Chenault, Tucker, and Cluke, the Federal garrison falling back to Lexington.

A force of rebels, under Pegram, about 2,500 strong, with six pieces of artillery, attacked a small Union garrison at this place July 27. After a severe fight of an hour, the Unionists were compelled to fall back to the Kentucky River.

Richmond, La., was captured by the Unionists June 13, 1863.

Richmond, Mo., was captured May 19, 1863, by guerrillas, who killed two or three men, and captured the whole guard of the town.

Richmond, Va., was, at an early period of the rebellion, chosen as the "Confederate Capital." (For the battles of 1862, see Fair Oaks, Cross Keys, Oak Grove, Mechanicsville, Gains's Mills, Peach Orchard, White Oak Swamp, Malvern Hill; for a history of Grant's movements against and final capture of the city, see Grant's Report.)

Rich Mountain, Va., was the scene of a battle July 11, 1861. 3,000 Confederates, under Pegram, was here strongly intrenched. The Unionists made the attack. General Rosecrans, with three Indiana and one Ohio regiments, made a circuit of the camp, and, by 3 o'clock P. M., attacked in the rear. After a fight of an hour and a half the Confederates were defeated, losing "all they had," with 60 killed and a large number wounded. Rosecrans lost 20 killed and 40 wounded. During the night the rebels retreated toward Beverly.

Rienzi, Miss.—The 3d battalion of the 5th Ohio Cavalry and a detachment of the 66th Illinois surprised and captured a force of between 3,000 and 4,000 rebels, encamped near this place, July 18, 1863. Sturgis's cavalry occupied the town June 7, 1864.

Rienzi, Mo., was the scene of an indecisive skirmish August 27, 1862.

Ringgold, Ga., was occupied by the Union forces, after some fighting, November 27, 1863, but evacuated December 1, the troops again concentrating at Chattanooga. The place was then held by the rebels, who left it January 31, 1864, and the Unionists occupied it again February 21.

Ripley, Miss., was occupied by Sturgis's cavalry June 5, 1864. A body of Confederates, posted at this place, were dispersed with considerable loss, by General A. J. Smith's forces, July 8, 1864.

Ripley, Tenn., was occupied, and the rebel camp there broken up, January 8, 1863. Rebel loss, 8 killed, 20 wounded, 45 prisoners; Union loss, small.

Roanoke Island. (See Burnside.)

Roan Springs, Tenn., was the scene of a skirmish and rebel defeat November 2, 1863.

Roan's Tan-yard, Randolph Co., Mo., was, on January 8, 1862, the scene of a battle between the rebels, 1,000 strong, and the Union forces, numbering 480 men.

After half an hour's feeble resistance, the rebels broke and fled, leaving every thing behind.

Rockingham, Ga., was occupied by General Howard December 12, 1864.

Rocky Face Ridge. (See Tunnel Hill.)

Rogersville, Ala., was occupied by General Negley May 13, 1862, after driving out the rebels, who crossed the river.

Rogersville, Tenn., was occupied November 5, 1863, by the rebels, who captured 800 men and 4 guns. The 13th Tennessee Cavalry met a band of guerrillas here August 22, 1864, of whom they killed 23 and wounded 35.

Romney, Va.—The Indiana Zouaves, Colonel Lew. Wallace, surprised a body of 500 Confederate troops at this place June 11, 1861, and routed them, killing two and wounding one seriously.

General Kelley, with 2,500 men, attacked the Confederate outposts at Mill Creek, about five miles from Romney, and drove them upon the main body, at Indian Mound Cemetery, to the west of the town, where they made a stand on a commanding position, and opened fire with 12-pounder rifled guns and a howitzer. General Kelley ordered a charge upon the batteries, which was being executed in gallant style, when the rebels broke and fled precipitately through the town toward Winchester. Rebel loss, 450 prisoners, a number killed and wounded, and a large amount of war material; Union loss, 2 killed, 11 wounded. General Lander occupied the place February 7, 1862.

Rosecrans, Wm. S., was, at the outbreak of the war, appointed as chief engineer on McClellan's staff. Governor Dennison appointed him Colonel of the 23d Ohio Volunteers June 10, 1861, and ten days later the President appointed him Brigadier-General in the Regular Army. He assumed command of the Department of the Ohio July 22. He took his place at the head of the Army of the Mississippi June 26, 1862, and he was made Major-General of volunteers soon after. He assumed command of the Army of the Cumberland October 30. On February 10, 1863, he issued an order declaring that rebel soldiers found in Federal uniforms, or carrying the Federal flag, shall not be treated as prisoners of war or receive quarter in battle.

A joint resolution of Congress, of March 3, thanked "General Rosecrans and his soldiers for gallantry and good conduct in the battle of Murfreesboro."

He was succeeded by General Thomas, October 25, 1863, and assumed command of the Missouri Department January 30, 1864. He held this position until December 2, when he was succeeded by General Dodge. (See Murfreesboro, Chickamauga, etc.)

Roseville, Ark.—About 400 Texan cavalry attempted to surprise a camp of 250 Federals, at this place, April 11, 1864. but were repulsed, losing 70 killed and wounded. Union loss about half as many.

Ross, John, the Cherokee chief, on June 19, 1861, urged neutrality upon his nation, reminding them of their obligations to the Government.

Rosswell, Ga. (See Rousseau.)

Rough and Ready, Ga., was the scene of General Howard driving General Iverson toward Jonesboro, November 16, 1864.

Round Top Mountain, Va.—General Sheridan's cavalry fought nearly the entire force of the rebel cavalry, at this place, October 9, 1864. The rebels were defeated, driven from the field, and pursued 26 miles; 11 pieces of artillery and 180 men taken, with ambulance and wagon trains.

Rousseau.—During the rebellion, perhaps no General in his sphere did more gallant service, or was better loved by his men, than General Rousseau. Raiding was his delight; one is mentioned as an example:

Rousseau left Decatur, Ala., July 10, 1864, with 2,700 cavalry. He crossed the Coosa River, on the 13th, and was immediately attacked by some Alabama cavalry, which he soon scattered, killing and capturing many He then visited Talladega, Tylocouga, Loachapoka, and Opelika, destroying quantities of niter and commissary stores; also large iron-works. He destroyed 30 miles of the Montgomery and West Point Railroad, burning all the bridges and culverts, with 13 depots, besides capturing a train, heavily laden with provisions and cotton At all of the aforementioned towns, he met with spirited opposition from large bands of rebels; as also at the crossing of the Tallapoosa River. General Rousseau returned to Marietta, Georgia, having been over a week out. He lost only some 50 killed and wounded. Nearly 1,000 of the enemy were captured and paroled, and over 100 killed and wounded; 600 horses and mules were among the spoils collected. He thus made a successful circuit of 250 miles, starting from Northern Alabama, penetrating two-thirds of the State, approaching close to Montgomery, and thence pushing a north-easterly course some days, reached Marietta.

Russelville, Ala., was occupied by Wilson's cavalry, without opposition, March 24, 1865.

Sabbath.—An order for the strict observance of the Sabbath in the army was issued, by General McClellan, September 7, 1861, and President Lincoln issued a similar order to the Army and Navy, November 18, 1862.

Sabine Pass, Texas.—At this place, January 21, 1863, the rebels captured the brig Morning Light and the schooner Velocity, 13 guns, $1,000,000 worth of property, and 109 prisoners. The Morning Light was afterward destroyed, to prevent its recapture by the Federals. An expedition was fitted out at New Orleans for the capture of this position, but failed in an attack September 8, and returned on the 12th, having lost two vessels.

Sabine Cross-roads. (See Mansfield.)

Salem, Ark., was, on March 16, 1862, the scene of a fight between 250 Union soldiers and 1,000 rebels; the rebels were surprised and defeated, with a loss of 100 killed and wounded. Union loss, 25 killed and wounded.

Salem, Ind. (See John Morgan.)

Salem, Miss., was the scene of an engagement October 8, 1863. S. D. Lee, with 4,000 rebels, attacked 1,500 Federals, under McCrellis and Phillips. After a stubborn fight, the latter were defeated, with the loss of 15 or 20 killed and wounded.

Salem, Mo.—About 300 rebels, under Freeman and Turner, surprised the Union garrison at this place. Major Bowen rallied his men, and the rebels were repulsed.

Salem, Tenn., was occupied by Averill's raiders December 16, 1863. They destroyed the railroad for 15 miles; 5 bridges, 3 large depot buildings, and an immense quantity of stores were burned.

Salem Heights. (See Fredericksburg, Va.)

Salisbury, N. C., was captured by Stoneman April 12, 1865. He took 1,165 prisoners, 19 guns, and 8 flags; destroyed a large quantity of supplies, including 7,000 bales cotton, 1,000,000 rounds of ammuntion, etc.; also a large arsenal and all its machinery, 6 depots in the vicinity, 2 engines and trains, several bridges, and several miles of railroad.

Salt-peter was ordered seized in the rebel States for the Government, and 50 cents per pound allowed therefor.

Saltville, Va., was the seat of the most extensive salt-works in the South, and upon its production the Confederates in a great measure depended. In September, 1864, General Burbridge, with a force of 2,500 men, moved from his camp in Kentucky, upon this place, October 2. He arrived near the town, and drove the rebels from Clinch Mountain and Laurel Gaps, and attacking them, forced them into their strong intrenchments around Saltville; but his ammunition giving out, he retired safely. The rebel force was double his. General Burbridge, with 4,000 cavalry, arrived at Bean Station, Tenn., December 2, and on the 11th was joined by Gillem's brigade, under Stoneman, who was to command a raid upon Saltville, which was immediately organized. General Stoneman, on the 13th, surprised, flanked, and defeated Colonel Morgan, with Duke's brigade, at Kingsport, killing and wounding 15, and taking 85 prisoners, the rebels retreating to Bristol, Tenn. About the same time, Breckenridge, with 3,000 troops, attacked General Gillem, near Morristown, routing him, and capturing his artillery (6 guns) and several hundred prisoners; the remainder of the command escaped to Strawberry Plains and Knoxville. Burbridge followed the rebels, and next morning, at three o'clock, entered Bristol, charging into the town, sword in hand, captured 300 prisoners and a train of cars with the mail for Richmond; the remainder of Duke's brigade fled. Burbridge at once proceeded toward Vaughn's position at Zollicoffer, 12 miles further. The latter retreated hastily toward Abington, but the Union forces reaching there two hours ahead, and capturing large quantities of stores and ammunition, Vaughn fled toward Wytheville, closely pursued by General Gillem, who captured 300 prisoners, 3 guns, a wagon train of ammunition, and some stores. Major Harrison, the same day, with 300 picked cavalry, cut the railroad east of Saltville, just after Breckenridge had gone thither with 200 militia from Lynchburg; took and burned 2 trains, and dashed up the railroad toward Wytheville, burning bridges. The 16th found Vaughn pursuing Harrison, while Gillem was trying to overtake Vaughn. Gillem overtook Vaughn's rear guard at Marion, capturing most of it. Then charging the main body, and being reinforced, drove it, and forced another battle at Mount Airy, again defeating the rebels, capturing 7 guns and many prisoners. The rebels continued *through* Wytheville, where Gillem met the home-guard, which he dispersed, taking their 4 guns, and continued his pursuit of Vaughn, who fled with 100 men—left out of 1,600—the rest being killed, wounded, prisoners, or dispersed. General Gillem having thus made atonement for his defeat at Morristown, proceeded to destroy the railroad bridge, 4 miles of track, the lead-works, and rebel stores. General Burbridge, in leaving Wytheville on the 19th, was repulsed by Breckenridge at Marion, but General Gillem coming up, again relieved the fortunes of the day, capturing 11 guns, 200 prisoners, 93 wagons, and Breckenridge's headquarters, that General retreating to Mount Airy, and thence into North Carolina. Saltville was occupied on the 20th, after driving out the rebels by a midnight attack. The salt-works and machinery were all destroyed, the wells being all filled up with stones and railroad iron. This raiding party marched 464 miles in eighteen days, and was among the most successful of the war: 11 founderies, 40 flouring-mills, 50 saw-mills, 30 large bridges, 13 locomotives, 100 cars, and immense amounts of provisions, ammunition, and military stores were destroyed; 20 guns, several thousand cattle, and 900 prisoners were captured—the whole damage to the rebels being over $3,000,000.

Salt-works, at Yellville, Ark., was destroyed December 15, 1862; those at Tampa Bay, Fla., July 11, 1864; those at Kingsbury, Ga., November 2, 1862; those near Wilmington, N. C., April 21, 1864; and those at Tazewell, Va., May 7, 1864.

Sandersville, Ga., was occupied by Sherman's right wing November 26, 1864.

Sandtown, Ga., was occupied by Kilpatrick August 19, 1864.

Sanitary Commission was authorized by the President June 8, 1861, and issued its first address to the people on the 26th. Branches were formed in nearly every town in the North. Many a poor sick soldier has blessed the Commission; and to it, under God's blessing, is many a one owing his life.

San Jacinto. (See Mason.)

Santa Fe, N. M., was occupied by rebel troops April 10, 1862, who evacuated it April 21, the Union forces driving them out. (See Apache Canon.)

Santa Rosa. (See Fort Pickens.)

Sartartia, Miss., was the scene of an action June 4, 1863, fought by 3,000 Unionists, under General Kimball, and 2,000 Confederates, under Wirt Adams, and lasted thirty minutes, when the rebels were routed, losing considerably in killed and wounded, and 100 prisoners. Union loss, 1 killed and 17 wounded. A detachment of Sherman's army, moving against Yazoo City, was fired upon near this place February 4, 1863, by 3,000 Texans from the shore. The troops were immediately landed, and, assisted by the gun-boats, succeeded in dislodging the rebels, losing 9 men killed of the 11th Illinois and 8th Louisiana. The rebel loss was unknown.

Savannah, Ga., was blockaded May 28, 1861. Fort Pulaski, at the mouth of the river, was taken possession of by the State authorities January 3, 1861. About February 1, 1862, battéries were erected on Venus Island, which cut the fort off from the main land. These were unsuccessfully attacked by four rebel gun-boats February 15. The siege was kept up until April 10, when a summons to surrender was sent in, which being refused, the bombardment immediately commenced, and continued vigorously through the day. At night new batteries were planted, and next morning breaches were discovered in the south-east face of the fort. The bombardment was continued vigorously, and, at 2 o'clock, the fort surrendered; 47 guns, 7,000 shot and shell, 40,000 pounds of powder, and 385 prisoners were taken with the fort. Union loss, one man killed and one slightly wounded; the Confederates had three severely wounded. Savannah, after this, rested in comparative quiet, until Sherman was known to be east of the Oconee, when the excitement was terrible. On December 9, 1864, General Howard was ten miles west of the city, and from thence communicated, on the 11th, with Admiral Dahlgren, commanding the fleet. General Sherman, on the 20th, demanded the surrender of the city. Hardee refused, but that night blowed up his rams and retreated northward. Sherman entered the city on the 21st, receiving its surrender from the Mayor. The captures included 800 prisoners, 33,000 bales of cotton, 150 cannon, 13 locomotives, 190 cars, 3 steamers, many stores, and much ammunition. General Geary was made Military Governor. Sherman's army, in three columns—one toward Charleston, and the other two, by different roads, toward Branchville, S. C.—started from Savannah January 17, 1865, and on the 27th the last division, under Geary, moved out.

Savannah, Tenn., was occupied by Union troops April 16, 1862, after defeating the rebels, who lost 5 killed and 65 wounded.

Schenck, Robert C., proved himself a patriot, and alike able to cope with rebels in the field as a soldier, or in Congress as a stateman.

Scottsville, Ky.—Rebel Colonel Hamilton, with 500 men, attacked the garrison of 150 men at this place January 28, 1864. After a desperate fight, the garrison capitulated; the rebels then, disregarding the agreement made to respect private property, destroyed the court-house and all the public documents.

Sea Brook Island. (See Charleston.)

Semmes. (See Alabama.)

Semmesport, La., was occupied by General Smith's forces March 13, 1864.

Seneca, Va., was the scene of a Union defeat March 21, 1863.

Senate of the U. S., on July 11, 1861, voted to expel from that body Senators James M. Mason and R. M. T. Hunter, of Virginia; Thomas L. Clingman and Thomas Bragg, of North Carolina; Louis T. Wigfall and J. W. Hemphill, of Texas; Charles B. Mitchell and William K. Sebastian, of Arkansas; and A. O. P. Nicholson, of Tennessee.

Seven Pines. (See Fair Oaks.)

Sevierville, Tenn. (See Fair Garden.)

Seward, Wm. H., was called into Mr. Lincoln's Cabinet as Secretary of State March 4, 1864. He has held that position during the rebellion. To him is, in a great measure, due the skillful management and successful issue of the nation's foreign policy. October 14, 1861, he issued a circular to Governors of States, advising sea-coast and lake defenses. He tendered his resignation December 18, 1862, which was not accepted. He was thrown from his carriage, in Washington, and had his arm and jaw broken, April 5, 1865. While confined to his room by his injuries, he was, on the evening of the 14th, (the same evening on which President Lincoln was assassinated,) attacked by one Payne, Booth's confederate. Payne made his way to Mr. Seward's residence about 10 o'clock in the evening, disabled several persons who opposed him, inflicting exceedingly serious wounds upon Mr. Frederick Seward, and, having made his way into the room where Secretary Seward was lying, stabbed him repeatedly, and would probably have killed him had he not rolled out upon the floor. The would-be assassin then escaped, despite all efforts to secure him.

Sewall's Point was the scene of artillery fighting May 19, 1861, and May 8, 1862.

Shakertown, Ky., was entered, and several cars destroyed, by guerrillas, February 20, 1863.

Shawnee Creek, Kansas.—The guerrillas captured a wagon train near this place May 24, 1863.

Shawneetown, Ark., was destroyed by guerrillas June 6, 1863.

Shawneetown, Ill.—Colonel Johnson, commanding guerrillas, crossed the Ohio River at Shawneetown, captured four steamers, and destroyed their cargoes, August 13, 1864.

Shelbyville, Tenn., was occupied by General Mitchell's forces April 6, 1862, and by Rosecrans' troops June 27, 1863. The rebels attacked the place October 4, but were repulsed.

Shell Mound, Tenn., was the scene of a battle and Union victory October 31, 1863.

Shepherdstown, Md. (See Maryland and Pennsylvania Invasion.)

Shepherdstown, Va., was the scene of a skirmish September 4, 1861.

Sheridan, Philip H., Major-General, although having previously done good service, was brought prominently before the public by being placed in command of the cavalry of the Potomac army in March, 1864. Between the 10th and 27th of May, he made a series of raids about Richmond, which were the wonder and admiration of all observers. He assumed command of the Middle Military Division August 7, whipped Early at Winchester September 19, and, on the 22d, again at Fisher's Hill; after which followed a series of most gallant victories, crowned by the complete triumph of Cedar Creek, October 19. He was, for gallantry here shown, promoted to Major-General in the Regular Army, dating from November 8, 1864. He left his camp at Winchester February 27, 1865, to join Grant in the final reduction of Richmond, for the history of which see Grant's Report. After the capture of Lee's army, General Sheridan was assigned to the command of the Texas Department.

Sherman, William Tecumseh, was born in Lancaster County, Ohio, February 8, 1820. His father dying when William was but 8 years old, he was taken into the family of the Hon. Thomas Ewing, through whose influence he entered West Point Military Academy in 1836, at the age of 16. He graduated June 20, 1840, ranking sixth in a class of forty. He next day entered the Regular Army as 2d Lieutenant of Artillery, connected with the 3d Regiment. He was ordered to Fort Sumter in 1841; to California, in 1846; to St. Louis, in 1850; and, subsequently, to New Orleans. He was, in 1851, breveted Captain in the Regular Army, for "meritorious service," dating from May 30, 1848. He resigned his position in the army in 1853, going to California, where he was connected with a banking-house. On his return to the States, he was invited to the Presidency of the Louisiana Military Academy, which position he promptly resigned upon Louisiana passing the secession ordinance. He had very flattering offers from the Confederate authorities, but, refusing all their overtures, he started North, where he took his place among the Union defenders, ranking as Colonel. He took an important part in the battle of Bull Run, acting as Brigadier-General, soon after being promoted to that rank, his commission dating from May 17, 1861, and placed second in command to General Anderson, then commanding the Department of the Cumberland. Upon General Anderson's resigning, General Sherman succeeded him October 8. He was relieved of this position, and assigned to a command in Western Missouri, November 10, and shortly after to Benton Barracks. Next, he was placed in command of Paducah, the base of supplies for General Grant's army, then operating against Forts Donaldson and Henry. He commanded a division at the battle of Shiloh, receiving special commendation for his services in the report of General Grant, commanding. The history of his movements against Vicksburg, on the Yazoo, etc., will be found under those heads. He was appointed to the command of the Army of the Tennessee October 27, 1863. He was, on March 12, 1864, assigned to the command of the Division of the Mississippi. The history of his movements against Atlanta, Savannah, his route through the Carolinas, etc., will be found under their appropriate headings. He bade his army farewell at Washington, May 30, 1865.

Sherwood, Mo., was the scene of a skirmish and Union defeat May 18, 1863.

Shiloh, Tenn.—The battle of Shiloh was commenced April 6, 1862. The Confederates, 45,000 strong, under Beauregard and Johnston, attacked the Union forces, 35,000 strong, under General Grant, at Pittsburg Landing. The battle raged fiercely all day. The Union army was driven to the river, with the loss of General Prentiss and 2,500 men, prisoners, 36 pieces of artillery, and a large amount of camp equipage. The army was saved from total defeat by the operations of the gunboats on the rebel right wing. General Johnston, the rebel commander, was killed. The advance of General Buell's army, from Nashville, appeared on the banks of the river late in the evening, and spent the night in crossing to the relief of General Grant. Early next morning the engagement became general; the fresh troops from General Buell's army checked the rebels, and turned the scale in favor of the Union army. The whole line advanced, and the rebels fell back, and were pursued by Sherman's division. The Union loss was 1,614 killed (including Brigadier-General W. H. L. Wallace), 7,721 wounded, and 3,963 missing and prisoners. The Confederate loss was never fully known. They left some 3,000 dead on the field.

Ship Gap, Ga., was occupied by General Sherman's forces on October 16, 1864. This secured railroad communications for Sherman's supplies.

Ship Island, at the entrance to Lake Borgne, Louisiana, was occupied by Union troops September 16, 1861. The Government had destroyed the fortifications in May, since which time the rebels held it. This island was used as a camp during the preparations for the capture of New Orleans.

Shippensburg. (See Pennsylvania Invasion.)

Shipping Point, Va., was occupied by Unionists March 28, 1862.

Shooter's Hill, Va., was the scene of a skirmish June 28, 1861.

Shreveport, La., was occupied March 16, 1864, by the rebels, who burned two steamers and 3,000 bales of cotton.

Sikeston, Mo., was a skirmish scene February 28, 1862.

Simmonsport, La., was destroyed by Union gunboats June 4, 1863.

Sisters Ferry, Ga.—Sherman's cavalry demonstrated against this place December 6, 1864, and, after a skirmish with two rebel brigades there, moved on toward Savannah.

Six-mile Station. (See Grant's Report.)

Skeet, N. C., was a skirmish scene March 4, 1863.

Skidaway, Ga.—The fortifications on Skidaway and Green Islands, in Warsaw Sound, were blown up, by order of Commodore Dupont, March 24, 1862.

Slate Creek, Ky., was the scene of a skirmish and Union defeat June 13, 1863.

Slater's Mills, Va., was the scene of an indecisive engagement May 9, 1862.

Slatersville, N. C., was occupied by General Stoneman April 13, 1865.

Slidell. (See Mason.)

Smith, Major-General Andrew J., proved himself a good soldier and the soldier's friend. He commanded a division, under Sherman, against Vicksburg. (See Mansfield, Louisiana; Pleasant Hill, Nashville, and Mobile.)

Smith's Ferry, Ala., was held by Rousseau July 16, 1864.

Smithfield, N. C., was occupied, April 11, 1865, by the 75th Indiana Regiment.

Smithfield, Va., was occupied by Union troops March 6, 1862. An indecisive skirmish occurred here February 12, 1863. A rebel mail was captured, and six of the escort wounded, at this point April 14, 1864. Sheridan drove Early through Smithfield August 28, 1864.

Snake Gap, 15 miles south of Dalton, Georgia, was captured by General McPherson May 8, 1864, thus flanking Rocky Face Ridge, and threatening Resaca.

Snicker's Gap, Va., was a skirmish scene October 28, 1862. The gap was occupied by General Hancock's forces, after driving out the rebels, November 2. They returned next day, but were driven off, losing heavily. General Stahl, on November 29, had a skirmish with the rebels, who were completely routed, and lost all their camp equipage, 50 killed and wounded, 40 prisoners, etc.; Union loss, 15 killed and wounded.

Crook overtook Early at this point July 17, 1864, capturing a portion of his plunder. The rebels burned part of their stores, and fled southward with the rest.

Snow Hill, near Auburn, Tenn.—General Stanley, with 2,000 cavalry and Colonel Matthews's infantry brigade, attacked Morgan and Wheeler, with eight regiments, at this place, April 2, 1863, and routed them. They lost 15 or 20 killed; 60 prisoners, and 300 horses were taken.

Snydersville, La.—There was an engagement at Brooks's plantation April 1, 1864, between 600 of the 1st Massachusetts Colored Cavalry and 1,000 rebels, lasting several hours, and resulting in the rout of the latter. Rebel loss unknown; Union loss, 46 killed and wounded.

Somerset Ky.—The battle of Somerset (or Mill Spring) was fought January 19, 1862, commencing at 6 o'clock, A. M. A rebel force 10,000 strong, under Generals Crittenden and Zollicoffer attacked the Union forces (four regiments) under General Thomas. The latter were dreadfully cut up, but after the first and severest engagement, they were reinforced by nine regiments and several batteries, and completely routed their antagonists, who were driven back to their intrenchments on the Cumberland River, which they recrossed during the night, and retreated in confusion. General Zollicoffer was killed during the fight. The Unionists captured 10 cannon, 100 wagons, 1,200 horses, 1,000 muskets, several boxes of arms, and large quantities of ammunition and subsistence stores, together with a number of boats. Rebel loss, 192 killed, 68 wounded, and 89 prisoners; Union loss, 39 killed and 207 wounded.

General Gillmore defeated the rebels at this place, March 31, 1863, driving them into the Cumberland. Union loss, 10 killed, and 25 wounded; rebel loss, 45 killed and wounded, and 400 prisoners. There was a skirmish at **Mill Spring,** near this place, April 28, and another May 31, in which the Unionists were defeated with a loss of 33 prisoners.

Sommerville, Tenn., was, on March 30, 1863, the scene of a rebel defeat, in which they lost 150 prisoners, and 200 cattle. Grierson's cavalry was beaten, with small loss, at this place, April 2, 1864.

South Carolina.—A bill to raise and equip 10,000 volunteers for the defense of the State passed the State Legislature November 10, 1860. The State Convention met at Columbia December 17, but on account of smallpox, adjourned to Charleston. A secession ordinance was passed December 20, and the following day a declaration of causes was adopted. Governor Pickens, on the 24th, issued a proclamation, declaring "South Carolina a sovereign, free, and independent nation." The Convention, on the 25th, passed a resolution, having in view the formation of a Southern Confederacy, and on the 31st commissioners were sent to the other slave States to lay the plan before them. An oath of abjuration and allegiance was adopted the same day. On January 4, 1861, the Convention appointed seven delegates to "the General Congress of the Seceding States," and next day adjourned, subject to the call of its President. The Legislature, on January 14, declared that any attempt to reinforce Fort Sumter would be an act of war, and on the 31st proposed to buy it. The Convention reassembled March 26, and April 3 ratified the Constitution of the Confederate States (146 *v.* 16).

South Mountain, Md.—A battle was fought here September 14, 1862. General McClellan attacked the main body of the rebel army, when a general engagement ensued. Rebels fell back slowly, contending stubbornly for every inch of ground. In this way the battle raged furiously all day. In the night the rebels retreated toward the Potomac, leaving their dead and wounded on the field. Union loss, 443 killed, including General Reno, 1,806 wounded, and 176 taken prisoners; Confederate loss, 4,300 killed, wounded, and prisoners.

South Union, Ky., was a skirmish scene—rebels defeated—May 13, 1863.

Spanish Fort. (See Mobile.)

Spanish Wells, S. C., was captured, and the signal station burned, March 13, 1863.

Spottsylvania. (See Grant's Report.)

Springfield, Mo., was occupied by General Lyon August 5, 1861, in his retreat before the rebels, and again by the Union forces, after the battle of Wilson's Creek, on the 11th. Major Zagonyi, at the head of about 300 of General Fremont's body-guard, charged against 2,000 rebels, drawn in line of battle, near this place, October 25, and routed them, killing and wounding a great number. They then cleared Springfield of rebels, where Generals Fremont and Sigel arrived next day, amid much enthusiasm. The town was occupied by rebels under McCulloch November 26. The Union forces, under General Curtis, took possession of the town February 13, 1862, the rebels having evacuated it during the previous night, leaving in the hospitals 600 sick and wounded. Marmaduke, with 5,000 rebels and 16 pieces of artillery, attacked the town January 8, 1863, defended by 2,000 men, and 5 pieces of artillery in bad order; the rebels were defeated. Union loss, 17 killed and a number wounded; rebel loss, 50 killed and many wounded.

St. Augustine, Florida, and the adjacent fort of five guns, was surrendered to Commodore Dupont March 11, 1862, the people of the town raising the Union flag.

St. Albans Raid.—A band of about 20 rebel refugees, from Canada, entered St. Albans, Vt., October 19, 1864, robbed three banks of $150,000, shot several men, stole each a horse, and fled whence they came. Eight of the raiders and $50,000 of the money were captured next day. The Canadian Judge Coursol discharged them December 13, on an unfounded legal pretense. The Canadian Parliament, January 23, 1865, reproved this action of their Judge, and he was removed from office. They were again discharged by Judge Smith, at Montreal, and immediately rearrested on another warrant. They were discharged, and again arrested April 5, and all but one again discharged April 10.

St. Charles, Mo., was occupied June 27, 1864, by General Carr, after defeating the rebels under Shelby, who lost 200 killed and wounded, and 500 prisoners. The guns of the "Queen City" were also retaken by the Unionists.

St. Genevieve, Mo., was occupied by Union troops, who captured $58,000, August 16, 1861.

St. John's Bluff, Fla.—The rebel batteries at this point were silenced September 17, 1862.

St. Marks, Fla.—The salt-works were here destroyed March 1, 1864.

St. Marys, Ga., was destroyed by Union gun-boats November 9, 1862.

Stafford's Store, Va., was a skirmish scene February 5, 1863.

Stamford, Ky.—The rebels captured and burned 60 wagons, near this place, July 31, 1863.

Stanton, Edwin M., was called into President Lincoln's Cabinet, as Secretary of War, January 13, 1862, *vice* Cameron, resigned.

Staunton, Va., was occupied by General Hunter June 6, 1864. After destroying $3,000,000 worth of public stores, he moved toward Lynchburg.

Stephens, Alex. H., in a speech at Milledgeville, November 15, 1860, opposed secession. He was elected Provisional Vice-President of the Confederate States February 9, 1861, and was inaugurated on the 18th, and July 11 upheld secession in a speech at Augusta.

Stewart's Landing, Tenn.—Wheeler attacked and murdered the colored garrison at this place August 20, 1864.

Stewart's Mill, Va., was a skirmish scene September 11, 1861.

Stone River. (See Murfreesboro.)

Strasburg, Va., was occupied January 1, 1862, by General Fremont, after driving out the rebels. There was an indecisive skirmish here March 27. General Banks's forces evacuated the town May 24, retreating to Winchester. On February 25, after skirmishing all day, the rebels were defeated, losing all the Union prisoners they had taken, and 20 others. The rebels, being reinforced, surprised the Unionists, and captured 200 of them. There were indecisive cavalry skirmishes here April 29 and November 17.

Strawberry Plains, Tenn., was the scene of a rebel defeat January 10, 1864. General Sturgis fell back from Dandridge to this place on the 7th, and, soon after leaving it, it was occupied by Longstreet, who retired toward Bull's Gap February 20.

Streight, Colonel A. D., left Nashville, Tenn., April 11, 1863, for a raid into Georgia. After doing the rebels immense damage, his whole command was captured on May 3, near Rome, Ga., by General Forrest and Colonel Roddy; 1,375 men, with all their horses and equipments, were surrendered. Colonel Streight lost 72 men killed, wounded, and missing, in his whole raid, while that of the rebels was between 500 and 600. He was carried to Libby Prison, where he was confined until May 10, 1864, when he and 106 other Union officers, after 51 days' work tunneling, made their escape. He and 54 others succeeded in making the Union lines, while 48 were recaptured. He was withheld from exchange on false pretenses of stirring up servile insurrection in Georgia. For a full history, and the manner of treating Union prisoners, see his publication, "The Prisoner of War." (See Day's Gap.)

Suden's Cove, Tenn., was a skirmish scene June 5, 1862.

Suffolk, Va., was occupied by Union forces May 18, 1862. The Union pickets were driven in November 19. A brisk skirmish occurred here December 12. Skirmishing commenced here again April 14, 1863, and was of frequent occurrence during the spring and summer.

Sugar Creek, Ark., was the scene of a brisk engagement February 17, 1862. Union loss, 5 killed and 13 wounded.

Sugar Loaf Mountain, Md., was occupied by Unionists September 10, 1862.

Sulphur Springs, Tenn., was the scene of a cavalry skirmish October 21, 1863. A sharp but indecisive battle was fought here August 11, 1864.

Sultanna, a transport steamer, with 1,886 souls aboard, mostly paroled prisoners, blew up, near Memphis, April 28, 1865. About 1,100 lives were lost in this disaster, due to the negligence or cupidity of those in charge of the Union prisoners, just paroled from the Southern starvation prisons.

Summersville, Va.—On August 26, 1862, while at breakfast, Colonel Tyler's 7th Ohio Regiment were surrounded by the Confederates. They rallied, however, and cut their way through four times their number; the casualities were few. The rebels were driven in a skirmish here February 9, 1863. (See Carnifex Ferry.)

Surratt, Mrs. (See Herold.)

Swan Quarter, N. C., was the scene of a rebel defeat March 4, 1863. Union loss, 20; rebel loss, 25.

Talladega, Ala., was occupied by Rousseau July 15, 1864. He paroled 140 sick rebels, and destroyed public stores, etc.

Tallahatchie, Miss., was evacuated by the rebels December 1, 1862.

Tampa Bay, Fla. (See Salt-works.)

Tappahannock, Va., was taken by the Union gunboats May 30, 1863.

Tazewell, Tenn., was the scene of brisk skirmishing August 5 and 6, 1862; the rebels were defeated. The garrison here repulsed the rebels 400 strong, January 26, 1864.

Tazewell, Va. (See Salt-works.)

Teche Country, La., was the scene of skirmishing, and a Union victory April 12, 13, and 14, 1863.

Telegraph.—By order of the Government, the United States Marshals seized the records of the telegraph offices throughout the North May 20, 1861. The object was to ascertain who were aiding the rebellion.

An order regulating the conveyance of intelligence concerning military operations was issued July 8. Congress, on January 31, 1862, authorized the President to take possession of the different lines, which he did February 25, 1862.

Tennessee.—The Legislature, on May 6, 1861, passed an ordinance of secession, which was termed a Declaration of Independence, and ordered it to be voted on by the people; passed by Senate (20 *v.* 4) and by House (46 *v.* 21). Next day the Governor announced a military league between that State and the Confederate States. On June 21, a Union Convention met at Knoxville. On the fourth day of its session it adopted a declaration of grievances against the usurping body which voted the State out of the Union and into the Confederate States. This ordinance of secession was submitted to the people and adopted, as per Governor Harris's proclamation, June 24. Ayes, 104,913; nays, 47,238. President Lincoln declared the State in insurrection August 16. The State was for some time represented in the Confederate Congress, though its actual position was nearly all the time with the Union. The State Convention passed an emancipation resolution January 15, 1865.

Texas.—The State Convention met at Austin January 28, 1861, and on February 1 passed an ordinance of secession (166 *v.* 7), to be submitted to the people on the 22d, and, unless rejected by a majority vote, to take effect on the 2d of March.

The ordinance was ratified by the people by 24,000 majority, the Union men there—many of them—not daring to vote. The State Convention ratified the Confederate Constitution March 25. The State was declared in insurrection May 19. (See Houston.) General A. J. Hamilton was appointed Military Governor November 15, 1862.

Thomas, George H., was commissioned as Lieutenant-Colonel April 25, 1861; promoted to Colonel May 5, to Brigadier-General of volunteers August 17; fought the battle of Mill Spring January 19, 1862; was promoted to Major-General of volunteers April 25. He succeeded General Buell in command of the Army of the Cumberland October 30. He was made Brigadier-General in the Regular Army October 27, 1863, and Major-General January 1, 1865. (See Stone River, Chickamauga, Mission Ridge, Atlanta, Nashville, etc.)

Thompson, Jacob, Buchanan's Secretary of the Interior, went to Raleigh, to persuade the North Carolina Legislature to vote for secession, November 18, 1860. He resigned January 8, 1861, after betraying the sailing of the "Star of the West" to reinforce Fort Sumter.

Thompson's Hill. (See Port Gibson.)

Thompson's Station. (See Franklin, Tenn.)

Thoroughfare Gap, Va., was occupied by Union troops April 2, 1862. General Stahl, on November 3, drove the rebels out of the gap and occupied it.

Three-mile Station, Va., was attacked January 14, 1864, by a party of 200 rebels, who were repulsed.

Tiger Creek, Ga., was the scene of a Union victory April 29, 1864.

Times, Chicago, was suppressed June 2, 1863, by order of General Burnside. President Lincoln revoked the order on the 4th.

Tishamingo. (See Guntown.)

Tolando, Miss., was occupied, and the 1st Alabama Cavalry captured, October 25, 1863.

Tomkinsville, Ky., was the scene of an engagement April 22, 1863. Court-house destroyed.

Trent. (See Mason.)

Triune, Tenn., was, on June 12, 1863, attacked by a rebel force, who were repulsed.

Tullahoma, Tenn., was occupied by General Rosecrans's advance July 1, 1863, Bragg evacuating the night before.

Tunnel Hill, Ga.—General Palmer left Chattanooga for a reconnoisance toward Tunnel Hill January 27, 1864. After considerable skirmishing, he next day drove in the rebel pickets, and then fell back to draw out the rebels, who retreated again at night. Union loss, 2 wounded; rebel loss, 10 killed and 20 or 25 wounded. The rebels then held the position. General Palmer again, February 23, after skirmishing with the rebels all day, drove them to Tunnel Hill, capturing over 300 prisoners. Union loss, 75 killed and wounded. On the 25th he occupied the town, and, after considerable skirmishing, his troops penetrated to the front of Dalton, losing 3 killed and 12 wounded. The rebels reported their loss at 150 killed and wounded. He fell back to Tunnel Hill next day. This was made a base in the commencement of operations against Buzzard Roost and Dalton.

Tupelo, Miss.—The railroad bridge at this place was destroyed December 28, 1862. The rebels were defeated here May 6, 1863, losing 100 prisoners.

Tuscaloosa, Ala., was occupied by Wilson's cavalry March 22, 1865.

Tuscumbia, Ala.—The Union troops, on December 13, 1862, surprised and defeated a rebel force at this place. The same thing was done February 22, 1863; 200 prisoners, one piece of artillery, a large quantity of ammunition, and a provision train were captured. The rebels attacked the Union gunboats April 2, but did no damage. The place was, on the 25th, occupied by Federal troops, the rebels being driven out. Federal loss, 100; rebel loss, not known.

Tuscumbia, Mo., was a skirmish scene September 20, 1861.

Union City, Ky., was surrendered by Colonel Hawkins to General Forrest March 24, 1864. Union loss, 425 men, prisoners, and a number of horses, mules, etc.

Union City, Tenn.—March 31, 1862, Colonel Buford,

with a force of infantry, cavalry, and artillery, captured Union City, dispersing the rebel force at that place.

Unionville, Tenn., was the scene of a battle March 7 1863, between General Minty's Union force and Russell's rebel cavalry, which resulted in the defeat of the rebels who lost 50 killed, 180 wounded, 58 prisoners, and a lot of horses.

Upperville, Va., was, after a few hours' engagement occupied by General Pleasanton March 3, 1862. The rebels were defeated in a cavalry engagement near this place June 21, 1863, and the Union forces were worsted in a like engagement February 26, 1864.

Vallandigham, Clement L., was, at the outbreak of the rebellion, member of Congress from the 3d District of Ohio. By his outspoken and persistent opposition to raising men and money for forcibly putting down secession, he soon became the acknowledged leader of the Peace party. In a public speech at the Cooper Institute, N. Y., he used the following words: "If any one or more of the States of this Union should at any time secede—for reasons of sufficiency and justice of which, before God, they alone may judge—much as I should deplore it, I never would, as Representative in Congress, vote one dollar of money whereby one drop of American blood should be shed in civil war." February 7, 1861, he proposed to amend the Constitution:

1st. Dividing the United States into four sections; the *North*, composed of the New England and Middle (except Delaware) States; the *West*, composed of Ohio, Indiana, Illinois, Michigan, Wisconsin, Missouri, Iowa, Kansas, and all new States formed out of territory north of 36° 30′, and east of the Rocky Mountains; the *Pacific*, composed of Oregon, California, and all new States formed out of territory west of the Rocky Mountains or Rio Grande; the *South*, composed of all the slave States, and all new States formed out of territory south of 36° 30′, and east of the Rio Grande and Rocky Mountains.

2d. A majority of the Senators from each section shall be necessary to the passage of any bill, order, or resolution, except adjournment.

3d. A majority of the electors in each section shall

be necessary to the choice of a President or Vice-President, and details under this provision.

4th. A State may secede with consent of the Legislatures to the section of which it belongs, the President, subject to the approval of Congress, having power to arrange the terms of the secession.

5th. Limiting the power of Congress.

He declared himself, February 20, rejoiced that the question was " peaceable disunion on one hand, or Union through adjustment and conciliation on the other." He declared the Union broken up, and predicted the recognition of the Southern Confederacy by European powers within three months. On January 14, 1863, in Congress, he declared : " You can not conquer the South. * * * Fight, tax, emancipate have become the trinity of your deep damnation. You can not abolish slavery by argument; as well try to abolish marriage, etc. * * * This is not a war of sections; it is the old war of the Cavalier and the Roundhead—the Liberalist and the Puritan. I propose informal, practical recognition (of the Confederacy). Stop fighting, withdraw and disband you armies, recall your fleets, and break up the blockade. Accept foreign mediation as proposed by France," etc. He all along professed a great regard for the Constitution and Union, and was sanguine of the success of his peace measures, or of secession.

May 1, 1863, while making a political speech at Mount Vernon, Ohio, he denounced the Government at Washington as aiming not to restore the Union, but to establish a despotism. He declared the war was waged to free the negro and enslave the white man; that the Government did not desire peace, having rejected the offer from the South. He denounced Order No. 38, (which forbid certain disloyal practices, giving notice that persons declaring themselves in sympathy with the rebels would be arrested for trial, etc.,) and proclaimed his intention to disobey it, and called upon those who heard him to resist and defeat its execution. For this speech he was arrested on the 5th, by order of General Burnside, and ordered to Cincinnati for trial. He applied for a writ of *habeas corpus*, which was denied, and the trial proceeded before a court-martial, which found him guilty of the principal charges, and he was sentenced to close confinement in Fort Warren. The President modified this sentence, by directing that he should be sent within the rebel lines, not to return to the United States during the war. This sentence was immediately carried into execution.

The opponents of the Administration denominated this a case of martyrdom, and held public meetings in many places, denouncing the action as tyrannical and highly dangerous to public liberty. Mr. Vallandigham was, on June 10, nominated by the Peace party of Ohio as their candidate for Governor, and on the 26th a committee from the Convention nominating him waited upon the President, and demanded his immediate recall. The President offered to restore him if a majority of the committee would subscribe to the following propositions:

1. "That there is now a rebellion in the United States, the object and tendency of which is to destroy the National Union, and that, in your opinion, an army and navy are constitutional means for repressing the rebellion.

2. That no one of you will do any thing which, in his own judgment, will tend to hinder the increase, or favor the decrease, or lessen the efficiency of the army or navy while engaged in the effort to suppress that rebellion; and,

3. That each of you will, in his sphere, do all he can to have the officers, soldiers, and seamen of the army and navy, while engaged in the effort to suppress the rebellion, paid, fed, clad, and otherwise well provided for and supported."

This they declined doing, and he was not restored. He ran the blockade, and July 15 arrived at Clifton House, on the Canada side of Niagara Falls, and issued an address to the people of Ohio, accepting the nomination for Governor. October 13 the election took place, at which he was defeated, Brough receiving 101,099 majority. He returned to his home in Dayton June 15, 1864. At the Chicago Convention he was Chairman of the Commmittee on Resolutions.

Van Buren, Ark., was captured by the Union forces under Herron and Blunt, December 28, 1862. A steamer and 400 rebels were captured at this place, January 28, 1863.

Vermillionville, La., was occupied by the Union troops under Banks, after driving out the rebels, April 17, 1863.

Vicksburg, Miss., was, at an early stage of the rebellion, taken possession of by the rebels, who fortified it in the strongest manner. As the possession of this point was an effectual blockade of the Mississippi, early efforts were made for its reduction by the Unionists. The mortar fleet, under command of Commodore Porter, arrived above Vicksburg June 20, 1862, and Farragut's fleet, from below, on the 25th. The bombardment was commenced next day, and on the 27th a canal, intended to isolate Vicksburg from the Mississipi River, and to alter the passage of the boats, was commenced, under the superintendance of Brigadier-General Williams. The fleet continued the bombardment of the batteries. Commodore Farragut, with his fleet, passed up above Vicksburg, silencing the rebel batteries, and communicated with General Halleck and Commodore Davis on the 28th.

The canal did not prove a success; the siege was abandoned. Another attempt was made, and General Sherman, December 27, attacked the outworks of the city, while the gun-boats engaged the Haines's Bluff batteries. A detachment was sent across the Mississippi River to destroy the Vicksburg and Shreveport Railroad, to prevent reinforcements to the garrison. The Union troops steadily advanced, driving the rebels out of their intenchments; and next day the first and second lines were taken, after a severe contest, and the attacking party reached within two and a half miles of the city.

On the 29th the Confederates, having been heavily reinforced, attacked the Federals with their full force, and succeeded in driving them back to their first line of defense. In the attack on Vicksburg, General Sherman was to have had the co-operation of General Grant, but that General had been compelled to fall back from Holly Springs, which not only made co-operation impossible, but had given the enemy the opportunity of bringing in reinforcements. The consequence was that the Federals had to withdraw from the contest, having lost 600 killed, 1,500 wounded, and about 1,000 prisoners. The Lake Providence Canal was then tried, then the Moon Lake, or Yazoo Pass Canal, and finally the Rolling Fork and Sunflower passage, all of which proved unavailing. Again, on February 18, 1863, the Union mortar-fleet commenced another bombardment, which proved unsuccessful.

The final siege commenced May 18, by General Grant, commanding. He said, in his report: "By this disposition, the three army corps covered all the ground that their strength would admit of, and by the morning of the 19th the investment of Vicksburg was made as complete as could be by the forces under my command."

An ineffectual assault was made on the 19th, and on the 22d a general assault, the gun-boats co-operating, was commenced at 10 o'clock A. M. Slowly and steadily the Union forces approached, without opposition, until within forty yards of the works, when suddenly they were met with a terrific fire, and compelled to retire, with a loss of nearly 1,000 men killed, wounded, and prisoners.

General Grant then determined upon a regular siege, and the troops commenced digging. The sappers constructed their corridors, passages, and pits amid a blazing fire of musketry, and in the fiercest rays of the summer sun, with a fortitude which has no parallel in history, and is equaled only by that of the Vicksburg garrison. Day after day—forty-six in all—did this process continue, one-half digging, while the other picked off the rebels who were endeavoring to interrupt them.

Admiral Porter co-operated heartily and vigorously with the army in all their operations. His gun-boats were constantly below the city, shelling the works, and the mortar-boats were at work for forty-two days, without intermission, throwing shells into all parts of the city. He also supplied the army with a large amount of artillery and ordnance, and prevented the depredations of guerrillas between Cairo and Vicksburg.

Every precaution was taken during the siege, to guard against an attack in the rear. Sherman was placed in command of all the troops designated to look after Johnston. The division of Osterhaus was sent to the Big Black to guard the crossings and repel any attack. A reconnoissance was also sent out under Blair, which reported no enemy within striking distance.

The sapping and mining progressed rapidly until the 25th of June, when one of the mines was ready to be sprung. The enemy, on their side, kept running counter-saps, so as to meet and cross those of the Union laborers, and, in two or three instances, only a thin wall of earth separated the combatants.

The mine under the principal fort of the enemy was exploded June 25. The explosion was terrific, the fort and every thing connected with it being blown into the air, and scattered around in all directions. Immediately the batteries along the whole line, with the mortar and gun-boat fleet, opened upon the enemy, who replied vigorously. As soon as the explosion had taken place, Leggett's brigade, of McPherson's corps, rushed into the sap and fort, and, after a severe contest of half an hour, the flag of the 45th Illinois Regiment appeared on the summit of the work. When the fort was gained, the pioneer corps mounted it, and commenced throwing up intrenchments and preparing to mount artillery.

After the explosion of this mine, the work of constructing parallels was resumed. As the Union lines advanced, the rebels retired, constructing inner lines of defense as the outer ones were taken.

Though the result of these operations must inevitably have been a surrender, it was known that the Vicksburg garrison had another enemy to contend with—exhaustion. It was soon evident that they were short of provisions, and must, in the end, be starved into surrender. The work upon the mines was then relaxed, a sufficient demonstration being kept up with artillery and musketry to annoy the enemy. The pear was ripe, and Grant only waited for it to drop into his hands. It was afterward learned that the garrison of Vicksburg were reduced to dregs of their commissaries. Mule meat, though not eaten as a necessity, had become preferable to their pickled beef. They had no pork or flour, and but a limited supply of unground corn. Their ammunition was nearly exhausted, and only ten percussion caps to the man were found in their pouches. The result was inevitable.

At eight o'clock A. M., July 3, a flag of truce came out from the rebel lines, with a communication for General Grant. It proved to be a proposition for an armistice, with a view to arranging terms of capitulation. General Grant promptly replied that his only terms were an unconditional surrender of the city and garrison. General Bowen, the bearer of the communication, requested that General Grant would meet General Pemberton, to consult concerning terms. This was readily agreed to, and at three o'clock P. M., after a brief renewal of hostilities, the two Generals met in front of General Burbridge's line, where they sat in close conversation for an hour and a half. The conference broke up without any definite decision. In the evening General Grant sent in a proposal, which was not replied to until daybreak the next morning, when Pemberton requested modifications of the terms offered. General Grant then sent his final note, agreeing to certain of the modifications, and General Pemberton promptly forwarded his acceptance of the terms proposed. Thus, at ten o'clock on the morning of the 4th of July, 1863, Vicksburg had surrendered, and the Mississippi Valley was held by Union forces.

The terms agreed upon were, that each brigade should march to the front of the lines occupied by it, stack arms, and then to return to the inside, to remain as prisoners of war until properly paroled. Officers were allowed to retain their private baggage and side-arms, and mounted officers one horse each. The rank and file were to be allowed their clothing, but no other property. Necessary rations might be taken from the rebel stores (there proved to be no rebel stores), and 30 wagons were allowed them.

The formal entry was made at one o'clock in the afternoon, by General Logan's division marching in as provost guard, and raising the Union flag on the public buildings. Rebel loss, 34,000, including one Lieutenant-General, and 19 Major and Brigadier-Generals, 102 field officers, 213 guns, 35,000 small arms, 87 stand of colors, and a small lot of ammunition and stores. About 1,200 women and children had been living in caves; 2,500 persons had been killed inside during the siege.

Vienna, Va., was the scene of a Union surprise and defeat—8 Union and 6 rebels killed—June 17, 1861. The rebels were successful in a cavalry skirmish here November 26.

Village Creek, Ark., was occupied June 12, 1862, by the Unionists, after defeating the rebels, who lost 28 killed, wounded, and prisoners. Union loss, 1 prisoner and 12 wounded.

Virginia.—The Governor, November 16, 1860, called an extra session of the State Legislature, which convened at Richmond January 7, 1861, and on the 15th passed a bill calling a State Convention—in the Senate, 45 to 1; in the House, unanimously. On the 18th they appropriated $1,000,000 for the defense of the State. An election for delegates to a State Convention was held February 4. It was reported that a majority of members chosen were Union men, and the vote on the question of referring the action of the Convention back to the people resulted in a majority of 56,000 in favor of such reference. The Convention met at Richmond on the 13th. Commissioners were sent to the Peace Conference; and after their return, April 4, the Convention, by the decisive vote of 89 to 45, refused to pass a secession ordinance. Governor Fetcher, on the 16th, refused to furnish troops under the President's proclamation. Next day the Convention passed an ordinance of secession—88 to 55—to take effect, if ratified by the people, on May 4; and the Governor recognized the Confederate States by proclamation. He soon afterward entered into an agreement with the Confederacy, through A. H. Stevens, whereby all the public property, naval stores, munitions of war, etc., acquired by the State from the United States, were turned over to the said Confederacy. This agreement was approved by the Convention on the 25th. It was understood that those who did not vote for secession in the eastern and southern parts of the State *had better not vote at all; that they had better leave the State.* Under this rule the result was announced, "125,950 for, and 20,373 against secession, not including several western counties." The Governor, on May 3, called out the militia to defend the State from the Northerners; and it was admitted into the Southern Confederacy May 6. President Lincoln declared the State in insurrection August 16. (See West Virginia.)

Wallerboro, S. C., was occupied March 3, 1865, by Kilpatrick, after he had driven out a small rebel force.

Warrensburg, Mo., was the scene of a Union victory—150 rebels captured—November 18, 1861. 200 of Quantrell's men were repulsed in an attack on this place March 26, 1862, by 60 Union troops, under Major Foster. Rebel loss, 9 killed, 16 wounded, and 25 horses; Union loss, 2 killed and 11 wounded. Captain Parker's guerrillas were, on the 28th, defeated near this place, losing 15 killed and 21 prisoners.

Warrenton, Va.—A brigade of cavalry, under Lieutenant-Colonel Karge, captured and paroled 1,600 rebels at this place September 29, 1862. The town was occupied by the Federal advance November 6. They left it on the 15th, moving toward Fredericksburg. Several Union signal officers were captured here August 14, 1863. White's rebel cavalry were here defeated September 18, and again October 31.

Warrenton Junction was the scene of skirmishes September 25 and November 19, 1862, and April 27 and May 3 and 30, 1863; none of them decisive.

Warsaw, Ky., was occupied and the State arms seized September 24, 1861.

Warsaw, Mo., was a skirmish scene October 16, 1861. The town was burned by the rebels November 19.

Washington, D. C.—Several demonstrations were made by the rebels against the Capital, but all unavailing.

Washington, John A. (See Elkwater.)

Washington, La., was occupied by General Banks April 20, 1863.

Washington, N. C., was occupied by General Burnside's troops March 21, 1862. An indecisive engagement occurred here June 10. The Union garrison at this place were, September 6, attacked by 1,200 rebels; after a fight of two hours, the enemy were repulsed and pursued 7 miles, with the loss of 4 guns and numerous prisoners.

The Union pickets were driven in, March 28, 1863, and the rebels attacked the town on the 30th. They were, with the assistance of the gun-boats, driven back. They renewed the attack next day, closely investing the place. The siege was continued two weeks, when it was raised without result.

Watauga Bridge, Tenn., was destroyed by Union forces December 30, 1862.

Waterloo Bridge, Va., was a skirmish scene August 25, 1862.

Waterproof, La.—800 rebel cavalry attacked the garrison of 200 colored troops, at this place, February 14, 1864; but, with the aid of gun-boats, after two and a half hours' fighting, were driven off; Union loss, 2 killed and 5 wounded; rebels left 8 killed and 5 prisoners.

Wachusett. (See "Florida.")

Waverly, Tenn., was the scene of skirmishes—rebels defeated each time—October 23, 1862, and April 11, 1863.

Waynesboro, Ga., was occupied and the public buildings burned by Sherman's forces November 27, 1864. Kilpatrick with his cavalry force attacked Wheeler, and drove him out of his works and through Waynesboro, with considerable loss. Wheeler was thus placed in the rear of Sherman's line of march, and the latter's cavalry force kept him there.

Weber Falls, Ark., was the scene of an engagement and rebel defeat, April 24, 1863.

Weongahick, Va., was occupied by General Sheridan March 16, 1865.

Wesley, Ky., was a skirmish scene—rebels defeated—March 16, 1863.

West Liberty, Ky., was the scene of a spirited engagement October 23, 1861. The rebels were defeated, with considerable loss.

Weston, Mo.—A train on the Platte County Railroad was seized, upon its arrival at Weston, by guerrillas, under the rebel Gordon, November 29, 1861. The town was occupied by 1,000 Kansas troops, under Colonel Jennison, after driving out the rebels, July 26, 1864.

West Point, Va.—On May 7, 1862, the rebels attacked the Union troops landing from transports, but, after a severe struggle, were routed, losing about 1,000 killed and wounded. Union loss, 250. The Union gunboats took part in the action. The town was occupied by Federal troops May 7, 1863; they evacuated the place June 2.

West Port, Mo., was a skirmish scene June 17, 1863. The Union forces, under Curtis, were driven out by Shelby, October 23, 1864. Shelby was, in turn, defeated next day by Pleasanton.

West Virginia.—An anti-secession convention of delegates, from the counties of Western Virginia, met at Wheeling, 35 counties being represented, May 13, 1861. After passing resolutions in favor of the Union, and recommending a division of the State of Virginia, it adjourned on the 15th, having called a Provisional Convention, to assemble at Wheeling June 11. The delegates to this convention were chosen May 26. About 40 counties chose delegates, and they met at the time and place designated. This body denounced as usurpers the Richmond Convention, which had passed the secession ordinance, repudiated the idea of allegiance to the Southern Confederacy, and vacated the offices of all who adhered to the rebellion. On the 20th, they unanimously resolved upon ultimate separation, and the same day elected F. H. Pierpont Governor. President Lincoln, on the 26th, acknowledged the Wheeling Government as the Government of Virginia. Congress ratified this action, and the new Legislature met at the same place July 2. On the 9th they elected John S. Carlile and Waitman T. Willey to the United States Senate, in place of Hunter and Mason. The bill admitting West Virginia into the Union as a State, distinct from Virginia, was approved December 31, 1862. The report of the new State's financial condition, December 31, 1863, showed *no debt*, and $209,683 in the treasury.

White House, Va. (See Grant's Report.)

White Oak Swamp. (See Charles City Cross-roads.)

White Point, North Edisto Island, S. C., was captured by Union troops May 1, 1862.

White Sulphur Springs, Va., was a skirmish scene November 13, 1862, and also October 12, 1863.

Wild Cat, Ky., was the scene of a hard-fought battle

October 21, 1861. The Unionists, under Schoepf, defeated the Confederates, under Zollicoffer. Union loss, 4 killed and 21 wounded; rebel loss, unknown.

Wilderness. (See Grant's Report.)

Wilks. (See Mason.)

Williamsburg, Va.—The advance of General McClellan's army overtook the rear of the Confederates at this place May 5, 1862, when a fight ensued. The battle raged furiously all day. Toward night General Hancock succeeded in turning the rebel left, when they broke and retreated under cover of the night. Union loss, 455 killed, 1,411 wounded, and 388 missing; rebel loss, about 3,000. The town was evacuated by the rebels during the night, leaving more than 1,000 wounded men in the hospitals. The place was occupied by the Federals next day. The rebel cavalry were repulsed here September 9. The Union cavalry fell into an ambush here February 7, 1863, losing 40 men. The rebels attacked the place March 29, but were repulsed, with considerable loss; the same action was repeated April 30.

Williamsport, Md. (See Pennsylvania Invasion.)

Williamsport, Tenn.—Several fights occurred at this place August 11, 1862, between guerrilla and Union forces, in each of which the rebels were defeated, with considerable loss.

Wilmington, N. C.—The forts at this place were seized by the State authorities January 2, 1861. This soon became notorious as a haven for blockade-runners, and so continued until the taking of Fort Fisher. (See Fort Fisher.) January 18, 1864, General Paine reconnoitered in force from Fort Fisher toward Wilmington, and, after some skirmishing, fell back to his intrenchments. This was repeated several times. General Terry, on the 11th, advanced, with two divisions, from Fort Fisher toward the city, the fleet co-operating, carried the rebel outer-works at the south end of Myrtle Sound, and intrenched close up to their main line, 12 miles from Wilmington.

General Schofield now co-operated with General Terry and the fleet and he, on the 18th, advanced from the land side, while Porter shelled the works from the boats. Fort Anderson was evacuated on the 19th, the rebels retiring toward Wilmington, the Unionists following, and next day took 2 guns and 340 prisoners. The Union forces, on the 21st, reached a point on the opposite side of the river from Wilmington, when the bridges were burning; the rebels, seeing this, burned 1,000 bales of cotton and 15,000 barrels of resin, and prepared to evacuate, which they did that night, the Union forces entering on the morning of the 22d. The entire rebel works in and about Wilmington and all the way down the river, 19 forts and batteries in all—being, perhaps, the strongest fortified harbor in the world—thus fell into Union possession. Three locomotives and a dozen cars were left in the railroad shops uninjured; 1 ram and 2 transports escaped up the river. The Union loss, in all, since the capture of Fort Fisher, was about 200.

Wilson's Creek, Mo. (See Lyon.)

Winchester, Va., was the scene of a skirmish and Union victory March 11, 1862, and also on the 22d. The Union army that night slept on their arms. Next morning at sunrise, the Confederates, 12,000 strong, under Jackson, attacked General Shields, with 10,000, at Kearnstown, near Winchester, Virginia. The fight was continued till noon, when a charge drove the rebels back half a mile. They rallied, and in turn drove the Unionists back. General Shields ordered the left flank turned, which was done in gallant style. Both sides fought desperately until 3 P. M., when a panic seized the rebels, and they fled toward Strasburg. Union loss, 115 killed and 450 wounded; rebel loss, 869 killed, wounded, and missing.

General Banks, in his retreat, occupied the town May 24. The town was again taken by the Federals December 3, who captured 140 prisoners. The Unionists, in a skirmish here May 19, 1863, captured a few prisoners. (See Grant's Report, and Pennsylvania Invasion.)

Winnsborough, S. C., was occupied by Slocum's forces February 21, 1865. The town was fired and a great part of it consumed, having caught from the cotton belonging to a rebel woman, who fired it herself.

Winton, N. C., was burned by Burnside's gun-boats February 20, 1862.

Woodbury, Ky.—Colonel Burbridge, with 250 men

and two pieces of artillery, attacked a body of 400 rebels in camp at Woodbury, routed them, and burned their camp October 29, 1861.

Woodbury, Tenn., was the scene of a severe fight and Union victory August 28, 1862. There was a skirmish here January 24, 1863, lasting an hour. Union loss, 9 wounded; rebel loss, 100 prisoners.

The Union forces, under General Hazen, marched to attack the rebels at this place April 2, but being apprised of the movement to capture them, they fled. The cavalry had a running fight for three miles. 15 rebels were killed and wounded, and 30 captured; 50 horses and a quantity of ammunition were also taken. Union loss, one wounded.

Woodburn, Tenn., was the scene of a skirmish and Union victory May 2, 1863. The depot at this place was burned by guerrillas August 20, 1864.

Woodville, Miss., was occupied, and the public buildings burned, by Union troops, August 15, 1863.

World. (See *Daily News* and Bogus Proclamation.)

Worthington, Va.—Colonel Crossman, September 2, 1861, with two companies, attacked a superior force of Confederates at this place, but were compelled to retire, losing two men.

Wytheville, Va., was occupied by Unionists July 15, 1863. They cut the line of the Virginia and Tennessee Railroad; 120 prisoners, 3 pieces of artillery, and 700 small arms were captured. Rebel loss, about 75 killed and wounded; Union loss, 65 killed and wounded. (See Saltville.)

Yazoo Pass Expedition.—This movement was undertaken to flank Vicksburg, cutting it off from supplies, but proved a failure. It cost both parties a vast amount of time and material, and was about equally disastrous to each. It occupied from February 22 until about May 25, 1863, including the other moves taken in connection with it.

Yellow Bayou, La.—During Banks's retreat from the Red River country, the rebels attacked him at this place May 18, 1864. They were met by Generals Mower and A J. Smith, who checked the rebels, with some loss.

Yellow Creek, Mo.—The rebels, under Poindexter, were scattered here August 13, 1862.

York, Penn. (See Pennsylvania Invasion.)

Yorktown, Va.—McClellan arrived in front of this place April 5, 1862. The rebels opened fire, which was returned. Union loss, 6 killed, 16 wounded. The rebels again, April 18, made a night attack, which was repulsed. The rebels left the city May 3, leaving all their heavy guns, large quantities of ammunition and camp equipage. McClellan occupied the place next day.

Young's Point. (See Vicksburg.)

Youngsville, Ala., was occupied by General Rousseau July 16, 1864. He burned four warehouses filled with corn and bacon.

Zollicoffer, Tenn., was the scene of a brisk but indecisive engagement September 20, 1863.

CITIZENS' MANUAL.

OUR NATIONAL SECURITIES

are of several different kinds. The bulk of the Public Debt, however, is embraced in the five following classes:

1st. The "SEVEN-THIRTIES," which bear seven and three-tenths per cent. interest, payable in currency, having three years to run, and then convertible into currency or Five-twenties, at the option of the holder.

2d. The "FIVE-TWENTIES," which bear six per cent. interest, payable semi-annually in gold, having twenty years to run, but which may be paid off in gold by the Government, on due notice to the holders, at any time after five years.

3d. The "TEN-FORTIES," which bear five per cent. interest, payable semi-annually in gold, having forty years to run, but which may be paid off in gold on notice to the holders, at any time after ten years.

4th. The "SIXES OF 1881," which bear six per cent. interest, payable semi-annually in gold, having twenty years to run (from 1861), and then payable in gold.

5th. The "LEGAL TENDER" or "Greenbacks," which are a legal tender for all debts, except duties on imports and interest on the gold-bearing bonds. There was, January 1, 1861, of these bills, including fractional currency, $640,780,861 37, of which $452,231,820 37 is free of interest, and $188,549,041 bears simple or compound interest, payable on the maturity of the notes, most of them six per cent., payable three years after 1864, the interest compounded in a table on the back of the note every six months.

In addition to the above, there are Oregon War Bonds, Texas Indemnity Bonds, Gold Certificates of Deposit, Certificates of Indebtedness, U. P. R. R. Bonds, and Temporary Loans.

THE NATIONAL DEBT.

The following is a statement of the public debt of the United States at certain dates:

Jan. 1, 1793	$75,463,476 52
Jan. 1, 1795	80,747,587 36
Jan. 1, 1800	82,976,294 35
Jan. 1, 1805	82,212,150 50
Jan. 1, 1810	53,173,217 52
Jan. 1, 1815	99,833,660 15
Jan. 1, 1820	91,015,566 15
Jan. 1, 1825	83,788,432 71
Jan. 1, 1830	48,565,408 50
Jan. 1, 1835	351,282 05
Jan. 1, 1840	5,025,077 63
Jan. 1, 1845	17,093,794 80
Jan. 1, 1850	64,228,238 37
Nov. 17, 1855	39,969,731 05
July 1, 1860	64,769,703 08

Jan. 1, 1866, the Public Debt was as follows:

Five-twenties	$665,370,800 00
Ten-forties	172,770,100 00
Sixes of 1881	282,645,800 00
Five and Six per cent. Bonds	46,361,591 80
Debt bearing Gold Interest	**1,167,148,291 80**
Seven-thirties	830,000,000 00
Compound Interest Notes	180,012,141 00
Sundry Items	169,463,094 50
Debt bearing Currency Interest	1,179,475,235 50
Debt due, not presented for payment	1,166,880 32
Debt bearing no Interest	459,519,950 37
Total Debt	$2,807,310,357 99
Cash in the Treasury	90,728,821 80
Balance	**$2,716,581,536 19**

NATIONAL DEBTS OF THE WORLD.

Country.	National Debt.	Population.	Per Capita.
Great Britain....	$3,913,324,000	29,000,000	$134 91
Netherlands.......	450,120,000	3,500,000	128 61
Hamburg	22,264,000	222,000	100 73
United States....	2,716,581,536	31,445,080	87 22
France	1,936,000,000	36,000,000	55 17
Portugal........	145,200,000	4,000,000	36 30
Spain...........	517,880,000	16,000,000	32 37
Austria.........	1,084,160,000	35,000,000	30 40
Belgium	126,808,000	4,500,000	28 17
Bavaria	122,840,000	4,600,000	26 70
Denmark........	58,080,000	2,600,000	22 34
Hanover........	33,396,000	1,800,000	18 55
Greece	19,360,000	1,070,000	18 09
Russia..........	1,118,040,000	75,000,000	14 91
Wurtemburg.....	24,200,000	1,700,000	14 23
Prussia	203,280,000	18,000,000	11 29
Brazil..........	75,020,000	7,700,000	9 74
Chili...........	7,260,000	1,400,000	5 19
Sweden.........	8,228,000	3,700,000	2 22

VOLUNTEERS AND BOUNTIES.

The several States furnished Volunteers during the rebellion, as follows:

States.	Aggregate No. of Men.	Aggregates reduced to a 3 yrs' standard.
Connecticut	57,270	50,514
Delaware	13,651	10,303
District of Columbia	16,872	11,506
Illinois	258,217	212,694
Indiana	196,147	152,283
Iowa	75,860	68,182
Kansas	20,097	18,654
Kentucky	78,540	70,348
Maine	71,745	56,595
Maryland	49,730	40,692
Massachusetts	151,785	123,844
Michigan	90,119	80,865
Minnesota	25,034	19,675
Missouri	108,773	86,192
New Hampshire	34,605	30,827
New Jersey	79,511	55,785
New York	455,568	380,980
Ohio	317,133	239,976
Pennsylvania	366,326	267,558
Rhode Island	23,711	17,878
Vermont	35,256	29,052
West Virginia	30,003	27,653
Wisconsin	96,118	78,985
Totals	**2,653,062**	**2,129,041**

The volunteers received bounties as follows:

1,156,868	received	$100 each	$115,686,800
10,606	"	200 "	2,121,200
396,709	"	300 "	119,012,700
158,507	"	400 "	63,402,800
930,372	"	no bounty.	
Total amount of bounties paid			**$300,223,500**

To equalize the bounties (at $400) will require, in addition to the amount already paid, $761,001,300.

PROCLAMATIONS.

[To save space, the usual closing, "In testimony whereof, etc.," the date and seal, with the signatures of the President and Secretary of State, are omitted.]

"THE SIXTY-DAYS' NOTICE."

By Abraham Lincoln, *President of the United States of America.*

Dated July 25, 1862.

In pursuance of the sixth section of the act of Congress, entitled "An act to suppress insurrection and to punish treason and rebellion, to seize and confiscate the property of rebels, and for other purposes," approved July 17, 1862, and which act, and the joint resolution explanatory thereof, are herewith published, I, Abraham Lincoln, President of the United States, do hereby proclaim to and warn all persons within the contemplation of said sixth section to cease participating in, aiding, countenancing, or abetting the existing rebellion, or any rebellion, against the Government of the United States, and to return to their proper allegiance to the United States, on pain of the forfeitures and seizures as within and by said sixth section provided.

A PROCLAMATION GIVING NOTICE OF THE EMANCIPATION PROCLAMATION, AND CALLING ATTENTION TO CERTAIN ACTS OF CONGRESS.

By Abraham Lincoln, *President of the United States of America.*

Dated September 22, 1862.

I, Abraham Lincoln, President of the United States of America, and Commander-in-chief of the army and navy thereof, do hereby proclaim and declare that hereafter, as heretofore, the war will be prosecuted for the object of practically restoring the constitutional relation between the United States and the people thereof, in which States that relation is, or may be, suspended or disturbed; that it is my purpose, upon the next meeting of Congress, to again recommend the adoption of a practical measure, tendering pecuniary aid to the free acceptance or rejection of all the slave States so called, the people whereof may not then be in rebellion against the United States, and which States may then have voluntarily adopted, or thereafter may voluntarily adopt, the immediate or gradual abolishment of slavery within their respective limits; and that the effort to colonize persons of African descent, with their consent, upon this continent or elsewhere, with the previously obtained consent of the governments existing there, will be continued; that on the first day of January, in the year of our Lord one thousand eight hundred and sixty-three, all persons held as slaves within any State, or any designated part of a State, the people whereof shall then be in rebellion against the United States, shall be thenceforward and forever free, and the Executive Government of the United States, including the military and naval authority thereof, will recognize and maintain the freedom of such persons, and will do no act or acts to repress such persons, or any of them, in any efforts they may make for their actual freedom; that the Executive will, on the first day of January aforesaid, by proclamation, designate the States and parts of States, if any, in which the people thereof respectively shall then be in rebellion against the United States, and the fact that any State, or the people thereof, shall, on that day, be in good faith represented in the Congress of the United States by members chosen thereto at elections wherein a majority of the qualified voters of such State shall have participated, shall, in the absence of strong countervailing testimony, be deemed conclusive evidence that such State and the people thereof are not then in rebellion against the United States.

[Attention is here called to certain Acts of Congress, and obedience to them enjoined. For the acts referred to, see *Anti-Slavery Progress*, "New Articles of War," and "An Act to suppress insurrection," etc.—Ed.]

And the Executive will, in due time, recommend that all citizens of the United States who shall have remained loyal thereto throughout the rebellion shall, upon the restoration of the constitutional relation between the United States and their respective States and people, if the relation shall have been suspended or disturbed, be compensated for all losses by acts of the United States, including the loss of slaves.

THE EMANCIPATION PROCLAMATION.

By Abraham Lincoln, *President of the United States of America.*

Dated January 1, 1863.

Whereas, on the twenty-second day of September, one thousand eight hundred and sixty-two, a proclamation was issued by the President of the United States, containing, among other things, the following, to-wit:

"That, on the first day of January, in the year of our Lord one thousand eight hundred and sixty-three, all persons held as slaves within any State, or designated part of a State, the people whereof shall then be in rebellion against the United States, shall be then, thenceforth, and forever free, and the Executive Government of the United States, including the military and naval authorities thereof, will recognize and maintain the freedom of such persons, and will do no act or acts to repress such persons, or any of them, in any efforts they may make for their actual freedom.

"That the Executive will, on the first day of January aforesaid, by proclamation, designate the States and parts of States, if any, in which the people thereof respectively shall then be in rebellion against the United States, and the fact that any State, or the people thereof, shall, on that day, be, in good faith, represented in the Congress of the United States by members chosen thereto at elections wherein a majority of the qualified voters of such State shall have participated, shall, in the absence of strong countervailing testimony, be deemed conclusive evidence that such State and the people thereof are not then in rebellion against the United States."

Now, therefore, I, Abraham Lincoln, President of the United States, by virtue of the power in me vested as Commander-in-chief of the Army and Navy of the United States in time of actual armed rebellion against the authority and Government of the United States, and as a fit and necessary war measure for suppressing said rebellion, do, on this first day of January, in the year of our Lord one thousand eight hundred and sixty-three, and in accordance with my purpose so to do, publicly proclaim for the full period of one hundred days from the day of the first above-mentioned order, and designate, as the States and parts of States wherein the people thereof respectively are this day in rebellion against the United States, the following, to-wit: Arkansas, Texas, Louisiana, (except the parishes of St. Bernard, Plaquemines, Jefferson, St. John, St. Charles, St. James, Ascension, Assumption, Terre Bonne, Lafourche, St. Mary, St. Martin, and Orleans, including the City of Orleans,) Mississippi, Alabama, Florida, Georgia, South Carolina, North Carolina, and Virginia, (except the forty-eight counties designated as West Virginia, and also the counties of Berkley, Accomac, Northampton, Elizabeth City, York, Princess Ann, and Norfolk, including the cities of Norfolk and Portsmouth), and which excepted parts are, for the present, left precisely as if this proclamation were not issued.

And by virtue of the power and for the purpose aforesaid, I do order and declare that all persons held as slaves within said designated States and parts of States are, and henceforward shall be, free; and that the Executive Government of the United States, including the military and naval authorities thereof, will recognize and maintain the freedom of said persons.

And I hereby enjoin upon the people so declared to be free to abstain from all violence, unless in necessary self-defense, and I recommend to them that, in all cases, when allowed, they labor faithfully for reasonable wages.

And I further declare and make known, that such persons, of suitable condition, will be received into the armed service of the United States, to garrison forts, positions, stations, and other places, and to man vessels of all sorts in said service.

And upon this act, sincerely believed to be an act of justice, warranted by the Constitution, upon military necessity, I invoke the considerate judgment of mankind and the gracious favor of Almighty God.

AMNESTY PROCLAMATION.

By Abraham Lincoln, *President of the United States of America.*

Dated December 8, 1863.

Whereas, in and by the Constitution of the United States, it is provided that the President shall have power to grant reprieves and pardons for offenses against the United States, except in cases of impeachment; and

Whereas, a rebellion now exists, whereby the loyal State governments of several States have, for a long time, been subverted, and many persons have committed and are now guilty of treason against the United States; and

Whereas, with reference to said rebellion and treason, laws have been enacted by Congress, declaring forfeiture and confiscation of property and liberation of slaves, all upon terms therein stated; and, also, declaring that the President was thereby authorized, at any time thereafter, by proclamation, to extend to persons who have participated in the existing rebellion, in any State or part thereof, pardon and amnesty, with such exceptions and at such times and on such conditions as he may deem expedient for the public welfare.

Whereas, the Congressional declaration for limited and conditional pardon accords with the well-established judicial exposition of the pardoning power; and whereas, with reference to the said rebellion, the President of the United States has issued several proclamations with provisions in regard to the liberation of slaves; and

Whereas, it is now desired by some persons heretofore engaged in the said rebellion to resume their allegiance to the United States, and to reinaugurate loyal State governments within and for their respective States; therefore,

I, Abraham Lincoln, President of the United States, do proclaim, declare, and make known to all persons who have directly or by implication participated in the existing rebellion, except as hereinafter excepted, a full pardon is hereby granted them and each of them, with restoration of all rights of property, except as to slaves, and in property cases where the rights of third parties shall have intervened, and upon condition that every such person shall take and subscribe an oath, and thenceforward keep and maintain said oath inviolate, and which oath shall be registered for permanent asseveration, and shall be of the tenor and effect following, to-wit:

I, —— ——, do solemnly swear, in the presence of Almighty God, that I will henceforth faithfully support, protect, and defend the Constitution of the United States and the Union of the States thereunder, and that I will, in like manner, abide by and faithfully support all acts of Congress passed during the existing rebellion, with reference to slaves, so long and so far as not repealed, modified, or held void by Congress or by decision of the Supreme Court, and that I will, in like manner, abide by and faithfully support all proclamations of the President made during the rebellion, having reference to slaves, so long and so far as not modified or declared void by decision of the Supreme Court, so help me God!

The persons excepted from the benefits of the foregoing provisions are, all who are or shall have been civil or diplomatic agents of the so-called Confederate Government; all who have left judicial stations under the United States to aid the rebellion; all who are or shall have been military or naval officers of said so-called Confederate Government, above the rank of colonel in the army and lieutenant in the navy; all who left seats in the United States Congress to aid the rebellion; all who have resigned commissions in the army or navy of the United States and afterward aided the rebellion; and all who have engaged, in any way, in treating colored persons or white persons in charge of such, otherwise than lawfully, as prisoners of war; and which persons may have been found in the United States service as soldiers, seamen, or in any other capacity.

And I do further proclaim, declare, and make known that whenever, in any of the States of Arkansas, Texas, Louisiana, Mississippi, Tennessee, Alabama, Georgia,

Florida, South Carolina, and North Carolina, a number of persons, not less than one-tenth of the votes cast in such States at the presidential election of the year of our Lord one thousand eight hundred and sixty, each having taken the oath aforesaid, and not having since violated it, and being a qualified voter by the election law of the State existing immediately before the so-called act of secession, and excluding all other, shall re-establish a State government which shall be republican and in no wise contravening said oath, such shall be recognised as the true government of the State, and the State shall receive thereunder the benefit of the constitutional provision which declares that the United States shall guarantee to every State in this Union a republican form of government and shall protect each of them against invasion on application of the Legislature, or of the Executive, when the Legislature can not be convened, against domestic violence.

And I do further proclaim and make known that any provision which may be adopted by such State, in relation to the freed people of such State which shall recognise and declare their permanent freedom, provide for their education, and which may yet be consistent as a temporary arrangement with their present condition, as a laboring, landless, and houseless class, will not be objected to by the National Executive.

And it is engaged as not improper that, in constructing a loyal State government in any State, the name of the State, the boundary, the subdivisions, the constitution, and the general code laws as before the rebellion, be maintained, subject only to the modifications made necessary by the conditions hereintofore stated, and such others, if any, not contravening said conditions, and which may be deemed expedient by those framing the new State government.

To avoid misunderstanding, it may be proper to say that this proposition, so far as it relates to State government, has no reference to States wherein loyal State governments have all the while been maintained; and for the same reasons it may be proper to further say, that whether members sent to Congress from any State shall be admitted to seats, constitutionally rests exclusively with the respective Houses and not, to any extent, with the Executive; and still further, that this proclamation is intended to present the people of the States, wherein the national authority has been suspended and loyal State governments have been subverted, a mode in and by which the national authority and loyal State governments may be re-established within said States or any of them; and while the mode presented is the best the Executive can suggest with his present impressions, it must not be understood that no other possible mode would be acceptable.

The above was limited, and explained by another, issued March 26, 1864, which declared that the objects of the proclamation were to suppress the insurrection and restore the national authority, and that the amnesty was offered with reference to these objects alone; that its benefits do not apply to those in military, naval, or civil confinement, under bonds or on parole as prisoners of war. That, on the contrary, it does apply to those only who, being at large, free from any arrest, confinement or duress, shall voluntarily come forward and take the oath, with the purpose of restoring peace and the national authority. The oath may be taken before any United States officer, or before any officer of a State or Territory, not in insurrection, who is, by law, qualified to administer oaths. Said officers to grant certificates to those taking the oath, transmitting the original records to the Department of State, where they shall be registered, and from which, in proper cases, certificates of such records may be issued.

THE AMNESTY PROCLAMATION,

By ANDREW JOHNSON, *President of the United States of America*, Dated May 29, 1865.

Grants to all persons who have, directly or indirectly, participated in the existing rebellion, except as hereinafter excepted, amnesty and pardon, with restoration of all rights of property, except as to slaves, and except in cases where legal proceedings, under the laws of the

United States providing for the confiscation of property of persons engaged in rebellion, have been instituted; but upon the condition that every such person shall take and subscribe the following oath (or affirmation), and which oath shall be registered for permanent preservation, to wit:

"I, ——— ———, do solemnly swear (or affirm), in presence of Almighty God, that I will henceforth faithfully support, protect, and defend the Constitution of the United States, and the Union of the States thereunder; and that I will, in like manner, abide by, and faithfully support all laws and proclamations which have been made during the existing rebellion with reference to the emancipation of slaves. So help me God."

The following classes of persons are excepted from the benefits of this proclamation: 1st, all who are or shall have been pretended civil or diplomatic officers or otherwise domestic or foreign agents of the pretended Confederate Government; 2d, all who left judicial stations under the United States to aid the rebellion; 3d, all who have been military or naval officers of said pretended Confederate Government, above the rank of Colonel in the army, or Lieutenant in the navy; 4th, all who left seats in the Congress of the United States to aid the rebellion; 5th, all who resigned or tendered resignations of their commissions in the army or navy of the United States, to evade duty in resisting the rebellion; 6th, all who have engaged in any way in treating otherwise than lawfully as prisoners of war persons found in the United States service, as officers, soldiers, seamen, or in other capacities; 7th, all persons who have been, or are absentees from the United States, for the purpose of aiding the rebellion; 8th, all military and naval officers in the rebel service, who were educated by the Government in the Military Academy at West Point, or the United States Naval Academy; 9th, all persons who held the pretended offices of governors of States in insurrection against the United States; 10th, all persons who left their homes within the jurisdiction and protection of the United States, and passed beyond the Federal military lines into the pretended Confederate States for the purpose of aiding the rebellion; 11th, all persons who have been engaged in the destruction of the commerce of the United States upon the high seas, and all persons who have made raids into the United States from Canada, or been engaged in destroying the commerce of the United States upon the lakes and rivers that separate the British Provinces from the United States; 12th, all persons who, at the time when they seek to obtain the benefits hereof by taking the oath herein prescribed, are in military, naval, or civil confinement or custody, or under bonds of the civil, military, or naval authorities or agents of the United States, as prisoners of war, or persons detained for offenses of any kind, either before or after conviction; 13th, all persons who have voluntarily participated in said rebellion, and the estimated value of whose taxable property is over twenty thousand dollars; 14th, all persons who have taken the oath of amnesty as prescribed in the President's proclamation of December 8, A. D. 1863, or an oath of allegiance to the Government of the United States since the date of said proclamation, and who have not thenceforward kept and maintained the same inviolate.

NATIONAL PLATFORMS OF 1864.

UNION PLATFORM.

Resolved, That it is the highest duty of every American citizen to maintain against all its enemies, the integrity of the Union, and the paramount authority of the Constitution and laws of the United States, and that, laying all political opinions aside, we pledge ourselves, as Union men, animated by a common sentiment, and aiming at a common object, to do everything in our power to aid the Government in quelling, by force of arms, the rebellion now raging against its authority, and bringing to the punishment due to their crimes, the rebels and traitors arrayed against it.

Resolved, That we approve the determination of the Government of the United States not to compromise with rebels, or to offer any terms of peace, except such as may be based upon an unconditional surrender of their hostility, etc., and a return to their just allegiance to the Constitution and laws of the United States, and that we call upon the Government to maintain this position, and to prosecute the war with the utmost possible vigor to the complete suppression of the rebellion, in full reliance upon the self-sacrifices, the patriotism, the heroic valor, and the undying devotion of the American people to their country and its free institutions.

Resolved, That slavery was the cause and now constitutes the strength of the rebellion, and that as it must be always and everywhere hostile to the principles of Republican Governments, justice and the national safety demand its utter and complete extirpation from the soil of the Republic, and that we uphold and maintain the acts and proclamations, by which the Government, in its own defence, has aimed a death blow at this gigantic evil. We are in favor, furthermore, of such an amendment to the Constitution, to be made by the people in conformity with its provisions, as shall terminate and forever prohibit the existence of slavery within the limits of the jurisdiction of the United States.

Resolved, That the thanks of the American people are due to the soldiers and sailors of the army and navy, who have periled their lives in defence of their country, and in vindication of the honor of the flag; that the nation owes them some permanent recognition of their patriotism and their valor, and ample and permanent provision for those of their survivors who have received disabling and honorable wounds in the service of their country, and that the memories of those who have fallen in its defense shall be held in grateful and everlasting remembrance.

Resolved, That we approve and applaud the political wisdom, the unselfish patriotism and unswerving fidelity to the Constitution and the principles of American liberty, with which Abraham Lincoln has discharged, under circumstances of unparalelled difficulty, the great duties and responsibilities of the Presidential office; that we approve and endorse, as demanded by the emergency and essential to the preservation of the nation, and as within the Constitution, the measures and acts which he has adopted to defend the nation against its open and secret foes; especially the Proclamation of Emancipation, and the employment, as Union soldiers, of men heretofore held in slavery, and that we have full confidence in his determination to carry these and all other Constitutional measures, essential to the salvation of the country, into full and complete effect.

Resolved, That we deem it essential to the general welfare, that harmony should prevail in the national councils, and we regard as worthy of public confidence and official trust those only who cordially endorse the principle proclaimed in these resolutions, and which should characterize the administration of the Government.

Resolved, That the Government owes to all men employed in its armies, without distinction of color, the full protection of the laws of war, and any violation of these laws and of the usages of civilized nations in the time of war, by the rebels now in arms, should be made the subject of full and prompt redress.

Resolved, That the foreign immigration, which in the past has added so much to the wealth and development of resources and increase of power to this nation, the asylum of the oppressed of all nations, should be fostered and encouraged by a liberal and just policy.

Resolved, That we are in favor of the speedy construction of the railroad to the Pacific.

Resolved, That the national faith is pledged for the redemption of the public debt and must be kept inviolate; and that for this purpose we recommend economy and rigid responsibilities in the public expenditures, and a vigorous and just system of taxation; that it is the duty of every loyal State to sustain the use of the national currency.

Resolved, That we approve the position taken by the Government, that the people of the United States can never regard with indifference the attempt of European power to overthrow by force, or to supplant by fraud, the institutions of any Republican Government on the Western Continent, and that they will view with extreme jealousy, as menacing to the peace and independence of this our country, the efforts of any such power to obtain new footholds for monarchical governments sustained by a foreign military force in near proximity to the United States.

DEMOCRATIC PLATFORM.

Resolved, That in the future, as in the past, we will adhere with unswerving fidelity to the Union under the Constitution as the only solid foundation of our strength, security and happiness as a people, and as a framework of government equally conducive to the welfare and prosperity of all the States, both Northern and Southern.

Resolved, That this Convention does explicitly declare, as the sense of the American people, that after four years of failure to restore the Union by the experiment of war, during which, under the pretense of military necessity or war power higher than the Constitution, the Constitution itself has been disregarded in every part, and public liberty and private right alike trodden down, and the material prosperity of the country essentially impaired, justice, humanity, liberty and the public welfare demand that immediate efforts be made for a cessation of hostilities with a view to an ultimate convention of the States, or other peaceable means, to the end that at the earliest practical moment peace may be restored on the basis of the Federal Union of the States.

Resolved, That the direct interference of the military authorities of the United States in the recent elections held in Kentucky, Maryland, Missouri and Delaware was a shameful violation of the Constitution, and a repetition of such acts in the approaching election will be held as revolutionary, and resisted with all the means and power under our control.

Resolved, That the aim and object of the Democratic party is to preserve the Federal Union and the rights of the States unimpaired, and they hereby declare that they considerthat the administrative usurpation of extraordinary and dangerous powers not granted by the Constitution, the subversion of the civil by military law in States not in insurrection, the arbitrary military arrest, imprisonment, trial and sentence of American citizens in States where the civil law exists in full force, the suppression of freedom of speech and of the press, the denial of the right of asylum, the open and avowed disregard of State rights, the employment of unusual test oaths, and the interference with, and denial of the right of the people to bear arms in their defense, is calculated to prevent a restoration of the Union and the perpetuation of the Government deriving its just powers from the consent of the governed.

Resolved, That the shameful disregard of the Administration to its duty in respect to our fellow-citizens who now are, and long have been, prisoners of war in a suffering condition, deserves the severest reprobation on the score alike of public policy and common humanity.

Resolved, That the sympathy of the Democratic party is heartily and earnestly extended to the soldiery of our army and sailors of our navy who are and have been in the field and on the sea, under the flag of their country, and in the event of its attaining power, they will receive all the care, protection and regard that the brave soldiers and sailors of the Republic have so nobly earned.

DECLARATION OF INDEPENDENCE.

In Congress, July 4th, 1776.

By the Representatives of the United States, in Congress assembled.

A DECLARATION.

When, in the course of human events, it becomes necessary for one people to dissolve the political bands which have connected them with another, and to assume among the powers of the earth the separate and equal station to which the laws of nature and of nature's God entitle them, a decent respect for the opinions of mankind requires that they should declare the causes which impel them to the separation.

We hold these truths to be self-evident:—that all men are created equal; that they are endowed by their Creator with certain unalienable rights; that among these are life, liberty, and the pursuit of happiness; that, to secure these rights, governments are instituted among men, deriving their just powers from the consent of the governed; that, whenever any form of government becomes destructive of these ends it is the right of the people to alter or to abolish it, and to institute a new government, laying its foundation on such principles, and organizing its powers in such form, as to them shall seem most likely to effect their safety and happiness. Prudence, indeed, will dictate that governments long established should not be changed for light and transient causes; and accordingly all experience hath shown that mankind are more disposed to suffer, while evils are sufferable, than to right themselves by abolishing the forms to which they are accustomed. But when a long train of abuses and usurpations, pursuing invariably the same object, evinces a design to reduce them under absolute despotism, it is their right, it is their duty, to throw off such government, and to provide new guards for their future security. Such has been the patient sufferance of these colonies; and such is now the necessity which constrains them to alter their former system of government. The history of the present king of Great Britain is a history of repeated injuries and usurpations, all having in direct object the establishment of an absolute tyranny over these states. To prove this, let facts be submitted to a candid world.

He has refused his assent to laws the most wholesome and necessary for the public good.

He has forbidden his governors to pass laws of immediate and pressing importance, unless suspended in their operation till his assent should be obtained; and, when so suspended, he has utterly neglected to attend to them.

He has refused to pass other laws for the accommodation of large districts of people, unless those people would relinquish the right of representation in the legislature—a right inestimable to them, and formidable to tyrants only.

He has called together legislative bodies at places unusual, uncomfortable, and distant from the depository of their public records, for the sole purpose of fatiguing them into compliance with his measures.

He has dissolved representative houses repeatedly, for opposing, with manly firmness, his invasions on the rights of the people.

He has refused, for a long time after such dissolutions, to cause others to be elected; whereby the legislative powers, incapable of annihilation, have returned to the people at large for their exercise; the state remaining, in the mean time, exposed to all the danger of invasion from without, and convulsions within.

He has endeavored to prevent the population of these states; for that purpose obstructing the laws for naturalization of foreigners, refusing to pass others to encourage their migration hither, and raising the conditions of new appropriations of lands.

He has obstructed the administration of justice, by refusing his assent to laws for establishing judiciary powers.

He has made judges dependent on his will alone for the tenure of their offices and the amount and payment of their salaries.

He has erected a multitude of new offices, and sent hither swarms of officers, to harass our people and eat out their substance.

He has kept among us, in times of peace, standing armies, without the consent of our legislatures.

He has affected to render the military independent of and superior to the civil power.

He has combined with others to subject us to a jurisdiction foreign to our Constitution and unacknowledged by our laws; giving his assent to their acts of pretended legislation,—

For quartering large bodies of armed troops among us:

For protecting them, by mock trial, from punishment for any murders which they should commit on the inhabitants of these states:

For cutting off our trade with all parts of the world:

For imposing taxes on us without our consent:

For depriving us, in many cases, of the benefits of trial by jury:

For transporting us beyond seas, to be tried for pretended offenses:

For abolishing the free system of English law in a neighboring province, establishing therein an arbitrary government, and enlarging its boundaries so as to render it at once an example and fit instrument for introducing the same absolute rule into these colonies:

For taking away our charters, abolishing our most valuable laws, and altering fundamentally the forms of our government:

For suspending our own legislatures, and declaring themselves invested with power to legislate for us in all cases whatsoever.

He has abdicated government here, by declaring us out of his protection, and waging war against us.

He has plundered our seas, ravaged our coasts, burned our towns and destroyed the lives of our people.

He is at this time transporting large armies of foreign mercenaries, to complete the works of death, desolation and tyranny, already begun, with circumstances of cruelty and perfidy scarcely paralleled in the most barbarous ages, and totally unworthy the head of a civilized nation.

He has constrained our fellow-citizens, taken captive on the high seas, to bear arms against their country, to become the executioners of their friends and brethren, or to fall themselves by their hands.

He has excited domestic insurrections among us, and has endeavored to bring on the inhabitants of our frontiers the merciless Indian savages, whose known rule of warfare is an undistinguished destruction of all ages, sexes, and conditions.

In every stage of these oppressions we have petitioned for redress in the most humble terms; our petitions have been answered only by repeated injury. A prince whose character is thus marked by every act which may define a tyrant is unfit to be the ruler of a free people.

Nor have we been wanting in attention to our British brethren. We have warned them, from time to time, of attempts made by their legislature to extend an unwarrantable jurisdiction over us. We have reminded them of the circumstances of our emigration and settlement here. We have appealed to their native justice and magnanimity, and we have conjured them, by the ties of our common kindred, to disavow these usurpations, which would inevitably interrupt our connections and correspondence. They, too, have been deaf to the voice of justice and consanguinity. We must, therefore, acquiesce in the necessity which denounces our separation, and hold them, as we hold the rest of mankind, enemies in war—in peace, friends.

We, therefore, the representatives of the United States of America, in General Congress assembled, appealing to the Supreme Judge of the world for the rectitude of our intentions, do, in the name and by the authority of the good people of these colonies, solemnly publish and declare, that these United Colonies are, and of right ought to be, free and independent states; that they are absolved from all allegiance to the British crown, and that all political connection between them and the state of Great Britain is, and ought to be, totally dissolved; and that, as free and independent states, they have full power to levy war, conclude peace, contract alliances, establish commerce, and do all other acts and things which independent states may of right do. And for the support of this declaration, with a firm reliance on the protection of Divine Providence, we mutually pledge to each other our lives, our fortunes, and our sacred honor.

Signed by order and in behalf of the Congress.

JOHN HANCOCK, President.

Attested, CHARLES THOMPSON, Secretary.

NEW HAMPSHIRE.

Josiah Bartlett,
William Whipple,
Mathew Thornton.

MASSACHUSETTS BAY.

Samuel Adams,
John Adams,
Robert Treat Paine.
Elbridge Gerry.

RHODE ISLAND, &c.

Stephen Hopkins,
William Ellery.

CONNECTICUT.

Roger Sherman,
Samuel Huntington,
William Williams,
Oliver Wolcott.

NEW YORK.

William Floyd,
Philip Livingston,
Francis Lewis,
Lewis Morris.

NEW JERSEY.

Richard Stockton,
John Witherspoon,
Francis Hopkinson,
John Hart,
Abramam Clark.

PENNSYLVANIA.

Robert Morris,
Benjamin Rush,
Benjamin Franklin,
John Morton,
George Clymer,
James Smith,
George Taylor,
James Wilson,
George Ross.

DELAWARE.

Cæsar Rodney,
George Read,
Thomas M'Kean.

MARYLAND.

Samuel Chase,
William Paca,

THOMAS STONE,
CHARLES CARROLL, of Carrollton.

VIRGINIA.

GEORGE WYTHE,
RICHARD HENRY LEE,
THOMAS JEFFERSON,
BENJAMIN HARRISON,
THOMAS NELSON, JR.,
FRANCIS LIGHTFOOT LEE,
CARTER BRAXTON.

NORTH CAROLINA.

WILLIAM HOOPER,
JOSEPH HEWES,
JOHN PENN.

SOUTH CAROLINA.

EDWARD RUTLEDGE,
THOMAS HEYWARD, JR.,
THOMAS LYNCH, JR.,
ARTHUR MIDDLETON.

GEORGIA.

BUTTON GWINNETT,
LYMAN HALL,
GEORGE WALTON.

ARTICLES OF CONFEDERATION

AND PERPETUAL UNION BETWEEN THE STATES OF NEW HAMPSHIRE, MASSACHUSETTS BAY, RHODE ISLAND, AND PROVIDENCE PLANTATIONS, CONNECTICUT, NEW YORK, NEW JERSEY, PENNSYLVANIA, DELAWARE, MARYLAND, VIRGINIA, NORTH CAROLINA, SOUTH CAROLINA AND GEORGIA.

ARTICLE 1. The style of this Confederacy shall be "The United States of America."

ARTICLE 2. Each State retains its sovereignty, freedom and independence, and every power, jurisdiction and right, which is not by this confederation expressly delegated to the United States in Congress assembled.

ARTICLE 3. The said States hereby severally enter into a firm league of friendship with each other, for their common defense, the security of their liberties, and their mutual and general welfare, binding themselves to assist each other against all force offered to, or attacks made upon them, or any of them, on account of religion, sovereignty, trade, or any other pretense whatever.

ARTICLE 4. The better to secure and perpetuate mutual friendship and intercourse among the people of the different States in this Union, the free inhabitants of each of these States—paupers, vagabonds, and fugitives from justice excepted—shall be entitled to all privileges and immunities of free citizens in the several States; and the people of each State shall have free ingress and regress to and from any other State, and shall enjoy therein all the privileges of trade and commerce, subject to the same duties, impositions and restrictions, as the inhabitants thereof respectively, provided that such restriction shall not extend so far as to prevent the removal of property, imported into any State, to any other State of which the owner is an inhabitant; provided, also, that no imposition, duties or restriction shall be laid by any State on the property of the United States, or either of them.

If any person guilty of, or charged with treason, felony, or other high misdemeanor in any State, shall flee from justice, and be found in any of the United States, he shall, upon demand of the Governor, or executive power of the State from which he fled, be delivered up and removed to the State having jurisdiction of his offense.

Full faith and credit shall be given in each of these States, to the records, acts, and judicial proceedings of the courts and magistrates of every other State.

ARTICLE 5. For the more convenient management of the general interest of the United States, Delegates shall be annually appointed, in such manner as the legislature of each State shall direct, to meet in Congress on the first Monday in November, in every year, with a power reserved to each State, to recall its Delegates, or any of them, at any time within the year, and to send others in their stead, for the remainder of the year.

No State shall be represented in Congress by less than two, nor by more than seven members; and no person shall be capable of being a Delegate for more than three years in any term of six years; nor shall any person, being a Delegate, be capable of holding any office under the United States, for which he, or another for his benefit, receives any salary, fees or emolument of any kind.

Each State shall maintain its own Delegates in any meeting of the States, and while they act as members of the Committee of the States.

In determining questions in the United States, in Congress assembled, each State shall have one vote.

Freedom of speech and debate in Congress shall not be impeached or questioned in any court or place, out of Congress, and the members of Congress shall be protected in their persons from arrests and imprisonments, during the time of their going to and from, and attendance on Congress, except for treason, felony, or breach of the peace.

ARTICLE 6. No State, without the consent of the United States in Congress assembled, shall send an embassy to, or receive an embassy from, or enter into any conference, agreement, alliance or treaty with any King, Prince or State; nor shall any person holding any office of profit or trust under the United States, or any of them, accept of any present, emolument, office or title of any kind whatever from any King, Prince or Foreign State; nor shall the United States in Congress assembled, or any of them, grant any title of nobility.

No two or more States shall enter into any treaty, confederation or alliance whatever between them, without the consent of the United States in Congress assembled, specifying accurately the purposes for which the same is to be entered into, and how long it shall continue.

No State shall lay any imposts or duties which may interfere with any stipulations in treaties, entered into by the United States in Congress assembled, with any King, Prince or State, in pursuance of any treaties already proposed by Congress, to the Courts of France and Spain.

No vessels of war shall be kept up in time of peace by any State, except such number only, as shall be deemed necessary by the United States in Congress assembled, for the defense of such State, or its trade; nor shall any body of forces be kept up by any State, in time of peace, except such number only, as in the judgment of the United States in Congress assembled, shall be deemed requisite to garrison the forts necessary for the defense of such State; but every State shall always keep up a well regulated and disciplined militia, sufficiently armed and accoutred, and shall provide and have constantly ready for use, in public stores, a due number of field pieces and tents, and a proper quantity of arms, ammunition and camp equipage.

No State shall engage in any war without the consent of the United States in Congress assembled, unless such State be actually invaded by enemies, or shall have received certain advice of a resolution being formed by some nation of Indians to invade such a State, and the danger is so imminent as not to admit of a delay, till the United States in Congress assembled can be consulted; nor shall any State grant commissions to any ships or vessels of war, nor letters of marque or reprisal, except it be after a declaration of war by the United States in Congress assembled, and then only against the Kingdom or State, and the subjects thereof, against which war has been so declared, and under such regulations as shall be established by the United States in Congress assembled, unless such State be infested by pirates, in which case vessels of war may be fitted out for that occasion, and kept so long as the danger shall continue, or until the United States in Congress assembled shall determine otherwise.

ARTICLE 7. When land forces are raised by any State for the common defense, all officers of, or under the rank of colonel, shall be appointed by the legislatures of each State respectively, by whom such forces shall be raised, or in such manner as such State shall direct, and all vacancies shall be filled up by the State which first made the appointment.

ARTICLE 8. All charges of war, and all other expenses that shall be incurred for the common defense or general welfare, and allowed by the United States in Congress assembled, shall be defrayed out of a common treasury, which shall be supplied by the several States, in proportion to the value of all land within each State, granted to or surveyed for any person, as such land and the buildings and improvements thereon shall be estimated according to such mode as the United States in Congress assembled, shall, from time to time, direct and appoint. The taxes for paying that proportion shall be laid and levied by the authority and direction of the legislatures of the several States within the time agreed upon by the United States in Congress assembled.

ARTICLE 9. The United States in Congress assembled shall have the sole and exclusive right and power of determining on peace and war, except in the cases mentioned in the 6th article—of sending and receiving ambassadors—entering into treaties and alliances, provided that no treaty of commerce shall be made whereby the legislative power of the respective States shall be restrained from imposing such imposts and duties on foreigners, as their own people are subjected to, or from prohibiting the exportation or importation of any species of goods or commodities whatsoever—of establishing rules for deciding in all cases what captures on land or water shall be legal, and in what manner prizes taken by land or naval forces in the service of the United States shall be divided or appropriated—of granting letters of marque and reprisal in times of peace—appointing courts for the trial of piracies and felonies committed on the high seas and establishing courts for receiving and determining finally appeals in all cases of captures, provided that no member of Congress shall be appointed a judge of any of the said courts.

The United States in Congress assembled shall also be the last resort on appeal in all disputes and differences now subsisting or that hereafter may arise between two or more States concerning boundary, jurisdiction, or any other cause whatever; which authority shall always be exercised in the manner following:—Whenever the legislative or executive authority or lawful agent of any State in controversy with another shall present a petition to Congress, stating the matter in question and praying for a hearing, notice thereof shall be given by order of Congress, to the legislative or executive authority of the other State in controversy, and a day assigned for the appearance of the parties by their lawful agents, who shall then be directed to appoint by joint consent, commissioners or judges to constitute a court for hearing and determining the matter in question; but if they cannot agree, Congress shall name three persons out of each of the United States, and from the list of such persons each party shall alternately strike out one, the petitioners beginning, until the number shall be reduced to thirteen; and from that number not less than seven, nor more than nine names, as Congress shall direct, shall in the presence of Congress be drawn out by lot, and the persons whose names shall be so drawn, or any five of them, shall be commissioners or judges, to hear and finally determine the controversy, so always as a major part of the judges who shall hear the cause shall agree in the determination; and if either party shall neglect to attend at the day appointed, without showing reasons which Congress shall judge sufficient, or being present shall refuse to strike, the Congress shall proceed to nominate three persons out of each State, and the Secretary of Congress shall strike in behalf of such party absent or refusing; and the judgment and sentence of the court to be appointed, in the manner above prescribed, shall be final and conclusive; and if any of the parties shall refuse to submit to the authority of such court, or to appear or defend their claim or cause, the court shall nevertheless proceed to pronounce sentence or judgment, which shall in like manner be final and decisive, the judgment or sentence and other proceedings being in either case transmitted to Congress and lodged among the acts of Congress for the security of the parties concerned: provided that every commissioner, before he sits in judgment, shall take an oath, to be administered by one of the judges of the Supreme or Superior Court of the State where the cause shall be tried, "well and truly to hear and determine the matter in question, according to the best of his judgment, without favor, affection, or hope of reward:" provided also that no State shall be deprived of territory for the benefit of the United States.

All controversies concerning the private right of soil claimed under different grants of two or more States, whose jurisdictions as they may respect such lands, and the States which passed such grants, are adjusted; the said grants or either of them being at the same time claimed to have originated antecedent to such settlement of jurisdiction, shall, on the petition of either party to the Congress of the United States, be finally determined as near as may be in the same manner as is before prescribed for deciding disputes respecting territorial jurisdiction between different States.

The United States in Congress assembled shall also have the sole exclusive right and power of regulating the alloy and value of coin struck by their own authority, or by that of the respective States—fixing the standard of weights and measures throughout the United States—regulating the trade and managing all affairs with the

Indians, not members of any of the States; provided that the legislative right of any State within its own limits be not infringed or violated—establishing or regulating post-offices from one State to another, throughout all the United States, and exacting such postage on the papers passing through the same as may be requisite to defray the expenses of the said office—appointing all officers of the land forces, in the service of the United States, excepting regimental officers—appointing all the officers of the naval forces, and commissioning all officers whatever in the service of the United States—making rules for the government and regulation of the said land and naval forces, and directing their operations.

The United States in Congress assembled shall have authority to appoint a committee, to sit in the recess of Congress, to be denominated "A Committee of the States," and to consist of one delegate from each State; and to appoint such other committees and civil officers as may be necessary for managing the general affairs of the United States under their direction—to appoint one of their number to preside; provided that no person be allowed to serve in the office of president more than one year in any term of three years—to ascertain the necessary sums of money to be raised for the service of the United States, and to appropriate and apply the same for defraying the public expenses—to borrow money, or emit bills on the credit of the United States, transmitting every half year to the respective States an account of the sums of money so borrowed or emitted—to build and equip a navy—to agree upon the number of land forces, and to make requisitions from each State for its quota, in proportion to the number of white inhabitants in such State; which requisition shall be binding, and thereupon the legislatures of each State shall appoint the regimental officers, raise the men, and clothe, arm and equip them in a soldier-like manner, at the expense of the United States; and the officers and men so clothed, armed and equipped, shall march to the place appointed, and within the time agreed on by the United States in Congress assembled: but if the United States in Congress assembled shall, on consideration of circumstances, judge proper that any State should not raise men, or should raise a smaller number than its quota, and that any other State should raise a greater number of men than the quota thereof, such extra number shall be raised, officered, clothed, armed and equipped in the same manner as the quota of such State, unless the legislature of such State shall judge that such extra number can not be safely spared out of the same, in which case they shall raise, officer, clothe, arm and equip as many of such extra number as they judge can be safely spared. And the officers and men so clothed, armed and equipped, shall march to the place appointed, and within the time agreed on by the United States in Congress assembled.

The United States in Congress assembled shall never engage in a war, nor grant letters of marque and reprisal in time of peace, nor enter into any treaties or alliances, nor coin money nor regulate the value thereof, nor ascertain the sums and expenses necessary for the defense and welfare of the United States, or any of them, nor emit bills, nor borrow money on the credit of the United States, nor appropriate money, nor agree upon the number of vessels of war to be built or purchased, or the number of land or sea forces to be raised, nor appoint a commander in chief of the army or navy, unless nine States assent to the same: nor shall a question on any other point, except for adjourning from day to day, be determined, unless by the votes of a majority of the United States in Congress assembled.

The Congress of the United States shall have power to adjourn to any time within the year, and to any place within the United States, so that no period of adjournment be for a longer duration than the space of six months, and shall publish the journal of their proceedings monthly, except such parts thereof relating to treaties, alliances, or military operations, as in their judgment require secrecy; and the yeas and nays of the delegates of each State on any question shall be entered on the journal, when it is desired by any delegate; and the delegates of a State, or any of them, at his or their request, shall be furnished with a transcript of the said journal, except such parts as are above excepted, to lay before the legislatures of the several States.

ARTICLE 10. The committee of the States, or any nine of them, shall be authorized to execute, in the recess of Congress, such of the powers of Congress, as the United States in Congress assembled, by the consent of nine States, shall, from time to time, think expedient to vest them with; provided that no power be delegated to the said committee, for the exercise of which, by the Articles of Confederation, the voice of nine States in the Congress of the United States assembled is requisite.

ARTICLE 11. Canada, acceding to this confederation, and joining in the measures of the United States, shall be admitted into, and entitled to all the advantages of this union; but no other colony shall be admitted into the same, unless such admission be agreed to by nine States.

ARTICLE 12. All bills of credit emitted, moneys borrowed, and debts contracted by, or under the authority of Congress, before the assembling of the United States, in pursuance of the present confederation, shall be deemed and considered as a charge against the United States, for payment and satisfaction whereof the said United States and the public faith are hereby solemnly pledged.

ARTICLE 13. Every State shall abide by the determinations of the United States in Congress assembled, on all questions which by this confederation are submitted to them. And the articles of this confederation shall be inviolably observed by every State, and the union shall be perpetual; nor shall any alteration at any time hereafter be made in any of them, unless such alteration be agreed to in a Congress of the United States, and be afterward confirmed by the legislatures of every State.

And Whereas, It hath pleased the Great Governor of the World to incline the hearts of the legislatures we respectively represent in Congress, to approve of, and to authorize us to ratify the said Articles of Confederation and perpetual union. Know Ye, that we, the undersigned delegates, by virtue of the power and authority to us given for that purpose, do, by these presents, in the name and in behalf of our respective constituents, fully and entirely ratify and confirm each and every of the said Articles of Confederation and perpetual union, and all and singular the matters and things therein contained. And we do further solemnly plight and engage the faith of our respective constituents, that they shall abide by the determinations of the United States in Congress assemblod, on all questions, which by the said confederation are submitted to them. And that the articles thereof shall be inviolably observed by the States we respectively represent, and that the union shall be perpetual. In witness whereof we have hereunto set our hands in Congress. Done at Philadelphia, in the State of Pennsylvania, the 9th day of July, in the year of our Lord, 1778, and in the 3d year of the Independence of America.

CONSTITUTION

OF THE

UNITED STATES.

We, the people of the United States, in order to form a more perfect union, establish justice, insure domestic tranquility, provide for the common defence, promote the general welfare, and secure the blessings of liberty to ourselves and our posterity, do ordain and establish this Constitution for the United States of America:

ARTICLE I.

SECT. I.—All legislative powers herein granted shall be vested in a Congress of the United States, which shall consist of a Senate and House of Representatives.

SECT. II.—1. The House of Representatives shall be composed of members chosen every second year by the people of the several states; and the electors in each state shall have the qualifications requisite for electors of the most numerous branch of the state legislature.

2. No person shall be a representative who shall not have attained the age of twenty-five years, and been seven years a citizen of the United States, and who shall not, when elected, be an inhabitant of the state in which he shall be chosen.

3. Representatives and direct taxes shall be apportioned among the several states which may be included within this Union, according to their respective numbers, which shall be determined by adding to the whole number of free persons, including those bound to service for a term of years, and excluding Indians not

taxed, three-fifths of all other persons. The actual enumeration shall be made within three years after the firt meeting of the Congress of the United States, and within every subsequent term of ten years, in such manner as they shall by law direct. The number of representatives shall not exceed one for every thirty thousand, but each state shall have at least one representative; and until such enumeration shall be made, the State of *New Hampshire* shall be entitled to choose three; *Massachusetts* eight; *Rhode Island and Providence Plantations*, one; *Connecticut*, five; *New York*, six; *New Jersey*, four; *Pennsylvania*, eight; *Delaware*, one; *Maryland*, six; *Virginia*, ten; *North Carolina*, five; *South Carolina*, five; and *Georgia*, three.

4. When vacancies happen in the representation from any state, the executive authority thereof shall issue writs of election to fill such vacancies.

5. The House of Representatives shall choose their Speaker and other officers, and shall have the sole power of impeachment.

Sect. III.—1. The Senate of the United States shall be composed of two Senators from each state, chosen by the legislature thereof, for six years; and each Senator shall have one vote.

2. Immediately after they shall be assembled in consequence of the first election, they shall be divided, as equally as may be, into three classes. The seats of the senators of the first class shall be vacated at the expiration of the second year, of the second class at the expiration of the fourth year, and of the third class at the expiration of the sixth year, so that one-third may be chosen every second year; and if vacancies happen by resignation or otherwise, during the recess of the legislature of any state, the executive thereof may make temporary appointments until the next meeting of the legislature which shall then fill such vacancies.

3. No person shall be a senator who shall not have attained to the age of thirty years, and been nine years a citizen of the United States, and who shall not, when elected, be an inhabitant of that state for which he shall be chosen.

4. The Vice-President of the United States shall be President of the Senate, but shall have no vote, unless they be equally divided.

5. The Senate shall choose their other officers, and also a president pro tempore in the absence of the Vice-President, or when he shall exercise the office of President of the United States.

6. The Senate shall have the sole power to try all impeachments. When sitting for that purpose, they shall be on oath or affirmation. When the President of the United States is tried, the chief justice shall preside; and no person shall be convicted without the concurrence of two-thirds of the members present.

7. Judgment, in cases of impeachment, shall not extend further than to removal from office, and disqualification to hold and enjoy any office of honor, trust, or profit under the United States; but the party convicted shall, nevertheless, be liable and subject to indictment, trial, judgment, and punishment, according to law.

SECT. IV.—1. The times, places, and manner of holding elections for senators and representatives shall be prescribed in each state by the legislature thereof; but the Congress may, at any time, by law, make or alter such regulations, except as to the places of choosing senators.

2. The Congress shall assemble at least once in every year; and such meeting shall be on the first Monday in December, unless they shall by law appoint a different day.

SECT. V.—1. Each house shall be the judge of the elections, returns, and qualifications of its own members; and a majority of each shall constitute a quorum to do business; but a smaller number may adjourn from day to day, and may be authorized to compel the attendance of absent members, in such manner and under such penalties as each house may provide.

2. Each house may determine the rule of its own proceedings, punish its members for disorderly behavior, and, with the concurrence of two-thirds, expel a member.

3. Each house shall keep a journal of its proceedings, and from time to time publish the same, excepting such

parts as may, in their judgment, require secrecy; and the yeas and nays of the members of either house on any question, shall, at the desire of one-fifth of those present, be entered on the journal.

4. Neither house, during the session of Congress, shall, without the consent of the other, adjourn for more than three days, nor to any other place than that in which the two houses shall be sitting.

SECT. VI.—1. The senators and representatives shall receive a compensation for their services, to be ascertained by law, and paid out of the treasury of the United States. They shall, in all cases, except treason, felony, and breach of the peace, be priviliged from arrest during their attendance at the session of their respective houses, and in going to or returning from the same; and for any speech or debate in either house they shall not be questioned in any other place.

2. No senator or representative shall, during the time for which he was elected, be appointed to any civil office under the authority of the United States which shall have been created, or the emoluments whereof shall have been increased, during such time; and no person holding any office under the United States shall be a member of either house during his continuance in office.

SECT. VII.—1. All bills for raising revenue shall originate in the House of Representatives; but the Senate may propose or concur with amendments, as on other bills.

2. Every bill which shall have passed the House of Representatives and the Senate, shall, before it becomes a law, be presented to the President of the United States; if he approve, he shall sign it; but if not, he shall return it, with his objections, to that house in which it shall have originated, who shall enter the objections at large upon their journal, and proceed to reconsider it. If, after such reconsideration, two-thirds of that house shall agree to pass the bill, it shall be sent, together with the objections, to the other house; and if approved by two-thirds of that house, it shall become a law. But in all such cases the votes of both houses shall be determined by yeas and nays; and the names of the persons voting for and against the bill shall be entered on

the journals of each house respectively. If any bill shall not be returned by the President within ten days (Sundays excepted) after it shall have been presented to him, the same shall be a law, in like manner as if he had signed it, unless Congress, by their adjournment, prevent its return; in which case it shall not be a law.

3. Every order, resolution, or vote, to which the concurrence of the Senate and House of Representatives may be necessary (except on a question of adjournment) shall be presented to the President of the United States, and before the same shall take effect shall be approved by him; or, being disapproved by him, shall be repassed by two-thirds of the Senate and House of Representatives, according to the rules and limitations prescribed in the case of a bill.

SECT. VIII.—The Congress shall have power,—

1. To lay and collect taxes, duties, imposts, and excises; to pay the debts and provide for the common defence and general welfare of the United States; but all duties, imposts and excises shall be uniform throughout the United States.

2. To borrow money on the credit of the United States:

3. To regulate commerce with foreign nations, and among the several states, and with the Indian tribes:

4. To establish a uniform rule of naturalization, and uniform laws on the subject of bankruptcies, throughout the United States:

5. To coin money, regulate the value thereof, and of foreign coin, and fix the standard of weights and neasures:

6. To provide for the punishment of counterfeiting the securities and current coin of the United States:

7. To establish post offices and post roads:

8. To promote the progress of science and useful arts, by securing, for limited times, to authors and inventors the exclusive right to their respective writings and discoveries:

9. To constitute tribunals inferior to the supreme court:

10. To define and punish piracies and felonies com-

mitted on the high seas, and offences against the law of nations:

11. To declare war, grant letters of marque and reprisal, and make rules concerning captures on land and water:

12. To raise and support armies; but no appropriation of money to that use shall be for a longer term than two years:

13. To provide and maintain a navy:

14. To make rules for the government and regulation of the land and naval forces:

15. To provide for calling forth the militia to execute the laws of the Union, suppress insurrections, and repel invasions:

16. To provide for organizing, arming, and disciplining the militia, and for governing such part of them as may be employed in the service of the United States, reserving to the states respectively the appointment of the officers, and the authority of training the militia, according to the discipline prescribed by Congress:

17. To exercise exclusive legislation, in all cases whatsoever, over such district (not exceeding ten miles square) as may, by cession of particular states, and the acceptance of Congress, become the seat of government of the United States, and to exercise like authority over all places purchased by the consent of the legislature of the state in which the same shall be, for the erection of forts, magazines, arsenals, dock-yards and other needful buildings: And,

18. To make all laws which shall be necessary and proper for carrying into execution the foregoing powers, and all other powers vested by this Constitution in the Government of the United States, or in any department or officer thereof.

Sect. IX.—1. The migration or importation of such persons as any of the states, now existing, shall think proper to admit, shall not be prohibited by the Congress prior to the year one thousand eight hundred and eight; but a tax or duty may be imposed on such importation, not exceeding ten dollars for each person.

2. The privilege of the writ of habeas corpus shall

not be suspended, unless when, in cases of rebellion or invasion, the public safety may require it.

3. No bill of attainder, or ex post facto law, shall be passed.

4. No capitation or other direct tax shall be laid, unless in proportion to the census or enumeration herein before directed to be taken.

5. No tax or duty shall be laid on articles exported from any state. No preference shall be given, by any regulation of commerce or revenue, to the ports of one state over those of another; nor shall vessels bound to or from one state be obliged to enter, clear, or pay duties in another.

6. No money shall be drawn from the treasury, but in consequence of appropriations made by law; and a regular statement and account of the receipts and expenditures of all public money shall be published from time to time.

7. No title of nobility shall be granted by the United States; and no person holding any office of profit or trust under them shall, without the consent of Congress, accept any present, emolument, office, or title of any kind whatever, from any king, prince, or foreign state.

SECT. X.—1. No state shall enter into any treaty, alliance, or confederation; grant letters of marque and reprisal; coin money; emit bills of credit; make anything but gold and silver coin a tender in payment of debts; pass any bill of attainder, ex post facto law, or law impairing the obligation of contracts; or grant any title of nobility.

2. No state shall, without the consent of Congress, lay any imposts or duties on imports or exports, except what may be absolutely necessary for executing its inspection laws; and the net produce of all duties and imposts laid by any state on imports or exports, shall be for the use of the treasury of the United States; and all such laws shall be subject to the revision and control of the Congress. No state shall, without the consent of Congress, lay any duty on tonnage, keep troops or ships of war in time of peace, enter into any agreement or compact with another state or with a foreign power,

or engage in war, unless actually invaded, or in such imminent danger as will not admit of delay.

ARTICLE II.

SECT. I.—1. The executive power shall be vested in a President of the United States of America. He shall hold his office during the term of four years, and, together with the Vice-President, chosen for the same term, be elected as follows:

2. Each State shall appoint, in such manner as the legislature thereof may direct, a number of electors, equal to the whole number of senators and representatives to which the state may be entitled in the Congress; but no senator or representative, or person holding an office of trust or profit under the United States, shall be appointed an elector.

3. [Annulled. See Amendments, Art. 12.]

4. The Congress may determine the time of chosing the electors, and the day on which they shall give their votes, which day shall be the same throughout the United States.

5. No person except a natural-born citizen, or a citizen of the United States at the time of the adoption of this Constitution, shall be eligible to the office of President; neither shall any person be eligible to that office who shall not have attained to the age of thirty-five years, and been fourteen years a resident within the United States.

6. In case of the removal of the President from office, or of his death, resignation, or inability to discharge the powers and duties of said office, the same shall devolve on the Vice-President; and the Congress may by law provide for the case of removal, death, resignation, or inability, both of the President and Vice-President, declaring what officer shall then act as President, and such officer shall act accordingly, until the disability be removed, or a President shall be elected.

7. The President shall, at stated times, receive for his services a compensation which shall neither be increased nor diminished during the period for which he shall

have been elected; and he shall not receive, within that period, any other emolument from the United States, or any of them.

8. Before he enter on the execution of his office, he shall take the following oath or affirmation:

"I do solemnly swear (or affirm) that I will faithfully execute the office of President of the United States, and will, to the best of my ability, preserve, protect, and defend the Constitution of the United States."

SECT. II.—1. The President shall be commander-in-chief of the army and navy of the United States, and of the militia of the several states, when called into the actual service of the United States: he may require the opinion, in writing, of the principal officer in each of the executive departments upon any subject relating to the duties of their respective offices; and he shall have power to grant reprieves and pardons for offences against the United States, except in cases of impeachment.

2. He shall have power, by and with the advice and consent of the Senate, to make treaties, provided two-thirds of the Senators present concur; and he shall nominate, and by and with the advice and consent of the Senate, shall appoint, ambassadors, other public ministers and consuls, judges of the Supreme court, and all other officers of the United States, whose appointments are not herein otherwise provided for, and which shall be established by law. But the Congress, may, by law, vest the appointment of such inferior officers as they think proper, in the President alone, in the courts of law, or in the heads of departments.

3. The President shall have power to fill up all vacancies that may happen during the recess of the Senate, by granting commissions, which shall expire at the end of their next session.

SECT. III.—He shall, from time to time, give to the Congress information of the state of the Union, and recommend to their consideration such measures as he shall judge necessary and expedient; he may, on extraordinary occasions, convene both houses, or either of them, and in case of disagreement between them with respect to the time of adjournment, he may adjourn them to such time as he shall think proper; he shall receive ambassadors, and other public ministers; he shall take care that the laws be faithfully executed; and shall commission all the officers of the United States.

Sect. IV.—The President, Vice-President and all civil officers of the United States, shall be removed from office on impeachment for, and conviction of, treason, bribery, or other high crimes and misdemeanors.

ARTICLE III.

Sect. I.—The judicial power of the United States shall be vested in one supreme court, and in such inferior courts as the Congress may, from time to time, ordain and establish. The judges, both of the supreme and inferior courts, shall hold their offices during good behavior, and shall, at stated times, receive for their services a compensation which shall not be diminished during their continuance in office.

Sect. II.—1. The judicial power shall extend to all cases, in law and equity, arising under this Constitution, the laws of the United States, and treaties made, or which shall be made, under their authority; to all cases affecting ambassadors, and other public ministers and consuls; to all cases of admirality and maritime jurisdiction; to controversies to which the United States shall be a party; to controversies between two or more States; between a state and citizens of another state; between citizens of different states; between citizens of the same state, claiming lands under grants of different states, and between a state, or the citizens thereof, and foreign states, citizens or subjects.

2. In all cases affecting ambassadors, other public ministers, and consuls, and those in which a state shall be a party, the supreme court shall have original jurisdiction. In all other cases before mentioned, the supreme court shall have appellate jurisdiction, both as to law and fact, with such exceptions, and under such regulations, as the Congress shall make.

3. The trial of all crimes, except in cases of impeachment, shall be by jury; and such trial shall be held in the state where the said crimes shall have been committed; but when not committed within any state, the trial

shall be at such a place or places as the Congress may by law have directed.

SECT. III.—1. Treason against the United States shall consist only in levying war against them, or in adhering to their enemies, giving them aid and comfort. No person shall be convicted of treason, unless on the testimony of two witnesses to the same overt act, or confessions in open court.

2. The Congress shall have power to declare the punishment of treason; but no attainder of treason shall work corruption of blood, or forfeiture, except during the life of the person attainted.

ARTICLE IV.

SECT. I.—Full faith and credit shall be given in each state to the public acts, records and judicial proceedings of every other state. And the Congress may, by general laws, prescribe the manner in which such acts, records and proceedings shall be proved, and the effect thereof.

SECT. II.—1. The citizens of each state shall be entitled to all privileges and immunities of citizens in the several states.

2. A person charged in any state with treason, felony, or other crime, who shall flee from justice, and be found in another state, shall, on demand of the executive authority of the state from which he fled, be delivered up to be removed to the state having jurisdiction of the crime.

3. No person held to service or labor in one state, under the laws thereof, escaping into another, shall, in consequence of any law or regulation therein, be discharged from such service or labor, but shall be delivered up on claim of the party to whom such service or labor may be due.

SECT. III.—1. New states may be admitted by the Congress into this Union; but no new state shall be formed or erected within the jurisdiction of any other state; nor any state be formed by the junction of two or more states, or parts of states, without the consent of the legislatures of the states concerned, as well as of the Congress.

2. The Congress shall have power to dispose of and make all needful rules and regulations respecting the territory or other property belonging to the United States; and nothing in this Constitution shall be so construed as to prejudice any claims of the United States, or of any particular state.

SECT. IV.—The United States shall guarantee to every state of this Union a republican form of government, and shall protect each of them against invasion, and, on application of the legislature, or of the executive (when the legislature can not be convened,) against domestic violence.

ARTICLE V.

The Congress, whenever two-thirds of both houses shall deem it necessary, shall propose amendments to this Constitution, or, on the application of the legislatures of two-thirds of the several states, shall call a convention for proposing amendments, which, in either case, shall be valid to all intents and purposes, as part of this Constitution, when ratified by the legislatures of three-fourths of the several states, or by conventions in three-fourths thereof, as the one or the other mode of ratification may be proposed by the Congress; provided that no amendment which may be made prior to the year one thousand eight hundred and eight shall in any manner affect the first and fourth clauses in the ninth section of the first article; and that no state, without its consent, shall be deprived of its equal suffrage in the Senate.

ARTICLE VI.

1. All debts contracted, and engagements entered into, before the adoption of this Constitution, shall be as valid against the United States under this Constitution as under the confederation.

2. This Constitution, and the laws of the United States which shall be made in pursuance thereof, and all treaties made, or which shall be made, under the authority of the United States, shall be the supreme law of the land; and the judges in every state shall be bound

thereby; anything in the constitution or laws of any state to the contrary notwithstanding.

3. The senators and representatives before mentioned, and the members of the several state legislatures, and all executive and judicial officers, both of the United States, and of the several states, shall be bound by oath or affirmation to support this Constitution; but no religious test shall ever be required as a qualification to any office or public trust under the United States.

ARTICLE VII.

The ratification of the conventions of nine states shall be sufficient for the establishment of this Constitution between the the states so ratifying the same.

Done in convention, by the unanimous consent of the states present, the seventeenth day of September, in the year of our Lord one thousand seven hundred and eighty-seven, and of the Independence of the United States of America the twelfth. In witness whereof, we have hereunto subscribed our names.

GEORGE WASHINGTON,
President, and Deputy from Virginia.

NEW HAMPSHIRE.

JOHN LANGDON,
NICHOLAS GILMAN.

MASSACHUSETTS.

NATHANIEL GORHAM,
RUFUS KING.

CONNECTICUT.

WM. SAMUEL JOHNSON,
ROGER SHERMAN.

NEW YORK.

ALEXANDER HAMILTON.

NEW JERSEY.

WILLIAM LIVINGSTON,
DAVID BREARLEY,
WILLIAM PATTERSON,
JONATHAN DAYTON.

PENNSYLVANIA.

BENJAMIN FRANKLIN,
THOMAS MIFFLIN,
ROBERT MORRIS,
GEORGE CLYMER,
THOMAS FITZSIMONS,
JARED INGERSOLL,
JAMES WILSON,
GOUVERNEUR MORRIS.

DELAWARE.

George Read,
Gunning Bedford, Jr.
John Dickinson,
Richard Bassett,
Jacob Broom.

MARYLAND.

James M'Henry,
Dan'l of St. Tho. Jenifer,
Daniel Carroll.

VIRGINIA.

John Blair,
James Madison, Jr.

NORTH CAROLINA.

William Blount,
Rich. Dobbs Spaight,
Hugh Williamson.

SOUTH CAROLINA.

John Rutledge,
Charles C. Pinckney,
Charles Pinckney,
Pierce Butler.

GEORGIA.

William Few,
Abraham Baldwin.

Attest, WILLIAM JACKSON, Secretary.

AMENDMENTS TO THE CONSTITUTION.

Art. I.—Congress shall make no law respecting an establishment of religion, or prohibiting the free exercise thereof: or abridging the freedom of speech, or of the press; or the right of the people peaceably to assemble and to petition the government for a redress of grievances.

Art. II.—A well regulated militia being necessary to the security of a free state, the right of the people to keep and bear arms shall not be infringed.

Art. III.—No soldier shall, in time of peace, be quartered in any house without the consent of the owner, nor in time of war, but in a manner to be prescribed by law.

Art. IV.—The right of the people to be secure in their persons, houses, papers and effects, against unreasonable searches and seizures, shall not be violated; and no warrants shall issue but upon probable cause, supported by oath or affirmation, and particularly describing the place to be searched, and the persons or things to be seized.

Art. V.—No person shall be held to answer for a capital or otherwise infamous crime, unless on a presentment or indictment of a grand jury, except in cases arising in the land and naval forces, or in the militia when in actual service, in time of war or public danger; nor shall any person be subject for the same offence to be twice put in jeopardy of life or limb; nor shall be compelled, in any criminal case, to be witness against himself, nor be deprived of life, liberty, or property, without due process of law; nor shall private property be taken for public use without just compensation.

Art. VI.—In all criminal prosecutions, the accused shall enjoy the right to a speedy and public trial by an impartial jury of the state and district wherein the crime shall have been committed, which district shall have been previously ascertained by law, and to be informed of the nature and cause of the accusation; to be confronted with the witnesses against him; to have compulsory process for obtaining witnesses in his favor; and to have the assistance of counsel for his defence.

Art. VII.—In suits at common law, where the value in controversy shall exceed twenty dollars, the right of trial by jury shall be preserved; and no fact tried by a jury, shall be otherwise re-examined in any court of the United States than according to the rules of the common law.

Art. VIII.—Excessive bail shall not be required, nor excessive fines imposed, nor cruel and unusual punishments inflicted.

Art. IX.—The enumeration in the Constitution of certain rights shall not be construed to deny or disparage others retained by the people.

Art. X.—The powers not delegated to the United States by the Constitution, nor prohibited by it to the states, are reserved to the states respectively, or to the people.

Art. XI.—The judicial power of the United States shall not be construed to extend to any suit in law or equity commenced or prosecuted against one of the United States by citizens of another state, or by citizens or subjects of any foreign state.

ART. XII.—1. The electors shall meet in their respective states, and vote by ballot for President and Vice-President, one of whom, at least, shall not be an inhabitant of the same state with themselves; they shall name in their ballots the person voted for as President, and in distinct ballots the person voted for as Vice President; and they shall make distinct lists of all persons voted for as President, and of all persons voted for as Vice-President, and of the number of votes for each; which lists they shall sign and certify, and transmit, sealed, to the seat of government of the United States, directed to the President of the Senate. The President of the Senate shall, in the presence of the Senate and House of Representatives, open all the certificates, and the votes shall then be counted; the person having the greatest number of votes for President shall be President, if such number be a majority of the whole number of electors appointed; and if no person have such majority, then from the persons having the highest number, not exceeding three, on the list of those voted for as President, the House of Representatives shall choose immediately, by ballot, the President. But, in choosing the President, the votes shall be taken by states, the representation from each state having one vote; a quorum for this purpose shall consist of a member or members from two thirds of the states, and a majority of all the states shall be necessary to a choice. And if the House of Representatives shall not choose a President, whenever the right of choice shall devolve upon them, before the fourth day of March next following, then the Vice-President shall act as President, as in the case of the death or other constitutional disability of the President.

2. The person having the greatest number of votes as Vice-President shall be the Vice-President, if such number be a majority of the whole number of electors appointed; and if no person have a majority, then from the two highest numbers on the list the Senate shall choose the Vice President; a quorum for the purpose shall consist of two-thirds of the whole number of senators, and a majority of the whole number shall be necessary to a choice.

3. But no person constitutionally ineligible to the office of President shall be eligible to that of Vice-President of the United States.

ART. XIII.—1. Neither slavery nor involuntary servitude, except as a punishment for crime, whereof the party shall have been duly convicted, shall exist within the United States, or any place subject to their jurisdiction.

2. Congress shall have power to enforce this article by appropriate legislation.

The XIII, or Anti-Slavery amendment was proposed in the United States Senate, February 1, 1864, and after a lengthy and searching debate, was adopted by that body April 8, as follows:

Ayes, 38—Republicans, 36; Democrats, 2.

Nays, 6—All Democrats.

Not voting, 6—Republicans, 1; Democrats, 5,

The House refused, June 15, to adopt it by the necessary two-thirds vote, (yeas, 95; nays, 66; not voting, 22; required two-thirds, 122.)

It was again called up, January 6, 1865, and adopted on the 31st, as follows:

Ayes, 119—Republicans, 103; Democrats, 16.

Nays, 56—All Democrats.

Not Voting, 8—All Democrats.

Secretary Seward officially announced its ratification, and declared it a part of the Constitution, December 18, 1865.

The following table shows which States, up to that time, had ratified the amendments:

Illinois	Feb. 1	Louisiana	Feb. 17
Rhode Island	Feb. 2	Wisconsin	Feb. 21
Michigan	Feb. 2	Missouri	Feb. 24
New York	Feb. 3	Vermont	Mar. 9
Maryland	Feb. 3	Tennessee	Apr. 5
Massachusetts	Feb. 3	Arkansas	Apr. 1
Pennsylvania	Feb. 3	Connecticut	May 4
West Virginia	Feb. 3	New Hampshire	June 30
Maine	Feb. 7	South Carolina	Nov. 13
Ohio	Feb. 8	North Carolina	Dec. 1
Kansas	Feb. 8	Alabama	Dec. 2
Minnesota	Feb. 8	Georgia	Dec. 6
Virginia	Feb. 9	Oregon	Dec. 11
Indiana	Feb. 13	California	Dec. 18
Nevada	Feb. 16		

The Legislatures of the following States declined to ratify the Amendment:

Delaware	Feb. 8	New Jersey	Mar. 1
Kentucky	Feb. 23		

WASHINGTON'S
FAREWELL ADDRESS.

FRIENDS AND FELLOW CITIZENS:—

The period for a new election of a citizen to administer the executive government of the United States being not far distant, and the time actually arrived when your thoughts must be employed in designating the person who is to be clothed with that important trust, it appears to me proper, especially as it may conduce to a more distinct expression of the public voice, that I should now apprise you of the resolution I have formed to decline being considered among the number of those out of whom the choice is to be made.

I beg you at the same time to do me the justice to be assured that this resolution has not been taken without a strict regard to all the considerations appertaining to the relation which binds a dutiful citizen to his country; and that, in withdrawing the tender of service which silence in my situation might imply, I am influenced by no diminution of zeal for your future interest; no deficiency of grateful respect for your past kindness; but am supported by a full conviction that the step is compatible with both.

The acceptance of, and continuance hitherto in, the office to which your suffrages have twice called me have been a uniform sacrifice of inclination to the opinion of duty, and to a deference for what appeared to be your desire. I constantly hoped that it would have been much earlier in my power, consistently with motives which I was not at liberty to disregard, to return to that retirement from which I had been reluctantly drawn. The strength of my inclination to do this previous to the last election had even led to the preparation of an address to declare it to you; but mature reflection on the then perplexed and critical posture of affairs with foreign nations, and the unanimous advice of persons entitled to my confidence, impelled me to abandon the idea. I rejoice that the state of your concerns, external as well as internal, no longer renders the pursuit of inclination incompatible with the sentiment of duty or propriety, and am persuaded, whatever partiality may be retained for my services, that in the present circumstances of our country you will not disapprove of my determination to retire.

The impressions with which I first undertook the arduous trust were explained on the proper occasion. In the discharge of this trust I will only say that I have, with good intentions, contributed towards the organization and administration of the government the best exertions of which a very fallible judgment was capable. Not unconscious, in the outset, of the inferiority of my qualifications, experience in my own eyes, perhaps still more in the eyes of others, has strengthened the motives to diffidence of myself; and every day the increasing weight of years admonishes me more and more that the shade of retirement is as necessary to me as it will be welcome. Satisfied that if any circumstances have given peculiar value to my services, they were temporary, I have the consolation to believe that while choice and prudence invite me to quit the political scene, patriotism does not forbid it.

In looking forward to the moment which is to terminate the career of my public life, my feelings do not permit me to suspend the deep acknowledgment of that debt of gratitude which I owe to my beloved country for the many honors it has conferred upon me; still more for the steadfast confidence with which it has supported me, and for the opportunities I have thence enjoyed of manifesting my inviolable attachment by services faithful and persevering, though in usefulness unequal to my zeal. If benefits have resulted to our country from these services, let it always be remembered to your praise, and as an instructive example in our annals, that under circumstances in which the passions, agitated in every direction, were liable to mislead—amidst appearances sometimes dubious—vicissitudes of fortune often discouraging—in situations in which not unfrequently want of success has countenanced the spirit of criticism—the constancy of your support was the essential prop of the efforts, and a guaranty of the plans, by which they were effected. Profoundly penetrated with this idea, I shall carry it with me to my grave, as a strong incitement to unceasing vows that Heaven may continue to you the choicest tokens of its beneficence; that your union and brotherly affection may be perpetual; that the free Constitution, which is the work of your hands, may be sacredly maintained; that its administration in every department may be stamped with wisdom and virtue; that, in fine, the happiness of the people of these States, under the auspices of liberty, may be made complete, by so careful a preservation and so prudent a use of this blessing, as will acquire to them the glory of recommending it to the applause, the affection, and the adoption of every nation which is yet a stranger to it.

Here, perhaps, I ought to stop. But a solicitude for your welfare, which cannot end but with my life, and the apprehension of danger natural to that solicitude, urge me, on an occasion like the present, to offer to your solemn contemplation, and to recommend to your frequent review, some sentiments which are the result of much reflection, of no inconsiderable observation, and which appear to me all-important to the permanency of your felicity as a people. These will be offered to you with the more freedom as you can only see in them the disinterested warnings of a parting friend, who can possibly have no personal motive to bias his counsel. Nor can I forget, as an encouragement to it, your indulgent reception of my sentiments on a former and not dissimilar occasion.

Interwoven as is the love of liberty with every ligament of your hearts, no recommendation of mine is necessary to fortify or confirm the attachment.

The unity of government which constitutes you one people is also dear to you. It is justly so; for it is a main pillar in the edifice of your real independence; the support of your tranquility at home, your peace abroad; of your safety, of your prosperity, of that very liberty which you so highly prize. But as it is easy to foresee that from different causes and from different quarters much pains will be taken, many artifices employed, to weaken in your minds the conviction of this truth--as this is the point in your political fortress against which the batteries of internal and external enemies will be most constantly and actively (though often covertly and insidiously) directed, it is of infinite moment that you should properly estimate the immense value of your national union to your collective and individual happiness; that you should cherish a cordial, habitual, and immovable attachment to it; accustoming yourselves to think and speak of it as of the palladium of your political safety and prosperity; watching for its preservation with jealous anxiety; discountenancing whatever may suggest even a suspicion that it can in any event be abandoned; and indignantly frowning upon the first dawning of every attempt to alienate any portion of our country from the rest, or to enfeeble the sacred ties which now link together the various parts.

For this you have every inducement of sympathy and interest. Citizens by birth, or choice, of a common country, that country has a right to concentrate your affections. The name of AMERICAN, which belongs to you in your national capacity, must always exalt the just pride of patriotism more than any appellation derived from local discriminations. With slight shades of difference, you have the same religion, manners, habits, and political principles. You have in a common cause fought and triumphed together; the independence and liberty you possess are the work of joint councils and joint efforts—of common dangers, sufferings, and successes.

But these considerations, however powerfully they address themselves to your sensibility, are greatly outweighed by those which apply more immediately to your interest. Here every portion of our country finds the most commanding motives for carefully guarding and preserving the union of the whole.

The North, in an unrestrained intercourse with the South, protected by the equal laws of a common government, finds in the productions of the latter great additional resources of maritime and commercial enterprise, and precious materials of manufacturing industry. The South, in the same intercourse, benefiting by the agency of the North, sees its agriculture grow and its commerce expand. Turning partly into its own channels the seamen of the North, it finds its particular navigation invigorated; and while it contributes, in different ways, to nourish and increase the general mass of the national navigation, it looks forward to the protection of a maritime strength to which itself is unusually adapted. The East, in like intercourse with the West, already finds, and in the progressive improvement of interior communications by land and water will more and more find, a valuable vent for the commodities which it brings from abroad or manufactures at home. The West derives from the East supplies requisite to its growth and comfort; and, what is, perhaps, of still greater consequence, it must of necessity owe the secure enjoyment of indispensable outlets for its own productions to the weight, influence, and the future maritime strength of the Atlantic side of the Union, directed by an indissoluble community of interest as one nation. Any other tenure by which the West can hold this essential advantage, whether derived from its own separate strength, or from an apostate and unnatural connection with any foreign power, must be intrinsically precarious.

While, then, every part of our country thus feels an immediate and particular interest in union, all the parts combined cannot fail to find in the united mass of means and efforts greater strength, greater resource, proportionally greater security from external danger, a less frequent interruption of their peace by foreign nations; and, what is of inestimable value, they must derive from union an exemption from those broils and wars between themselves which so frequently afflict neighboring countries not tied together by the same government, which their own rivalships alone would be sufficient to produce, but which opposite foreign alliances, attachments, and intrigues would stimulate and imbitter. Hence, likewise, they will avoid the necessity of those overgrown military establishments which, under any form of government, are inauspicious to liberty, and which are to be regarded as particularly hostile to republican liberty. In this sense it is that your union ought to be considered as a main prop of your liberty, and that the love of the one ought to endear to you the preservation of the other.

These considerations speak a persuasive language to every reflecting and virtuous mind, and exhibit the continuance of the union as a primary object of patriotic desire. Is there a doubt whether a common government can embrace so large a sphere? Let experience solve it. To listen to mere speculation in such a case were criminal. We are authorized to hope that a proper organization of the whole, with the auxiliary agency of governments for the respective subdivisions, will afford a happy issue to the experiment. It is well worth a fair and full experiment. With such powerful and obvious motives to union, affecting all parts of our country, while experience shall not have demonstrated its impracticability, there will always be reason to distrust the patriotism of those who, in any quarter, may endeavor to weaken its bands.

In contemplating the causes which may disturb our union, it occurs as a matter of serious concern that any ground should have been furnished for characterizing parties by geographical discriminations—NORTHERN and SOUTHERN, ATLANTIC and WESTERN; whence designing men may endeavor to excite a belief that there is a real difference of local interests and views. One of the expedients of party to acquire influence within particular districts is to misrepresent the opinions and aims of other districts. You cannot shield yourselves too much against the jealousies and heartburnings which spring from these misrepresentations; they tend to render alien to each other those who ought to be bound together by fraternal affection. The inhabitants of our western country have lately had a useful lesson on this head. They have seen in the negotiation by the executive, and in the unanimous ratification by the Senate of the treaty with Spain, and in the universal satisfaction at that event throughout the United States, a decisive proof how unfounded were the suspicions propagated among them of a policy in the general government and in the Atlantic States unfriendly to their interests in regard to the Mississippi. They have been witnesses to the formation of two treaties—that with Great Britain and that with Spain—which secure to them everything they could desire, in respect to our foreign relations, towards confirming their prosperity. Will it not be their wisdom to rely for the preservation of these advantages on the union by which they were procured? Will they not henceforth be deaf to those advisers, if such there are, who would sever them from their brethren and connect them with aliens?

To the efficacy and permanency of your union a government for the whole is indispensable. No alliances, however strict, between the parts can be an adequate substitute; they must inevitably experience the infractions and interruptions which all alliances in all times have experienced. Sensible of this momentous truth, you have improved upon your first essay by the adoption of a constitution of government better calculated than your former for an intimate union, and for the efficacious management of your common concerns. This government—the offspring of your own choice, uninfluenced and unawed, adopted upon full investigation and mature deliberation, completely free in its principles, in the distribution of its powers, uniting security with energy, and containing within itself a provision for its own amendment—has a just claim to your confidence and your support. Respect for its authority, compliance with its laws, acquiescence in its measures, are duties enjoined by the fundamental maxims of true liberty. The basis of our political systems is the right of the people to make and to alter their constitutions of government. But the Constitution which at any time exists, until changed by an explicit and authentic act of the whole people, is sacredly obligatory upon all. The very idea of the power and the right of the people to establish government presupposes the duty of every individual to obey the established government.

All obstructions to the execution of the laws, all combinations and associations, under whatever plausible character, with the real design to direct, control, counteract, or awe the regular deliberation and action of the constituted authorities, are destructive of this fundamental principle, and of fatal tendency. They serve to organize faction, to give it an artificial and extraordinary force; to put in the place of the delegated will of the nation the will of a party, often a small but artful and enterprising minority of the community; and according to the alternate triumphs of different parties, to make the public administration the mirror of the ill-concerted and incongruous projects of faction, rather than the organ of consistent and wholesome plans, digested by common councils, and modified by mutual interests.

However combinations or associations of the above description may now and then answer popular ends, they are likely, in the course of times and things, to become potent engines by which cunning, ambitious, and unprincipled men will be enabled to subvert the power of the people, and to usurp for themselves the reins of government, destroying afterwards the very engines which have lifted them to unjust dominion.

Towards the preservation of your government, and the permanency of your present happy state, it is requisite not only that you steadily discountenance irregular oppositious to its acknowledged authority, but also that you resist with care the spirit of innovation upon its principles, however specious the pretext. One method of assault may be to effect in the forms of the Constitution alterations which will impair the energy of the system, and thus to undermine what cannot be directly overthrown. In all the changes to which you may be invited, remember that time and habit are at least as necessary to fix the true character of government as of other human institutions; that experience is the surest standard by which to test the real tendency of the existing Constitution of a country; that facility in changes upon the credit of mere hypothesis and opinion exposes to perpetual change, from the endless variety of hypothesis and opinion; and remember, especially, that for the efficient management of your common interests, in a country so extensive as ours, a government of as much vigor as is consistent with the perfect security of liberty is indispensable. Liberty itself will find in such a government, with powers properly distributed and adjusted, its surest guardian. It is indeed little else than a name where the government is too feeble to withstand the enterprises of faction, to confine each member of the society within the limits prescribed by the laws, and to maintain all in the secure and tranquil enjoyment of the rights of person and property.

I have already intimated to you the danger of parties in the State, with particular references to the founding of them on geographical discriminations. Let me now take a more comprehensive view, and warn you in the most solemn manner against the baneful effects of the spirit of party generally.

This spirit, unfortunately, is inseparable from our nature, having its root in the strongest passions of the human mind. It exists under different shapes in all governments, more or less stifled, controlled, or repressed; but in those of the popular form it is seen in its greatest rankness, and is truly their worst enemy.

The alternate domination of one faction over another, sharpened by the spirit of revenge natural to party dissension, which, in different ages and countries, has perpetrated the most horrid enormities, is itself a frightful despotism. But this leads at length to a more formal and permanent despotism. The disorders and miseries which result, gradually incline the minds of men to seek security and repose in the absolute power of an individual; and, sooner or later, the chief of some prevailing faction, more able or more fortunate than his competitors, turns this disposition to the purposes of his own elevation on the ruins of public liberty.

Without looking forward to an extremity of this kind, (which, nevertheless, ought not to be entirely out of sight,) the common and continual mischiefs of the spirit of party are sufficient to make it the interest and duty of a wise people to discourage and restrain it.

It serves always to distract the public councils and enfeeble the public administration. It agitates the community with ill-founded jealousies and false alarms; kindles the animosity of one part against another; foments occasionally riot and insurrection. It opens the door to foreign influence and corruption, which find a facilitated access to the government itself, through the channels of party passions. Thus the policy and the will of one country are subjected to the policy and will of another.

There is an opinion that parties in free countries are useful checks upon the administration of the government, and serve to keep alive the spirit of liberty. This, within certain limits, is probably true; and in governments of a monarchical cast, patriotism may look with indulgence, if not with favor, upon the spirit of party. But in those of the popular character, in governments purely elective, it is a spirit not to be encouraged. From their natural tendency it is certain there will always be enough of that spirit for every salutary purpose. And there being constant danger of excess, the effort ought to be, by force of public opinion, to mitigate and assuage it. A fire not to be quenched, it demands a uniform vigilance, to prevent its bursting into a flame, lest, instead of warming, it should consume.

It is important, likewise, that the habits of thinking, in a free country, should inspire caution in those intrusted with its administration, to confine themselves within their respective constitutional spheres, avoiding, in the exercise of the powers of one department, to encroach upon another. The spirit of encroachment tends to consolidate the powers of all the departments in one, and thus to create, whatever the form of government, a real despotism. A just estimate of that love of power, and proneness to abuse it, which predominate in the human heart, is sufficient to satisfy us of the truth of this position. The necessity of reciprocal checks in the exercise of political power, by dividing and distributing it into different depositories, and constituting each the guardian of the public weal against invasions by the others, has been evinced by experiments, ancient and modern; some of them in our country, and under our own eyes. To preserve them must be as necessary as to institute them. If, in the opinion of the people, the distribution or modification of the constitutional powers be in any particular wrong, let it be corrected by an amendment in the way which the constitution designates. But let there be no change by usurpation; for, though this, in one instance, may be the instrument of good, it is the customary weapon by which free governments are destroyed. The precedent must always greatly overbalance in permanent evil any partial or transient benefit which the use can at any time yield.

Of all the dispositions and habits which lead to political prosperity, religion and morality are indispensable supports. In vain would that man claim the tribute of patriotism who should labor to subvert these great pillars of human happiness, these firmest props of the duties of men and citizens. The mere politician, equally with the pious man, ought to respect and to cherish them. A volume could not trace all their connections with private and public felicity. Let it simply be asked, where is the security for property, for reputation, for life, if the sense of religious obligations desert the oaths which are the instruments of investigation in courts of justice? And let us with caution indulge the supposition that morality can be maintained without religion. Whatever may be conceded to the influence of refined education on minds of peculiar structure, reason and experience both forbid us to expect that national morality can prevail in exclusion of religious principle.

It is substantially true that virtue, or morality, is a necessary spring of popular government. The rule indeed extends with more or less force to every species of free government. Who that is a sincere friend to it can look with indifference upon attempts to shake the foundation of the fabric?

Promote, then, as an object of primary importance, institutions for the general diffusion of knowledge. In proportion as the structure of a government gives force to public opinion, it is essential that public opinion should be enlightened.

As a very important source of strength and security, cherish public credit. One method of preserving it is to use it as sparingly as possible, avoiding occasions of expense by cultivating peace; but remembering, also, that timely disbursements to prepare for danger frequently prevent much greater disbursements to repel it; avoiding, likewise, the accumulation of debt, not only by shunning occasions of expense, but by vigorous exertions in time of peace to discharge the debts which unavoidable wars may have occasioned, not ungenerously throwing upon posterity the burden which we ourselves ought to bear. The execution of these maxims belongs to your representatives; but it is necessary that public opinion should co-operate. To facilitate to them the performance of their duty, it is essential that you should practically bear in mind that towards the payment of debts there must be revenue; that to have revenue there must be taxes; that no taxes can be devised which are not more or less inconvenient and unpleasant; that the intrinsic embarrassment inseparable from the selection of the proper objects (which is always a choice of difficulties) ought to be a decisive motive for a candid construction of the conduct of the government in making it, and for a spirit of acquiescence in the measures for obtaining revenue which the public exigencies may at any time dictate.

Observe good faith and justice towards all nations; cultivate peace and harmony with all. Religion and morality enjoin this conduct, and can it be that good policy does not equally enjoin it? It will be worthy of a free, enlightened, and, at no distant period, a great nation, to give to mankind the magnanimous and too novel example of a people always guided by an exalted sense of justice and benevolence. Who can doubt that in the course of time and things the fruits of such a plan would richly repay any temporary advantages which might be lost by a steady adherence to it? Can it be that Providence has not connected the permanent felicity of a nation with its virtue? The experiment, at least, is recommended by every sentiment which enobles human nature. Alas! is it rendered impossible by its vices?

In the execution of such a plan, nothing is more essential than that permanent inveterate antipathies against particular nations, and passionate attachments for others, should be excluded; and that in place of them just and amicable feelings towards all should be cultivated. The nation which indulges towards another an habitual hatred or an habitual fondness is in some degree a slave. It is a slave to its animosity or to its affection, either of which is sufficient to lead it astray from its duty and its interest. Antipathy in one nation against another disposes each more readily to offer insult and injury, to lay hold of slight causes of umbrage, and to be haughty and intractable when accidental or trifling occasions of dispute occur.

Hence frequent collisions, obstinate, envenomed, and bloody contests. The nation, prompted by ill will and resentment, sometimes impels to war the government, contrary to the best calculations of policy. The government sometimes participates in the national propensity, and adopts, through passion, what reason would reject; at other times it makes the animosity of the nation subservient to projects of hostility instigated by pride, ambition, and other sinister and pernicious motives. The peace often, sometimes perhaps the liberty, of nations has been the victim.

So, likewise, a passionate attachment of one nation for another produces a variety of evils. Sympathy for the favorite nation, facilitating the illusion of an imaginary common interest in cases where no real common interest exists, and infusing into one the enmities of the other, betrays the former into a participation in the quarrels and wars of the latter, without adequate inducement or justification. It leads, also, to concessions to the favorite nation of privileges denied to others, which are apt doubly to injure the nation making the concessions, by unnecessarily parting with what ought to have been retained, and by exciting jealousy, ill will, and a disposition to retaliate, in the parties from whom equal privileges are withheld; and it gives to ambitious, corrupted, or deluded citizens (who devote themselves to the favorite nation) facility to betray or sacrifice the interests of their own country without odium, sometimes even with popularity; gilding with the appearance of a virtuous sense of obligation, a commendable deference for public opinion, or a laudable zeal for public good, the base or foolish compliances of ambition, corruption, or infatuation.

As avenues to foreign influence, in innumerable ways, such attachments are particularly alarming to the truly enlightened and independent patriot. How many opportunities do they afford to tamper with domestic factions, to practice the arts of seduction, to mislead public opinion, to influence or awe the public councils! Such an attachment of a small or weak towards a great and powerful nation dooms the former to be the satellite of the other. Against the insidious wiles of foreign influence (I conjure you to believe me, fellow-citizens) the jealousy of a free people ought to be constantly awake, since history and experience prove that foreign influence is one of the most baneful foes of republican governments. But that jealousy, to be useful, must be impartial; else it becomes the instrument of the very influence to be avoided, instead of a defence against it. Excessive partiality for one foreign nation, and excessive dislike of another, cause those whom they actuate to see danger only on one side, and serve to veil and even second the arts of influence on the other. Real patriots, who may resist the intrigues of the favorite, are liable to become suspected and odious; while its tools and dupes usurp the applause and confidence of the people, to surrender their interests.

The great rule of conduct for us, in regard to foreign nations, is, in extending our commercial relations, to have with them as little political connection as possible. So far as we have already formed engagements, let them be fulfilled with perfect good faith. Here let us stop.

Europe has a set of primary interests which to us have none, or a very remote, relation. Hence she must be engaged in frequent controversies, the causes of which are essentially foreign to our concerns. Hence, therefore, it must be unwise in us to implicate ourselves, by artificial ties, in the ordinary vicissitudes of her politics, or the ordinary combinations and collisions of her friendships or enmities.

Our detached and distant situation invites and enables us to pursue a different course. If we remain one people, under an efficient government, the period is not far off when we may defy material injury from external annoyance; when we may take such an attitude as will cause the neutrality we may at any time resolve upon to be scrupulously respected; when belligerent nations, under the impossibility of making acquisitions upon us, will not lightly hazard the giving us provocation; when we may choose peace or war, as our interest, guided by justice, shall counsel

Why forego the advantages of so peculiar a situation? Why quit our own to stand upon foreign ground? Why, by interweaving our destiny with that of any part of Europe, entangle our peace and prosperity in the toils of European ambition, rivalship, interest, humor, or caprice?

It is our true policy to steer clear of permanent alliances with any portion of the foreign world; so far, I mean, as we are now at liberty to do it; for let me not be understood as capable of patronizing infidelity to existing engagements. I hold the maxim no less applicable to public than to private affairs, that honesty is always the best policy. I repeat it, therefore, let those engagements be observed in their genuine sense. But, in my opinion, it is unnecessary, and would be unwise, to extend them.

Taking care always to keep ourselves, by suitable establishments, on a respectable defensive posture, we may safely trust to temporary alliances for extraordinary emergencies.

Harmony, and a liberal intercourse with all nations, are recommended by policy, humanity, and interest. But even our commercial policy should hold an equal, an impartial hand; neither seeking nor granting exclusive favors or preferences; consulting the natural course of things; diffusing and diversifying, by gentle means, the streams of commerce, but forcing nothing; establishing, with powers so disposed—in order to give trade a stable course, to define the rights of our merchants, and to enable the government to support them—conventional rules of intercourse, the best that present circumstances and mutual opinion will permit, but temporary, and liable to be from time to time abandoned or varied, as experience and circumstances shall dictate; constantly keeping in view that it is folly in one nation to look for disinterested favors from another; that it must pay with a portion of its independence for whatever it may accept under that character; that by such acceptance it may place itself in the condition of having given equivalents for nominal favors, and yet of being reproached with ingratitude for not giving more. There can be no greater error than to expect or calculate upon real favors from nation to nation. It is an illusion which experience must cure, which a just pride ought to discard.

In offering to you, my countrymen, these counsels of an old and affectionate friend, I dare not hope they will make the strong and lasting impression I could wish; that they will control the usual current of the passions, or prevent our nation from running the course which has hitherto marked the destiny of nations; but if I may even flatter myself that they may be productive of some partial benefit, some occasional good; that they may now and then recur to moderate the fury of party spirit, to warn against the mischiefs of foreign intrigue, to guard against the impostures of pretended patriotism; this hope will be a full recompense for the solicitude for your welfare by which they have been dictated.

How far, in the discharge of my official duties, I have been guided by the principles which have been delineated, the public records and other evidences of my conduct must witness to you and to the world. To myself, the assurance of my own conscience is, that I have at least believed myself to be guided by them.

In relation to the still subsisting war in Europe, my proclamation of the 22d of April, 1793, is the index to my plan. Sanctioned by your approving voice, and by that of your representatives in both houses of Congress, the spirit of that measure has continually governed me, uninfluenced by any attempts to deter or divert me from it.

After deliberate examination, with the aid of the best lights I could obtain, I was well satisfied that our country, under all the circumstances of the case, had a right to take, and was bound in duty and interest to take, a neutral position. Having taken it, I determined, as far as should depend upon me, to maintain it with moderation, perseverance, and firmness.

The considerations which respect the right to hold this conduct is not necessary, on this occasion, to detail. I will only observe that, according to my understanding of the matter, that right, so far from being denied by any of the belligerent powers, has been virtually admitted by all.

The duty of holding a neutral conduct may be inferred, without any thing more, from the obligation which justice and humanity impose on every nation, in cases in which it is free to act, to maintain inviolate the relations of peace and amity towards other nations.

The inducements of interest for observing that conduct will best be referred to your own reflections and experience. With me, a predominant motive has been to endeavor to gain time to our country to settle and mature its yet recent institutions, and to progress, without interruption, to that degree of strength and consistency which is necessary to give it, humanly speaking, the command of its own fortunes.

Though in reviewing the incidents of my administration I am unconscious of intentional error, I am nevertheless too sensible of my defects not to think it probable that I may have committed many errors. Whatever they may be, I fervently beseech the Almighty to avert or mitigate the evils to which they may tend. I shall also carry with me the hope that my country will never cease to view them with indulgence; and that after forty-five years of my life, dedicated to its service with an upright zeal, the faults of incompetent abilities will be consigned to oblivion, as myself must soon be to the mansions of rest.

Relying on its kindness in this as in other things, and actuated by that fervent love towards it which is so natural to a man who views in it the native soil of himself and his progenitors for several generations, I anticipate with pleasing expectation that retreat in which I promise myself to realize, without alloy, the sweet enjoyment of partaking, in the midst of my fellow-citizens, the benign influence of good laws under a free government—the ever favorite object of my heart, and the happy reward, as I trust, of our mutual cares, labors, and dangers.

G. WASHINGTON.

United States, September 17, 1796.

SECOND INAUGURAL ADDRESS.

BY ABRAHAM LINCOLN, MARCH 4, 1865.

FELLOW-COUNTRYMEN: At this second appearing to take the oath of the Presidential office, there is less occasion for an extended address than there was at the first. Then a statement, somewhat in detail, of a course to be pursued, seemed very fitting and proper. Now, at the expiration of four years, during which public declarations have been constantly called forth on every point and phase of the great contest which still absorbs the attention and engrosses the energies of the nation, little that is new could be presented.

The progress of our arms, upon which all else chiefly depends, is as well known to the public as to myself, and it is, I trust, reasonably satisfactory and encouraging to all. With high hope for the future, no prediction with regard to it is ventured.

On the occasion corresponding to this, four years ago, all thoughts were anxiously directed to an impending civil war. All dreaded it; all sought to avoid it. While the inaugural address was being delivered from this place, devoted altogether to saving the Union without war, insurgent agents were in the city seeking to destroy it without war—seeking to dissolve the Union and divide the effects by negotiation. Both parties deprecated war, but one of them would make war rather than let the nation survive; and the other would accept war rather than let it perish, and the war came.

One-eighth of the whole population were colored slaves, not distributed generally over the Union, but localized in the southern part of it. These slaves constituted a peculiar and powerful interest. All knew that this interest was somehow the cause of the war. To strengthen, perpetuate and extend this interest, was the object for which the insurgents would rend the Union, even by war, while the Government claimed no right to to do more than to restrict the territorial enlargement of it.

Neither party expected for the war the magnitude or the duration which it has already attained. Neither anticipated that the cause of the conflict might cease with, or even before the conflict itself should cease. Each looked for an easier triumph, and a result less fundamental and astounding.

Both read the same Bible, and pray to the same God; and each invokes His aid against the other. It may seem strange that any men should dare to ask a just God's assistance in wringing their bread from the sweat of other men's faces; but let us judge not, that we be not judged. The prayers of both could not be answered. That of neither has been answered fully. The Almighty has His own purposes. "Woe unto the world because of offences, for it must needs be that offences come; but woe to that man by whom the offence cometh." If we shall suppose that American slavery is one of these offences, which, in the providence of God, must needs come, but which, having continued through His appointed time, He now wills to remove, and that He gives to both North and South this terrible war as the woe due to those by whom the offence came, shall we discern therein any departure from those divine attributes which the believers in a living God always ascribe to Him? Fondly do we hope, fervently do we pray, that this mighty scourge of war may soon pass away. Yet, if God wills that it continue until all the wealth piled by the bondman's two hundred and fifty years of unrequited toil shall be sunk, and until every drop of blood drawn with the lash, shall be paid with another drawn by the sword; as was said three thousand years ago, so still it must be said, "The judgments of the Lord are true and righteous altogether."

With malice toward none, with charity to all, with firmness in the right, as God gives us to see the right, let us strive on to finish the work we are in; to bind up the nation's wounds; to care for him who shall have borne the battle, and for his widow and his orphans; to do all which may achieve and cherish a just and a lasting peace among ourselves and with all nations.

THE UNITED STATES OF AMERICA.

From the moment that the Declaration of Independence was published, July 4, 1776, the thirteen Colonies ceased to form a part of the British Empire, and became thirteen separate, independent, sovereign nations, each possessed of the power of self-government.

Immediately after the Declaration, a committee prepared Articles of Confederation, which were adopted by the several Colonies. A new nation, the United States of America, was thus formed and went into operation March 23, 1781.

The powers conferred by these articles were found to be too limited for the purposes of a National Government. It was merely a league between sovereign nations. The bond of Union was too feeble for permanency. The people felt this, and remedied it by adopting a Constitution, which binds the people of each and all of the states together under one National Government.

The Constitution was adopted September 17, 1787, and upon it and the amendments thereto is based our present Government, all the powers of which are granted through this instrument, as set forth in the preamble, by "We, the people of the United States, in order to form a more perfect union, &c."

These powers are exercised by the three co-ordinate branches of the Government, viz: the legislative, judicial, and executive.

The legislative, or law-making power, is vested in a Congress, consisting of two branches, the Senate and House of Representatives. For full information in relation to Congress, see the Constitution, Art. 1. As there are thirty-six states in the Union, the whole number of Senators is seventy-two; the whole number of Representatives is two hundred and forty-two, exclusive of the Territorial Delegates—one from each territory—who has the privileges of a Representative, except that of voting. As some of the states lately in rebellion are not represented in Congress the actual attendance is considerably less than the above figures.

The judicial, or law-interpreting power, is vested in "one Supreme Court and other inferior Courts," for the particulars of which see the Constitution, Art. III.

The executive, or law-enforcing power, is vested in the President. For his qualifications, election, powers, duties, &c., see the Constitution, Art. II. For the veto power, see Art. I, Sec. VII, Par. 3. The President is assisted in the performance of his duties by several officers who compose his cabinet, and who are his constitutional advisers. They are the Secretaries of State, of the Treasury, of War, of the Navy, and of the Interior, the Postmaster General, and the Attorney General. They are all executive officers. They are nominated by the President, and approved by the Senate, and are removable by the will of the President.

SALARIES.

The principal officers of the Government ere paid for their services as follows:

President	$25,000 per annum.
Vice-President	8,000 per annum.
Cabinet Officers	8,000 per annum.
Chief Justice	6,500 per annum.
Associate Justices	6,000 per annum.
Speaker of the House	3,000 per annum.
Senators	3,000 per annum.
Representatives	3,000 per annum.

Congressmen are also allowed mileage at the rate of eight dollars for every twenty miles of estimated distance by the most usual road from his place of residence to the seat of Congress, at the commencement and at the end of every regular session.

Habeas Corpus.—When a person is arrested or imprisoned, he is not compelled to wait for a hearing till the regular term of the court, but he may have a writ of "habeas corpus," and be immediately brought before a judge. And if it appears that he is illegally detained, he is entitled to an immediate discharge. The term habeas corpus, means you may have the body, and authorizes the officer to whom it is directed, to bring forth the body of the prisoner from confinement, to have an immediate hearing. This writ has justly been considered the "bulwark of personal liberty," and the Constitution declares that this privilege "shall not be suspended, unless when in cases of rebellion or invasion the public safety may require it." For the privileges and duties of citizens, see Constitution, Art. IV, Sec. II, and Amendments 1 to 11, inclusive. For State Rights, see Constitution, Art. I, Sec. X, Art. IV, and Amendment X.

THE STATES:

THEIR SETTLEMENT, FORMATION AS TERRITORIES, ADMISSION INTO THE UNION, AREA, POPULATION IN 1860, SUFFRAGE LAWS, GENERAL ELECTION, &C., &C.

Alabama—Was settled near Mobile, by the French, in 1702; was formed into a territory, from the eastern portion of Mississippi, March 3, 1817; framed a Constitution August 2, 1819, and was admitted into the Union December 14, of the same year. Area, 50,722 square miles. Population, 964,201, of whom 435,080 were slaves. Free white male persons, twenty-one years of age, citizens of the United States, who have resided one year in the State and three months in the county, are entitled to vote. State election, first Monday in August. The Legislature meets biennially, on the second Monday in November.

Arkansas—Was settled at Arkansas Post in 1685, by the French, and was part of the Louisiana purchase ceded by France to the United States, April 30, 1803. It was formed into a territory by act of Congress, March 2, 1819, from the southern part of the territory of Missouri; its western boundary was settled May 26, 1824, and its southern May 19, 1828, and the State admitted into the Union June 15, 1836. Area 52,198 square miles. Population 435,450, of whom 111,115 were slaves. It is an agricultural State, its staples being corn and cotton. The State Constitution makes every free white male citizen of the United States, twenty-one years of age, who shall have resided six months in the State, a qualified voter in the district where he resides, except that no soldier, seaman, or marine in the United States' service can vote in the State. State election, first Monday in August. The Legislature meets biennially on the first Monday in November.

California—Was settled at Diego in 1768, by Spaniards, and was part of the territory ceded to the United States by Mexico, by the treaty concluded at Guadaloupe Hidalgo, February 22, 1848. After several ineffectual attempts to organize it as a territory or admit it as a State, a law was passed by Congress for the latter purpose, which was approved September 9, 1850. Area 188,981 square miles. Population 305,439. It is the most productive gold mining region on the continent, and also abounds in many other minerals. Every white male citizen of the United States (or of Mexico who shall have elected to become a citizen of the United States under treaty of Queretaro) of full age, resident six months in the State and thirty days in the district is a qualified elector. The Legislature, which meets biennially on the first Monday in December, has power to extend the right to Indians and their descendants. State election, first Monday in September.

Connecticut—Was settled at Windsor, in 1633, by English Puritans from Massachusetts, and continued under the jurisdiction of that province until April 23, 1662, when a separate charter was granted, which continued in force until a Constitution was formed, September 15, 1818. It was one of the original thirteen States, and ratified the United States Constitution, January 9, 1788. Area 4,750 square miles. Population 460,147. It is one of the most densely populated and principal manufacturing States in the Union. Connecticut gives the ballot to all persons, whether white or black, who were freemen at the adoption of her Constitution (1818) and subsequently to "every white male citizen of the United States," of full age, resident six months in the town, and owning a freehold of the yearly value of $7, or who shall have performed militia duty, paid a State tax, and sustained a good moral character within the year. This was amended in 1845 by striking out the property and tax-paying qualification, and fixing the residence at one year in the State, and six months in the town. Only those negroes have voted in Connecticut who were admitted freedmen prior to 1818. State election first Monday in April. The Legislature meets annually, on the first Wednesday in May.

Delaware—Was settled at Wilmington, in 1638, by Swedes and Finns; was granted to William Penn in 1682, and continued under the government of Pennsylvania until the adoption of a Constitution, September 20, 1776; a new one was formed June 12, 1792. It was one of the original thirteen States, and ratified the United States Constitution, December 7, 1787. Area 2,120 square miles. Population 112,216, of whom 1,798 were slaves. It is a grain and fruit growing State, with some extensive manufactories. This State gives the elective franchise to every free white male citizen of the age of twenty-two years, who has resided one year in the State, and the last month thereof in the county, and who has, within two years, paid a county tax, assessed at least six months before the election; every free white male citizen over twenty-one and under twenty-two may vote without paying any tax. Idiots, insane persons, paupers and felons, are excluded from voting, and the Legislature may impose forfeiture of the right of suffrage as a punishment for crime. State election, first Tuesday in November. The Legislature meets biennially, on the first Tuesday in January.

Florida—Was settled at St. Augustine, in 1565, by Spaniards; was formed from part of the territory ceded by Spain to the United States, by treaty of February 22, 1819. An act to authorize the President to establish a temporary government was passed March 3, 1819; articles of surrender of East Florida were framed July 10, and of West Florida, July 17, 1821, and it was then taken possession of by General Jackson as Governor. An act for the establishment of a territorial government was passed March 30, 1822, and by act of March 3, 1823, East and West Florida were constituted one territory. Acts to establish its boundary line between Georgia and Alabama were passed May 4, 1826, and March 2, 1831. After several ineffectual attempts to organise it into two territories, or into a State and territory, an act for its admission into the Union was passed March 3, 1845. Area 59,268 square miles. Population 140,425, of whom 61,745 were slaves. It is an agricultural State, tropical in its climate and products. Florida limits the suffrage to "every free white male person," of twenty-one years of age, a citizen of the United States, two years a resident of the State, and six months of the county, duly enrolled in the militia, and duly registered; provided that no soldier or seaman quartered therein shall be deemed a resident, and the Legislature may exclude from voting for crime. State election, first Monday in October. The Legislature meets biennially on the first Monday in November.

Georgia—Was settled at Savannah, in 1733, by the English under General Oglethorpe. It was chartered June 9, 1732; formed a Constitution February 5, 1777; a second in 1785, and a third May 30, 1798. It was one of the thirteen original States, and ratified the United States Constitution January 2, 1788. Area 58,000 square miles. Population 1,057,286, of whom 462,198 are slaves. It is a large cotton and rice growing State. The new Constitution declares that "the electors of the General Assembly shall be free white male citizens of the State, and shall have attained the age of twenty-one years, and shall have paid all taxes which may have been required of them, and which they have had an opportunity of paying agreeable to law, for the year preceeding the election, shall be citizens of the United States; and shall have resided six months either in the district or county, and two years within the State. State election, first Wednesday in October. The Legislature meets annually, on the first Thursday in November.

Illinois—Was settled at Kaskaskia, in 1633, by the French, and formed part of the Northwestern territory ceded by Virginia to the United States. An act for dividing the Indiana territory and organizing the territory of Illinois, was passed by Congress, February 3, 1809; and an act to enable it to form a State Constitution, Government, etc., was passed April 18, 1818, a Constitution was framed August 26, and it was admitted into the Union December 23, of the same year. Area 55,409 square miles. Population 1,711,951. It is the chief "Prairie" State, mainly devoted to grain-growing and cattle-raising. Illinois gives the vote to "every white male citizen," of full age, residing one year in the State, and "every white male inhabitant" who was a resident of the State at the adoption of this

Constitution. State election, first Tuesday in November. The Legislature meets biennially, on the second Monday in January.

Indiana—Was settled at Vincennes in 1690, by the French, and formed part of the Northwestern territory ceded by Virginia to the United States. It was organized into a territory May 7, 1800, from which the territory of Michigan was set off in 1805, and Illinois in 1809. An act was passed to empower it to form a State Constitution, Government, etc., April 19, 1816, and it was admitted into the Union December 11, of the same year. Area 33,809 square miles. Population 1,350,428. It is an agricultural State chiefly devoted to grain growing and cattle raising. Indiana gives the right of suffrage to "every white male citizen of the United States," of full age and six months' residence in the State, and every white male of foreign birth and full age, who has resided one year in the United States, and six months preceding the election in the State, and who has declared his intention to become a citizen. State election, second Tuesday in October. The Legislature meets biennially, on the first Wednesday in January.

Iowa—Was first settled at Burlington by emigrants from the Northern and Eastern States. It was part of the rigion purchased from France; was set off from the territory of Wisconsin and organized as a separate territory June 12, 1838; an act for its admission as a State was passed and approved March 3, 1845, to which the assent of its inhabitants was to be given, to be announced by proclamation of the President, and on December 28, 1846, another act for its admission was passed. Area 55,000 square miles. Population 674,913. It is an agricultural State, resembling Illinois, and contains important lead mines. White male citizens of the United States, having resided in the State six months, and county twenty days, are entitled to vote. State election, second Tuesday in October. The Legislature meets biennially, on the second Monday in January.

Kansas—Was formed out of the original Louisiana purchase, and organized into a territory by act of Congress, May —, 1854, and after several ineffectual attempts was finally admitted into the Union in January,

1861. Area 114,798 square miles. Population 107,206. It is an agricultural State, with a soil of rich and deep black loam, except the central portion, which is partly a desert. The western portion is a fine grazing country, well wooded. It also abounds in minerals. Kansas gives the ballot to every white male adult resident six months in the State and thirty days in the town, who is either a citizen or has declared his intention. State election first Tuesday in November. The Legislature meets annually on the second Thursday in January.

Kentucky—Was settled in 1775 by Virginians; formed into a territory by act of the Virginia Legislature, December 18, 1789, and admitted into the Union June 1, 1792, by virtue of an act of Congress, passed February 4, 1791. Area 37,680 square miles. Population 1,155,684, of whom 225,483 were slaves. It is an agricultural State, raising more flax and hemp than any other. In Kentucky "every white male citizen of the age of twenty-one years," who has resided two years in the State, one year in the county, and sixty days in the precinct, is a voter. State election first Monday in August. The Legislature meets biennially, on the first Monday in December.

Louisiana—Was settlod at Iberville, in 1699, by the French, and comprised part of the territory ceded by France to the United States, by treaty of April 30, 1803, which purchase was erected into two territories by act of Congress, March 26, 1804, one called the territory of Orleans, the other the district of Louisiana, afterward changed to that of Missouri. Congress, March 2, 1806, authorized the inhabitants of Orleans territory to form a State Constitution and Government when their population should amount to 60,000; a Constitution was adopted January 22, 1812, and the State admitted into the Union April 8, of the same year, under the name of Louisiana. Area 41,346 square miles. Population 708,002, of whom 331,726 were slaves. It is the chief sugar producing State of the Union. Louisiana gives the ballot to every free white male who has attained the age of twenty-one years, and has resided twelve months in the State, and six months in the parish. State election first Monday in November. The Legislature meets biennially, on the third Monday in January.

Maine—Was settled at York, in 1623, by the English, and was formerly under the jurisdiction of Massachusetts. October 29, 1819, the inhabitants of the District of Maine framed a Constitution, applied for admission December 8, 1819. Congress passed an act March 3, 1820, and it was admitted as a State March 15, of the same year. Area 35,000 square miles. Population 628,279. It is largely engaged in the lumber trade and ship-building. Citizens of the United States, except paupers, and persons under guardianship, who have resided in the State for three months next preceding the election, are entitled to vote. State election, second Monday in September. The Legislature meets annually on the first Wednesday in January.

Maryland—Was settled at St. Mary, in 1634, by Irish Roman Catholics, having been chartered June 20, 1632. It was one of the original thirteen States; formed a Constitution August 14, 1776, and ratified the Constitution of the United States April 28, 1788. Area 11,124 square miles. Population 687,049, of whom 87,189 were slaves. It is mainly an agricultural State, producing grain and tobacco. Maryland allows "every free white male person of twenty-one years of age, or upward," who has resided one year in the State, six months in the county, and is a citizen of the United States, to vote in the election district in which he resides, but no adult convicted of an infamous crime unless pardoned, and no lunatic or person *non compos mentis* shall vote. State election, first Tuesday in November. The Legislature meets annually on the first Wednesday in January.

Massachusetts—Was settled at Plymouth, November 3, 1620, by English Puritans, and charters were granted March 4, 1629, January 13, 1630, August 20, 1726, and October 7, 1731. It was one of the original thirteen States; adopted a Constitution March 2, 1780, which was amended November 3, 1820, and ratified the Constitution of the United States February 6, 1788. Area 7,800 square miles. Population 1,231,066. It is a largely commercial, the chief manufacturing and most densely populated State in the Union. The ballot belongs to every male citizen, twenyt-one years of age (except paupers and persons under guardianship), who shall have paid any tax assessed within two years, or who shall be exempted from taxation. But no person has the right to vote, or is eligible to office under the Constitution of this Commonwealth, who is not able to read the Constitution in the English language, and write his name. State election, first Tuesday in November. The Legislature meets annually on the first Wednesday in January.

Michigan—Was settled at Detroit in 1670, by the French, and was part of the territory ceded to the United States by Virginia. It was set off from the territory of Indiana, and erected into a separate territory January 11, 1805; an act to attach to it all the territory of the United States west of the Mississippi river, and north of the State of Missouri, was passed June 28, 1834. Wisconsin was organized from it April 30, 1836; in June of the same year an act was passed to provide for the admission of the State of Michigan into the Union, and a Constitution having been adopted, it was admitted January 26, 1837. Area 56,243 square miles. Population 749,113. It is a grain-growing and cattle-rearing State, with rich and extensive mines of copper and iron in the Northern Peninsula. Michigan gives the ballot to every white male citizen, to every white male inhabitant residing in the State June 24th, 1835, and to every white male inhabitant residing in the State January 1st, 1850, who has declared his intention, etc., or who has resided two and a half years in the State, and declared his intention, and to every civilized male Indan inhabitant, not a member of any tribe. But no person shall vote unless of full age, and a resident six months in the State and six days in the town. State election, first Tuesday in November. The Legislature meets biennially on the first Wednesday in January.

Minnesota—Was settled about 1846, chiefly by emigrants from the Northern and Western States. It was organized as a territory by act of Congress, approved March 3, 1849, and admitted into the Union February 26, 1857. Area 83,531 square miles. Population 172,123 whites, and about 25,000 Indians, many of the tribes being of a warlike character. It is an agricultural State, chiefly devoted to Northern grains. The right to vote is extended to male persons of twenty-one years of age, of the following classes, if they have resided in the United States one year, the State four months, and the election district ten days: 1. A white citizen of the United States. 2. A white alien who has declared his intention. 3. Civilized persons of mixed white and Indian blood. 4. Civilized Indians certified by a district court to be fit for citizenship. State election, first Tuesday in November. The Legislature meets biennially on the first Tuesday in January.

Mississippi—Was settled at Natchez, in 1716, by the French, and was formed out of part of the territory ceded to the United States by South Carolina in 1787, and Georgia in 1802. It was organized as a territory by act of Congress, April 7, 1789, and enlarged on the north March 27, 1804, and on the south May 14, 1812. After several unsuccessful attempts to enter the Union, Congress finally passed an act March 1, 1817, enabling the people of the western part of the territory to form a State Constitution and Government, which being complied with August 15, it was admitted December 10 of the same year. Area 46,156 square miles. Population 791,305, of whom 436,631 were slaves. It is the second cotton growing State of the Union. Mississippi makes every free white male person of twenty-one years of age, who shall be a citizen of the United States, who has resided one year in the State, and four months in the county, a qualified elector. State election, first Monday in October. The Legislature meets biennially on the first Monday in January.

Missouri—Was settled at Genevieve in 1763, by the French, and was part of the territory ceded by France by treaty of April 30, 1803. It was created under the name of the district of Louisiana, by an act approved March 26, 1804, and placed under the direction of the officers of the Indiana territory, and was organized into a separate territory June 4, 1812, its name being changed to that of Missouri; and was divided March 2, 1819, the territory of Arkansas being then created. An act authorizing it to form a State Constitution and Government, was passed March 6, 1820, and it was admitted into the Union December 14, 1821. Area 67,380 square miles, or 43,123,200 acres. Population, in 1860, 1,182,012, of which 114,931 were slaves. It is an agricultural and mining State. Citizens of the United States who have resided in the State one year, and county three months, are entitled to vote. State election, first Tuesday in November. The Legislature meets biennially on the last Monday in December.

Nevada—Was organized as a territory March 2, 1861. Its name signifies snowy, and is derived from the Spanish word nieve (snow.) It comprises 81,539 square miles, or 52,184,960 acres, lying mostly within the Great Basin of the Pacific coast. Congress, at its session in 1864, passed an act, which was approved March 21, to enable the people of the territory to form a Constitution and State Government, in pursuance of which a government was organized and the territory admitted as a State by proclamation of the President, October 31, 1864. At the time of its organization the territory possessed a population of 6,857 white settlers. The development of her mineral resources was rapid and almost without parallel, and attracted a constant stream of immigration to that territory. As the population has not been subject to the fluctuations from which other territories have suffered, the growth of Nevada has been rapid and steady. At the general convention election of 1863, 10,934 votes were cast. During 1864 great accessions to the population were made. It is probably the richest State in the Union in respect to mineral resources. No region in the world is richer in argentiferous leads. It also contains an immense basin of salt, five miles square. Quartz mills are a very important feature in mining operations. The State is barren for agricultural purposes, and is remarkably healthy. Every white male citizen of full age, six months a resident in the State, and every white male alien, of full age, resident in the United States one year, who has declared his intention, may vote, but "no negro, Chinaman, or mulatto." State election, first Tuesday in November. The

Legislature meets annually on the first Monday in January.

New Hampshire—Was settled at Dover, in 1623, by English Puritans, and continued under the jurisdiction of Massachusetts until September 18, 1679, when a separate charter was granted. It was one of the original thirteen States, and ratified the United States Constitution June 21, 1788; its State Constitution was framed January 5, 1776, and amended in 1784 and 1792. Area 9,280 square miles. Population 326,073. It is a grazing and manufacturing State. New Hampshire gives the ballot to "every male inhabitant" of twenty-one years, except paupers and persons excused from paying taxes at their own request. State election, second Tuesday in March. The Legislature meets annually on the first Wednesday in June.

New Jersey—Was settled at Bergen, in 1624, by the Dutch and Danes; was conquered by the Dutch in 1655, and submitted to the English in 1664, being held thereafter under the same grants as New York, until it was surrendered to the crown in 1702. It was one of the original thirteen States, adopted a State Constitution July 2, 1776, and ratified the United States Constitution December 18, 1787. Area 8,320 square miles. Population 672,035. It is a grain and fruit growing region, its orchard and market products being relatively greater than those of any other State. New Jersey gives the ballot to "every white male citizen" of the United States, of full age, residing one year in the State and five months in the county, except that no pauper, idiot, insane person, or person convicted of a crime which excludes him from being a witness, shall vote. State election, first Tuesday in November. The Legislature meets annually on the second Tuesday in January.

New York—Was settled at Manhattan in 1614, by the Dutch; was conceded to the English by grants to the Duke of York, March 20, April 26, and June 24, 1664; was retaken by the Dutch in 1673, and surrendered again by them to the English, February 9, 1674. It was one of the original thirteen States, ratified the United States Constitution July 26, 1788; framed a Constitution April 20, 1777, which was amended October 27, 1801, and November 10, 1821; a new one was adopted November 3, 1846. Area 46,000 square miles. Population 3,880,735. It is the most populous, wealthy, and commercial of the States. New York admits to the suffrage "every male citizen" of full age, who shall have been ten days a citizen, one year in the State, four months in the county, and thirty days in the district. But no man of color shall vote unless he has been three years a citizen of the State, and for one year the owner of a freehold worth $250, over incumbrances, on which he shall have paid a tax, and he is to be subject to no direct tax unless he owns such freehold. Laws are authorized and have been passed, excluding from the suffrage, persons convicted of bribery, larceny, or infamous crime; also persons betting on the election. No person gains or loses a residence by reason of presence or absence in the service of the United States—nor in navigation—nor as a student in a seminary—nor in an asylum or prison. A registry law also exists. State election, first Tuesday in November. The Legislature meets annually on the first Tuesday in January.

North Carolina—Was settled at Albemarle, in 1650, by the English, and was chartered March 20, 1663. It was one of the original thirteen States, and ratified the United States Constitution November 21, 1789; its State Constitution was adopted December 18, 1776, and amended in 1835. Area 50,700 square miles. Population 992,622, of whom 331,059 were slaves. It is an agricultural State, with some mines and extensive pine forests. All freemen twenty-one years of age, living twelve months in the State, and owning a freehold of fifty acres for six months, should vote, except that "no free negro, free mulatto, or free person of mixed blood, descended from negro ancestors to the fourth generation inclusive (though one ancestor of each generation may have been a white person), shall vote for members of the Senate or House of Commons." State election, second Thursday in August. The Legislature meets biennially on the third Monday in November.

Ohio—Was settled at Marietta in 1788, by emigrants from Virginia and New England; was ceded by Virginia to the United States October 20, 1783; accepted by the latter March 1, 1784, and admitted into the Union April 30, 1802. Area 39,964 square miles. Population 2,339,511. It is the most populous and wealthy of the agricultural States, devoted chiefly to wool-growing, grain and live stock. Ohio limits the elective franchise to "every white male citizen" of the United States, of full age, resident one year in the State. (Constitution of 1851.) But the courts of Ohio having held that every person of one-half white blood is a "white male citizen" within the Constitution and that the burden of proof is with the challenging party, to show that the person is more than half black, which is impracticable. State election, second Tuesday in October. The Legislature meets bienniully on the first Monday in January.

Oregon—Although it had previously been seen by various navigators, was first taken possession of by Capt. Robert Gray, who entered the mouth of its principal river May 7, 1792, naming it after his vessel, the Columbia, of Boston. Exploring expeditions soon followed, and fur companies sent their trappers and traders into the region. In 1811 a trading post was established at the mouth of the Columbia river by the American Fur Company, who named it Astoria. For some time a provisional territorial government existed, but the boundary remained unsettled until the treaty with Great Britain in 1846, when the 49th parallel was adopted. It was formally organized as a territory August 14, 1848; was divided March 2, 1853, on the 46th parallel, the northern portion being called Washington, and the southern Oregon. November 9, 1857, a State Constitution was adopted, under which it was admitted February 14, 1859, about one-third of it on the east being added to Washington territory, its northern boundary following the Columbia river until its intersection with latitude 46° north. Area about 95,274 square miles. Population 52,465. It is an agricultural State, possessed of a fertile soil, extensive pastures, genial climate, and is well wooded. Gold and other precious metals are found in considerable abundance. Suffrage qualification, same as in Nevada. State election, first Monday in June. The

Legislature meets biennially on the second Monday in September.

Pennsylvania—Was settled at Philadelphia, in 1681, by English Quakers, and was chartered February 28 of the same year. It was one of the original thirteen States, ratifying the United States Constitution December 12, 1787; adopted a State Constitution September 28, 1776, and amended it September 2, 1790. Area 47,000 square miles. Population 2,906,115. It is the second State in wealth and population, and the principal coal and iron mining region in the Union. Pennsylvania gives a vote to "every white freeman," of full age, who has resided one year in the State, and ten days in the election district, and has within two years paid a tax, except that a once qualified voter, returning into the State after an absence which disqualifies him from voting, regains his vote by a six months' residence, and except that white free citizens under twenty-two and over twenty-one vote without paying taxes. State election, second Tuesday in October. The Legislature meets annually, on the first Tuesday in January.

Rhode Island—Was settled at Providence in 1636, by the English from Massachusetts under Roger Williams. It was under the jurisdiction of Massachusetts until July 8, 1662, when a separate charter was granted, which continued in force until the formation of a Constitution in September 1842. It was one of the original thirteen States, ratifying the United States Constitution, May 29, 1790. Area 1,306 square miles. Population 174,620. It is largely engaged in manufactures. Rhode Island gives the right of suffrage: 1. To every male citizen, of full age, one year in the State, six months in the town, owning real estate worth $134, or renting $7 per annum. 2. To every native male citizen of fulll age, two years in the State, six months in the town, who is duly registered, who has paid one dollar tax, or done militia service within the year. State election, first Wednesday in April. The Legislature meets annually on the last Tuesday in June.

South Carolina—Was settled at Port Royal, in 1670, by the English, and continued under the charter of Carolina or North Carolina until they were separated in 1729. It was one of the original thirteen states, ratifying the United States Constitution May 23, 1798; it framed a State Constitution March 26, 1776, which was amended March 19, 1778, and June 3, 1790. Area 34,000 square miles. Population 703,708, of whom 402,406 were slaves, an excess of 101,270 over the whites. It is the principal rice growing State. South Carolina gives the right of voting to every person who has the following qualifications: He shall be a free white man who has attained the age of twenty-one years, and is not a pauper, nor a non-commissioned officer or private soldier of the army, nor a seaman or a marine of the navy of the United States. He shall, for two years preceding the election, have been a citizen of the State, or for the same period, an emigrant from Europe, who has declared his intention to become a citizen of the United States. He shall have resided in the State at least two years preceding the election, and for the last six months in the district. State election, fourth Monday in November. The Legislature meets annually, on the third Wednesday in October.

Tennessee—Was settled at Fort Donelson, in 1756 by emigrants from Virginia and North Corolina; was ceded to the United States by North Carolina, December, 1789, conveyed by the Senators of that State February 25, 1790, and accepted by act of Congress, April 2, of the same year; it adopted a Constitution February 6, 1799, and was admitted into the Union the first of June following. Area 45,000 square miles. Population 1,109,801, of whom 275,170 were slaves. It is a mining and agricultural State, and is largely productive of live stock. Tennessee gives the elective franchise to every free white man of the age of twenty-one years, being a citizen of the Uuited States, and for six months a resident of the county. State election, first Thursday in August. The Legislature meets biennially, on the first Monday in October.

Texas—Was first settled at Bexar, in 1694, by Spaniards; formed a part of Mexico until 1836, when she revolted from that Republic and instituted a separate government, under which she existed until admitted into the Union by a joint resolution, approved March 1,

1845, imposing certain conditions which were accepted, and a Constitution formed July 4, of the same year, and another joint resolution adopted by Congress, consummating the annexation, was approved December 29, 1845. Area 274,356 square miles. Population 604,215, of whom 182,566 were slaves. It is an agricultural region, principally devoted to grain, cotton and tropical fruits. Texas gives the vote to "every free male person" who shall have attained the age of twenty-one years, a citizen of the United States or of the Republic of Texas, one year a resident of the State, and six months of the county, (Indians not taxed, Africans and the descendants of Africans excepted). State election, first Monday in August. The Legislature meets biennially, on the first Monday in November.

Vermont—Was settled in in 1724, by Englishmen from Connecticut, chiefly under grants from New Hampshire; was formed from a part of the territory of New York by act of its Legislature, March 6, 1760; framed a State Constitution December 25, 1777, and was admitted into the Union March 4, 1791, by virtue of an act of Congress passed February 18 of the same year. Area 10,212 square miles. Population 315,098. It is a grazing region, producing more wool, live stock, maple sugar, butter, cheese and hay, in proportion to its population, than any other State. Any citizen of the United States, who has resided in the State one year, and will take the oath to vote "so as in your conscience you shall judge will most conduce to the best good" of the State, may vote. State election, first Tuesday in September. The Legislature meets annually, on the second Thursday in October.

Virginia—Was settled at Jamestown, in 1607, by the English, and was chartered April 10, 1606, May 23, 1609, and March 12, 1612. It was one of the original thirteen States, ratifying the United States Constitution June 25, 1788; it framed a State Constitution July 5,1776, which was amended January 15, 1830. Area 61,352 square miles. Population 1,596,318, of whom 490,865 were slaves. It is a large corn producing, and the chief tobacco growing State. Virginia admits to vote "every white male citizen of Virginia of twenty-one years, who has resided two years in the State and twelve months in the county, except persons of unsound mind, paupers, non-commissioned officers, soldiers, seamen or marines in the United States service, or persons convicted of bribery, or some infamous offence; persons in the military and naval United States service not to be deemed residents by virtue of being stationed therein." State election, fourth Thursday in May. The Legislature meets biennially, on the second Monday in January.

West Virginia—Was formed as set forth in the body of this work. State election, fourth Thursday in October. The Legislature meets annually, on the third Thursday in January.

Wisconsin—Was settled at Green Bay, in 1669, by the French; was a part of the territory ceded by Virginia, and was set off from Michigan December 23, 1834, and organized into a territory April 30, 1836. Iowa was set off from it June 12, 1838, and acts were passed at various times settling its boundaries; March 3, 1847, an act for its admission into the Union was passed, to take effect on the issuing of a proclamation by the President, and by act of May 29, 1848, it was admitted into the Union. Area 53,924 square miles. Population 775,881. It is an agricultural State, chiefly engaged in grain-raising and wool-growing. Wisconsin gives the ballot to every male person of full age, resident one year in the State, and being either: 1. A white citizen of the United States. 2. A white alien who has declared his intention. 3. A person of Indian blood who has been declared a citizen by act of Congress. 4. Civilized persons of Indian descent not members of any tribe. In November 1865 a vote was taken on a proposed amendment to the State Constitution, to strike out the word "white" in the qualification of voters. The amendment was rejected by a majority of 8,059. State election, first Tuesday after the first Monday in November. The Legislature meets annually on the second Wednesday in January.

Arizona—Was organized as a territory February 24, 1863. It contains all of New Mexico west of a line from the point where the southwest corner of Colorado joins New Mexico, being the 109 Meridian (32d west from Washington) due south to the southern line of New Mexico (or northern line of Mexico.) The territory forms a block nearly square, and contains 126,141 square miles, or 80,730,240 acres. Its white population is about 10,000. The wealth of Arizona is but just becoming known. Its ancient ruins were among the best in the world, yet they have had to give way, in interest and value, to the newly opened placers and veins. The territory is literally veined with the precious metals, but the terrible aridity of the soil and the presence of those irrepressible tigers of the plains—the Comanches and the Apaches—renders the territory less tempting to wealth-hunters than the more northerly regions where gold and silver are as plenty, water and wood more accessible, and the Indians are less troublesome.

Colorado—Was organized March 2, 1861, from parts of Kansas, Nebraska, and Utah, and is situated on each side of the Rocky Mountains, between latitude 37° and 41°, and longitude 25° and 32° west from Washington. Area 106,475 square miles. Population 80,000, besides numerous tribes of Indians. It is a superior grazing and cattle-producing region, with a healthy climate and rich soil; an extensive coal bed, and also gold, iron and other minerals abound. Its population is rapidly increasing. Several fine towns serve as centres of supply and trade, and offer fine facilities for schools, churches, etc. The direct route from Fort Kearney to Salt Lake passes through the northern part of the territory, and a fine road from Denver City to the overland route makes the region around Pike's Peak easily accessible. The Colorado mines differ somewhat from those of California, where placer and gulch mining permits single operatives to do a good business. The Colorado metals run in beds, mixed with quartz and pyrites, necessitating all the appliances of underground mining, crushing mills, etc., to render the ores available.

Dakota—Was first settled by employees of the Hudson Bay Company, but is now being peopled by emigrants from the Northern and Western States. It was set off from the western portion of Minnesota when that territory became a State in 1857, and was organized March 2, 1861. Area 148,932 square miles, or 95,336,480 acres. Population in 1864 was 2,576 whites, and 2,261 Indians, beside the roving tribes. Being easily accessible by the Missouri river, which runs through it from the southeast to its northwestern corner, and bounded on its entire northeastern line by the Red river of the north, this territory offers unusual facilities for agricultural and grazing operations.

Idaho—Was organized by the Thirty-Seventh Congress, at its second session, in the winter of 1863. Its name means Bead of the Mountains, and it embraces the whole breadth of the Rocky Mountain region, and has within its bounds the head waters of nearly all the great rivers that flow down its either slope, but the greater portion lies east of the mountains. Its southern boundary is the 41st, its northern the 46th parallel of latitude. It extends from the 104th meridian on the east to the 110th on the west. Area 326,373 square miles. Gold has been discovered on nearly all the tributaries and head-waters of the Missouri and Yellow Stone rivers. Copper and iron exist in abundance, and salt is plentiful in many localities. Coal also is found on the Upper Missouri and Yellow Stone, upon the Pacific slope of the Rocky Mountains.

Montana—Was settled by emigrants from the northern and western States. Organized in 1864, with the following boundary: Commencing at a point formed by the intersection of the 27° L. W. from Washington with the 45° N. L.; thence due west on said 45th degree to a point formed by its intersection with the 34th degree W. from Washington; thence due south along said 34th degree of longitude to its intersection with the 44th degree and 30 minutes of N. L.; thence due west along said 44th degree and 30 minutes of N. L. to a point formed by its intersection with the crest of the Rocky

Mountains; thence following the crest of the Rocky Mountains northward till its intersection with the Bitter Root Mountains; thence northward, along the crest of said Bitter Root Mountains, to its intersection with the 39th degree of longitude W. from Washington; thence along said 39th degree of longitude northward to the boundary line of the British possessions; thence eastward, along said boundary, to the 27th degree of longitude W. from Washington; thence southward, along said 27th degree to the place of beginning. The population is put at 35,822. It is a good mining and agricultural region.

Nebraska—Was settled by emigrants from the North, and was formed out of a part of the territory ceded by France, April 30, 1803. Attempts to organize it were made in 1844 and 1848, but it was not accomplished until May 30, 1854, Area 75,955 square miles, or 44,796.160 acres. Population 38,841, besides a few roving tribes of Indians. It is an agricultural region, its prairies affording boundless pasture lands.

New Mexico—Was formed from a part of the territory ceded to the United States by Mexico, by the treaty of Guadalupe, Hidalgo, February 2, 1848, and was organized into a territory September 9, 1850. Area 121,201 square miles, or 77,568,640 acres. Population 83,000, besides large tribes of warlike Indians. The principle resources of the country is its minerals, though enormous "ranches" scattered over the whole territory produced immense droves of horses and cattle, who thrive on the rich "gramma" grass. The mines of New Mexico are noted for their variety and richness.

Utah—Was settled by the Mormons, and was formed from a part of the territory ceded to the United States by Mexico, by the treaty of Gaudalupe Hidalgo, February 2, 1848, and was organized into a territory September 9, 1850. Area 106,392 square miles, or 68,084,-480 acres. Population 60,000. Brine, sulphureous and chalybeate springs abound; limestone, granite, sandstone and marble are found in large quantities; iron is abundant, and gold, silver, copper, lead and zinc have been found. Not one-fiftieth part of the soil is fit for tillage, but on that which is, abundant crops of grain and considerable cotton are raised.

Washington—Was settled by emigrants from the North, and was organized into a territory March 2, 1853, from the northern portion of Oregon, to which was added another portion from the eastern part when the latter territory was admitted as a State, February 14, 1859. Area 69,994 square miles, or 48,636,800 acres. Population 22,168, besides numerous tribes of Indians.

THE OFFICIAL REPORT

OF

LIEUTENANT-GENERAL ULYSSES S. GRANT,

As submitted July 22, 1865.

(SYNOPSIS.)

FROM an early period in the rebellion, I had been impressed with the idea that active and continuous operations of all the troops that could be brought into the field, regardless of season and weather, were necessary to a speedy termination of the war.

I was firm in the conviction that no peace could be had that would be stable and conducive to the happiness of the people, both North and South, until the military power of the rebellion was entirely broken.

I therefore determined, first, to use the greatest number of troops practically against the armed force of the enemy, preventing him from using the same force at different seasons against first one and then another of our armies. Second, to hammer continuously against the armed force of the enemy and his resources, until, by mere attrition, if in no other way, there should be nothing left to him but an equal submission with the loyal section of our common country to the Constitution and laws of the land.

These views have been kept constantly in mind, and orders given and campaigns made to carry them out. Whether they might have been better in conception and execution is for the people, who mourn the loss of friends fallen, and who have to pay the pecuniary cost, to say. All I can say is, that what I have done has been done conscientiously, to the best of my ability, and in what I conceived to be for the best interests of the whole country.

At the date when this report begins, the situation of the contending forces was about as follows: The Mississippi River was strongly garrisoned by Federal troops from St. Louis to its mouth. The line of the Arkansas was also held, thus giving us armed possession of all west of the Mississippi, north of that stream. A few points in southern Louisiana, not remote from the river, were held by us, together with a small garrison at and near the mouth of the Rio Grande. All the balance of the vast territory of Arkansas, Louisiana, and Texas was in almost undisputed possession of the enemy. East of the Mississippi we held substantially with the line of the Tennessee and Holston Rivers, running eastward to include nearly all of the State of Tennessee; south of Chattanooga a small foothold in Georgia, sufficient to protect East Tennessee from incursions from the enemy's force at Dalton, Ga.; West Virginia was substantially within our lines. Virginia, with the exception of the northern border, the Potomac River, a small area about the mouth of James River, covered by the troops at Norfolk and Fortress Monroe, and the territory covered by the Army of the Potomac, lying along the Rapidan, was in the possession of the enemy. Along the sea-coast footholds had been obtained at Plymouth, Washington, and Newbern; Beaufort, Folly, and Morris Islands; Hilton Head, Fort Pulaski, and Port Royal; Fernandina, St. Augustine, Key West, and Pensacola, while all the important ports were blockaded by the navy.

Behind the Union lines there were many bands of guerrillas and a large population disloyal to the Government, making it necessary to guard every foot of road or river used in supplying our armies. In the South a reign of military despotism prevailed, which made every man and boy capable of bearing arms a soldier, and those who could not bear arms in the field acted as provosts for collecting deserters and returning them. This enabled the enemy to bring almost his entire strength into the field.

The enemy had concentrated the bulk of his forces east of the Mississippi into two armies, commanded by Generals R. E. Lee and J. E. Johnston, his ablest and best Generals. The army commanded by Lee occupied the south bank of the Rapidan, extending from Mine Run westward, strongly intrenched, covering and defending Richmond. The army under Johnston occupied a strongly intrenched position at Dalton, Ga., covering and defending Atlanta. In addition to these armies, he had a large cavalry force, under Forrest, in North-east Mississippi, a considerable force in the Shenandoah Valley, and in the western part of Virginia and extreme eastern part of Tennessee, and also confronting our sea-coast garrisons, and holding blockaded ports where we had no foothold upon land.

These two armies, and the cities covered and defended by them, were the main objective points of the campaign.

Major-General Sherman, who was appointed to the command of the Military Division of the Mississippi, had the immediate command of the armies operating against Johnston.

Major-General Meade had the immediate command of the Army of the Potomac, from where I exercised general supervision of the movements of our armies.

I may here state that, commanding all the armics as I did, I tried, as far as possible, to leave General Meade in independent command of the Army of the Potomac. My instructions for that army were all through him, and were general in their nature, leaving all the details and the execution to him. The campaigns that followed proved him to be the right man in the right place. His commanding always in the presence of an officer superior to him in rank has drawn from him much of that public attention that his zeal and ability entitle him to.

General Sherman was instructed to move against Johnston's army, to break it up, and to go into the interior of the enemy's country as far as he could, inflicting all the damage he could upon their war resources. If the enemy in his front showed signs of joining Lee, to follow him up to the full extent of his ability, while I would prevent, if possible, the concentration of Lee upon him. General Meade was instructed that Lee's army would be his objective point; that wherever Lee went he would go also. For his movement two plans presented themselves—one to cross the Rapidan below Lee, moving by his right flank; the other above, moving by his left. Each presented advantages over the other, with corresponding objections. It was decided to take the lower route.

In co-operation with the main movements against Lee

and Johnston, I was desirous of using all other troops necessarily kept in departments remote from the fields of immediate operations, and also those kept in the background for the protection of our extended lines, and instructions were issued accordingly.

Owing to the weather and bad condition of the roads, operations were delayed until the 1st of May, when, every thing being in readiness, and the roads favorable, orders were given for a general movement of all the armies not later than the 4th of May.

The Army of the Potomac commenced its movement on the morning of May 4. Before night the whole army, with the greater part of its trains (about 4,000 wagons), was across the Rapidan, having met but little opposition.

Early on the 5th, the advance corps met and engaged the enemy outside his intrenchments near Mine Run. The battle raged furiously all day, the whole army being brought into the fight as fast as the corps could be got upon the field.

General Burnside, with the 9th Corps, was left to hold the road back to Bull Run, and instructions to move promptly as soon as he received notice that a crossing of the Rapidan was secured. This notice he received on the afternoon of the 4th. By 6 o'clock A. M. of the 6th, he was leading his corps into action near the Wilderness Tavern, some of his troops having marched a distance of over thirty miles, crossing both the Rappahannock and Rapidan Rivers.

The battle of the Wilderness was renewed by us at 5 o'clock on the morning of the 6th, and continued with unabated fury until darkness set in, each army holding substantially the same position that they had on the evening of the 5th. After dark the enemy made a feeble attempt to turn our right flank, capturing several hundred prisoners, and creating considerable confusion. But the promptness of General Sedgwick, who commanded that part of our line, soon reformed it and restored order. Morning showed that the enemy had fallen behind his intrenched lines. From this it was evident to my mind that the two days' fighting had satisfied him of his inability to further maintain the contest in open field, notwithstanding his advantage of position, and that he would wait an attack behind his works. I therefore determined to push on and put my whole force between him and Richmond; and orders were at once issued for a movement by his right flank. On the night of the 7th, the march was commenced toward Spottsylvania Court-house. But the enemy having become apprised of our movement, and having the shorter line, was enabled to reach there first. On the 8th, General Warren met a force of the enemy which had been sent out to oppose and delay his advance, to gain time to fortify the line taken up at Spottsylvania. This force was steadily driven back on the main force, within the recently-constructed works, after considerable fighting, resulting in severe loss to both sides. The 9th, 10th, and 11th were spent in maneuvering and fighting, without decisive results. The able and distinguished Major-General Sedgwick was killed on the 9th. Major-General Wright succeeded him in command.

Early on the 12th, a general attack was made on the enemy. General Hancock carried a salient of his line, capturing most of Johnston's division of Ewell's corps and twenty pieces of artillery. But the resistance was so obstinate that the advantage gained did not prove decisive. The 13th, 14th, 15th, 16th, 17th, and 18th were consumed in maneuvering and awaiting the arrival of reinforcements from Washington. Orders were issued for a movement to the North Anna, to commence at 12 o'clock on the night of the 19th. Late in the afternoon of the 19th, Ewell's corps came out of its works on our extreme right flank; but the attack was promptly repulsed, with heavy loss. This delayed the movement until the night of the 21st, when it was commenced. But the enemy again having the shorter line, and being in possession of the main roads, was enabled to reach the North Anna in advance of us, and took position behind it. The 2d, 5th, 6th, and 9th Corps reached the North Anna on the afternoon of the 23d, General Warren effecting a crossing with little opposition. He was violently attacked, but repulsed the enemy with great slaughter. General Sheridan, having started on a raid on the 9th, rejoined the main body again on the 25th, having destroyed the depots at Beaver Dam and Ashland

Stations, four trains of cars, large supplies of rations, and many miles of railroad track; recaptured about four hundred of our men, on their way to Richmond as prisoners of war; met and defeated the enemy's cavalry at Yellow Tavern; carried the first line of works around Richmond; but, finding the second line too strong to be carried by assault, recrossed to the north bank of the Chickahominy at Meadow Bridge, under heavy fire, and moved by a *détour* to Haxall's Landing, on the James River, where he communicated with General Butler.

General Butler moved up James River May 4. He sent a force of 1,800 cavalry, by way of West Point, to form a junction with him wherever he might get a foothold, and a force of 3,000 cavalry, under General Kautz, from Suffolk, to operate against the roads south of Petersburg and Richmond. On the 5th he occupied, without opposition, both City Point and Bermuda Hundred, his movement being a complete surprise. On the 6th he was in position, and commenced intrenching; on the 7th he made a reconnoissance against the Petersburg and Richmond railroad, destroying a portion of it. On the evening of the 13th and morning of the 14th he carried a portion of the first line of defenses at Fort Darling, with small loss. The time thus consumed lost to us the surprise and capture of Richmond and Petersburg, enabling Beauregard to collect his loose forces in North and South Carolina. On the 16th the enemy attacked General Butler. He was forced back into his intrenchments between the forks of the James and Appomattox Rivers, the enemy intrenching strongly in his front. His army, therefore, though in a position of great security, was as completely shut off from further operations directly against Richmond as if it had been in a bottle, strongly corked.

The position at Bermuda Hundred was as easy to defend as it was difficult to operate from against the enemy. I determined, therefore, to bring from it all available forces, leaving enough only to secure what had been gained, and, accordingly, on the 22d, I directed that they be sent forward to join the Army of the Potomac.

General Burnside's corps was, on the 24th, constituted a part General Meade's command

Finding the enemy's position on the North Anna stronger than either of his previous ones, I withdrew on the night of the 26th to the north bank of the North Anna, and moved to turn the enemy's position by his right. The cavalry, under Sheridan, and the 6th Corps leading the advance, crossed the Pamunky River at Hanovertown after considerable fighting, and on the 28th, the two divisions of cavalry had a severe but successful engagement with the enemy at Hawe's Shop. We advanced to Hanover Court-house and Cold Harbor Road, and developed the enemy's position north of the Chickahominy. Late on the 30th, the enemy came out and attacked our left, but was repulsed. An attack was immediately ordered by General Meade along his whole line, which resulted in driving the enemy from a part of his intrenched skirmish line.

An attack was made at 5 P. M., June 1, by the 6th Corps and by General Smith, the other corps being held in readiness to advance on receipt of orders. This resulted in our carrying and holding the enemy's first line of works in front of the right of the attacking troops. During the attack, the enemy made repeated assaults on each of the corps not engaged in the main attack, but were repulsed with heavy loss in every instance. That night he made several assaults to regain what he had lost in the day, but failed. The 2d was spent in getting troops into position for an attack on the 3d, when we again assaulted the enemy's works, in the hope of driving him from his position. In this attempt our loss was heavy, while that of the enemy, I have reason to believe, was comparatively light.

From the proximity of the enemy to his defenses around Richmond, it was impossible, by any flank movement, to interpose between him and the city. I was still in a condition to either move by his left flank, and invest Richmond from the north side, or continue my move by his right flank to the south side of the James. I determined to hold substantially the ground we then occupied, taking advantage of any favorable circumstances that might present themselves, until the cavalry could be sent to Charlottsville and Gordonsville, to effectually break up the railroad connection between Richmond and the Shenandoah Valley and Lynchburg; and, when the cavalry got well off, to move the army to the south side of the James River, by the enemy's right flank, where I felt I could cut off all his sources of supply except by the canal.

During the three long years the armies of the Potomac and Northern Virginia had been confronting each other, they had fought more desperate battles than it probably ever fell to the lot of two armies to fight, without materially changing the vantage-ground of either. The Southern press and people, with more shrewdness than was displayed in the North, finding that they had failed to capture Washington and New York, assumed that they only defended their Capital and Southern territory. Hence, Antietam, Gettysburg, and all the other battles that had been fought, were by them set down as failures on our part, and victories for them. Their army believed this. It produced a morale which could only be overcome by continuous and desperate hard fighting. The battles of the Wilderness, Spottsylvania, North Anna, and Cold Harbor, bloody and terrible as they were on our side, were even more damaging to the enemy, and so crippled him as to make him wary ever after of taking the offensive. Not regarding the operations of General Sigel in the Kanawha and Shenandoah Valleys as satisfactory, I asked for his removal. He was succeeded by General Hunter, who immediately took up the offensive, and met the enemy at Piedmont, June 5, and routed him, capturing 1,500 men, 3 guns, and 300 small arms. On the 8th he formed a junction with Crook and Averill, at Staunton, from which place he moved direct on Lynchburg, *via* Lexington, which he invested June 16. To meet this movement, General Lee sent a force, which reached Lynchburg a short time before Hunter, who, being out of ammunition, retired from before the place on the 18th. Unfortunately, this want of ammunition forced his return by way of Kanawha, which lost to us the use of his troops for several weeks from the defense of the North.

The Second Corps (Potomac army) commenced crossing the James River on the morning of the 14th, by ferry-boats, at Wilcox's Landing. The crossing having commenced, General Butler was ordered to send General Smith immediately, that night, with all the troops he could give him without sacrificing the position he then held, for the capture of Petersburg. General Smith got off as directed, and confronted the enemy's pickets near Petersburg before daylight next morning, but, for some unexplained reason, did not assault his main lines until near sundown. Then, with a part of his command only, he made the assault, and carried the lines north-east of Petersburg, from the Appomattox River for a distance of over two and a half miles, capturing fifteen pieces of artillery and three hundred prisoners. This was about 7 P. M. Between the line thus captured and Petersburg there were no other works, and there was no evidence that the enemy had reinforced Petersburg with a single brigade from any source. The night was clear—the moon shining brightly—and favorable to further operations. General Hancock, with large reinforcements, waived rank, that Smith, who was supposed to know the ground, might act; yet no attack was made. By the time I arrived the next morning, the enemy was in force. An attack was made at 6 o'clock that evening, and continued, with but little intermission, until 6 o'clock the next morning, and resulted in our carrying the advance and some of the main works of the enemy, to the right (our left) of those previously captured by General Smith. Attacks were renewed on the 17th and 18th, which forced the enemy to an interior line, from which he could not be dislodged. The army then proceeded to envelop Petersburg toward the Southside Railroad.

On the 6th the enemy, to reinforce Petersburg, withdrew from a part of his intrenchment in front of Bermuda Hundred. General Butler at once moved a force on the railroad between Petersburg and Richmond. To retain the advantage thus gained, I ordered two divisions to report to General Butler, of which he was notified, and the importance of holding a position in advance of his present line urged upon him. About 2 o'clock P. M. Butler was forced back to the line from which the enemy had withdrawn in the morning. This position he held until the 17th, when he was joined by the two divisions before named. Instead of putting these into the enemy's works, to hold them, he permitted them to halt and rest some distance in the rear of his old line. General Butler, with one brigade, on the night of the 20th, effected a lodgment on the north bank of the James, at Deep Bottom, and connected the pontoon bridge with Bermuda Hundred.

On the 19th, General Sheridan, on his return from his expedition against the Virginia Central Railroad, met the enemy's cavalry at the White House, and compelled it to retire. During this expedition, General Sheridan, on June 11, near Trevillian Station, met the enemy's cavalry, whom he drove from the field in complete rout, capturing 400 prisoners, several hundred horses, etc. The dead and wounded were left in our hands. He destroyed the railroad from this place to Louisa Court-house, and advanced toward Gordonsville. He found the enemy behind rifle-pits, about five miles from the latter place, and too strong to successfully assault. On the extreme right, however, his reserve brigade carried the enemy's works twice, and was twice driven therefrom by infantry. Night closed the contest. Not having sufficient ammunition to continue the engagement, and his animals being without forage, he withdrew his command, and rejoined the Army of the Potomac.

General Wilson, on the 22d, moved against the enemy's railroads south of Richmond. Striking the Weldon Railroad at Ream's Station, destroying the depot and several miles of the road and the Southside Road, about fifteen miles from Petersburg, to near Nottaway's Station, where he defeated the enemy's cavalry, he reached Burksville Station on the 23d, and from there destroyed the Danville Railroad to Roanoke Bridge (twenty-five miles), where he found the enemy in a position from which he could not dislodge him. He then commenced his return march, and on the 28th met the enemy's cavalry at the Weldon Railroad crossing of Stony Creek, where he had a severe but not decisive engagement. Thence he made a *détour* from his left. At Ream's Station he was met by the enemy's cavalry, supported by infantry, and forced to retire, with the loss of his artillery and trains. This expedition severed all connection by railroad with Richmond for several weeks.

On the night of July 26, with a view of cutting the enemy's railroad from near Richmond to the Anna River, and making him wary of the situation of his army in the Shenandoah, and, in the event of failure in this, to take advantage of his necessary withdrawal of troops from Petersburg, to explode a mine that had been prepared in front of the 9th Corps, and assault the enemy's lines at that place, the 2d Corps and two divisions of the cavalry corps and Kautz's cavalry were crossed to the north bank of the James River, and joined the force General Butler had there. On the 27th the enemy was driven from his intrenched position, with the loss of four pieces of artillery. On the 28th our lines were extended from Deep Bottom to New Market road, but were attacked by the enemy, resulting in considerable loss to both sides. The first object of this move having failed, by reason of the very large force thrown there by the enemy, I determined to take advantage of the diversion made, by assaulting Petersburg before he could get his force back there.

On the 30th, between 4 and 5 A. M., the mine was sprung, blowing up a battery and most of a regiment. The advance of the assaulting column immediately took possession of the crater, but, for some cause, failed to advance promptly to the ridge beyond. Had they done this, I had every reason to believe that Petersburg would have fallen. Other troops were immediately pushed forward, but the time consumed in getting them up enabled the enemy to rally from his surprise (which had been complete) and get forces to this point for its defense. The captured line thus held being untenable, and of no advantage to us, the troops were withdrawn, but not without heavy loss. Thus terminated in disaster what promised to be the most successful assault of the campaign.

Immediately upon the enemy's ascertaining that General Hunter was retreating from Lynchburg by way of the Kanawha River, thus laying the Shenandoah Valley open for raids into Maryland and Pennsylvania, he returned northward and moved down that valley. Owing to low water and breaks in the railroad, General Hunter could not reach Harper's Ferry in time to check this movement. The garrisons of Baltimore and Washington were at this time made up of heavy artillery regiments, hundred days' men, and detachments from the Invalid Corps. General Ricketts, with one division of the 6th Corps, was sent to Baltimore, and the other two divisions, under General Wright, were subsequently sent to Washington. On the 3d of July the enemy approached Martinsburg. General Sigel, in command there, retreated across the Potomac at Shepardstown, and General Weber, commanding at Harper's Ferry, crossed the river and occupied Maryland Heights. On the 6th the enemy occupied Hagerstown, moving a strong column toward Frederick City. General Wallace, with Ricketts's division and his own command, mostly new and undisciplined troops, pushed from Baltimore with great promptness, and met the enemy in force on the Monocacy, where, although defeated, he detained the enemy, and thereby enabled General Wright to reach Washington, upon which place the enemy moved, his cavalry advance reaching Rockville on the evening of the 10th. On the 12th a reconnoisance was thrown out in front of Fort Stevens, to ascertain the enemy's position and force. A severe skirmish ensued, in which we lost about 280 killed and wounded. The enemy's loss was probably greater. He commenced retreating during the night.

General Wright was assigned to the command of all troops in the field operating against this invasion, and commenced the pursuit on the 13th. On the 18th the enemy was overtaken at Snicker's Ferry, when a sharp skirmish occurred; and on the 20th General Averill encountered and defeated a portion of the rebel army at Winchester, capturing four pieces of artillery and several hundred prisoners.

About the 25th the enemy was again advancing upon Maryland and Pennsylvania; he moved down the valley and sent a raiding party into Pennsylvania, which, on the 30th, burned Chambersburg, and then retreated, pursued by our cavalry, toward Cumberland. They were met and defeated by General Kelly, and with diminished numbers, escaped into the mountains of West Virginia.

From where I was I hesitated to give positive orders for the movement of our forces at Monocacy, lest by so doing I should expose Washington. I therefore visited General Hunter on the 5th, and, after consultation with him, gave him his instructions, among which were "Bear in mind, the object is to drive the enemy south, and to do this you want to keep him always in sight. Be guided in your course by the course he takes."

From the time of the first raid the telegraph wires were frequently down between Washington and City Point, making it necessary to transmit messages a part of the way by boat. It took from twenty-four to thirty-six hours to get dispatches through and return answers back, often causing confusion and an apparent contradiction of orders that was very embarrassing to those executing them, and detrimental to effective operations. To remedy this evil, some one should have supreme command of the forces operating against Early. General Hunter having, in our conversation, expressed a willingness to be relieved from command, the Middle Military Division was constituted August 7, and General Sheridan was assigned to command of the same. His operations during the month of August and the forepart of September were both of an offensive and defensive character, resulting in many severe skirmishes, principally by the cavalry, in which we were generally successful, but no general engagement took place. The two armies lay in such position that either could bring on a battle at any time. Defeat to us would lay open to the enemy the States of Maryland and Pennsylvania. Under these circumstances I hesitated about allowing the initiative to be taken. Finally, the use of the Baltimore and Ohio Railroad and the Chesapeake and Ohio Canal, which were both obstructed by the enemy, became so indispensably necessary to us, and the importance of relieving Pennsylvania and Maryland from continuously threatened invasion so great, that I visited General Sheridan at his head-quarters to decide, after conference with him, what should be done. I met him at Charleston, and he pointed out so distinctly how each army lay, what he could do the moment he was authorized, and expressed such confidence of success, that I saw there were but two words of instructions necessary—Go in! I asked him if he could get out his teams and supplies in time to make an attack on the ensuing Tuesday morning. His reply was that he could, before daylight on Monday. He was off promptly to time, and I may here add that the result was such that I have never since deemed it necessary to visit General Sheridan before giving him orders.

On the morning of September 19 he attacked Early at the crossing on Opequan Creek, and, after a most sanguinary and bloody battle, lasting until five o'clock in the evening, defeated him with heavy loss, carrying his entire position from Opequan Creek to Winchester, capturing several thousand prisoners and five pieces of artillery. The enemy rallied and made a stand in a strong position at Fisher's Hill, where he was attacked and again defeated on the 20th. Sheridan pursued him with great energy through Harrisonburg, Staunton, and the gaps of the Blue Ridge. After stripping the upper valley of most of the supplies and provisions for the rebel army, he returned to Strasburg and took position on the north side of Cedar Creek.

Having received considerable reinforcements, General Early again returned to the valley, and on October 9 his cavalry encountered ours near Strasburg, where he was defeated, losing 11 guns and 350 prisoners. On the night of the 18th the enemy crossed the mountains which separated the branches of the Shenandoah, forded the north fork, and, early on the morning of the 19th, surprised and turned our left flank, capturing the batteries which enfiladed our whole line. Our troops fell back with heavy loss and in much confusion, but were finally rallied between Middletown and Newton. At this juncture General Sheridan, who was at Winchester when the battle commenced, arrived on the field, arranged his lines just in time to repulse a heavy attack of the enemy, and immediately assuming the offensive, he attacked in turn with great vigor. The enemy was defeated with great slaughter, and the loss of most of his artillery and trains, and the trophies he had captured in the morning. The wreck of his army escaped during the night, and fled in the direction of Staunton and

Lynchburg. Pursuit was made to Mount Jackson. Thus ended this the enemy's last attempt to invade the North, *via* the Shenandoah Valley.

Supposing the enemy had sent a force from Petersburg to reinforce Early, I, on the night of August 13, threatened Richmond from the north side of the James, to prevent him from sending troops away, and, if possible, to draw back those sent. We captured six guns and several hundred prisoners, detained troops that were under marching orders, and ascertained that but one division of the three reputed detached had gone. On the 18th we took possession of the Weldon Railroad, to regain which the enemy made repeated and desperate assaults, but was each time repulsed with great loss.

On the 25th, our cavalry, while at Ream's Station destroying the railroad, were forced back, losing 5 guns.

The extension of our lines across the Weldon Railroad compelled the enemy to so extend his that it seemed he could have but few troops north of the James for the defense of Richmond. On the night of September 28, the 10th and 18th Corps were crossed to the north side of the James, and advanced on the morning of the 29th, carrying the very strong fortifications and intrenchments below Chapin's Farm, known as Fort Harrison, capturing fifteen pieces of artillery and the New Market road and intrenchments. This success was followed up by a gallant assault upon Fort Gillmore, in which we were repulsed with heavy loss. Kautz's cavalry was pushed forward on the road to the right of this, supported by infantry, and reached the enemy's inner line, but was unable to get further. The position captured from the enemy was so threatening to Richmond that I determined to hold it. The enemy made several desperate attempts to dislodge us, all of which were unsuccessful, and for which he paid dearly.

General Meade, on the 30th, with a view to attacking the enemy's line, if it was found sufficiently weakened by withdrawal of troops to the north side, sent out a reconnoisance which captured and held the enemy's works near Poplar Spring Church.

On October 7 the enemy attacked Kautz's cavalry north of the James, and drove it back, with heavy loss in killed, wounded, and prisoners, and the loss of all the artillery, eight or nine pieces. This he followed up by an attack on our intrenched infantry line, but was repulsed with severe slaughter. On the 13th a reconnoissance was sent out by General Butler, with a view to drive the enemy from some new works he was constructing, which resulted in very heavy loss to us.

On the 27th, the Army of the Potomac, leaving only sufficient men to hold its fortified line, moved by the enemy's right flank, and forced a passage of Hatcher's Run, and moved up the south side of it toward Southside Railroad, until the advance reached the Boydtown Plank Road. At this point we were six miles distant from the Southside Railroad, which I had, by this movement, to reach and hold. But finding that we had not reached the end of the ememy's fortifications, and no place presenting itself for a successful assault by which he might be doubled up and shortened, I determined to withdraw within our fortified line, which was done after repulsing an attack of the enemy. General Butler's cooperative movement was partially successful, but his forces withdrew to their former position.

From this time forward the operations in front of Petersburg and Richmond, until the spring campaign of 1865, were confined to the defense and extension of our lines, and to offensive movements for crippling the enemy's line of communications, and to prevent his detaching any considerable force to send south. By the 7th of February our lines were extended to Hatcher's Run, and the Weldon Railroad had been destroyed to Hicksford.

General Sherman moved from Chattanooga on May 6, with the Armies of the Cumberland, Tennessee, and Ohio, commanded, respectively, by Generals Thomas, McPherson, and Schofield, upon Johnston's army at Dalton. The enemy's position at Buzzard's Roost being too strong for assault, McPherson was sent through Snake Gap to turn it, while Thomas and Schofield threatened it in front and north. Johnston retreated to Resaca on the 15th, and he again fled southward. His rear-guard was overtaken near Adamsville on the 17th, and at Cassville on the 19th, when at night he crossed the

Etowah. He was driven to New Hope Church, near Dallas, on the 25th. On the 28th he assaulted McPherson at Dallas, but was bloodily repulsed. He abandoned New Hope Church June 4, retreating to Kenesaw, Pine, and Lost Mountains. He yielded the two last-named places on the 27th, and Kenesaw July 3, going to Atlanta, where he was succeeded by Hood, who assumed the offensive-defensive policy, and made several attacks during the latter part of July, in all of which he was repulsed with heavy loss. General Sherman moved his main force by the enemy's left flank, thus drawing him from the fortifications; and after defeating him near Rough and Ready, Jonesboro, and Lovejoys, forced him south, and, on September 2, occupied Atlanta, thus closing a movement that was prompt, skillful, and brilliant. The history of his flank movements and battles during that memorable campaign will ever be read with an interest unsurpassed by any thing in history.

During these movements, Forrest annoyed us considerably, and his successes seemed to embolden others. Early in April he captured Fort Pillow; and, after our men threw down their arms, proceeded in an inhuman and merciless massacre of the garrison.

The Red River expedition left Vicksburg March 10, under command of General A. J. Smith. The rebel forces, thinking to defeat him in the open field, left Fort DeRussy on the 14th. Smith stole a march on them, and captured the fort with its garrison of 350 men, 11 guns, and small arms. Our loss was slight. He defeated the enemy, capturing 210 prisoners and 4 guns, at Henderson Hill on the 21st. General Banks pushed forward from Grand Ecore April 6, and defeated the enemy near Pleasant Hill on the 7th, and again the same evening, eight miles beyond. On the 8th, at Sabine Cross-roads and Peach Hill, the enemy attacked and defeated his advance, capturing 10 pieces of artillery and an immense amount of transportation and stores. During the night General Banks fell back to Pleasant Hill, where another battle was fought on the 9th, and the enemy repulsed with great loss. During the night General Banks continued his retrograde movement to

Grand Ecore, and thence to Alexandria, which he reached on the 27th, leaving that place May 14. The disastrous termination of this expedition, and the lateness of the season, rendered impracticable the capture of Mobile General Canby, who had been assigned to the command was therefore directed to send the 19th Corps to join the armies operating against Richmond, and to limit the remainder of his command to such operations as might be necessary to hold the positions and lines he then occupied.

Late in July General Granger was sent, with such forces as he could collect, to co-operate with Admiral Farragut against the defenses of Mobile Bay. On the 8th of August Fort Gaines surrendered to the combined naval and land forces. Fort Powell was blown up and abandoned.

On the 9th Fort Morgan was invested, and, after a severe bombardment, surrendered on the 23d. The total captures amounted to 1,464 prisoners and 104 guns.

About the last day of August, Price was reported on his way to Missouri, with a force of 10,000 men. He captured Pilot Knob September 26. He was forced to battle on the Big Blue, and defeated, with the loss of nearly all his artillery and train, and a large number of prisoners. He made a precipitate retreat to Northern Arkansas.

The enemy's cavalry made an extensive raid during the latter part of September and forepart of October, through Tennessee, and escaped to Corinth, Mississippi.

General Burbridge met the enemy, October 2, about three miles from Saltville, Virginia, and drove him into his strongly-intrenched position around the salt-works, from which he was unable to dislodge him. During the night he withdrew his command and returned to Kentucky.

General Sherman, immediately after the fall of Atlanta, put his armies in camp in and about the place, and made all preparations for refitting and supplying them for future service; and, after a full interchange of opinions and reasons, he commenced his preparations for his proposed movement to the sea, keeping his army in position, in the mean time, to watch Hood. Having concentrated his troops at Atlanta by the 14th of November, he commenced his march, threatening both Augusta and Macon. His coming-out point could not be definitely fixed. Having to gather his subsistence as he marched through the country, it was not impossible that a force inferior to his own might compel him to head for such point as he could reach, instead of such as he might prefer. The blindness of the enemy, however, in ignoring his movement, and sending Hood's army (the only considerable force he had west of Richmond and east of the Mississippi River) northward, on an offensive campaign, left the whole country open, and Sherman's route to his own choice.

How that campaign was conducted, how little opposition was met with, the condition of the country through which the armies passed, the capture of Fort McAllister, on the Savannah River, and the occupation of Savannah on the 21st of December, are all clearly set forth in General Sherman's admirable report.

Hood, instead of following Sherman, continued his move northward, which seemed to me to be leading to his certain doom. At all events, had I had the power to command both armies, I should not have changed the orders under which he seemed to be acting. His advance reached Decatur, Alabama, October 24, but, failing to carry the place, he withdrew and effected a lodgment on the north side of the Tennessee River, near Florence. General Hood pressed General Thomas back toward Nashville, and coming up with our main force, commanded by General Schofield, at Frankfort, on the 30th, assaulted our works during the afternoon repeatedly, until late at night, but was in every instance repulsed. His loss in this battle was 1,750 killed, 700 prisoners, and 3,800 wounded; our entire loss was 2,300. This was the first serious opposition the enemy met with, and I am satisfied was the fatal blow to all his expectations. During the night General Schofield fell back toward Nashville. This left the field to the enemy—not lost by the battle, but voluntarily abandoned—so that General Thomas's whole force might be brought together. The enemy followed up, and commenced the establishment of his line in front of Nashville December 2, General Smith having arrived there two days earlier. On the morning of December 15, General Thomas attacked Hood in position, and, in a battle lasting two days, defeated and drove him from the field in the utmost confusion.

Before the battle of Nashville I grew very impatient over, as it appeared to me, the unnecessary delay, and I was quite disposed to censure, but his final defeat of Hood was so complete that it will be accepted as a vindication of that distinguished officer's judgment.

After this defeat, Hood, though closely followed by our troops, made his escape southward.

During the above movements Breckenridge made a raid in the eastern part of the State, but Stoneman soon drove him back, dispersed his forces, and captured and destroyed Saltville, Virginia.

The nature of the outlet of Cape Fear River was such that, without possession of the land north of New Inlet, or Fort Fisher, it was impossible for the navy to entirely close Wilmington harbor against blockade-runners. To secure this a land force of 6,500 troops were detached, to co-operate with the navy. The expedition got off December 13, and arrived near Fort Fisher on the evening of the 15th. Admiral Porter arrived three days later; but a rough sea, lack of coal and water, with stormy weather, delayed action until the 24th. A landing was effected without opposition on the 25th, and a reconnoissance, under General Curtis, pushed up toward the fort. But before receiving a full report of the result of this reconnoissance, General Butler, in direct violation of the instructions given, ordered the re-embarkation of the troops and the return of the expedition.

The instructions which I had given December 6 (which military courtesy required should go through General Butler, he commanding that department,) to General Weitzel, that General has since officially informed me he never received, nor was he aware of their existence until he read General Butler's published official report of the Fort Fisher failure. General Curtis and others, officers and men, afterward voluntarily reported to me that, when recalled, they were nearly into the fort, and, in their opinion, it could have been taken without much loss.

The next expedition was under General Terry, with whom I communicated direct, the instructions being materially those given for the first expedition. The troops, also, were the same, with a small brigade (about 1,500 men) and a small siege train. The latter it was never found necessary to land.

The expedition reached its destination January 12, 1865, and by 3 o clock P. M. next day the troops were landed, under cover of the fleet, without loss. The fort was assaulted, and, after desperate fighting, was captured on the 15th. We thus secured one of the most important successes of the war. At my request General Ord succeeded General Butler in command of the department.

The State of North Carolina was constituted into a military department, and General Schofield, who had been ordered from the West, as not necessary in General Thomas's army, assigned to the command, and, January 31, placed under the orders of General Sherman.

In obedience to his instructions, General Schofield proceeded, in co-operation with the navy under Admiral Porter, to reduce Wilmington, which, after fighting on the 20th and 21st, our troops entered on the morning of the 22d, the enemy having retreated toward Goldsboro during the night.

Having information of the defeat and utter route of Hood's army, I asked General Sherman on the 18th for his views of operations, and, on the 19th, directed him to make preparations to start, as he proposed, without delay, to break up the railroads in North and South Carolina, and join the armies operating against Richmond as soon as he could. January 21, I informed him that the 23d Corps, General Schofield commanding, numbering 21,000 men, would go to Wilmington or Newbern; that we had at Fort Fisher 8,000 men; at Newbern, 4,000; and that the surplus force at both these points would move to the interior toward Goldsboro, in co-operation with his movement; that from either point railroad communication could be run out, and that all these troops would be subject to his orders as he came into communication with them.

By the 1st of February General Sherman's whole army was in motion from Savannah. He captured Columbia, S. C., on the 17th; then moved on Goldsboro, N. C., *via* Fayetteville, reaching the latter place March 12, opening up communication with General Schofield. On the 18th the combined forces of the enemy, under Joe Johnston, attacked his advance at Bentonville, capturing three guns and driving it back upon the main body. General Slocum, who was in the advance, ascertaining that the whole of Johnston's army was in the front, arranged his troops on the defensive, intrenched himself, and awaited reinforcements, which were pushed forward. On the night of the 21st the enemy retreated to Smithfield, leaving his dead and wounded in our hands. From there Sherman continued to Goldsboro, which place had been occupied by Schofield on the 21st, and forced the fall of Charleston, S. C.

General Sheridan moved from Winchester February 27, with 10,000 cavalry, and made Staunton March 2, the enemy retreating to Waynesboro, where he went. Finding the enemy intrenched and in force, an immediate attack was made, the position carried, and 1,600 prisoners, 11 guns, 200 wagons, and 17 battle-flags were captured. He reached Charlottesville on the 3d, destroying effectually the railroad and bridges as he went. He remained two days, destroying the railroad toward Richmond and Lynchburg. On the 6th, dividing his force into two columns, he sent one to Scottsville, whence it marched to New Market. From here a force was pushed out to Duiguidsville, to obtain possession of the bridge across the James River at that place, but failed. The enemy burned it and the one at Hardwicksville on our approach. The other column moved down the railroad toward Lynchburg, destroying it as far as Amherst C. H., 16 miles from Lynchburg; thence across the country, uniting with the column at New Market. From here he followed the canal toward Richmond, destroying every lock upon it, and cutting the banks wherever practicable, to a point eight miles east of Goochland, concentrating the whole force on the 10th at Columbia, from which he moved in a direction to threaten Richmond, to near Ashland Station; he crossed the Annas, and after having destroyed all the bridges and many miles of the railroad, proceeded to White House, which place he reached on the 19th.

The situation in March, 1865, showed that General Canby was moving an adequate force against Mobile; Thomas was pushing out two large cavalry expeditions—one, under General Wilson, against the enemy's vital points in Alabama; the other, under General Stoneman, toward Lynchburg, and assembling the remainder of his available forces preparatory to offensive operations from East Tennessee. Sheridan's cavalry was at the White House; the Armies of the Potomac and James were confronting the enemy under Lee; Sherman, with his armies reinforced by that of Schofield, was at Goldsboro; Pope was making preparations for a spring campaign against the enemy, under Kirby Smith and Price, west of the Mississippi; and Hancock was concentrating a force in the vicinity of Winchester, Va., to guard against invasion or to operate offensively, as might prove necessary. Sheridan joined the Army of the Potomac in front of Petersburg on the 27th. On the morning of the 25th the enemy assaulted our lines, and carried Fort Steadman and a part of the line to the right and left of it, established themselves, and turned the guns of the fort against us; but our troops on either flank held their ground until reserves were brought up, when the enemy was driven back, with a heavy loss in killed and wounded, and 1,900 prisoners. Our loss was 68 killed, 337 wounded, and 506 missing. General Meade at once felt the enemy's respective fronts, and captured and held the enemy's strongly intrenched picket line, in front of the 2d and 6th Corps, and 834 prisoners. The enemy made desperate attempts to retake this line, but without success. Our loss in front of these was 52 killed, 864 wounded, and 207 missing. The enemy's loss in killed and wounded was far greater.

General Sherman, on the 27th, reported his troops in camp at Goldsboro, and added they would be ready for work by April 10. He proposed a movement to threaten Raleigh, and then, by turning suddenly to the right, reach the Roanoke or Gaston, or thereabouts, whence he could move on to the Richmond and Danville Railroad, striking it in the vicinity of Burkesville, or join the armies operating against Richmond, as might be deemed best. This plan he was directed to carry into execution, if he received no further directions in the mean time.

I had spent days of anxiety lest each morning should bring the report that the enemy had retreated the night before. I was firmly convinced that Sherman's crossing the Roanoke would be the signal for Lee to leave. I was therefore anxious for the movement, which commenced on the morning of the 29th. At night the cavalry was at Dinwiddie C. H., and the left of our infantry line extended to the Quaker road, near its intersection with the Boydton Plank-road. The position of the troops from right to left was as follows: Sheridan, Warren, Humphreys, Ord, Wright, Parke.

Every thing looked favorable to the defeat of the enemy, and the capture of Petersburg and Richmond, if the proper effort was made.

From the night of the 29th to the morning of the 31st the rain fell in such torrents as to make it impossible to move wheeled vehicles, except as corduroy roads were laid in front of them. During the 30th, Sheridan advanced toward Five Forks, where he found the enemy in force. Warren advanced and extended his line across the Boydton Plank-road to near the White Oak road, where he fortified. Humphreys drove the enemy from his front into his main line on the Hatcher, near Burgess's Mills. Generals Ord, Wright, and Parke made examinations in their fronts, to determine the feasibility of an assault on the enemy's lines. The two latter reported favorably. Humphreys's corps was ordered to report to Sheridan; but the condition of the roads prevented immediate movement. On the 31st, Warren was directed to get possession of the White Oak road. To accomplish this he moved with one division, which was attacked by the enemy in superior force, and driven back on the second division, and it, in turn, forced back upon the third division, when the enemy was checked. A division of the 2d Corps was immediately sent to his support, the enemy driven back with heavy loss, and possession of White Oak road gained. Sheridan advanced, and, with a portion of his cavalry, got possession of the Five Forks, but the enemy reinforced the rebel cavalry defending that point with infantry, and forced him back toward Dinwiddie C. H. Here Sheridan displayed great generalship. Instead of retreating with his whole command on the main army, to tell the story of superior forces encountered, he deployed his cavalry on foot, leaving only mounted men enough to take charge of the horses. This compelled the enemy to deploy over a vast extent of woods and broken country, and made his progress slow. He dispatched to me what had taken place, and that he was dropping back slowly on Dinwiddie C. H. Next morning, being reinforced by Warren, he drove the enemy back on Five Forks, where, late in the evening, he assaulted and carried his strongly-fortified position, capturing all his artillery, and between 5,000 and 6,000 prisoners.

Some apprehensions filled my mind lest the enemy might desert his lines during the night, and by falling upon Sheridan before assistance could reach him, drive him from his position, and open the way for retreat. To guard against this, one division was sent to reinforce him, and a bombardment was commenced and kept up until four o'clock in the morning (April 2), when an assault was ordered on the enemy's lines. General Wright penetrated the lines with his whole corps, sweeping every thing before him and to his left, toward Hatcher's Run, capturing many guns and several thousand prisoners. He was closely followed by two divisions of General Ord's command, until he met the other division of Ord's that had succeeded in forcing the enemy's lines near Hatcher's Run. Generals Wright and Ord immediately swung to the right, and closed all the enemy on that side of them in Petersburg, while Humphreys pushed forward with two divisions and joined Wright on the left. General Parke succeeded in carrying the enemy's main line, capturing guns and prisoners, but was unable to carry his inner line. Sheridan, being advised of the condition of affairs, returned General Miles to his proper command. On reaching the enemy's lines immediately surrounding Petersburg, a portion of General Gibbon's corps, by a most gallant charge, captured two strong inclosed works—the most salient and commanding south of Petersburg—thus materially shortening the line of investment necessary for taking the city. The enemy south of Hatcher's Run retreated westward to Sutherland's Station, where they were overtaken by Miles's division. A severe engagement ensued, and lasted until both his right and left flanks were threatened by the approach of Sheridan, who was moving from Ford's Station toward Petersburg, and a division sent by Meade from the front of Petersburg, when he broke in the utmost confusion, leaving in our hands his guns and many prisoners. This force retreated by the main road along the Appomattox River.

During the night of the 2d, the enemy evacuated Petersburg and Richmond, and retreated toward Danville. On the morning of the 3d pursuit was commenced. Sheridan pushed for the Danville road, keeping near the Appomattox, followed by Meade, with the 2d and 6th Corps, while Ord moved from Burkesville along the Southside road, the 9th Corps stretching along that road behind him. On the 4th, Sheridan struck the Danville road near Jettersville, where he learned that Lee was at Amelia Court-house. He immediately intrenched himself, and awaited the arrival of Meade, who reached there the next day. Ord reached Burkesville on the evening of the 5th.

On the morning of the 6th, it was found that General Lee was moving west of Jettersville, toward Danville. General Sheridan moved with his cavalry, to strike his flank, while the 2d and 6th Corps pressed hard after, forcing him to abandon several hundred wagons and several pieces of artillery. General Ord advanced from Burkesville toward Farmville, sending two regiments of infantry and a squadron of cavalry, under General Read, to reach and destroy the bridges. This advance met the head of Lee's column near Farmville, which it heroically attacked and detained until General Read was killed and his small force overpowered. This caused a delay in the enemy's movements, and enabled Ord to get well up with the remainder of his force, on meeting which the enemy immediately intrenched himself. In the afternoon Sheridan struck the enemy south of Sailor's Creek, captured 16 pieces of artillery and about

400 wagons, and detained him until the 6th Corps got up, when a general attack of infantry and cavalry was made, which resulted in the capture of 6,000 or 7,000 prisoners, among whom were many general officers. The movements of the 2d Corps and Ord's command contributed greatly to the day's success.

On the morning of the 7th the pursuit was renewed, the cavalry (except one division) and the 5th Corps moving by Prince Edward's Court-house; the 6th Corps, General Ord's command, and one division of cavalry, on Farmville, and the 2d Corps by the High-bridge road. It was soon found that the enemy had crossed to the north side of the Appomattox, but so close was the pursuit that the 2d Corps got possession at High-bridge before the enemy could destroy it, and immediately crossed over. The 6th Corps and a division of cavalry crossed at Farmville to its support.

Feeling now that Lee's chance of escape was utterly hopeless, I addressed him a note, asking for the "surrender of that portion of the Confederate States army known as the Army of Northern Virginia." A correspondence ensued, which resulted in the following:

"APPOMATTOX COURT-HOUSE, VA.,
April 9, 1865.

"GENERAL: In accordance with the substance of my letter to you of the 8th instant, I propose to receive the surrender of the Army of Northern Virginia on the following terms, to-wit: Rolls of all the officers and men to be made in duplicate, one copy to be given to an officer to be designated by me, the other to be retained by such officer or officers as you may designate. The officers to give their individual parole not to take up arms against the Government of the United States until properly exchanged, and each company or regimental commander sign a like parole for the men of their commands. The arms, artillery, and public property to be packed and stacked, and turned over to the officers appointed by me to receive them. This will not embrace the side-arms of the officers, nor their private horses or baggage. This done, each officer and man will be allowed to return to his home, not to be disturbed by United States authority so long as they observe their paroles and the laws in force where they may reside. U. S. GRANT, *Lieutenant-General.*

General R. E. LEE.

HEAD-QUARTERS ARMY OF NORTHERN VIRGINIA, *April* 9, 1865.

GENERAL: I received your letter of this date containing the terms of surrender of the Army of Northern Virginia, as proposed by you. As they are substantially the same as those expressed in your letter of the 8th instant, they are accepted. I will proceed to designate the proper officers to carry the stipulations into effect. R. E. LEE, *General.*

Lieutenant-General U. S. GRANT.

The commands of Generals Gibbon and Griffin, and McKenzie's cavalry, were designated to await the paroling of the surrendered army, and take charge of the public property. The remainder of the army immediately returned to the vicinity of Burkesville.

General Lee's great influence throughout the whole South caused his example to be followed, and to-day the result is that the armies lately under his leadership are at their homes, desiring peace and quiet, and their arms are in the hands of our ordnance officers.

On the 14th, a correspondence was opened between Generals Sherman and Johnston, which resulted, on the 18th, in an agreement for a suspension of hostilities, and a memorandum or basis for peace, subject to the approval of the President. The President's disapproval I communicated to General Sherman at Raleigh, North Carolina, on the 24th. He at once notified General Johnston of the termination of the truce. Another meeting between them on the 26th terminated in the surrender and disbandment of General Johnston's army, upon substantially the same terms as were given to General Lee.

The expedition under General Stoneman from East Tennessee got off on the 20th of March, moving by way of Boone, N. C., and struck the railroad at Wytheville, Chambersburg, and Big Lick, and thence to within a few miles of Lynchburg. At Salisbury he attacked and defeated a force of the enemy under General Gardiner, capturing 14 guns and 1,364 prisoners, and destroyed large amounts of army stores. At this place he destroyed fifteen miles of railroad, and the bridges toward Charlotte. Thence he moved to Slatersville.

The expedition under General Wilson, consisting of 12,500 mounted men, was delayed by rains until March 22, when it moved from Chickasaw, Ala. April 1, he met Forrest, in force, near Ebenezer Church, drove him in confusion, captured 300 prisoners and 3 guns, and destroyed the central bridge over the Cahawba River. On the 2d he captured Selma, defended by Forrest with 7,000 men and 32 guns, destroyed the arsenal, armory, naval foundry, machine shops, vast quantities of stores, and captured 3,000 prisoners. He captured Tuscaloosa on the 4th, and occupied Montgomery on the 14th, the enemy having abandoned it. At this place many stores and five steamboats fell into our hands. Thence a force marched direct on Columbus, and another on West Point, both of which places were assaulted and captured on the 16th. At the former place we got 1,500 prisoners and 52 guns, destroyed two gun-boats, the navy-yard, foundries, arsenal, many factories, and much other public property. At the latter place we got 300 prisoners, 4 guns, and destroyed 19 locomotives and 300 cars. On the 20th he took possession of Macon, Ga., with 60 guns, 1,200 militia, and 5 generals. General Wilson, hearing that Jefferson Davis was trying to make his escape, sent forces in pursuit, and succeeded in capturing him on the morning of May 11.

General Canby commenced his movement against Mobile March 20, invested Spanish Fort on the 27th, which was captured April 8, and Fort Blakely next day. Mobile was evacuated on the night of the 11th, and occupied by our forces next morning. General Dick Taylor surrendered to General Canby all the remaining rebel forces east of the Mississippi May 4.

General Sheridan, with a force sufficient to insure an easy triumph over Kirby Smith, west of the Mississippi, was immediately put in motion for Texas; but on May 26 (before Sheridan reached his destination), Smith surrendered his entire command to General Canby. The bad faith was exhibited of first disbanding most of his army and permitting an indiscriminate plunder of public property.

Owing to the report that many of those lately in arms against the Government had taken refuge upon the soil of Mexico, carrying with them arms rightfully belonging to the United States, which had been surrendered to us by agreement—among them some of the leaders who had surrendered in person—and the disturbed condition of affairs on the Rio Grande, the orders for troops to proceed to Texas were not changed.

There have been severe combats, raids, expeditions and movements to defeat the designs and purposes of the enemy, most of them reflecting great credit on our arms, and which contributed greatly to our final triumph, that I have not mentioned.

It has been my fortune to see the armies of both the West and the East fight battles, and, from what I have seen, I know there is no difference in their fighting qualities. All that it was possible for men to do in battle they have done. The Western armies commenced their battles in the Mississippi Valley, and received their final surrender of the remnant of the principal army opposed to them in North Carolina. The armies of the East commenced their battles on the river from which the Army of the Potomac derived its name, and received the final surrender of their old antagonist at Appomattox Court-house, Va. The splendid achievements of each have nationalized our victories, removed all sectional jealousies (of which we have unfortunately experienced too much) and the cause of crimination and recrimination that might have followed had either section failed in its duty. All have a proud record, and all sections can well congratulate themselves and each other for having done their full share in restoring the supremacy of law over every foot of territory belonging to the United States. Let them hope for perpetual peace and harmony with that enemy, whose manhood, however mistaken the cause, drew forth such Herculean deeds of valor.

PARLIAMENTARY RULES.

FOR THE GOVERNMENT OF PUBLIC ASSEMBLIES.

A knowledge of the rules which regulate the formation and order of business in public assemblies, is essential to every well informed citizen. Every citizen is obliged, at some time, to take part in the primary assemblies of the people. These are constantly held, not merely for political purposes, but for those of business—commercial, literary, benevolent, or religious. In addition to these primary assemblies, there are various and numerous organized associations, with some one or more of which almost every citizen is connected. The rules for the transaction of business in the assemblies, or associations, are substantially the same in all of them, the most important of which are substantially as follows:

ORGANIZATION.

1. In regularly *organized* bodies, such as Congress, the State Legislatures, religious, political, or other associations, the Constitution under which they act usually designates the title of their presiding officer, defines his duties, and provides for the mode of his appointment.

2. When a *primary assembly* of the people, or of any part of them, is called together for any purpose, the first thing to be done is to choose a presiding officer, usually designated as *Chairman*.

3. At the proper time some one rises, and moves that A. B. be appointed Chairman of the meeting. When this is seconded *the person making the motion* puts the question, and if it be carried, A. B. takes the chair as presiding officer.

4. Regularly every public assembly should have a *Secretary*, who is chosen in such manner as the body may direct.

5. The assembly may appoint such other officers as is deemed expedient; and on important occasions there are usually appointed several vice-presidents and additional secretaries.

6. In deliberate bodies composed of delegates, it is usual to effect a *primary organization* as above; then appoint a committee on "Permanent Organization," who *nominate* permanent officers for the assembly; and a committee on "Credentials," who prepare a list of those entitled to take part in the proceedings.

7. Immediately before or after (usually after) the permanent organisation there is appointed committees on Order of Business, Resolutions, Address, and such others as the case may require.

DUTIES OF OFFICERS.

8. The *presiding officer* opens each sitting of the body by taking the chair and calling the members to order; he announces the business in order; receives all communications, messages. motions, and propositions; puts to vote all questions coming before the body for their decision; and enforces the rules of order. He may read sitting, but should rise to state a motion or put a question.

9. The *Secretary* keeps a record of the proceedings of the body; reads all papers as ordered; calls the roll of members and records their votes during a call for the ayes and nays; notifies committees of their appointment, and the business referred to them; and takes charge of all papers and documents belonging to the assembly.

10. The *Vice President* takes the chair in the absence of the presiding officer, or when he leaves the chair to take part in the proceedings of the meeting.

11. When other officers are chosen their duties are set forth in the resolution appointing them, or in the by-laws of the association.

ORDER.

12. In all assemblies any member may at any time rise to a point of order. He must distinctly state his question or objection, which the presiding officer will decide.

13. Any member dissatisfied with the ruling of the

chair may appeal to the assembly; and the presiding officer may call upon the house to sustain him in preserving order. The decision of the meeting is final.

14. Every member must treat every other member with respect and decorum; and especially must he acknowledge the dignity of the body at large, and of the officers thereof.

15. The chairman of an assembly cannot regularly speak to any thing but a point of order, or a question of fact.

16. In general the chairman has his own vote no more, but in primary meetings he is usually entitled to the casting vote.

17. If two persons rise to speak together, the chairman determines which shall have precedence; it may, however, be referred to the house.

18. A person speaking cannot regularly mention another member of the assembly by name. He must describe him as "The gentleman who has just sat down," "the gentleman on the other side of the question, etc.

19. When a person rises to speak, he must address the presiding officer, who should call him by name, that the assembly may know who he is.

20. The person speaking should confine himself to the question under debate, and avoid personality. If he transgress the rules of order, he may be called to order by the presiding officer, or any member.

21. No one should be interrupted while speaking, except he be out of order, or to ask, or to make an explanation.

22. A speaker may allow others to ask questions or make explanations; but if he yield the floor, he cannot claim it again as his right.

ORDER OF BUSINESS.

23. All business should be presented by a motion—and in writing, if so required—the motion to be made by one member and seconded by another.

24. A question is not to be discussed until it is moved, seconded, and distinctly stated by the presiding officer.

25. A question before the meeting cannot be withdrawn, except by unanimous consent.

26. A motion should contain but one distinct proposition, or question. If it contains more than one, it may be divided at the request of any member, and the questions acted on separately.

27. A motion before the meeting, must be put to vote, unless withdrawn, laid on the table, or postponed.

28. A motion lost should not be renewed at the same meeting, unless under circumstances of peculiar necessity.

29. While a motion is under debate, no other motion can be allowed, except

THE PRIVILEGED QUESTIONS.

1. To adjourn.
2. To lay on the table.
3. For the previous question.
4. To postpone to a day certain.
5. To commit or amend.
6. To postpone indefinitely.

Which several motions shall have precedence in the order in which they are arranged; and no motion to postpone to a day certain, to commit, or to postpone indefinitely, being decided, shall be again allowed on the same day, and of the same stage of the proposition.

30. Motions to adjourn, to lay on the table, for the previous question, to commit, and to indefinitely postpone, are not debatable. But when they are modified by some condition of *time*, *place*, or *purpose*, they become debatable, and subject to the rules of other motions.

31. A motion to *adjourn* is always in order, except while the body is engaged in voting, on another question, or while a member is speaking.

32. A body may adjourn to specified time. But if no time is mentioned, then it is understood to be adjourned to the time of its next meeting; or if it have no other fixed time for meeting, then an adjournment without date is equivalent to a dissolution.

33. If a meeting votes to adjourn at a specified hour, no vote is requisite when that hour arrives. The chair simply announces that the meeting stands adjourned.

34. By adjournment the condition of things is not

changed; and when the body meet again, every thing is renewed at the point where it was left.

35. Immediate and decisive action, on any question, may be deferred by a vote to *lay* the resolution pending *on the table*, whence it can be ordered up when it suits the convenience of the assembly.

36. When any question is before the House, any member may move the *previous question*, which is: "Shall the main question be now put;" if it pass, then the main question is to be put immediately, without debate or amendment; but if lost, then the main question is not put, and the discussion goes on.

37. A postponement to *a day certain*, is used when a proposition is made which it is proper to act on—but information is wanted, or something more pressing claims present attention.

38. An *indefinite postponement* is considered equivalent to a final dismissal of the question.

39. The meeting may decide to take up some particular business, at a specified time. That business becomes the *order of the day*, and when the hour specified arrives the chair announces the order of the day and other business is suspended.

40. Questions relating to the *rights* and *privileges* of the meeting, and of its members, are of primary importance, and for the time take precedence of all other business, and supercede all other motions, except that of adjournment.

41. When a question has been decided it is in order for any member who voted with the majority to move at the same or next succeeding sitting of the body for a *reconsideration* thereof. A question reconsidered is placed again before the body for action.

COMMITTEES.

42. All committees shall be appointed by the presiding officer, unless otherwise directed. If voted for by the body it requires a majority (in the absence of any other rule) of all the votes cast to elect.

43. The first one named in the appointment of a committee is by courtesy considered the chairman; but the committee have the right to appoint their own chairman.

44. Any subject in debate, or matter of business, may be referred to a committee, with or without instructions; the committee to report the result of their investigations to the meeting.

45. The report of a committee is accepted by a vote, which simply acknowledges the service of the commitee, and places their report before the meeting for its action. Afterwards, any distinct proposition or recommendation contained in the report, is separately acted on, and may be *adopted* or *rejected*.

46. A majority of a committee constitutes a *quorum* for business, who may meet where they please, but they cannot act except when together; and nothing can be the report of the committee except what is agreed upon in committee.

AMENDMENTS.

47. Amendments may be made to motions by omitting, adding or substituting, words or sentences, and amendments to amendments, are in order.

48. The amendment should be discussed and voted on first, and then the original resolution, as amended.

49. No amendment should be made, which essentially changes the nature or design of the original resolution.

50. But a *substitute* may be offered for any motion or amendment under debate, which may or may not change the design of the motion.

51. It is in order to move an amendment to strike out certain words and insert others;—this being rejected, it is in order to move to strike out, and insert a different set of words; this being rejected, it is in order to move to strike out the same words, and insert nothing; because each of these is a distinct proposition differing from the others. But it must be recollected, that it is *not in order*, if the motion to strike out and insert A. *is carried*, to move an amendment to *strike out* A. and *insert* B. To avoid this dilemma, the mover of B. must *give notice*, pending the motion to insert A., that he intends to move the insertion of B., in which case, he will gain the votes of all who prefer the amendment B. to the amendment A., in opposition to A. But, after A. *is inserted*, it is in order to move an amendment by striking out the whole, or part of the *original paragraph*, in-

cluding A.; for this is essentially *a different proposition* from that to strike out A. merely.

QUORUM.

52. In every constitutionally organized body, there must be some number fixed, which are sufficient to do business. This number is called a *quorum*, and is usually designated in the Constitution under which the body acts. Sometimes a quorum consists of a definite number of members; sometimes of two-thirds of all the members; but usually, as in Congress, of a majority of the members.

53. When a quorum is necessary to do business, in general, the chair should not be taken by the presiding officer till *that quorum* is present. And whenever, in the progress of business, it is observed that a quorum is not present, any member may call for a count of the House; and a quorum being found wanting, business must be suspended.

54. In primary assemblies of the people, there is, of course, no number requisite to constitute a quorum, and it frequently happens that a very small number of persons act for a large community.

MISCELLANEOUS.

55. The question is *first* put on the *affirmative*, and then on the *negative* side; till which, it is not a full question; but in the cases of small matters, such as receiving reports, petitions, reading papers, etc., the presiding officer may presume consent unless some objection be formally made; which saves the time of taking votes on matters of mere routine.

56. In putting a question the presiding officer declares whether the yeas or nays have it by the *sound*, if he be himself satisfied; if he be not satisfied, or if any member express dissatisfaction, the body is divided, usually by rising. The ayes first rise, and are counted standing in their places, by the chair or by tellers, as the case may be, then they sit; and the noes ries, and are counted in the same manner.

57. If the result be a *tie* (unless the chair give the casting vote, or if his vote makes the tie) *the motion is lost*.

58. A *mistake* in the announcement of a vote may be rectified after the result is announced.

59. There is precedent that a member may change his vote if it be done before any other business is taken up.

60. Where different numbers are suggested for *filling blanks*, the highest number, greatest distance, and longest time, are usually voted on first.

61. A rule of order may be *suspended* by a vote of the meeting, to allow of transacting business which could not otherwise be done.

62. The chair has a right to name any one to act for him, but this substitution does not extend beyond the first adjournment.

INDEX.

THE REGISTER AND MANUAL.

Is a large 12 mo. volume, of 384 pages, printed from new stereotype plates, on fine paper, in neat and substantial binding, and furnished at the following prices:

In Muslin Binding............................$2.00
In Leather Binding.......................... 2.50
In Half Calf Binding........................ 3.00

Sold Exclusively by Canvassing Agents.

The Title-page, Preface, and Index, together with the sample pages here presented, exhibit, to some extent, the plan and scope of the work. This book has received the unqualified commendation of many of our public and literary men, and meets with large patronage wherever introduced.

I wish to Engage Good, Reliable Agents, (Male or Female),

In every town. Will you, (if you cannot personally engage in the business), hand this Circular to some energetic friend, who will earnestly engage in the work? If you desire an Agency, please state your age and experience, if any, in this business. Send a list of the towns you can canvass, in the order of your preference, and the retail price for a copy of the work. By return mail you will receive a copy of the book, a certificate of agency for the first territory on your list unassigned, together with Order Book, Instructions, Hints to Agents, &c., &c.

www.ingramcontent.com/pod-product-compliance
Lightning Source LLC
Chambersburg PA
CBHW030904270326
41929CB00008B/563

* 9 7 8 3 3 3 7 2 0 2 5 5 2 *